The Economics of Creativity

The Economics of Creativity

Art and Achievement under Uncertainty

PIERRE-MICHEL MENGER

Harvard University Press

Cambridge, Massachusetts
London, England
2014

This book is an abridgment of a work originally published in French as
Le Travail Créateur, © Seuil/Gallimard, 2009

Library of Congress Cataloging-in-Publication Data

Menger, Pierre-Michel.
[Travail créateur. English]
The economics of creativity : art and achievement under uncertainty /
Pierre-Michel Menger.
    pages   cm
Includes bibliographical references and index.
ISBN 978-0-674-72456-3
1. Creation (Literary, artistic, etc.)   2. Artists—France—Social conditions.
3. Art and society—France.   I. Title.
NX160.M4513   2014
700.1'03—dc23   2013040100

For Béatrice Longuenesse

Contents

Translated by:

Steven Rendall

Amy Jacobs

Arianne Dorval

Lisette Eskinazi

Emmanuelle Saada

Joe Karaganis

Introduction

LABOR is a familiar subject for study in the social sciences. The literature is replete with studies of occupations, careers, labor markets, contractual relations in employment, unemployment, the relations between training and professionalization, and various aspects of remuneration, including its distribution, its relation to investments in training, and its evolution in individuals' careers. When the labor in question is artistic, however, such analysis is somewhat harder to find. This no doubt reflects the unusual nature of artistic labor.

Research shows that artists are better educated than most other workers, but also that on-the-job training and learning through experience play such a decisive role in many artistic domains that initial training acts as a very imperfect lever for entering the field. Surprisingly enough, even with steadily growing demand for artistic and cultural products and services, labor supply increases faster than demand. Thus artists show higher rates of unemployment and of several forms of constrained underemployment (nonvoluntary part-time work, intermittent work, fewer hours of work), are more often multiple jobholders, and earn less than workers with comparable human capital (education, training, and age) in their broad occupational category, that of professional, technical, and kindred workers.

Artists increasingly work under contingent arrangements. Long-term artistic employment has been vanishing except in heavily subsidized and sponsored organizations like orchestras and opera houses. Casual employment and self-employment prevail. The number of small artistic and cultural organizations has been growing as fast as the number of artists. These firms compete increasingly under flexible production schemes that revolve around spot transactions. It may be that vertically disintegrated systems of production, common in the arts, favor only loose employment relationships. Filtering mechanisms and selective matching processes generate transactional stability as well as labor force segmentation. Employers use artists' reputations as screening devices and signals of employability; artists learn how to cultivate a balance of recurrent and nonrecurrent hiring ties in order to secure a living, as well as to increase their human capital. Talent agencies mediate the contingent labor market and increasingly broker artistic projects.

There are considerable inequalities among artists in how much they work and what they earn. These inequalities trace their origins to the skewed distribution of talent and to the joint consumption technologies that magnify the importance of small differences in talent. Since quality in a context of infinite differentiation cannot be measured directly, but only revealed through a series of trials, inequalities also arise from competitions, tournaments, and other mechanisms for relative comparison. These are ubiquitous in art worlds in order to rank artists and artworks, to attract the demand of professionals and consumers, and to create the benefits arising from critical awards or market hit parades. No other professional world, with the exception of sports, depends so heavily on the format of the tourney of comparison. And art, compared with sports, has many more temporal scales for weighing merit: *daily,* with the indexes of audiovisual audiences, box-office receipts for films, and the number of downloads; *weekly,* with the lists of best sellers and hits; *annually,* with prizes awarded in ever-increasing numbers for books, films, musical albums, shows, and exhibits, and to their authors; and *very long-term or indefinitely,* when the most famous or accomplished artists are invited into the various pantheons that celebrate and consecrate art as a great and enduring human achievement and artists themselves as worthy of universal and eternal admiration. Moreover, no other world of activity preserves and places a value on so many traces of the process of production (artists' drafts, models, exercises, and so on), not only in order to archive them, but also to offer them for analysis and to marvel at.

Inequalities are increased by the way a disintegrated labor market operates, since both the allocation of piecemeal work based on reputational rankings and the formation of teams based on selective matchings magnify the advantages accruing from talent. Large parts of the business risk are transferred down to the artistic and technical workforce in a highly flexible and disintegrated organizational setting. The study of artistic careers illuminates how individuals learn to manage the consequent risks of their trade: through multiple jobholding, occupational role versatility, portfolio diversification of employment ties, and transfer incomes from public support, social insurance, and social security programs. Institutional arrangements regarding artists' legal status and what financial support they can expect may differ greatly among countries and states, yet occupational risk management is a constant, and it is basic to economic survival and personal success. Ironically enough, it brings to the foreground how rationally artists must behave, although artistic work and innovative spirit may symbolize the high end of idiosyncrasy.

Taken together, these features in economic terms amount to a disequilibrium of oversupply. They have been documented for so long that excess supply of artistic labor appears to be permanent and may act as a true structural condition of the arts' unbalanced growth.

The Principle of Uncertainty

In this book, I propose to explain these peculiarities by a principle that unifies their analysis and comprehension, the principle of uncertainty. I will show how, from the intimacy of creative activity to analyses of the broadest labor market, one and the same set of analytical tools can be used on the basis of this principle.

The initial hypothesis is simple: Artistic labor is shaped by uncertainty. An artist's activity follows an uncertain course, and its end point is neither defined nor guaranteed. If art were a programmable activity, work would be determined by a clear specification of the problems to be resolved, by precise instructions that must be respected, by knowledge to be implemented without difficulty, by well-defined rules of choice, and by optimization of the choices to be respected. And it would be easy to evaluate, because the result could be judged by whether it met the goal clearly specified at the beginning. But if uncertainty about goals, processes, and results creates challenges, it is also a precondition for originality and invention, and for more long-range innovation. It is both necessary to the satisfaction taken in creating, and a trial to be endured. It is characteristic of activities that are not very routine (art being paradigmatic) that they provide satisfactions proportionate to the degree of uncertainty about success. We are speaking here, of course, of activities that are uncertain but not chaotic: If an activity were completely unpredictable it could not be organized or evaluated.

By saying that the creator is never assured of arriving at the goal of his enterprise, or of arriving at it in complete conformity with what he hoped to do, I mean that uncertainty is not solely exterior to creative labor, and that it does not concern simply the reaction of an audience or a market. If that were the case, entering upon an artistic career would be very quickly assimilated to buying a lottery ticket: Each individual, feeling in himself the call of an artistic vocation, could have a go at it, trusting it to chance, since the ingredients of original invention cannot be specified *a priori*. This schema would lead everyone to overestimate his chances of success by underestimating the power of selective comparisons. Artistic activity is, in the highest sense, a kind of labor, not a lottery, but more precisely a kind of labor whose course and outcome are uncertain. This means that in projects to which the artist attaches great importance, creative activity has to deviate from tasks that are easily mastered and repetitive, that are not very exciting, to be sure, but which are also not very risky, because their results are foreseeable. But deviating from repetitive activities also constitutes a trial. And it is indeed the trial of uncertainty that gives creative work its human depth and its highest satisfactions. Since Aristotle, this is why art has been considered one of the loftiest forms of human action. Uncertainty regarding the result leads us to ask on whom success depends. The answer is always given in four points: Success depends (1) on the artist himself; (2) on the environment in which his activity takes place and the conditions (material, legal, political) in which his labor is undertaken; (3) on the quality of the labor done by the team put together to create a work or a show; and (4) on the evaluation of those peers, professionals, or ordinary consumers who receive the finished work.

To reduce the question of uncertain success to that of the public's admiration, indifference, or rejection with regard to the work and its creator, is to cover only half the course of analysis. Inversely, to consider the creative act as this fragile, uncertain impulse threatened by its own inner problems, without attending to the circumstances of creation, to the external conditions of the activity, and to the relations of competition and cooperation among all those who constitute artistic worlds, is to focus solely on the part of artistic work that is centered on the self. In short, each aspect of the analysis, considered separately, is a source of stereotypes, the kind of stereotypes that are found in commonsense discourse on artistic creation. To the stereotype according to which the creative act, in its highest form, is supposed to be a kind of labor undertaken with indifference to the expectations of any audience whatsoever, is opposed the idea, just as conventional, according to which the artist cannot ignore the expectations and reactions of his contemporaries, even if he cannot determine them with certainty. Similarly, to designate artistic creation as an activity that is thoroughly collective, that would not exist without the multiple cooperations and collaborations required for its achievement, may establish the conditions that make the action possible, but doing so effaces the individualization of acts and interventions, and the uncertainty that weighs on teamwork's chances of success.

All kinds of paradoxes have been invented to resolve these ambivalences and antinomies. The most famous of them consists in claiming that in creative activity, solipsistic purity of intention and absolute indifference to success is in fact the best guarantee of success, through a sort of ruse of reason. In other words, the less success is sought, the more likely it is to be found. There is a related commonplace about time, endurance, and compensatory justice: The most rapid successes are the most ephemeral, and inversely, the longer success is in coming, the more enduring and ample the consecration will be. These formulas cannot take the place of reasoning in helping us to understand the artist's activity and the dimension of uncertainty inherent in it. In the course of this book's analyses, I will show, for instance, that the activity of creation would not be so profoundly stimulating and desirable if the individual did not learn, gradually, through the possibilities he invents and the choices he makes, to know himself and to discover himself as one and as multiple. The main resource of imaginative work is to invent and experiment on the basis of oneself, whether the dominant feeling is that of freedom and conscious mastery of creative decision or that of urgency and passion—or more probably, the sequence or alternation of these two mental states.

I will also show that the artist's behavior is neither univocal nor monolithic, that its variability is one of the most fertile sources of creative tension. If nonroutine activities in fact have this much-sought property of constantly teaching new things to those who carry them out, it would nonetheless be absurd to overemphasize this instructive value: No one could work to constantly reinvent all the essential aspects of one's activity. Without conventions, without rules of interaction, without more or less stable procedures of dividing up tasks and mutually adjusting expectations, without routines, no cooperation is possible among all those who have to participate in the production, dissemination, consumption, evaluation, and preservation of artworks. It remains that the very prestige and seductive power of artistic vocations are measured by the degree to which the result and success are unpredictable. Whence the composite character of artistic work, which is constructed of challenges and inventions, but also of reliance on solutions that have already been tested, and whence also the diversity of behaviors that may result depending on the proportion, chosen deliberately or not, of proven elements and new experiments. The multiplicity of an artist's manners, or the variety of the phases of his work, which lead him to alternate exploratory works with more conventional ones that are also more in conformity with his public image, or sudden and durable change, or even the artist's splitting himself into several identities, constitute so many forms of individualization situated along an axis whose two extremities would be the pure exploitation of a formula of creation that is entirely analyzable and reproducible from one work to the next, and, at the other pole, constant change, resistant to any recognizable stabilization of a personal manner, and thus to any identification of an individual style.

Outline of the Book

This book is organized in the following way.

In the first chapter, I present the social-science tools that I require to establish the principles for analyzing creative work. I start out from the opposition between two models of the analysis of action, the determinist, or causal-continuist model as I also call it, and the interactionist. I examine the way in which this opposition runs through the two sciences whose contributions I seek to connect, sociology and economics.

If I try to specify as precisely as possible all the characteristics and resources of the individual, such as I can know them at the moment when he engages in action, I also have to consider that this specification will allow me not only to evaluate the probabilities of the actor's behavior and choices, but also to define the system of relations within his environment. But this specification, which makes the development of the activity predictable, in the manner of a dynamic propulsion entirely contained in the premises of the action, will accept uncertainty in itself only as a concession that is exceptional in the normal and regular course of things. Its key operation, in sociology, is the conversion of all interindividual differences into products of the hierarchies of social position. Of course, we differ from one another first of all in our social and economic capital. But in a relatively homogeneous group (consisting of, say, the members of a profession or a community of people with similar social characteristics), what can I explain about our differences in behavior and action without invariably referring all differences to deep causes whose determining power tends to be postulated more often than demonstrated empirically?

Let us now turn toward the second group of models. In these models, the variability of situations is a given, as is uncertainty regarding the course of events: What needs to be explained are stability and the recurrence of actions and behaviors. The process of learning that triggers this variability, and the strategically uncertain character of relationships with others, become essential elements for understanding how individuals negotiate, cooperate, exchange points of view (putting themselves in the place of the other as much as they communicate with the other), observe one another, imitate one another, engage in rivalry, and compete with one another. By proceeding in this way, the analysis moves more easily in universes defined by a process of exchange and the learning of roles and competences (including relational ones), and by the management of networks of relations. But it seems to lose sight of the properties that define social hierarchies, and it seems to sacrifice the inscription of the actors in the social structure to their inscription in the situation of action. I take the same route, first in sociology, then in economics, in order to bring out the properties of the model that I need in order to analyze activities that are highly variable in content and that have a high degree of intrinsic and extrinsic uncertainty.

At the end of the long opening chapter, I describe the conception of time to which action has to be referred in order to define the determinants and the indeterminate nature of the emergence of what is original and new, and which can by definition not be reduced to an extrapolation from the past. Then, in Chapter 2, I discuss conceptions of labor in the more familiar terms of the social sciences. But I distance myself from the diverse conceptions that try to detach the exercise of a creative activity from any presumption of substantial rationality. Creative activity is a rational behavior: This statement acquires its full meaning only if this rationality is specified as being that of behavior in an uncertain horizon.

I must therefore define and isolate the properties of labor that are appropriate for treating creation as an act of labor. The best strategy seems to me to be to start out from the conception most opposed to the one that I need, the one which, to put it in terms of economic analysis, assimilates labor to a negative magnitude. In this conception, labor is given the restrictive value of "disutility," of the expense of individual energy in exchange for a salary and the consumer goods to which this salary provides access. Leisure and consumer goods are the source of individual satisfaction and well-being; labor appears, in the economic vocabulary, to be negative consumption. In this way involvement in the labor market and the choice to engage in this or that kind of employment depend entirely upon a classic axiomatics of the rationality of behavior, that of maximization under constraint.

Nevertheless, the essential correlate of such an analysis is an extreme simplification of labor, and in particular its homogenization, which constitutes an obstacle to the most elementary observation of situations of employment and the very variable degrees of disutility experienced in carrying out labor. I show how to enrich the conception of labor in order to move from its characterization as a simple means, a cost, an expense, or a sacrifice, to a conception of labor as a vector of individual accomplishment. But in conformity with the framework adopted in the first chapter, I also have to examine the question of interindividual differences. Among the factors acting on professional choices and on the differences in remuneration associated with them, there are two elements on which socioeconomic analysis chiefly concentrates: the nature and the level of initial training, and interindividual differences in ability that lead to dissimilar returns on the investment in training made by two different individuals. Sociological theories that seek to account for inequalities in academic success criticize the argument that abilities differ: According to these theories, differences in individuals' abilities and differences in the investments in education made by individuals and their families arise from intergenerational reproduction of inequalities of the agents' social condition. Inversely, some economic analyses attribute to abilities a determining explanatory role, prior to educational investments: Individuals differ in their demand for educational training, not only as a result of their parents' ability to finance and manage studies at the family level, but also because of the abilities they show. Whence the hypothesis that, *ceteris paribus,* individuals with the most ability are led to invest in an elevated level of training.

Involvement in artistic vocations makes heavy demands on these two factors: the acquisition of training and the more or less precocious manifestation of abilities that generate a "vocation." How is their influence distributed, with respect to the general analysis of professional situations? The argument I develop emphasizes that access to artistic vocations is only partially connected with the acquisition of training, because the requisite of a specific initial training varies a great deal, and because the acquisition of such training provides only a partial explanation of success and the capacity for originality. What the abilities for the practice of an art (often discerned as the residuals of a heterogeneity unexplained in the econometrics of earnings functions) actually are is revealed only gradually in many artistic vocations. And it is only as they practice that art that individuals endowed with the same level of initial training can reveal themselves to be (to an unequal extent) the bearers of abilities sufficiently (poorly) in demand to provide them with a successful (middling or failed) professional career. If practice of the activity is much more formative in the arts than in the majority of professions, that is because careers and chances of success are more uncertain.

The title of Chapter 3 refers to one of the questions that has become classic in the social sciences: How does an actor behave rationally when confronted with the uncertainty of the environment in which his action and its development over time are situated? By applying the problem to the case of the artist, I have sought to forge new tools for understanding and modeling in order to explore careers and labor markets that are governed by a high degree of uncertainty regarding success. First we have to explain why people might be attracted to professions in which success is very uncertain and in which it is probable that one will earn less than individuals with equivalent characteristics in other professions would earn.

The main economic explanation of the attraction of the artistic professions resides in the combination of two arguments. On the one hand, taking risks is encouraged by the hope of elevated gains (this is the steep profile of the distribution of revenues), whereas a calculation based on taking into account average revenues is dissuasive. On the other hand, the nonmonetary part of the revenues (the flow of remunerations and psychological and social gratifications, attractive working conditions, fewer routine tasks, and such) provisionally or durably compensates for the lost revenue.

The value of uncertainty is the pivotal argument for the integration of sociological and economic studies of the artistic professions. On the individual level, uncertainty as to success is part of the very essence of the satisfactions provided by the pursuit of an artistic activity. On the collective level, the dimension of uncertainty weaves together the indetermination of artistic competition and the disequilibria of the labor market. Taking risks can be interpreted in accord with the theory of job matching, because the jobs in which success is highly uncertain are also those that, *a posteriori,* provide the individual with the most information regarding his abilities. Taking risks is a demand for information, and the high rate of variance in revenues in the artistic professions can be considered in part the consequence of the market's showing the individual what he is worth.

The study of the conditions of professionalization in the various artistic disciplines allows us to provide a more precise graduation of professional risk. Risk varies greatly depending on whether the job market is highly integrated and protected by elevated entry requirements, whether the resources of multiactivity (such as the activities of interpretation and teaching in the field of art music) are thus multiplied, whether the artistic activity is sufficiently discontinuous or open in its material organization to allow artists to have second jobs and to allow a very gradual or partial professionalization (for example, journalism and teaching, among writers), or whether the requirements of training and practice force people very early on to make choices or bets on professional talent and very brief careers, and difficult reconversions (such as classical dance). One way of modeling these combinations of resources and jobs is, I will argue, to draw on Markowitz's portfolio theory.

In the last part of the chapter, I show that the structural imbalance between the supply and demand for artistic work must be connected in particular with the strategies for managing uncertainty implemented by artistic organizations.

Having examined artists' activities and careers as a remarkable form of behavior under uncertainty, and having shown how artists manage the occupational risks that result from the uncertain course of careers, I come to the analysis of the two main determinants of professional success: training and abilities. In Chapter 4 I seek to explain the considerable differences in gains and reputation that are observed in the arts. Why does training explain so little about the chances for gain in artistic professions? And if we say that the probabilities of success and the inequalities of success are determined primarily by inequalities of ability, how can the latter be defined? If these abilities were easily defined and observable, there would be no uncertainty regarding success. But uncertainty is the fuel for creative labor, innovation, and competition in artistic worlds. These worlds constantly carry out comparisons because it is impossible to determine completely the sources of artistic invention and originality. But in the trials that compare, classify, select, eliminate, and give to creative artists' careers their peculiar profile, what is the value of the procedures of evaluation? Aren't there countless possible biases? Analysis can take two different paths that are presented successively. The first is that of normative and critical analysis, which seeks to show that inequalities in reputation and gains are the product of a contingent organization of activities, the one that gives priority to mercantile competition and the industrial organization of cultural production. Another mode of organization could lead to a radical equalization of talents and to a complete liberation of individual creativity instead of reserving implementation for specialized professions. I examine especially two versions of this normative critique. One is based on the hope of complete social and economic transformations, and the other counts on the expected effects of contemporary technological innovations. The first, whose condition is the abolition of competition and an abundance of resources available to everyone, leads to the elimination of the uncertainty of creative labor, and runs into insurmountable contradictions. The second, which amounts to abolishing or softening Pareto's law, is contradicted by the facts.

The other path for analysis is the one offered by explanatory models of the considerable disproportion between inequalities of gain and the underlying differences of quality and ability. I examine two approaches. One involves the study of demand and shows how the sensitivity of demand to perceptible differences in quality gives rise to a strong concentration of attention on the artists deemed most talented. The argument can be maintained, even in the presence of almost negligible differences in quality, but then it assumes that mechanisms of interdependency between the judgments and opinions of consumers and evaluators are in place. The other approach is situated at the point of departure for individuals' careers and shows that even if differences in ability between two candidates for professional success are minimal or even nonexistent, there is a mechanism of cumulative advantage that amplifies, from one career sequence to another, differences in performance that were initially small and possibly attributable to chance. This second model, which comes from the sociology of science, can easily be applied to the arts. But its coherence is guaranteed only if in each case the tests of relative comparison that govern careers subject to strong competition and lacking in statutory employment security cause discernible differences in performance to surface. The analysis developed in this chapter leads to a model with four components. In particular, this model brings to bear the collective reality of artistic labor (its organization into teams and collaborative networks) to show how selective matchings, intended to reduce uncertainty regarding the result and to increase the productivity of the labor done by individuals of comparable quality who are associated in teams, are made.

The conclusions at which this chapter arrives are then developed in Chapter 5, which examines the first part of Beethoven's career. The composer's career and the artistic challenges he faced are connected with the series of changes that transformed, at the dawn of the nineteenth century, the social position of composers and the import of their innovations. In the social history of the arts, the great artist is often seen as an innovator on both the aesthetic and social levels, whether because he represents the rising power of new social forces that are the bearers of new aspirations and new ways of seeing the world, or because he marks the transition from an old regime to a new way of organizing the system of artistic production, and from the former's aesthetic system to the latter's. Analyses of artistic greatness or genius are torn between two formulas. One postulates that the exceptional individual is merely an incarnation of historical necessity: Changes had to occur, and if one person had not been their agent, another would have been. The other formula sees the great creator as an artist-entrepreneur who mobilizes resources for his own benefit and who incarnates the strategist capable of seeking the optimal formula of organization for his activity in order to establish an artistic and social power equal to the talent he knows he has. These formulas lead to dead ends.

It is to demonstrate this that I discuss the constructionist thesis according to which Beethoven's success, and the attribution of the qualities that make him a paradigmatic embodiment of an extraordinary creative power, are in reality the product of investments made by patrons who were very effectively mobilized by the composer. If that is the case, according to the counterfactual reasoning practiced by constructionist argumentation, then another composer comparable in talent (it is suggested that there must have been one among Beethoven's immediate competitors) would have achieved the same success had he benefited from the same social support and the same opportunities to express his qualities completely. If counterfactual reasoning goes wrong, we have to show why, and substitute for it an analytical model that does not limit itself to asserting, tautologically, that Beethoven's superiority is obvious and demonstrated by the considerable quality of his works. The solution I propose is based on the model presented at the end of Chapter 6.

In the course of artists' first formative experiences, abilities are manifested differently and unequally, depending on the individuals concerned. It remains to determine what kind of difference in talent exists between creators who will succeed and others who will be less well off. Expressed in terms of probabilities of success, the advantage obtained by recognized qualities early in one's career may be small, but it suffices that there be, at each trial of competitive comparison, a perceptible difference, whether small or large, in order to attract investments and wagers made by the system's actors (the artist's teachers, professional musicians, concert organizers, publishers, critics, patrons, audiences). The intrinsically formative character of labor situations operates the same lever: There is an optimal profile of the growth of competences that is a function of the number and the variety of work experiences and of the quality of the networks of collaboration mobilized by the artist in the sequence of his projects.

This dynamic reasoning indicates how differences in talent initially perceived as small can give rise to an increasing differentiation of careers. In addition, analyzing differences in success assigns a determining role to the networks of relationships constructed by the artist. Whether it is a matter of patrons, instrumental partners, or the diverse categories of professions with which Beethoven established working and collaborative relations, it is in accord with a formula of selective matchings that his networks of activity are organized. Among the benefits derived from this structuration of partnerships, the least is not mutual learning, as is shown by the fertile collaborations between Beethoven and the famed interpreters with whom he worked (Clement, Duport, Kreutzer, Rode, Schuppanzigh, Stich, and others).

In the twentieth century, many poets, plastic artists, composers, novelists, and filmmakers contributed to the elaboration of a poetics of creative activity. At first sight, two of the essential goals of this poetics seem contradictory: recognizing the role of chance or the unpredictable, and bringing fully to light the labor of creation in its most sinuous, most arduous, most uncertain aspects. Rodin's aesthetic audacities highlight these two aspects, as I show in Chapter 6. What we know about the details of creative labor we owe chiefly to the fact that it was no longer relegated to invisible operations in the studio or confined to the artist's secret mental laboratory. Gradually, the value of creative engagement has come to be measured no longer by the perfection or imperfection of the work alone, but also by the material evidence of the groping process of invention: Trials, errors, corrections, pentimenti, new starts, and bifurcations characterize, as we know, the artist's everyday labor, and the artist may seek to admit them, record them, or exhibit them, not simply in order to invent a superior form of narcissistic heroizing of the creative act (in its double form, that of labor connected with the pain of giving birth, and that of a triumph over oneself, of recovery), but because, for the artist, the documentation of creative labor is the indispensable reflexive support for an activity governed by the uncertainty of the result. One consequence of this is the relativization of the state of completion. And starting in the nineteenth century, the qualification of incompletion has constantly moved away from a simple definition that recognized only two possible states of the interrupted course of work, voluntary abandonment or involuntary suspension of the work under way.

In reality, insofar as the aesthetic quest challenged the criteria of the work's perfection and organic unity, attention was concentrated on the two extremes of the creative process. The initial states of labor, the outlines, the preliminary sketches, were found intriguing, especially starting at the end of the eighteenth century: They harbored qualities that brought to light the complexity of the creative process with its phases of springing forth, elaboration, and revision, to the point of strengthening the privilege of the artistic act's initial moment of invention over the terminal state of elaboration. At the other extreme, what did the work's state of completion signify? Without the canons of formal perfection and increasing approximation to an ideal, the artist's labor became more paradoxical: What was Flaubert trying to achieve by obstinately continuing to revise and rewrite a novel? To what absolute was Cézanne trying to relate his endless quest for perfection on the basis of a limited repertory of motifs and subjects? When artists produced genetic documents retracing certain steps or moments in creative labor, or when they multiplied series or sketches, as in painting, or again when they made the production of the work itself, or its impossible completion, the subject of the work, they may have wanted to demonstrate that particular works are situated in the long course of a career, and that the creative process is more important than its particular realizations. They might also suggest that they were the first to solve the mystery of the act of invention, by shaking up the whole range of the tools of reflexivity. Or again they make changes and revision a right to test a work's possible adjustments to the multiple situations that shape its reception and dissemination. Here, this questioning is applied to the study of Rodin's creative practice, which made virtuoso use of the resources of his medium, sculpture, to discover in the varied degrees of the work's completion a source of invention and at the same time a means of increasing his productivity, by taking systematic advantage of the uncertainty of the course of his activity.

CHAPTER ONE

Time, Causes, and Reasons in Action

ACTION ANALYSIS in both sociology and economics faces a persistent tension. To understand how individuals differ in their behavior, we may need to define each individual's characteristics, preferences, and resources at the onset of the course of action. This essentially leads to a long-term, propelling view of the causal determination of individual action. However, as action unfolds sequentially, within an environment of interactions, people learn from each other and about themselves in ways that cannot be fully anticipated. Can we, simultaneously, fully define the identities of social actors and the situations that bring those actors together? My view is that any attempt to do so needs to bring into play the related notions of temporality of action and differences among individuals, and that these notions represent a link between sociology and economics rather than a line of separation. My approach focuses on the sets of theories in the two disciplines that most effectively facilitate the comparative analysis of coordinated treatment of individual differences and temporality of action.

I begin with a critical comparison of two families of theories in sociology and then consider how the same questions are handled in economic theory. In looking at each discipline, the first type of model we will consider compresses or effaces the dynamic properties of action and individual behaviors.

Actors and Time in Sociology

It is common to mark the opposition between the two sciences by associating sociology with deterministic causal analysis and economics with intentional, strategic causal analysis. Elster and Dupuy[1] note that one of the two elementary structuring principles of this antagonism is the temporal orientation of causation; that is, determination by the past versus determination by intentional aim or focus on a goal, and therefore by anticipation of the future (in particularly reductive versions, this polarization takes the form of mechanism versus finalism). Critiques of goal-oriented action theory and, symmetrically, of a theory that understands action as a mere routine automatically adopted through the functionally stabilizing power of habit have become ritualized. They lead to either an attempt to absorb the opponent's objections and viewpoint—a kind of strategy of imperialist encirclement discernible in the respective aspirations of Gary Becker[2] and Pierre Bourdieu[3]—or to more eclectic compromises in which the behavior categories and the environments for action and interaction implied by the respective paradigms are selectively assigned. Following an obviously asymmetrical distribution, the sociologist is confined to routine, normed behaviors and the economist to rational, goal-oriented ones, with very few exceptions.

In fact, the distinction between deterministic and nondeterministic models runs through both sciences; the two sets of theories face off against each other within both. Before going further, it is important to preclude any confusion arising from my choice of vocabulary. The debate about determinism in science at large and in the social sciences that concern us here would be incomprehensible if we merely assimilated determinism to causal analysis.[4]

It is important to define clearly what is at issue. What type of dependence exists among the states, behaviors, and initiatives of successive moments in the actor's existence? Do we have to understand each act or behavior as an event linked to the act and behavior immediately preceding, through a strict relation of causal dependence? If so, do we have to remain within the boundaries of a deterministic model of causal engendering in which the successive points on an individual trajectory are all derived from "determined initial conditions," with the environment acting only as a disruptive milieu that the agent has to deal with, its power to shape outcomes only in exceptional cases having a significant effect on the trajectory of behavior? How should we model temporal dependence as a constraint that is in turn encompassed within the probabilizable space of a "course of action" so as to let the actor come to exercise a variable degree of control on, in accordance with the situations he encounters and his particular objectives?

Deterministic Theories in Sociology

In deterministic theories, causal analysis places the agent under the control of a set of forces that constrain individual action. The actor is propelled by her past in the manner of a *vis a tergo* (as a force from behind), and the situation in which she moves amounts to an "arena," a field in which the factors that determine an individual's behavior and action fully operate. There are, of course, several possible ways of specifying the deterministic paradigm, but in all cases it is crucial to provide the actor with a past, and to decipher his behavior by means of this past, using a grammar-like logic. The concepts of role, status, norm, and value are to be understood as crystallizations of collective influence on individual behavior. They are "in charge" of making the individual's actions coherent and coordinating the multiple individual behaviors, and they are what make it possible to explain the (recognized or unrecognized) adjustment or maladjustment of those behaviors. These concepts are bearers of a history, that of the supra-individual constraints determining action and action coordination, and they serve to characterize the homeostatic properties of the functioning of social groups. But using them amounts to hollowing out the action arena, evacuating its particularities, transforming it instead into a medium or receptacle for the causal influence of the supra-individual forces understood to govern individual behavior.

In deterministic theories, specification of the actor's environment is generally aligned with specification of the determinants of his action. In Durkheim's homeostatic model, achieving the stability of the social order amounts to establishing the conditions in which the individual will have a sufficiently strong perception of the relation of dependence between her set of preferences and the social whole—the idea being that she can only contribute to the harmonious functioning of that whole if she allows herself to be guided by the force of collective ideals.[5]

Another canonical example is Parsons's structural-functionalist theory, where a correspondence is understood to exist between, on the one hand, normative and value systems, and, on the other hand, the interaction situation or environment, the latter defined as a set of constraints that are stable and coherent for the actor. Clearly this amounts to congruence between situation and functions. Institutions are themselves crystallized systems of positions: a time, a past, frozen into arrangements that are constantly being reactivated without having to be remotivated. The social system could not preserve its equilibrium without this quadrilateral of functional imperatives—normative stability, the attainment of goals, adaptation, integration—or without socialization, which ensures that the individual internalizes those imperatives.

Parsons does not overlook the differences among individuals, but he argues that socialization makes people similar, allowing mutual comprehension and social cohesion. Although socialization creates autonomous actors, interdependence is also characteristic of the fully developed socialized being. Interactions in which Self and Other are mutually dependent could not have a determined outcome and could not therefore be stable if expectations and roles were not complementary. As shown by Bourricaud,[6] a world of autonomous and interdependent actors could not reach an equilibrium in the Parsonian system if actors' autonomy were not firmly fastened to mechanisms—constraints, obligations, norms—that bring about the convergence of actions. What is most likely to ensure social equilibrium is early socialization, which guarantees strong, enduring internalization. Once contracted and compressed to generate individual behavior, the active power of inherited time does indeed ensure the harmonious differentiation of actors—the severely restricted form of differentiation represented by the relation of complementarity.

Deterministic theories seldom claim they can produce outlines for strict conditioning of individual action. They generally include a probabilistic dimension[7] that makes it possible to specify the conditions in which the determining power of the actor's initial socialization operates. They also make it possible, perhaps, to link that first socialization to later socialization and to attribute strategic capacities to the actor, if only in the form of a felicitous disposition to choose what is "best suited" in each situation.

However, most of the theoretical contortions that deterministic theories go through to preserve a probabilistic margin for the analysis of action prove inadequate or at the very least mysterious, because they lack explicit, duly instrumented probabilistic reasoning and a notion of social facts as dynamic.

Among the many breathtaking instances of this sort of contortion, we can cite Bourdieu's rejection of the accusation that his thinking is deterministic. In the following sentence he first protests against that accusation, then proceeds to reject antideterministic concessions:

> The habitus is not destiny as some have made it out to be. As the product of history, it is an open system of dispositions, which is then constantly being confronted with new experiences and thus constantly being affected by them. It is lasting but not immutable. *That being said, I should immediately add* that most people are statistically destined to encounter circumstances consis-

tent with those that originally fashioned their habitus, and therefore to have experiences that will work to reinforce their dispositions.[8]

The next paragraph displays the same winding argument, yet the order is reversed. First comes the deterministic affirmation, then the concession:

> All stimuli and conditioning experiences are perceived at every moment through categories already constructed by previous experiences. The result is that privilege inevitably goes to first experiences and consequently, the system of dispositions making up the habitus is a *relatively* closed one. But this is not all: The habitus is only revealed—it must be remembered that this is a system of dispositions, meaning virtualities, potentialities—in *relation* to a determined situation.[9]

Twisting in one direction, then the other. The final result, as expressed one page later, looks very much like a folding of the individual back onto itself, managed by means of a quite singular version of self-determinism:

> Social agents actively determine the situation that determines them, through the intermediary of socially and historically constituted categories of perception and valuation. It can even be said that social agents are determined *only* to the extent that they determine themselves. But the perception and valuation categories that are the first principle of this (self-)determination are themselves in large measure determined by the economic and social conditions in which they were constituted.[10]

Detailed analysis of the wording here would show how each term is twisted by the speaker's use of its opposite, as well as the considerable effort exerted to ensure that emancipation remains subordinate to determinism, while qualifications such as "in large measure" and "*relatively* closed" offer a sort of impossible probabilistic compensation, no sooner mentioned than annulled.

How does this paradoxical probabilism affect the notion of temporality of action?

Bourdieu himself noted a kinship between his constructive structuralism and phenomenological analyses of action and temporality, the understanding being that the first had critically overtaken the second. Rejecting "the detemporalized notion of action that informs structuralist and rationalist visions of action" (Wacquant's wording), Bourdieu claimed to have temporalized the habitus, and thus to have moved beyond both Husserlian understandings of temporality and rational choice theory. There are two aspects to this operation.

The first of these—which remains perfectly within the boundaries of phenomenology rather than going beyond them—consists in inscribing determinism in a kind of temporality where the future gets folded back onto the past via the actualizing power of the present.[11] The close proximity of this understanding to phenomenological theory has been analyzed with great insight by Héran (1987), who shows Bourdieu's use of the kind of switching or "toggle" move central to Husserl's phenomenology:

> We have to presuppose, however mysterious this may be, that the deposited disposition somehow reverses itself; we have to assume the existence of something that activates the passive, actualizes the past. The habitus is, at the very least, a way of naming this switching system . . . Most definitions of the habitus seem to involve activation of something passive. These definitions readily take the form of diptychs in which two sides of the concept—the passive and the active, the before and the after—are juxtaposed, without our understanding very clearly how that reversal occurs or is genetically constituted: "as a product of history, the habitus produces individual and collective practices, and therefore history"; "as incorporated history, history-that-has-been-made-into-nature and is therefore forgotten as history, the habitus is the active, effective presence of the entire past that produced it"; the autonomy that [the habitus] confers on practices, in contrast to external determinations of the immediate present, is "that of the [already] enacted and [yet] active, effective past [*passé agi et agissant*], which, functioning as accumulated capital, produces history out of history."[12]

This phenomenologized structural constructivism requires three spectacular simplifications, which may be described as follows:

- Sedimentation of past experience into a habitual body occurs without loss or cost. The body is conceived as a surface that allows for perfect inscription and retrieval of exchanges with the environment through continuous activation of an internalization-externalization mechanism;
- The grammar of the habitus recognizes very few behavior-determining predicates. In deterministic analyses that take into account biographical determinants, individual history is given the shape of an accumulation trajectory. In theory, and consistent with the phenomenological source of Bourdieu's analysis in terms of complete incorporation of experience, the actor's entire past is retained, stocked, reactivatible. But the perception and representation filters form grids for categorizing perceptual information that in fact configure and predetermine the meaning of experiences, so the knowledge content of past experiences is inherently reduced from the outset. The next move is to assign a single origin—social class position—to the various filters and the way they function, thereby drastically simplifying the sedimentary accumulation hypothesis;

- Since individuals can only meet others who resemble them in situations that reinforce the determinants of their actions and confirm their representations—better yet, since individuals are destined to anticipate that what is the most probable for them, and therefore to bring into being, via their representations, that which determines them to be nothing but the product of their determinations—then *by definition* the range of actualizable possibilities open to them is limited to the characteristics of regularly encountered situations.

Looking at the obverse of this move to temporalize the habitus will enable us to locate the margin of chance that Bourdieu says provides this determinism with its probabilistic dimension. On the one hand, reproduction of the social structure is ensured by the switching game that goes on between (1) the set of habituses and (2) reproduction strategies that are "at once independent, often to the point of conflict, and orchestrated by all the agents involved, all working continuously to reproduce the social structure." On the other hand we have "unknown factors" and "failures"— that is, the sum of individual deviations from the trajectories that would ensure strict perpetuation of inherited positions in social space—and these are due to "contradictions inherent in the structures and to conflict or competition among agents operating in those structures."[13] Competition is thus invoked to explain both the properties that keep the social system stationary and chance departures from the rule, departures that taken together do affect the system, but only by shifting it as a structural whole.

There is not enough space here to demonstrate that the problems caused for this theory by recognizing a margin of indetermination are rooted in a quite mysterious understanding of collective realities, an understanding in terms of classes, fractions of classes, and institutions. Those collective levels are at times conceived as the product of aggregated individual practices and destinies, with "clashes" and "conflicts" working as a kind of yeast for instability and "contradiction." At other times they are seen as homogeneous realities endowed with common interests, undifferentiated identity, and strategic capacities of resistance that limit possible changes to the system to a reduced dynamic and explain why the power game only ever gives rise to structural shifts—a formula for "preservation through change."

Bourdieu's affirmation of the probabilistic character of causal relations, a defining feature that works to perpetuate a "relatively" stationary state, obviously raises the question of what historical time we are moving in, or, to put the question differently, the nature of deviation from the logical course of things. Individuals with deviant trajectories are individuals who, by distancing themselves from their class or class fraction, have singular destinies, and the sum of these deviant trajectories plus the adaptation, reestablishment, or protest strategies they engender help bring about change in the social system and the way its "instruments of reproduction" function by redistributing positions. These changes in turn engender deviation probabilities. But the question then arises how to explain the initial deviation. As in economics—as we shall see further on—the primitive functions of the model may be specified in a way that situates us in logical time or a way that situates us in historical time.

Lastly, the temporalization of action differs radically depending on whether the individual is acting individually or as a member of a group. In the family of theories examined here, an individual's expectations about her future situation or the course of her action is subject to a notion caught twice over in the deterministic circle. First, the individual's forming expectations about the future is primarily adaptive in that it derives directly from past experience. Second, the formation of that expectation is directly socialized, as it is understood to develop entirely in reference to the social group of which the individual is a member. This is so both because the individual's position is the equivalent of a statistical component in a homogeneous class of positions—with the understanding that perception of self and self's being in time is homogeneous within this class—and because the level of an individual's aspirations and how he assesses opportunities for action can only derive from comparison with the situation and opportunities for action of other groups, precisely those groups with whom the group he belongs to is competing.

In deterministic sociology, time is condensed in such a way as to have meaning only as the origin of the system of action. It is responsible for endowing actors with material and cognitive resources, and it is sedimented in the values and norms that orient the system of their preferences. In these models, history and the unfolding of time primarily relate to continuous, stationary, or evolving processes where the future state of the system is contained in its present. The social "dynamic" is that of predictable evolution, as in the schema of linear transformation through increasing social complexity and differentiation (for example, the division of labor in Durkheim's thought) or that of perpetuating a system's structure by way of a simple reproduction mechanism. An unchanging order prevails within an overall structure that is moving: Differences are preserved in a context where living conditions are improving over the long term. Agent behavior is predictable; value systems remain constant (Parsons); macrosocial trends can be extrapolated from, regardless of whether balances are stationary (and based on self-maintaining and self-reinforcing situations of class conflict and domination) or cyclical (change being understood as a disturbance that is corrected by the system's fundamental homeostatic properties and balancing mechanisms).

We see that the stability of the system may be attained by way of diametrically opposed hypotheses. Conflicts and struggles in a society based on inequality and domination can serve social integration, as long as people continue to invest energy in economic competition under the misapprehension that the results of the game are not fixed in advance by the deeply unequal points from which players begin. This form of integration obviously differs radically from one deriving from a system of values shared by all members of the given society and working to the advantage of each on the basis of individual differences—a society where expression of those differences is made to serve the group as a whole within the tolerable limits of a hierarchical ordering and rewarding of individual merits and efforts. Still, these opposing visions of social stability build on the same functional mechanism of internalization, itself produced by constraining socialization. This mechanism ensures endogenization of all determinants of action and actor relations while justifying understanding of the two analytic levels—macrosociological and microsociological—as two homologous expressions of the same reality, with the intermediate levels (fields, subsystems) replicating and refracting the general properties of the system in particular domains, in accordance with the same structuration variables.

If the different scale realities are isomorphic, then it does not really make sense to speak of a social *environment* the actor has to respond to or act upon. And if the properties of both action determinants and social relations are similar, then there cannot really be any uncertainty intrinsic to the course of action. Time in deterministic theory only serves to make actual what has already been determined by the origin of individual trajectories. Traces of past experiences are sedimented in it, and it reactivates those traces—this is nonproductive time. The time of the individual amounts primarily to *amor fati*, love of necessity; "meanwhile," stationarity works to prevent the individual from understanding that what he considers desirable is really only inevitable.

Interactionist Theories in Sociology

Interactionist theories restore intentionality to actors and attribute a fundamental role to their representations of their resources and the goals of their action. The mental operations referred to in these theories have nothing to do with states of a mystified "consciousness." How do the actor's past and present come together and work together in these theories? The socialization of the actor is understood not as a matter of conditioning but of adaptive processes: The cognitive resources and attitudes resulting from the socialization process guide the individual's behavior, but not according to the prescriptions of an action grammar. Instead, the newness of a situation carries information that elicits a change in behavior and produces enriched experience. The optimization hypothesis—that the actor in a given action context consciously seeks the best solution, that solution being a function of his preferences, interests, and resources as he perceives them—differs significantly from an understanding of individual behaviors in terms of strategy. That understanding, as we have seen, reintroduces teleology into action, using notions of ambiguous if not untenable epistemological status, such as Bourdieu's "unconscious strategy," a hard-to-conceive passive variety of strategy.

Interactionist theories as analyzed by Boudon and Bourricaud[14] loosen even further the hypothesis of the constraining power of an individual's primary socialization. They do so by ranking socialization-produced normative and cognitive combinations by degree of internalization and power of constraint, but also and above all by including learning phenomena that occur *after* the initial socialization phases.[15] The effect is to preclude thinking of first socialization in terms of indelible imprints or molds that organize all later acquisition of new knowledge and experience. Here socialization is differentiated, or may be said to become a particular case of a more general rule—learning—whose temporal horizon is much vaster than that of the individual's very first experiences, these understood to be particularly intense because inculcated in a contracted period of time.

In this understanding, individual action is not entirely determined by, but is instead deployed within, a system of constraints into which the actor manages to fit her preferences and resources. Those situations form a complex, dynamic environment. There is no one-to-one correspondence here between situation characteristics and actor characteristics—in contrast to theories that establish affinities between actors' dispositions and the positions offered by the field of action, or between internalized values and stable, coherent constraints particular to action environments, as in structural functionalism.

For our purposes we can identify two categories in this family of theories, noting that these do not cover the entire set of criteria used earlier by Boudon to subdivide interactionist theories more finely into four types: Marxian, Tocquevillian, Mertonian, and Weberian.[16]

In the first type of theory, actors act independently of each other and are not in a situation of strategic interaction. The pursuit of individual interest is guided by preferences, whether these are considered exogenous or influenced by an individual's socialization; individuals are maximizers operating under resource constraints; social facts and the social dynamic are produced by the combining of individual actions, and the aggregation of those actions engenders results that were not systematically produced by a collective will. This category of interactionist model shares two fundamental characteristics with economics models of perfect competitive behavior: maximization of individual interest and individualism. Two of its essential traits are discussed later in connection with perfect-competition General Equilibrium models in economics. Ideally, we would consider the differences between interactionist models in the two disciplines, but the scope of this chapter once again prevents me from doing so. Suffice it to say here that in sociology there is no hypothesis on conditions for balancing the social system, so the independence of individual-maximizing behaviors leads to a variety of stable and unstable collective results and emerging effects.

The second category of interactionist models postulates that actors are interdependent and that social situations are configured by way of particular procedures for managing those strategic interdependencies, for example, negotiation, mutual adjustment, and conflict resolution. We begin with the interactionist theories developed by symbolic interactionists in the United States—Becker, Goffman, Hughes, and Strauss—and with ethnomethodology as developed by and derived from Garfinkel, in line with the work of Mead and Blumer and descending from German phenomenology as rethought by Schütz.

In direct contrast to what is required by deterministic models, this category of interactionist analyses specifies the social identity of actors exclusively in terms of the nature of their involvement in strategic interaction games, work situations, interindividual cooperation, and collective activity networks.[17] In contrast to sociological or psychological approaches that conceive of social interactions as an arena in which the factors that determine individuals' behavior and action operate and are expressed, these models stress that interaction is also a training process wherein "individuals each orient, control, inflect and modify their lines of action in light of what they learn about others' actions."[18] The vocabulary used by these sociologists is much more that of cooperation and coordination than conflict. It is not that they err on the side of irenicism; their thinking is simply more in line with game theory, where situations are positioned on a continuum ranging from wholly conflictual to wholly coordinated. Cooperation among actors is at the center of this analysis precisely because the various categories of participants have at least one interest or aim in common, that of making the given type of activity or group exist.

While cases of imperfect overlapping of participants' interests and problematic coordination are legion, these analyses all stress (in contrast to interpretations that deduce invariant structural properties of domination and dependence from the inequality of actors' respective resources) that dependence cannot be conceived outside a framework of interdependence, if only because of the strategic uncertainties that make it impossible to perfectly predict others' behavior.

Movement—change—is the explanatory principle in these analyses, focused as they are on the interindividual relations and behavior adjustment mechanisms that found collective action. Here stability and regularity of practices, the inertia of habit, and the perpetuity of institutions are the dependent variables. Clearly this stands in direct contrast to theories like those of Parsons. This in turn explains how it is that interaction dynamics analysis can proceed from such notions as role or convention, the latter taken from game theory and analytic philosophy. In interactionist theory the recurrences constantly observed in collective activities, and the rules and norms that create them, are conceived as stable but revisable social arrangements.

The intersubjective dimension of agreement, which is what produces a convention and silently maintains its efficacy, serves to bring together and establish correspondences among an entire range of realities—practices, techniques, objects, perceptions, meanings, shared knowledge, institutional arrangements. The stability of those realities implies both advantage and cost: They are modified more or less readily, depending on how much is required from actors in the way of individual investments and mobilization. In this approach, interaction situations and the procedures and rules that organize them may be placed on an axis ranging from the most routine, formalized, strictly repeatable situations to the least stable, rapidly changing ones.

The relationship that interactionist theories posit between individual differences and the timing of an action reverses the deterministic model equation. Action is fully temporalized, to the point where the individual himself changes from one point in time to another. And the reason the individual is able to put himself in the other's place for the purpose of assessing and regulating the course of strategic interaction is precisely that he experiences his self as differing over time. In characterizing these differences, no reference is made to any initial actor endowment (resources, preferences) in order to explain a series of individual actions independently of each other. To understand how the link between time and otherness operates, it is necessary to take a detour through phenomenology, one of the foundations of interactionism.

In the fifth of his *Cartesian Meditations* and in his lectures *On the Phenomenology of the Consciousness of Internal Time*,[19] Husserl develops a notion of the sense of otherness as both developing in and being fundamentally conditioned by time. The present would seem the time of consciousness and identity par excellence: Consciousness is situated at the "point" of each present instant and relates to itself in the immediacy of this living present. However, as Derrida puts it,

> The presence of the perceived present can appear as such only inasmuch as it is *continuously compounded* with a nonpresence and nonperception, with primary memory and expectation (retention and protention). These nonperceptions are neither added to, nor do they *occasionally* accompany, the actually perceived now; they are essentially involved in its possibility.[20]

The seeming simplicity of self's immediate relation to consciousness-of-self in a pure present actually involves a complex temporality that extends "simultaneously" in the direction of a passed present, with its nonrealized possibilities, and a present-to-come—that is, the possibilities discernible on the horizon of the present. This is a future whose difference from the present means that it cannot be merely extrapolated from that present; but it is also a future about which there *are* expectations, expectations that belong to the substance of the present.

The complex time structure of consciousness makes it possible to understand not only self-reflection—without distance from self, there can be no turning around to consider self—but also the self's relation to others. Just as self-consciousness is created by awareness of self's existing at different times, so, too, consciousness of the other, of otherness, is attained only by *analogy* to the experience of difference between self and self in time.[21] Herein lies the power of time: The individual moves within it perceiving himself as both identical to and different from what he was and will be, and this fundamental experience allows him to understand the other as another self. That other's otherness is *similar to* the otherness experienced by self in the meeting and combining of identity (present) with difference (past as another present) that constitutes reflexive, temporalized consideration of self.

These two themes—experience through consciousness of a complex temporality and experience of otherness by way of time—are at the heart of interactionism. To fully demonstrate this, however, it would be necessary to detail not only George Herbert Mead's work but also Alfred Schütz's. Here Strauss's suggestive synthesis of these two currents of thought in *Mirrors and Masks* may serve as a guide.[22] To establish that interaction is a highly complex process, Strauss points out all the temporal dimensions of action that come to light when it is considered from the following double perspective:

- In the course of acting, the actor is continually assessing, reassessing, and developing revisable expectations.
- The actor's having a view of her action within the situation implies her taking into account the other actors involved, representing to herself their possible reactions and adjusting her behavior.

In the first postulate, behavior and reflexivity are intertwined. The course of action is an occasion for learning, and for as long as it lasts, it continually elicits assessment of actions already performed and possible ways of reorganizing choices and behavior. These mechanisms are particularly clearly at work in problematic, ambiguous situations, situations that most directly reveal the uncertainty of the future and the risk of error. It is in these difficult-to-predict situations that learning proceeds by trial and error, correction, reformulation of objectives, and revision of modes of engagement. The process-like character of action thus conceived means that the expectations made possible by past experience are necessarily imperfect and that the probability of assessment or judgment error requires some degree of reflexive control.

People adjust their behaviors to the situation at hand. In a stable environment, behaviors may indeed be akin to automatic responses to predictable situations, responses understood by all. Activities are conventional, routine; expectations are correct; action is akin to ritual; the future can indeed be extrapolated from past experiences—and there is no learning. On the contrary, explains Strauss, change and innovation occur in uncertain, confusing environments where surprise requires the actor to reassess his past acts and invent new values, new responses, and draw lessons from mistaken expectations. It is precisely this kind of experience that points out the indeterminacy of the future, with its wealth of productive possibilities and its risks.

Interactionist analysis differentiates situations by type of appeal or how they prompt the actor: Is she called upon to invent responses, or, on the contrary, to apply a preestablished, routine schema? Through reflexive oversight and control—incessant comparing of past decisions with the present circumstances and the more or less predictable future of the course of action—the actor becomes involved in a multiplication of self. It is when the course of things is undetermined and fluid, that the temporality of action is particularly clear and reflexive work particularly intense and productive. In such cases, what may be called self-interaction—made up of reconsiderations of self in the form of self-criticism, regret, avoidance, the invention of new hypotheses—is itself an open process, partially undetermined, and subject to continual revision.

The second postulate enlarges the scope of the analysis to include interactions with others. Strategic interdependence, arising as the actor anticipates others' reactions and adjusts his course in light of what he anticipates, lies at the heart of his assessment of the course of action. Here uncertainty lies in the differences that may exist between the actor's understanding of his act and the meaning that others will impute to it, differences and divergences that may cause perplexity for the actor as to the real meaning of his action and lead him to question himself. Here, too, there are, on the one hand, codified, conventional situations that do not require agents to have much information in order to act, or that require readily accessible and widely shared information—these are also situations where convergence of interpretations of the situation and the resulting actions is highly probable, even nearly automatic. On the other hand, there are ambiguous, new, not-yet-experienced situations where the deciphering and adjusting of assessments that each actor must do with regard to his own acts and those of others do not appear a homogeneous process. In these cases, adopting behavioral norms or frameworks such as roles—a move which serves to coordinate actions at a lower cost—precludes neither self-distancing nor a degree of maneuvering room.

When actions are strategically interdependent, action causation becomes complex. This point has of course been discussed and debated among social scientists from Wright Mills to the ethnomethodologists in connection with motivations and justifications for action. When an individual undertakes a less-than-routine action, he also makes an effort to provide a motive for that action, to find a justification for it that will be acceptable to others. Motivation here has two meanings: A reason to act in accordance with determined, explicit motives, and an effort to rid action of its arbitrariness in the eyes of others. In questioning one's own motives for action and the value of those motives, the actor includes others; that is, he anticipates the need for justifications that will be acceptable to them. He only chooses a course of action after working to assess others' anticipated reactions and possibly correcting his own first intentions.

But given that actors' beliefs and representations can vary greatly, it becomes important to determine a foundation for mutual comprehension among actors. At the very least it has to be assumed, following Davidson,[23] that interindividual differences in beliefs and desires can only be expressed without intercomprehension's being destroyed if we can attribute a real measure of rationality and consistency to others' behavior and arguments (beliefs and desires). Without this rationality or consistency, interpersonal communication would be impossible. If we are to be able to attribute expressive coherence to the words of a speaker we do not know and do not fully understand—an expressive coherence similar to the one we would manifest in circumstances similar to the ones that that speaker is in—there needs to be a translation operation. Without this mental game of matching another's sentences with the self's sentences in response to a given context—without, in sum, forming a theory of others' beliefs that grants them a minimum of coherence and relevance—we cannot arrive at what others mean and we cannot grasp the errors or differences of opinion that constitute in part the foundation of interpersonal exchange. Others' language and behavior are accessible to me, interpretable by me, in reference to an overarching system that would be inconceivable without rationality criteria: "In the case of language, this is apparent, because understanding it is *translating* it into our own system of concepts. But in fact the case is no different with beliefs, desires and actions."[24]

C. Wright Mills developed a similar analysis in his influential early article, "Situated Actions and Vocabularies of Motive."[25] Wright Mills places such a strong emphasis on verbalization of action motives that he sometimes seems to disconnect those motives from the function of reasoned choice, meanwhile insisting on the intrinsically social character of motive, consistent with Weber's theses on actor rationality. These two dimensions are clear in the following passages from the article:

> Motives are words. . . . They do not denote any elements "in" individuals. They stand for anticipated situational consequences of questioned conduct. Intention or purpose (stated as a "program") *is* awareness of anticipated consequences; motives are names for consequential situations, and surrogates for actions leading to them. . . .
>
> Motives are accepted justifications for present, future or past programs or acts. To term them justification is *not* to deny their efficacy. Often anticipations of acceptable justifications will control conduct. ("If I did this, what could I say? What would they say?") Decisions may be, wholly or in part, delimited by answers to such queries. . . .
>
> The vocalized expectation of an act, its "reason," is not only a mediating condition of the act but it is a proximate and controlling condition for which the term "cause" is not inappropriate. It may strengthen the act of the actor. It may win new allies for his act. . . .
>
> When an agent vocalizes or imputes motives, he is not trying to *describe* his experienced social action. He is not merely stating "reasons." His is influencing others—and himself. . . . The motives actually used in justifying or criticizing an act definitely link it to situations, integrate one man's action with another's, and line up conduct with norms. . . . When they constitute compo-

nents of a vocabulary of motives, i.e., are typical and relatively unquestioned accompaniments of typal situations, such words often function as directives and incentives by virtue of their being judgments of others as anticipated by the actor.[26]

The theoretical tools of accountability and reflexivity developed by Garfinkel in ethnomethodology are closely related to this understanding of verbalized interaction. They refer to the work of describing and interpreting that the actor is continually (and more or less automatically) undertaking: The contextualized, indexed imputations of meaning that work to orient and control action; and the (routine or rationally organized) work of producing categories of meaning on the basis of which behaviors can be adjusted to each other. This conceptual framework implies temporalizing behavior and contextualizing reflexive activity so that the "action description" resource may be applied to the singular characteristics of the given situation; it also implies that action coordination is characteristically flexible, negotiable, and revisable.[27] In simple terms, reflexivity is the ability to account for oneself to oneself; that is, to realize-verbalize the motives of one's action.

It should be noted here that quite different uses have been made of Wright Mills's notion, depending on whether it was being linked to the phenomenology of experience or applied to inflect action analysis toward exploring the descriptive forms offered by language.

While each actor in an interaction situation engages in a labor of reflexivity and anticipation, convergence of expectations works best when there is perfect interchangeability of viewpoints, otherwise known as common knowledge. Strategic interdependence has the following pair of properties: (a) It links each actor's perceptions and assessments of the given situation to the justifiable decisions that each of them selects, and in so doing (b) it compels the individual to "multiply" his self. In other words, upon encountering others, the individual must himself become other than himself through reflexivity, in order to represent others' reactions to himself.

The simple-seeming idea of intentionality gets more complicated when it becomes temporalized and includes others. To summarize, it implies an undetermined future for situations where interactions are not rituals, reflexivity, by which the individual "acts" on himself through distanced examination of his past acts and motives and anticipation of the possible consequences of his future acts. And it implies the interchangeability of viewpoints. The interaction is with self (speaking to oneself, deliberating, criticizing oneself, justifying oneself, projecting oneself) as much as with others. This interaction would be impossible if otherness and temporality were not co-determined.

The interwining of otherness and temporality in interactionist theories leads to the last point I wish to focus on here, the theme of multiple selves. Since the writings of Strauss and Goffman, this notion has had a highly successful career in sociology, particularly among authors interested in the paradoxes of actor rationality and in working to account for changes in behavior over time without turning to the radical solution of endogenous preference-changing.[28] As Elster recalls in the collective work he edited on the subject,[29] numerous theoretical formulas have been used to analyze the multiple self. Strauss's, developed in phenomenological terms and inspired by Mead,[30] emphasizes the distance from self introduced by the process-like dynamics of action, that is, by temporalization of the reflexive apprehension of self. Goffman's analysis of the multiple self emphasizes instead the context of strategic interdependence; this is the point of his critical understanding of social roles, a central issue in the debate between functionalist and interactionist approaches. Whereas in functionalism roles are combined systems of normative constraints to which actors must submit, as well as systems of rights linked to those constraints, in interactionism the actor's distance from his role is the sign of his reflexive handle on the action and allows for introducing a capacity for the play, negotiation, and maneuvering that comes to control the interaction situation. Goffman writes in *Encounters:*

> It is common in sociology to study the individual in terms of the conception he and others have of him, and to argue that these conceptions are made available to him through the role that he plays. In this paper, the focus of role is narrowed down to a situated activity system. And it is argued that the individual must be seen as someone who organizes his expressive situational behavior *in relation* to situated activity roles, but that in doing this he uses whatever means are at hand to introduce a margin of freedom and maneuverability, of pointed disidentification, between himself and the self virtually available to him in the situation . . .
>
> The individual does not embrace the situated role that he finds available to him while holding all his other selves in abeyance. I have argued that a situated activity system provides an arena for conduct and that in this arena the individual constantly twists, turns, and squirms, even while allowing himself to be carried along by the controlling definition of the situation. The image that emerges of the individual is that of a juggler and synthetiser, an accommodator and appeaser, who fulfils one function while he is apparently engaged in another . . .
>
> I have also argued that these various identificatory demands are not created by the individual but are drawn from what society allots him. He frees himself from one group, not to be free, but because there is another hold on him.

While actively participating in an activity system, he is, nevertheless, also obliged to engage in other matters, in relationships, in multi-situated systems of activity, in sustaining norms of conduct that crosscut many particular activity systems.[31]

The question is what happens to the actor and to his or her unified self when the different situations in which that actor is involved are differentiated from and considered in relation to each other? Structural-functionalist and structuralist-deterministic models locate that unity in the determination of conditions that preexist action-taking and coordination—shared adherence to values, nonnegotiable submission to action constraints—or in the much more costly hypothesis (which, as we have seen, cannot be rigorously specified) that there exist structural affinities between the field of action and the distribution of actors' characteristics, the latter understood as products of earlier states of society.

In interactionist models, on the other hand, the actor has to be attributed a reflexive power of adjustment if he is to maintain some ability to act in diverse situations. When the situation is imperfectly determined, nonroutine, or ambiguous, the actor has to be able to distance himself in some way from both himself and all available roles so as to maintain some room for maneuver. This strategic flexibility is the precondition of an action's efficacy in interaction situations, and it is what accounts for the dynamism of action coordination procedures (in contrast to mere dependence on the characteristics of individual actors considered separately).

Where We Are Thus Far

At this point we can say that sociological theories that explain action in the deterministic terms of internalized values and norms, types of socialization, or homologies between action variables and interaction structures differentiate actors and situations in terms of an actively determining, sedimented, reactivated past that is somehow contained in those actors and situations. The historical substance of the action is reduced to stationary time that actualizes what are mainly predictable situations. In models like Durkheim's or Parsons's, internalized values and norms ensure, or are supposed to ensure, coordination of individual actions while limiting expression of individual differences. It is by containing and limiting expression of these differences—an ever more pressing need given the evolution of societies—that society as a whole manages to attain balance above and beyond class conflict. In deterministic sociologies of conflict, differentiation propels struggle but is itself immobile in a world doomed to reproduce itself, with the exception of accidents and chance occurrences. While differentiation variables keep the class struggle going, their effect is to engender stable differences between individuals' situations, due to actors' ignorance of the fundamental properties defining social stratification (this lack of knowledge being particularly likely to characterize the least well-endowed actors). This means that time teaches individuals little of substance beyond the mechanical play of forces among exclusively collective actors and the understanding that situations have been ordained once and for all by a sort of Newtonian social physics. Actors' differentiation, when occurring identically at the various aggregation levels (groups, fractions, classes), results in a self-reinforcing social reproduction scheme. The critical stance arising from that scheme readily prompts a voluntarist eschatology and advocates social emancipation. However, any reallocation of power will run up against the structural properties of a system that perpetuates its order beyond any local changes brought about by intergenerational mobility as well as by exogenous shocks (scientific discoveries, technical revolutions, natural accidents). This is due to the understanding that actor interdependencies are entirely absorbed by the structure of a struggle between sets (classes, class fractions) that in themselves crystallize individual differences.

The ease and appeal of deterministic reasoning has to do with (1) the power of the causal language of variables, which often operates outside any explicit model specifying the conditions how to check and explain the hypothesis (it is left up to the reader to devise how much of the variance is explained); (2) the use of a "cleaned-up" if not eviscerated notion of the environment of action: Facts can be linked directly to variables merely by locating the environment at a macrosociological level or by matching environments by means of simple transformation laws like structural homology; (3) the homogenizing of behavior: All behaviors become subject to causal determination, since individual identity is fixed by socialization and initial endowments and remains stable (with the exception of chance occurrences) in all the various spheres—private, educational, economic, cultural, and so on—that the thread of an individual history unwinds in.

The understanding in interactionist theories, on the other hand, is that interindividual differences reveal themselves in time. The individual is a synthesis of different temporalized selves, and the wellspring of the action dynamic is the interdependence of actors—that is, the procedures for coordinating actions between or among agents defined by their otherness. Action situations are differentiated by the degree to which they do or do not elicit conventional behaviors (perceptions, assessments, decisions).

Keeping collective forms of arrangement and coordination stable in an evolving environment carries high opportunity costs. Actors' initial socialization does not underpin all their decisions. Time—on condition that it not be the stationary time of routine or ritual situations—leads to learning, since the information required for taking action is not contained in the initial state of the system, but rather drawn from observation and analysis of situations and reflexive assessment of one's own contribution to the action. Individuals act on each other and coordinate with each other because each is acting on himself or herself. And because interindividual differences do not come down to differences in initial endowment, they are not conceived of as arguments in a "struggle" that can be fully transposed to every context. On the contrary, those differences engender interaction dynamics precisely because they teach the individual to assess possible courses of action by way of retrospection and anticipation of others' reactions. The learning one does about oneself is coordinated with learning about others.

Does the antideterminism of interactionist theories fail to appreciate how powerful are the forces that structure and determine the contexts in which we act? Not at all. The reality of the opposition to deterministic models is particularly clear in research on organizations. As Strauss in his studies of negotiation[32] and Crozier and Friedberg in their sociology of organizations[33] are careful to explain in different but related ways, antideterminism is not directed against either the idea that there are constraints on action or that interaction contexts have a structure.

The structure of strategic interaction involves organizational rules, an individual behavior function—actors select goals based on their resources and the constraints imposed by the action system—and a game dynamic based on interdependent intentional behaviors. Such a dynamic exists when power as distributed among the given actors cannot be summed up in terms of each actor's initial resource endowment or the conditions prescribed by the rules of the system for investing those resources. The power to act in interactionist theory is by nature relational. Uncertainty here—exogenous chance occurrences, management of uncertainty involving individual behavior, strategic uncertainty linked to the imperfect predictability of others' behavior—constitutes a wellspring for the relational game; it fuels and fortifies the power to act. The understanding is that purely routine situations that are perfectly predictable, characterized by social programming that empties behavior of all choice and reflexivity, and by interindividual relations devoid of uncertainty, are extreme cases. All we have to do to engender dynamic play, with its asymmetries, incompleteness, and uncertainties, is to lower by one degree the probability of these extreme conditions' being realized. Once this is done, the game is framed—in a probabilized space—by specifically defined gain-and-loss matrixes and by actors typified in terms of preferences and the resources they invest in the situation.

Elster proposes another way of describing things.[34] He hypothesizes that individual behavior results from a filtering process that occurs at two levels. At one level, structural constraints over which the actor has no control restrict his possibilities for action to a set of realizable initiatives; at the other, he or she makes a choice from among the possibilities. Mechanistic analysis takes into account only the first type of filtering, where all possibles are immediately reduced to a single one, necessarily chosen without any conscious deliberation. An analysis that includes both levels might appear antimechanistic, but would in fact be deterministic in that it would stipulate that the field of possibility be structured in such a way that "choice" follows an entirely predictable, stable, restrictive selection principle (unrecognized as such) to be deduced from the initially determined parameters of behavior. (Behavioral constraint receives various names in deterministic theories: disposition, practical sense, implicit knowledge, prereflexive steering.) Intentional analysis postulates instead that at the second level, choice is the result of deliberation aimed at maximizing satisfaction or gain.

The antideterministic stance of interactionist models has a clearly longitudinal dimension. The point is to reject the idea of any *a priori* causal relation between the power to act and cognitive resources as initially capitalized, then invested, in deciphering the context of action. It is here that interactionist models posit an actor transformed by accumulation of selectively memorized experiences.[35] If, in order to act, an actor had nothing more available to her than a set of categories for deciphering and interpreting situations—a set of cognitive resources whose content and structure derive from the earliest and most vivid experiences of socialization, and whose power is furthermore a direct function of the extent of her linguistic competence—then everything would already be *determined*. In fact, all research into the dynamics of how people acquire skills brings to light more complex, evolving relations between an actor's existing knowledge and know-how and the potential for learning that is present in that actor's interaction with his or her different environments.

But the blind spot for all interaction analysis is the extent to which actors are different: Actors are not so different from one another as to preclude common frameworks for perceiving and defining a situation or to preclude credible, repeatable interindividual transactions or negotiations or mutually advantageous cooperation or negotiation. Whence the two classical foundations of dynamic interaction.

First, no intersubjective relations or exchange of viewpoints would be possible if there were not some balance between similarity and diversity in what defines individual behavior. Beyond the fact that interindividual diversity is a matter of the most elementary realism, that diversity is what makes exchange possible and gives interaction its substance; and the characteristics that individuals share are what make mutual comprehension possible. One of the standard ways of designating this foundation of shared characteristics is the imputation of rationality. What elicits such devastating accusations of "irrealism" against models that attribute calculating, modeling capacities to the actor is usually the imputation of (1) "reflexive-consciousness" rationality (knowing one's reasons for action, or at the very least, coming to know them gradually, through the clarification that emerges in the course of interactions); (2) the completeness and transitivity of preferred relations; and (3) optimizing behavior in the sense that the individual is understood to try every time to choose what will be most advantageous for him, a constancy that it would be costly for him to abandon. This is the price to pay for steering clear of ad hoc explanations. It is only by overloading the model that the individual can be endowed, as in the economics of perfect competition, with both an ideally powerful ability to process information, which enables him to flawlessly optimize in the way defined by the model, and perfect information about the situation, which enables him to flawlessly apply his cognitive power.

On the other hand, unless what is acquired from repeated interactions (defined as habitual or minimally recurring, to give them some salience) is stabilized, there can be no shared culture and no capital of tried and tested solutions and conventional routines that free actors from having to continually reinvent procedures of exchange. Blumer's interactionism as revised and enriched by Becker[36] (1988) thus deposits into the notion of convention the semantic values of (1) the anthropological understanding of culture—Redfield's, for example,[37] and (2) tacit coordination as identified by the philosopher Lewis, a conception that goes in the direction of game theory.[38]

Analysts regularly discern in the interactionist paradigm a weakness inversely symmetrical to the one affecting propulsive causation determinism. Just as determinism was faulted for exaggerating the extent to which an actor is socialized, propelled from behind by his past—a past he shares with many similarly fashioned actors—so interactionism is faulted for underemphasizing these things. This diagnosis may be put differently: Emphasizing interaction leads to endowing individuals with communicative rationality: "Given what I know of the situation and the choices I myself have made, choices that best suit what I'm looking for, I act so as to inform others of my intention to act in that way and, simultaneously, to inform them of my intention to inform them through my acts."[39] But if the intersubjective relation comes down to mere well-conducted introspection—"If I were in Y's place, I would do thus. And when I act, I have to assume that Y, too, can reason in the way I just have," and so on—then interindividual differences are effaced: In temporal terms, as Pierce explains,[40] this type of intersubjectivity is the equivalent of a relation between a present self and a self-to-come, a self engaged in fundamentally dialogical thinking. The otherness of the intersubjective relation is here analytically reduced to an intentional relation between self and a future, determinable state of self, a relation that can exist because every actor is identically able to decipher the situation and its earlier states. Clearly this is the same result as Husserl's: The self comes to experience others as other via the temporal flow of self-presence. But if intersubjectivity is merely a matter of inner dialogue or—what amounts to the same thing—perfect specularity, the specularity of perfect interchangeability of viewpoints, the "shared knowledge" postulated in game theory, then the other is not really constituted as different from self, nor is time constituted as an irreversible flow. Dupuy shows quite clearly that unless a minuscule dose of imperfection is introduced into each actor's information about the game and the other players—that is, unless there is a certain degree of situational opaqueness—then we cannot conceive of anything real.[41] Without such imperfection, we cannot conceive of an individual differentiated from others, of the collective as an external force and a restrictive and stabilizing reference for interindividual exchanges, or of the temporal dynamic that transforms actor reflexivity from mere introspective mobility into an evolving process directly related to the grip that each one wants to get on the action situation. To define differences in terms of how different each actor's information (differing information on the self, on others, on the rules and past of the situational game) is generically to designate what will move those actors to "get to know each other" sequentially, in the course of cooperative or conflictual interaction.

Actors and Time in Economics

We can now do a symmetrical exercise to assess how economic actors and time are conceived in economic analysis. This will provide a framework for comparison with the sociological approach.

Neoclassical Axiomatics and Determinism
in Economics

The most influential and mathematically powerful set of models in economics research is of course neoclassical theory. Given the multiple understandings of this doctrine and how variously it gets applied to all the points we have been considering, it would be grossly simplistic to speak of a unified "neo-classical theory." Still, there is obviously a much higher degree of homogeneity in economics than in sociology, and this makes possible a schematic review of the cornerstones of this set of theories.

Neoclassical theory is a theory of equilibrium which posits that (1) a given agent's various intentional actions under given constraints are compatible with each other, and, more importantly (2) the actions of all agents are compatible. The first hypothesis can rightly claim a certain realism as a representation of individual behavior, whereas the second is merely a mathematical necessity for defining how the parameters under study are systematically related to each other. One of the major advantages of the idea of equilibrium is that it allows the construction of models that can make some claim to forecast accurately. Sociologists' conceptual toolbox contains no such radically simple postulate, in large part because the ideas of methodological individualism and the rationality of actors that economists need to make the concept of equilibrium work are not at all as widely accepted in sociology.

Neoclassical theorists look for mathematical solutions to the problem of aggregating agents' behaviors; that is, getting from diversity to integrative synthesis without introducing bias. The less heterogeneity allowed to actors' behavior, the better the solution. Sociologists, on the other hand, construct intermediate concepts to apprehend interindividual heterogeneity, and give much greater weight than economists to the logic of action situations.

Furthermore, for modeling purposes, economic analysis involves much more thorough decontextualization than its sociological counterpart. The environment of the phenomena studied is treated as exogenous and schematized by reducing temporal, spatial, and qualitative considerations. This is why many models reason in terms of two commodities, two agents, two periods, or, on the contrary, an infinite number of agents and periods. The cost of such schematic reduction seems excessively high. But when economists attempt to construct a locally valid model by stacking interindividual heterogeneity factors (for example, information asymmetry) on top of intertemporal heterogeneity ones (such as a dynamic, random frame), they, like sociologists, run into problems of synthesis or complexity that interfere with mathematical processing of the data.

At a more general level, economics and sociology are sharply distinguished from each other by the way they classify components as either endogenous or exogenous. General equilibrium models treat agents' initial endowments, property structure (proportion of a company that is agent-owned), technologies, consumer preferences (namely with regard to paid work versus leisure), and the information that agents possess as exogenous variables, while prices, quantities traded, and income are treated as endogenous. Restricting ourselves to the psychological, social, and cultural dimensions of behavior, we can say that economists treat agents' preferences and representations as exogenous while sociologists consider them endogenous. The endogenization involved in extending the economic approach into new areas (such as the family, the organization) raises problems when it comes to modeling heterogeneous behavior (for example, whether an agent is optimally maximizing or not) and deviations from the blueprint of theoretical competitive equilibrium.

The two disciplines' different distributions of exogenous and endogenous variables affect how they understand individual action and the coordination of action. In the basic equilibrium model, uncertainty is necessarily exogenous; it results from changes in the state of the world that in turn affect fundamental economic variables. The chances of these changes occurring are dealt with by calculations of probability. But exogenous uncertainty has identical effects on all agents and cannot differentiate among them in terms of information. The picture changes significantly if we think of agents as interacting in situations where the decisions of each affect those of all the others, and where, in trying to make optimal choices and decisions, each agent tries to predict the actions of the others and anticipate their predictions when making his own predictions, and so on. The result is *endogenous* uncertainty, uncertainty about how others are going to behave. Exogenous and endogenous uncertainty get linked through individuals' beliefs about the probability of a chance event occurring that will affect the state of the world.[42] The notion that an event which in itself does not affect economic fundamentals becomes causally influential if beliefs about its effect on the behavior of nature or individuals differ by agent and become interdependent.

Lastly—and despite the fact that economists have debated this point long and hard, either to amend or enrich it—economists' fundamental assumption about individual behavior is the rationality of actors. The postulate of rationality is more of a theoretical construct than an anthropological truth. One reason it does not have the same central position in sociology is that it cannot work there as a logical operator. Sociologists strongly opposed to methodological individualism are likely to attack economics by criticizing the postulate of rationality. In so doing, not only do they mistakenly assimilate methodological individualism with the rationality postulate, but they dissociate or desolidarize the rationality postulate as a logical operator from the system that endows it with meaning.

In simple terms, the rationality postulate may be defined thus: Individuals have preferences and reasons to act (desires, needs) that they are perfectly knowledgeable about and that they seek to satisfy intelligently within their budget constraints. Moreover, they have absolute knowledge of the consequences of their acts once performed, and they therefore perform those acts assuming that the expected consequences will be realized. The backbone of rationality as understood by economists is not so much the idea of making perfect use of existing information or knowledge as it is the maximization principle itself. Rationality can only produce all of its effects if (1) each actor is pursuing her own interest only and maximizing her utility function as a consumer or profit function as a producer; (2) everyone is proceeding this way; and (3) everyone knows that everyone else is doing so.

Under these conditions, interdependent individual actions result in equilibrium through the transactions between "suppliers" and "demanders," sellers and buyers. But these transactions are understood to be instantaneous, costless, and to be based on information about prices and the quantities of available goods and services that is perfectly accessible to all agents. The transactions themselves therefore cannot influence individual behavior. Agent behavior in this understanding is extremely simple: What makes their needs and actions mutually compatible is precisely that all of them are acting independently of each other and have no other choice but to act this way. Prices contain and convey all information needed for transactions; parties to transactions have nothing to learn from exchange situations or each other; they need only optimize; price adjustment will coordinate their individual decisions.

But how do the prices that decisions coordinate around—the prices whose virtue is to generate equilibrium prices—get determined? The obvious logical tension in this analysis is what elicited the Walrasian fiction of the auctioneer or planning agent. For, if each actor is keeping an eye on prices that his or her action helps determine, then clearly price is simultaneously—and contradictorily—a given for agents as "price-takers" and an economic variable. How can actions whose individual influence must remain negligible be coordinated unless agents can consult with each other? The solution to this question in the general equilibrium model is to posit the existence of a set of production factor prices and product prices, such that if firms and consumers simultaneously optimized on their basis, the resulting production and purchasing would determine just those prices. This answer points up two of the essential conditions for realizing a world of perfect competition:

1. When interindividual differences are inoperative, they are insignificant;
2. The basic model runs in strictly logical time and can only be made "chronological" by radically contracting transaction time, forcing it into the fiction of perfect instantaneity, perfect simultaneity, and perfect predictability.

The Insignificance of Interindividual Differences in a World of Perfect Competition

To produce a strictly deterministic model, Arrow-Debreu's general equilibrium theory[43] had to specify individual difference variables (tastes, initial endowments, the structure of company ownership rights) as exogenous. In this way, it was possible to use the methodological fiction of a single representative agent and maintain the hypothesis that the determinants of individual behavior are independent of the contexts of and rules for interindividual confrontation on transaction markets.

In other words, while the model in no way restricts agents' interindividual differences before they meet on the market, neither does it grant any role to these differences. Since the wellspring of the economy is determination of equilibrium prices—the equivalent of aggregate supply and demand—it does not matter whether agents are endowed differently or identically. The axiomatics require them to make choices and transactions in isolation, and to do so without taking into consideration any information other than their own preferences, needs, and budget constraints. It is worth considering this point in greater detail. The equilibria specified by the theory are to be understood in relation to a given environment: An initial distribution of income or utility among the members of a given society is defined by a number of different individual abilities, amounts of human capital, and financial wealth. This distribution is what defines the configuration of consumer demand in the economy thus specified. If the distribution of the initial endowment varies, demand for goods and services will vary correlatively, which will in turn induce correlative variation in equilibrium prices and quantities. Theoretically, the various initial distributions can be associated with an infinite number of possible Pareto-effective distributions, on condition that the market is perfectly competitive.

This last clause is of course a cruel one because it dissociates concern about economic efficiency from concern about equitable distribution. The first fundamental theorem of welfare economics specifies the conditions governing individuals' behavior regardless of their endowments—they can only act in isolation as self-interest maximizers and "price-takers"—and does not rank the Pareto-optimal equilibria associated with different initial distributions by degree of equity. Discussions of impediments to realizing Pareto-optimal efficiency do not generally take up equity considerations; most go no further than examining whether a perfectly competitive economy is possible. But they do look into whether modifying the distribution of initial endowments in the direction of greater interindividual equity is compatible with competitive equilibrium. This is the point of the second fundamental theorem of welfare economics: Without changing the premises (consumers and producers are price-takers individually pursuing their respective self-interests), Pareto-optimal equilibria can be reached by implementing tax and social-transfer policies that will change the initial distribution of wealth among individuals or among firms.

Whether or not the system's efficiency can be preserved if considerations of equity are introduced is of course a crucial question for economic theory; unfortunately, it cannot be discussed in the confines of this analysis. It is interesting to note, however, that the tax system generally understood to be most congenial to the general equilibrium efficiency principle is flat-rate taxation, which by definition cannot be affected by the individual and which consequently precludes his modifying the characteristics that taxation is based on (income, trade-off between work and leisure, choosing to be employed or self-employed, level of savings and capitalization). The problem is of course that such a tax is identical for all—at most it can be modulated in terms of characteristics that individuals have no control over (age, sex)—meaning that if the initial endowment distribution is strongly inegalitarian, taxation can only perpetuate the system's inequity. It will be objected that this is a theoretical instrument whose main purpose is to determine a norm for measuring the various efficiency losses generated by the different fiscal systems currently in use. But it is interesting that the same conditions apply on this point: The flat-rate tax transfer is made before the market opens and before equilibrium-producing exchanges occur, an arrangement that maintains the original distribution of exogenous/endogenous variables. The "snag" of actual tax systems is that they endogenously modify behavior and endowment distribution, thereby undermining the optimal competition criterion.

Though many Pareto-effective distributions do allow for the expression of individual differences, the general equilibrium model nonetheless limits agent differentiation in the exchange economy by means of another of its essential axioms—agent "atomicity." This is actually a size requirement: Individual agents have to be "small" enough that no single one of them can influence the price level at which supply and demand are balanced—that is, no individual agent can have market power—or find it more in his interest to act in coalition or collusion with others than alone. The best way of approximating this condition is to assume that the number of participants on each side of a market is high enough to make each individual insignificant enough that it is reasonable to postulate that agent identity or interchangeability provides a good logical-mathematical approximation.

The mathematical argument of numerical insignificance does not imply a refusal to accept differences among agents, but rather situates those differences on a continuum. In other words, agents are endowed with a set of determinable, measurable individual characteristics which, once determined and measured, can be said to describe interindividual differences. Individual characteristics are thus distributed in such a way that agents are heterogeneous enough to differ from each other nonarbitrarily. The mathematics of the model then allows for reducing these multiple individual agents' behaviors in the economy to the fiction of an entire economy behaving like *the* individual in whom those traits are distributed precisely as they are among the entire set of agents. This logical condition makes freedom to act, as defined by the individualist axiomatics of maximizing rationality, consistent with the condition of "sufficiently" equal distribution of endowments (or distribution so minimally unequal as to have no significant effect on the system as a whole) among a high enough number of agents (firms or individuals) as to ensure that exchange will not be thrown off balance by the market power of *some* of those agents. Obviously such mathematical equality constitutes an idealizing abstraction, but it is common practice to consider this abstraction a guiding approximation for modeling purposes. This points up the fact that in a deterministic system, the individual is nothing more than a logical operator, the understanding being either that there is no need to differentiate individuals from each other or that, as far as system operating is concerned, no efficiency property, either negative or positive, is to be derived from interindividual differences. As Granger explains, perfect competition modeling neutralizes action, replacing it with calculation:

> Economic actors are reduced here to passive elements in a force field whose unity derives from the highly familiar hypotheses defining the perfect competition market: perfect fluidity, complete and immediate information, free market entry, etc. All that subsists of the intuitive content of action is the

utility maximization norm, which limits from the inside, as it were, the protagonists' otherwise total heteronomy. But let us make no mistake: this is only seeming. . . . In order to have action in the intuitive sense I continue to give the term, we have to superimpose an organized field of relations among competing subjects onto the organized utilities field.[44]

It is striking that two radically opposed ideas of competitive society produce the same result. Structural-constructivist sociology differentiates individuals or classes of individuals or fractions of classes of individuals by the marked inequality of their initial endowments. It conceives of society as a field of competitive struggle for domination, an arena whose structure is, for all intents and purposes, preserved through time by the very power of the instruments of domination and the self-sustaining mechanism of competition— all these mechanisms remaining largely unknown and unrecognized so they can maintain their efficiency. In this version of sociology, equilibrium (if it can be called that) comes of the imperfection intrinsic to such competition; this imperfection is due to differences in initial endowments that in turn create determinant gaps that are perpetuated in profiles for accumulating and exploiting economic, cultural, and social capital, even as individual conditions actually change.[45]

The society defined by the general equilibrium theory in economics is quite the opposite of that described by structuralist-constructivist sociology. Here, the desires and actions of all individuals are mutually compatible— and there is no possible preferable alternative—the understanding being that such a society is particularly easy to produce (deduce) when interindividual differentiation is negligible. Once the initial conditions have been set, equilibrium is attained by means of a somewhat mysterious "operator" called equilibrium price determination. We know little about the processes that determine those prices. The prices themselves, however, impress themselves on everyone as givens that ensure the system is coordinated and endures on the basis of poor knowledge about the principles that determine them. The first of these worlds may be defined as being in a state of perfect disequilibrium, the second in a state of perfect equilibrium, but the theoretical logic that produces these diametrically opposed societies is, oddly, the same.

Temporality in General Equilibrium

We can now consider the other cornerstone of the analysis, the conception of time. In order for the market to coordinate actions in the context of a balanced competitive economy, the flexibility of communication and interaction has to be perfect. This explains the favor shown to immediacy, instantaneity, and the move to eliminate duration from trade relations. We can begin with the classic model of general equilibrium in a static world.

In such a model, agents all act simultaneously, that is, in such a way as to preclude situations of interdependent decision-making. The adjustments that allow for attaining equilibrium are made without delay; the price system reacts with infinite speed to market imbalance at any given moment. The interindividual relations that consumers engage in on the occasion of goods and services exchange have no duration; on the contrary, the hypothesis requires those relations to come apart immediately and perfectly. They cannot last, and there can be no memory of the relation that might acquire value, for this would generate a situation of inequality between Agent A, for example, who trades repeatedly with Producer X, and Individual B, who has dealt and will deal with X only once.

In a static model there is a list of different commodities and a market and price for each. All markets function simultaneously and all contribute to the attainment of general equilibrium. This static or atemporal model has been extended to an intertemporal general equilibrium theory whose essential principles we may briefly review.[46] Time is divided into a series of dates. Commodities are distinguished from each other by physical characteristics and the date and place delivered. For each commodity, then, there are as many markets as delivery periods; a seller commits under contract to deliver a unit of commodity X on date T. Production and consumption dates may differ, but all trades in this complete system of futures markets have to be made on the initial date. Transactions therefore take place for all later periods.

Each agent thinks of the price system in all these markets as a given, and her preferences and constraints are defined for the entire set of periods. Likewise her consumption (or production) plans are valid for all periods. Supply and demand are balanced by all present and future markets for all goods, and transactions take place only after equilibrium has been attained. Since the economy is already in a state of equilibrium on the initial date, production and trade can take place in calendar time, but all actors' decisions will have been coordinated on a single date, and that coordination holds for all future markets. This intertemporal market is of course merely the static economy logically multiplied.

Since the model includes no uncertainty about the way the world will go, forecasts in it are perfect. It is possible, however, to introduce uncertainty into the model nondisruptively. If the environment behaves randomly, agents will consider all possible states of that environment and associate an objective probability with each. If the environment is evolving in ways that agents are uncertain about, subjective probabilities alone will be associated with all possible results. In all cases, the environment is treated as if it were exogenous, and agents' expectations in a situation of uncertainty are reduced to probability distributions across the variables. The main point is that expectations, whether objective or subjective, do not radically differ from each other. The results of the basic model then apply, and we have a system of balanced contingent markets.

By itself, then, uncertainty—at least about the state of the world—introduces little that is new into this modeling of the economic system. Things would be different if agents had imperfect information on the state of the world and if the degree of "imperfection" were not identical for all. If individuals possessed information that differed in quality or quantity, they would develop different probabilistic beliefs, and in that case, instead of being concerned only with themselves (their own preferences, consumption plans, the consequences of their decisions), they would start taking into account what others might know about the state of the world. In sum, information asymmetry would work against the condition of independent behavior. This is precisely what the general equilibrium model averts by identically reducing exogenous uncertainty for all. But the price to pay for the model's supreme axiomatic clarity is high, for we simply cannot endorse the two hypotheses implied in the model's domestication of uncertainty about the future course of the world, that is, the hypothesis of a complete system of futures markets, and the correlative hypothesis of the existence of a complete system of insurance markets for protecting agents against all imaginable imponderables.

From Logical Time to Historical Time: Temporary Equilibrium and Sequential Economic Models

Conceiving of time as a continuum makes it a negligible category in general equilibrium models that compress it to program the whole set of future transactions. Instead, let us break it up into periods—let us differentiate it. There are three facets to this operation, or three coordinated moves.

First, time has to be of infinite or indefinite length. In a deterministic framework, infinite time, or at least a time span of undetermined length, best approximates uncertainty. Were the temporal horizon understood as finite, it would always be possible to look backward and forward in time and to use backward induction to impose conditions on the present that have been determined by taking into account the ultimate end and all preceding periods as they "recede" one by one back to the present. The reduction to finiteness adopted in the Arrow-Debreu intertemporal model was also a mathematical constraint that allowed for overcoming the complications of extending the temporal horizon to infinity.

Second, differentiating time implies loosening the grip of macroeconomics' longstanding preference for the long term. As Malinvaud points out, the long term makes the hypothesis of a perfectly predictable price system "fairly satisfactory," in that "agents have time to adapt their predictions to developments they observe under way and that they can reasonably assume to be slow and regular."[47] Price flexibility here seems due to a kind of smoothing down of changes produced by regular trends that agents can anticipate. Inversely, short-term macroeconomics analyzes immediate, situated phenomena, thus bringing wage and price rigidities to the fore, rigidities linked to market imbalances and to a variety of deviations from the law of supply and demand equalization. It is in just such a short-term world that macroeconomists observe unemployment, delays in delivery, transaction rigidities due, for example, to the mutual advantages for suppliers and customers, or employers and employees, of maintaining stable, enduring ties, or to the costs of collecting information or making contracts. Here we have a paradox: The trade-stabilizing factor of the *duration* of a relationship between two agents—what economists call a rigidity factor—comes into view and takes shape on the *short-term* temporal horizon.

Third, time needs to be broken up into periods that each have their own length or "breadth." In the intertemporal general equilibrium model, each unit of time was a mere logical atom in an order of succession. In deterministic programming of the complete chain of events or set of probabilizable scripts (after introduction of uncertainty), no point in time could have any effect on those following. Time was therefore modeled just as individuals were. Individuals' coexistence was purged of any substantial interdependence, and as "atoms" they were all of equal "size." In historical time, on the contrary, every period is heir to a past, whose traces it both preserves and allows to fade away, and period sequencing is fairly "myopic": The time barrier cannot be crossed by reducing time to a neat series of dates and logically interpolating future and present by postulating the existence of futures markets, on which products are negotiated today that will only be available later.

Economic models that take history into account are sequential economic models. There is irreducible uncertainty about the future, and the supply and demand that develop on a market are equalized only step by step and much more myopically than in the earlier model. But in order to introduce an uncertain horizon that *ipso facto* dynamizes and orients the economy thus conceived, we need to posit the existence of planning, of agents who try to anticipate the future. In temporalized economics, agents anticipate and expectations appear.

Because futures markets do not exist for all goods (and it suffices for there to be no futures market for one good), and because agents do not make their production and consumption decisions once and for all, markets reopen with each new period. There is nothing to prevent agents from committing themselves for the future, but they do so knowing that markets are going to open anew at later periods—knowing, therefore, that the prices and quantities of those future goods can vary.

At each date, economic agents (individuals, companies) make plans and decisions to produce, invest, save, and consume as a function of current prices, current interest rates, and expectations about their future environment, which environment includes future prices and interest rates. In other words, the shrinking of the temporal horizon implied by reasoning in terms of temporary equilibrium shifts attention to the interdependence between future and present and brings out the fact that expectations—which are, of course, what ensure the intertemporal structure of decision-making—are elastic. The effect of this is that, in contrast to logical time, there is no guarantee of economic stability.

This way of handling time combines with differentiation of active system components—individuals, financial assets, currency—as follows.

1. In an economy composed of short-term equilibrium sequences, agents' expectations are correct only if equilibrium variables remain constant over time; in other words, only if short-term equilibrium sequences taken together form a long-term, stationary equilibrium. This would amount to "de-differentiating" time by linearizing it. Expectation accuracy would then produce intertemporal equilibrium—a "particular case." In temporary equilibrium reality, agents make plans on the basis of their current information and expectations. But the plans are made with an eye to immediate consequences only, those related to operations that take place in the very near term. In sum, temporary equilibrium ensures that those operations are consistent with each other, but not that plans related to future operations will be likewise consistent. This means that even if there are no unforeseen changes in the economic environment, there is a possibility that agents' current plans will not have been

realized when the following period opens, and this in turn would require them to modify those plans, the effect of which is that their current expectations will turn out to have been at least partially inaccurate. This in turn leads agents to revise their expectations. Observed reality is produced by interaction between expectations and the actual performances of the economy.

2. In a model where the price system reacts infinitely quickly to market imbalance, thereby absorbing both diversity and variability in the accuracy of agents' expectations, the operative hypothesis is still that of a perfectly competitive market. In the historical time of a sequential economy, on the other hand, interindividual differences play their role to the full. Agents' plans are compatible with each other, but for one period only, because those plans are determined on the basis of expectations that may vary in the future. If they never varied, we would once again find ourselves in the framework of intertemporal general equilibrium.

3. In a sequential economy, currency and financial assets come into play at last as wealth reserves, as goods factored into calculations about time, that make time work and bring similarities and differences among periods into play. The same analysis applies for all forms of accumulation, specifically the formation of human capital and the accumulation of technical advances. These forms are what ensure that there are links between periods—links that may be associated with negative or positive results: waste, bankruptcy for agents who forecast incorrectly or invested badly, entrepreneurial success, financial gain, or technical advances and innovations.

The fact that the future is irreducibly ambivalent means it cannot be understood as a mere increment or continuous accumulation vector. The economic theory of innovation offers a perfect illustration of this. If we conceive of innovation as resulting only from a continuous learning process, then we will fail to understand that knowledge and skills themselves become obsolete and that innovations, by outdating knowledge, techniques, and products, can destroy them. It is crucial to be aware of the power of the negative (loss, forgetting, error) in creative processes—Schumpeter's "creative destruction." The most valuable innovation is not incremental. It involves a break, the sudden appearance of something new—radical innovation *exploits* uncertainty. It can occur *because* the future is unpredictable. And this analysis may be readily extended to work: The most highly valued work tends to involve the experience of uncertainty, as I will show in Chapter 2.

Modeling Interindividual Differences
in Historical Time

What of agents? We can now differentiate them in the same way we have differentiated time.

The first move pertains to number. We have seen that in perfect competition theory the number of agents has to be for all intents and purposes infinite, in order for them to meet the condition of being insignificant atoms. When the number of agents is high, differences among them get distributed along a continuum and cancel each other out in the system as a whole, a state of affairs that allows for using the highly valued notion of a "representative agent." Because individuals have no real weight in relation to the whole, they have no influence on it and their transactions are fundamentally passive. They are "price-takers," and since price constitutes all the information necessary for exchange, interindividual communication is reduced to naught. Interestingly, there is a kind of symmetry with what is prescribed for traded objects: Just as the number of individuals is extremely high, making them mathematically similar, so the commodities exchanged are homogeneous products, perfectly, infinitely divisible, and thus require no rationing. In this "world without qualities," where the individual is forced to be concerned exclusively with his or her own behavior, communication among agents via transactions may be described as continuous, costless, and insubstantial.

If we let go of the postulate of an infinite or extremely high number of agents, we simply define the properly *historical* (rather than merely logical) space-time coordinates of an action and interaction context. When there are fewer agents, those agents see themselves as different from each other, differently endowed, and they see themselves as in a position to affect supply and demand because their individual influence is no longer negligible.

The second differentiation move is to endow agents with memory and an ability to form expectations. Since each period is distinguished from the preceding one (except in the "stationary" case), the information that agents receive about economic developments, that is, the information required for forecasting, varies by period. To describe sequential market adjustment in real time, it therefore becomes necessary to specify the equilibrium relation by specifying how agents foresee the future on each date by the information they possess about present and past states of the economy. Expectations are not *ipso facto* accurate, any more so than individuals are all identical. If there has been error, there will be revision—learning by trial and error.

The third move is just that: to allow agents to learn. When we posit that agents have to anticipate, critically compare their expectations with realizations, correct or adjust the representations they based their expectations on; when we posit that they have to draw a sizable amount of information from observation of economic variable behavior during each period, we are taking short-term learning processes explicitly into account. Shrinking the temporal horizon sets individuals groping about in what is no longer a fully determined world, and differentiates them by their respective abilities to process available information. Errors, disagreements, or differences in assessment express agents' myopia in limited time, a kind of time in which the future is not a mere logical replica of the present or the unfolding of a program that encompasses the economy as a whole. In other words, in order for economic agents to be able to learn, change, or differ from one period to the next, the future has to be uncertain.

This is what brings temporary equilibrium economic analysis[48] closer to sociology's interactionist theories. The differences have to do with the degree to which features of behavior are formalized. The two disciplines readily agree that for an expectation-forming agent, the acquisition of new information—particularly by comparing expectations to realizations—triggers a learning process that leads her to modify the representations she based those expectations on. But though they converge on this point, they do not reason out from it in the same direction. Economists want to determine the most accurate way of modeling how expectations get formed (statistical inferences, estimation of unknown parameters, backward induction procedures), how agents revise their representations of the future (fixed rule, Bayesian revision, model reestimating), and the temporality of revision (do agents revise continually or only after accumulating observations?). The answer to these questions is far from univocal or stable in economics, and there is no guarantee that learning mechanisms can be understood in general terms.

If agents' expectations amounted to no more than subjective probabilities about the state of their environment made on the basis of identically incomplete information, and if those expectations reflected different attitudes toward risk, for example, or different time-related preferences, then the diversity of behaviors triggered by expectations could be handled as an exogenous factor, just as differences in preference are handled. But once we acknowledge that diversity in expectation is due to agents' working with different quantities and qualities of information, things become more complicated. Then expectations are no longer exogenous but endogenous variables, and this amounts to acknowledging the economy's sequential dynamic when operating outside the bounds of any perfect forecast schema. Expectations vary by the changes in the economic situation and by the various lessons agents learn from the quantity and quality of the information that each obtains about those changes.

The other, more serious difficulty for a sequential economy lies in the very nature of expectations. Expectations based on a past from which information has been extracted and lessons have been drawn involve adaptation and extrapolation only. Since such expectations are not in the least dynamic, in a stationary world they could only be confirmed. But then they would have no raison d'être.

The limitation to the learning and expectation functions that we see looming here is easy to understand if we consider the different parameters of the sequential economic model. We have introduced interindividual differences, and ensured that time affects agents by inducing them to learn and to revise their expectations and representations. What is missing is the introduction of actors' interdependence.

Strategic Interdependence and Temporality

When the expectations required of agents in temporary equilibrium run up against the limitations of extrapolating from the past, the postulate of actors' rationality runs into trouble. Rational expectations economists have solved this problem by introducing actor interdependence into expectation formation: Each agent integrates observable variables of his fellow agents' behavior—endowments, preferences, expectations—into his own expectations. But the complexities here are obvious. If two agents determine their respective behaviors on the basis of their respective expectations, and if each one predicts the other's action by trying to anticipate the other's expectations, this gives rise to a system of multilevel, intersecting expectations that may not converge toward equilibrium, that is, toward a correct forecast about the future designated by the vanishing point of all those multiple expectations. The solution is then to redefine the actor differentiation variable. The strong rationality hypothesis is sound if, as Walliser observes,[49] there is one and only one expectation-forming actor, or if—second-best—all agents' expectations about their shared environment are coordinated. Agents here have been reduced to either unity or identity, and the point of anticipating is to avoid error. If the rationality assumed by the theory is to be preserved under these conditions, those agents have to be endowed with extensive knowledge of the economic system. In fact, each agent has to have an accurate model of the entire economy, a model identical to the economist's. Furthermore, because an agent's forecasts depend on those of other agents, his knowledge can only be common knowledge. Expectations thus become self-fulfilling. They can only be correct, but under exorbitant conditions, as is often pointed out.

We see that by introducing interdependence *and* restoring rationality to the expectation function, economic theory abolishes the temporal dimensions it introduced by way of that function. Anticipating the future on the basis of fully shared knowledge of how to make it advene in the present amounts to predicting it perfectly—and therefore abolishing it. In just the same way, the theory abolishes the temporal dynamic of individual behavior: Forming a complete model of the economy is either a long, arduous activity requiring extremely costly learning (how could the system assume that cost?) or a logical fiction that obliterates agents' diversity along with changes in agents' behavior over time. Once again, the plausibility of the model improves only if the economy is running in a regular regime—which is just another way of substituting logical for historical time. Unless, of course, as Grossman suggests,[50] perfect forecasting is actually an equilibrium concept rather than a condition of individual rationality.

The World's Imperfection

We have seen how letting go of certain basic postulates of perfect competition makes it possible to apprehend and model the individual and time as components that are something other than logical. The analogies with sociological theory are partial, of course, but suggestive. The way models handle time is strongly correlated with the way they handle differences among individuals: Deterministic analysis and interactionist analysis reflect two different understandings of action situations. In the axiomatics of both categories of theories, action logic and the action environment are co-determined, but in different ways.

Economic theory offers the canonical example of this. Its chosen way of stylizing reality makes mathematization imperative. The requirements that actors (1) engage in strictly selfish maximizing of their individual interests, (2) be numerically insignificant, and (3) obtain perfect information from prices are particularly radical in perfect-competition theory, and this theory produces a logical machinery, a kind of blueprint it can then use for measuring imperfect realities. Logic precludes taking into account time, the individual, and the uncertainties attaching to the historical course of the world with all its interactions.

If we combine and compound deviations from this logical blueprint, we enter into the world of imperfect economic competition, for which there is no general theory but rather a multitude of competing modeling approaches. Game theory today claims to provide a unifying analytical framework for these approaches.[51] Let us look briefly at how the main features of the economics of imperfect competition restore substance to the dimensions of action we have been examining.

In imperfect competition, individuals influence each other. There are no longer so many of them as to be all indifferently small; they are instead of unequal size, and this inequality means that some market actors have the power and ability to influence others. Information here is a key variable differentiating actors, particularly since information in a context of strategic interdependence is an endogenous rather than exogenous behavior variable. Whereas in perfect competition the individual is axiomatically solipsistic, indifferent to others—ignorant of their characteristics—here interactions depend on the information that each actor has about the others and the environment, and interactions themselves produce information that modifies actors' behavior. This is why actor differentiation primarily amounts to difference in information held by each actor. This in turn means that in order for the agent to act at all, several things need to be brought into play: her representations, beliefs, and conjectures about the situation she is in, how it will evolve, and what her prospects are for action in that situation, given her assessment of the other agents' characteristics, actions, and reactions.

Commodities in this approach are as nonhomogeneous as agents. Their characteristics and qualities may be observable or not so observable; meanwhile, agents have full knowledge of neither themselves nor, more importantly, each other. Since prices are no longer the sum total of information and since information is now necessarily incomplete and imperfect, it costs agents something to acquire some. In strategic interaction situations, having and using information are action resources. And time itself is a nonhomogeneous factor. Actors do not act simultaneously or once and for all; they grope around, seek out, assess, get informed, and learn. It takes *time* to reach equilibrium. Actors pay out the time the action requires, but they also use time differently from one another and absorb it in different ways: as information, stocked knowledge, and investment in skills.

The functioning of the economy here implies costs—research costs, transaction costs, the costs of making or breaking contracts, and the costs of organizing work—that point to the compounded effects of information imperfection, agent and commodity heterogeneity, and time required to gather information, decide, act, and balance the market. The links between agents (producers and consumers) are no longer anonymous: Mechanisms such as recurring relations, trust, and reputation developed on the basis of lasting acquaintanceship, make it possible to lower trade relation costs and organize a world of interactions where individuals learn to know and evaluate each other. Inversely, difficulty accessing information and moves to provide misleading information about oneself create mistrust, monitoring costs, demands for contract guarantees, and insurance. Because individuals are unequally informed, they are also unequally uncertain about the course of the world, and this in turn precludes the assumption that competition among them will produce the best possible world (that is, a Pareto-efficient one). The fact is that the environment the individual makes decisions about is determined not only by the uncertain state of the world passively "chosen" by nature—nature has no particular objectives—but also by other decision-making individuals whose strategic choices affect those of every other actor.

Game theory's claim to have what it takes to unify imperfect competition models is founded directly on the fact that it purports to analyze situations of strategic interaction.[52] Specifically, interaction in game theory is modeled in such a way as to take into account the entire range of situations, from conflict to cooperation, in which each agent has to take all the other participating agents into account—either altogether and from the outset, or sequentially—when shaping his or her decisions and plans. This explains how game models capture all the main characteristics of imperfect competition situations: conflicts of interest, coalition forming, unequal powers to act, information asymmetries, recurrence or nonrecurrence of relations, nonsimultaneity of decision-making and action, the power to undermine conditions for trusting cooperation or, on the contrary, to create such conditions, and so on.

Much has been written about the gain in realism made by multiplying the tools used to analyze interactions. Hypotheses about each player's knowledge of the game's characteristics, the strategies available to each, the outcomes produced by the entire set of strategies and by strategy combinations, to say nothing of the corresponding mathematical processing, become particularly complicated when it comes to modeling situations that simultaneously bring into play strategic interdependence and actor differentiation, particularly those involving incomplete information and private information. The most sophisticated game theory analyses—which are also the most threatening for the unity and robustness of game theory—involve fully differentiated actors. In imperfect information games, some players are uncertain about other players' characteristics (their winnings, their knowledge of the game) and they therefore have to make conjectures (probability distributions) on the basis of signals received and beliefs about those other players' potential actions. Diversity in conjecture may lead to multiple solutions (i.e., multiple equilibria) and therefore imply an indeterminate result. To eliminate some of these solutions, game theorists have introduced such concepts as "rationalizability."

While the guiding ideas are still individualism and rational behavior, the "mere" demand that actors take into account their own knowledge, information, and expectations about other decision-makers' behavior shifts the dualist divide in neoclassical axiomatics so that the slash now falls between "perfect competition-solipsistic world" and "imperfect competition-world of interactions." The distinction between noncooperative and cooperative games introduces new complexities that come spectacularly to light in observed deviations from equilibrium solutions (the Prisoner's Dilemma being the most famous example).

Changing the general theoretical framework allows us to focus on quite a long list of other issues: conflicts of interest instead of convergent choices and decisions by actors who influence each other by the mere fact of belonging to one and the same space of action; the genesis of distinct types of group organizations (coalitions, teams with a common interest and objective); decision-making coordination as a response to decision interdependence; the same participants playing together repeatedly rather than once-only transactions; the emergence of institutions and norms for guaranteeing cooperation viability, and so on. This list brings to light the link between actor differentiation (asymmetry) and interaction dynamics. On the one hand, we have figures of an enriched temporality—move sequence and the questions of whether moves are made simultaneously or not, whether players have knowledge of how the game has gone in the past or not, whether game decisions are sequential, and whether players are repeating the game or playing once only. On the other hand, by mathematically compressing this enriched time into an initial plan of action founded on fully elaborated strategic calculation, we compress the behavior dynamic in a way that satisfies the calculability required for modeling. Clearly, the modeler's renewed handle on temporalization may block intuitive understanding of how behavior develops in the course of the game.

Sequential games, then, have the three fundamental characteristics we are looking for:

- The situation of interdependence temporalizes action: "If I act in such and such a way, how is the other person going to react, and what will come of my choice to act that way given [what I think] others' reactions [will be]?";
- Actors provide each other with information in the very "act" of observing each other's actions;

- Expectations are gradually modified through a process of trial and error; beliefs and expectations are revised; actions are adjusted, rectified. The sequentiality of games and the fact that actors are differentiated by the information they possess move us away from the swirl of solipsistic reasoning implied by the perfect interchange-ability of viewpoints, with the specular circularity of common knowledge that characterizes them. This circularity comes clearly to the fore in simultaneous games (or games played separately, where one of the players is ignorant of what the other is doing, has done, or will do): "In deciding to act in such and such a way, I can only use the information I obtain from my hypotheses about others' reactions to my decision, so I have to formulate a second-degree hypothesis that will serve as supplementary information, and so forth."

In order for this modeling compression to appear both remarkable *and* only a special case, we cannot simply adjust arguments about the "realism of calculability," but must once again modify the temporal horizon. Analy-sis of repeated games, for example, enables us to substitute a learning dy-namic (learning about others' characteristics and the structure of the game or winnings) for perfect knowledge and bring to light the emergence of cooperation norms for obtaining mutually advantageous results that are less than optimal from a selfish perspective (as in the Prisoner's Dilemma). But we also have to move from a closed horizon, where the result of a game can be accurately anticipated and may lead by backward induction to a mutually disadvantageous optimum (as in the prisoner's game), and ensure that the game is (or is perceived to be) repeatable an indefinite number of times. What this gets us is an association between two figures of time—time determined by a definite, knowable limit versus open-horizon time with its uncertainty about the outcome of the game. And it gets us two possible expressions of composite individual differences: conflict that can-not be resolved through cooperation, and cooperative coordination con-strained by the threat of retaliation if any player unilaterally breaks the mutually advantageous agreement that has emerged.

Causation and Temporality

Obviously no deterministic model would "settle" for being a mere mecha-nistic formula for how action is conditioned. Symmetrically, no interac-tionist model of intentional causation claims to free the actor from the gravitational power of situational constraints on action or the constraints of biographical experiences that affect preferences or choices. Might not these symmetrical concessions from the two approaches be a means of facilitating convergence toward a wholesome realism, a commonsensical sort of theorizing where no one should fail to take into account the ambiguities and ambivalences of the real, including action? This seems a fitting moment in the argument to invoke Paul Valéry's concise, elegant appraisal: "'Determinism' is the only way to represent the world, indeterminism the only way to live in it."[53] The statement leaves the problem whole; indeed, in its very brio the antinomy acknowledges our analytic impotence—in contrast to so much pompous epistemological writing.

To move forward, is it enough to specify a range of typical action situations, with the understanding that such-and-such explanatory model applies to such-and-such category of situations or even to such-and-such borderline situation? To a situation of tightly constrained choice, for example, which could then be characterized as either typological (a given borderline category of "forced choice" corresponds to a given set of factors) or historical (there exist exceptionally constraining economic situations)? That can only work if the basic arguments concerning action temporality have been fully expounded. Indeed, we need to specify yet another dimension in which deterministic and interactionist models of action stand sharply opposed: the continuist versus noncontinuist understandings of actor behavior and integration of an actor's actions into the course of the social world. It will be seen that this opposition is correlated to the one between propulsive causation and intentional causation.

When, in either sociology or economics, the understanding of social agents' behavior is rooted in the continuist conception of actor experience—in other words, that actors retain and reactivate at every point in time all they have experienced since birth—this renders the anticipatory dimension of action either (1) an empty frame or mere adaptive adjustment based entirely on extrapolations from past information or experience or (2) a power to calculate that is equal to the modeler's, in other words, a logical-mathematical abstraction. The agent is endowed with either a general ability to act in compliance with internalized norms (this is a Parsonian agent) or an infallible ability to discern almost automatically, on the basis of meanings already sedimented in him, what is relevant to him in each situation and thereby to frame each situation in the best possible way given his cumulative *ab initio* cognitive capital and representation-forming resources (this is the Bourdieusian agent). Or he might have the same infallible ability to determine the optimum in an equilibrium context (this is the economic agent of intertemporal General Equilibrium theory, fully rational and fully informed about the past and all properties of the action system, including other agents). And it changes nothing to add the qualification "unforeseeable situations excepted" since such situations are understood as exogenous to individual behavior.

The approach to causation most likely to organize deterministic-continuist behavior analysis is Hume's. The subject in this kind of analysis is defined in the same way Hume defined the spirit: a mechanism able to sum the frequencies of past events and estimate their possible repetition. If to Hume's understanding we add Husserl's thesis of the original prepredicative foundation of all judgment, we will establish a relation between the subject and her environment such that the environment is immediately and continuously assimilable by her, as in Bourdieu's structural definition of the immediacy of our understanding of the world:

> The world is comprehensible, immediately endowed with meaning, because the body, which, thanks to its senses and its brain, has the capacity to be present to what is outside itself, in the world, and to be impressed and durably modified by it, has been protractedly (from the beginning) exposed to its regularities. Having acquired from this exposure a system of dispositions attuned to theses regularities, it is inclined and able to anticipate them practically in behaviours which engage a *corporeal knowledge* that provides a practical comprehension of the world quite different from the intentional act of conscious decoding that is normally designated by the idea of comprehension. In other words, if the agent has an immediate understanding of the familiar world, this is because the cognitive structures that he implements are the product of incorporation of the structures of the world in which he acts: the instruments of construction that he uses to know the world are constructed by the world.[54]

It is worth noting that in this deterministic system, the regularities alluded to are not emerging properties—emerging, that is, out of the combination of situation variability and correlative distributions around a central tendency. Each unit in social space is imprinted with a system of structural relations of opposition to and affinity with the environment, understood as an environment to which it is regularly exposed.

In an early work, Granger[55] identified three figures of time: causal, historical, and stochastic. Causal time is the undated, reversible time of rational mechanics: How the initial state is specified entirely determines the sequence of later states. All sociology that derives behavioral structure from the initial programming of conditions are fueled to varying degrees by this understanding of time, as is all economic analysis bearing on the conditions in which a system attains intertemporal equilibrium.

The difference between historical time and causal time, according to Granger, is that in historical time the content of each instant depends on the content of all of the instants preceding it. This is clearly a concept of accumulation: A system's successive states and evolution are determined by the full set of its prior states and therefore by its history. It remains to be seen what conception of causality fits this accumulation scheme. Granger mentions Freudian epistemology. To provide a basis for the theory of the unconscious, Freud set out to replace classical etiology, where the only determinant causal factors are initial conditions, with the model of accumulated marks or traces left in the subject by successive events. The same type of model is operative in Husserl's phenomenology of consciousness and the intentional grip of consciousness on the world, and in later variants of this understanding, namely the thinking of Merleau-Ponty as Granger analyzes it.

Here Granger makes two decisive remarks. First, whereas in causal time the notion of a functional link between initial conditions and an effect is clear and simple, the concept of a system determined by the entire set of its earlier states is not only richer in causal substance but also much more obscure. A phenomenology or sociology of action systems may well present itself as fully historical, but unless it substantiates the accumulation argument, it does not increase by one whit the degree of intelligibility offered by a mechanistic deterministic model. We can see the difficulty if, as Husserl understood—and Bourdieu after him when, by radically socializing the *habitus,* he generalized Husserl's analysis to include all experience of the social world—the *habitus* preconstructs our expectations and interests from the very outset by systematically filtering representations and perceptions in such a way as to preserve only that part of information delivered by the intentional relation to the world that is already adjusted to the preconstruct. If indeed that is so, then how can the genetic thesis of the original, prepredicative foundation of all intentional activity (perception, judgment, representation, and so forth) be made consistent with that of continuous incorporation of new information made available to the subject by his multiple-mode relations with the world of things, beings and meanings? In this way of thinking, is not the newness of a piece of information always already evacuated by the perceptive and cognitive structure that handles it?

Second, if the law governing temporal variation of successive states engenders continuous transformation, then the historical time of accumulation may well be nothing more than a variant devoid of any original properties. Taking evolution to be the continuous accumulation of transformations is not at all different from talking about the propagation of a cause's effects over time. Nor, ultimately, is it different from atemporal analysis, as in the intertemporal general equilibrium models described above. The phenomenological conception of time-consciousness, together with habitualist models of behavior causation, are strictly continuist both in their micrological presentation (the matrix for this breakdown being the way they temporalize intentionality) and their macrological specification (that is, the requirement that the world be characterized by stable states and regular developments).

Inversely, and following Granger once again, we can only speak coherently of the historicity of a changing system if we break time down into distinct periods in discontinuist fashion, as this enables us not only to include crises (as in a continuist model seeking to correct its mechanistic linearity) but also to generate action situations with specific time coordinates and inner workings. In establishing the traits of sequential economics, as described previously in this chapter, I showed how it is the property of discontinuity that reveals historicity. We can now briefly review the problem in more general terms.

There are four strictly interdependent requisites for the noncontinuist model:

1. In place of the postulate of spontaneous disposition adjustment, the agent is endowed with reflexivity and understood to differentiate his cognitive operations by situation characteristics;
2. The agent is endowed with a capacity for intentional behavior;
3. The present course of action is compared to possible alternatives, thereby recovering the virtual, including through retrospective readings (like in counterfactual reasoning);
4. Action sequences are conceived of as isolatable and as separately modelizable.

In a continuist model, reflection and reflexivity are mere derivative characteristics, subordinate capacities, devoid of spontaneity. The continuist temporal model inclines us to understand the continuous grasp the subject has on his past not as an *act* but rather an essential *property* of the temporalization of the subject's relation to the world.

It is therefore not the subject who has a grip on her past but the past that has a grip on the subject, and this is so all the way down to the gravitational pull of this past. It will be objected that the phenomenological understanding of the constitutive power of knowledge and the multiple modes for attributing meaning should provide a means of actively recovering what has been obtained through the intertwining of perceptual receptiveness and predicative shaping. But when that understanding is integrated into a continuist causal schema of accumulative time, what becomes of the active dimension of reinterpretive apprehension, a dimension whose variability is indexed on the situations in which the activity is triggered? When constrained by the causal influence of first causes perpetually propagating their effects across all events affecting the subject, Husserl's answer, with its on-off switch from passivity to activity via the *habitus* so clearly identified by Héran,[56] becomes a mere simulacrum of the move to acting.

Can we, as Héran does in the aforementioned text, bring together Bourdieu's *habitus* and Garfinkel's reflexivity to make the point that reflexivity, too, involves nearly automatic reaction? This leaves aside a key dimension of Garfinkel's analysis, namely, the notion that being reflexive is the strict correlative of taking into account a *range* of action possibilities. If reflexivity were no more than a passive, automatic self-control function, it would have no depth; it would not allow for positing the past as reinterpretable or the present as a source of possible initiatives to be taken in light of a rereading of the past. This is what Garfinkel, in his critical discussion of Parsons's theory of socialization determinism, with its internalizing of behavior-conditioning norms, puts down to nonintentional causation, a kind of causation devoid of an actor's deliberate decision-making.

In sharp contrast to this understanding, nonmechanistic models are concerned to indicate, and to include on the horizon of individual behavior, the alternative courses of action on the basis of which choices, negotiations, and arbitration may be made or conducted, and to bring into play correlative components: learning, information acquisition, expectations, and analysis of the uncertainties related to a strategic interdependence environment. Behavior in interaction models is oriented by something other than action programming schemata or merely adaptive responses to constraints. There are two parts to the reasoning. If the experience accumulated by an actor has meaning, that meaning inheres in the fact that his experience provides him with memory of situations and acts performed in response to variable situations and environments—a catalogue of tried and tested routines, stocked and memorized information, lessons learned from previous trial and error, acquired, transposable, and extrapolatable schemata. However, once the actor's past becomes something other than a tight, conditioning force constraining all behavior and preventing it from being anything more than an automatic adaptive response triggered by external stimuli, then the present must be conceived as always oriented both toward selective reappropriation of the past and anticipatory grasp of action possibilities. The price to pay, if action is to bring learning in its wake, is the work of analyzing agreement and/or discrepancy between expectations and results, between hypotheses about others' probable behavior and observations of actual behavior, between investments made and results obtained. In other words, we have to conceive of the actor as able to find a set of responses in her past experiences that she can assess on the basis of experienced successes, satisfactions, and failures, then correct accordingly and then make use of in the new situations she encounters.

Once it has been established that an actor's reflexivity should occupy a central position, the question arises as to the exact nature of the individual's reflexive twisting back upon himself, the move that in fact enables him to make his past a selective learning resource. Do we need to endow the individual with a permanent ability to perceive and evaluate the causes and motives that oriented his earlier behavior? If so, how can this self-knowledge be rescued from the illusion of a straight, direct path between self and self? Or is the point rather to reestimate the relation between prior and present states of the individual situation, within the time of action, in light of the actor's aims and observed performances?

The first of these options would imply inventing a meta-actor who is permanently organizing the individual's relation with his different states, intervening to perform the necessary switching operations in response to the various action situations. This fiction of a multiplying self leaves intact the paradox of self-consciousness, renowned for the aporia it led philosophical idealism into—an aporia summed up in the idea that consciousness-of-self has to be partnered with a second entity, consciousness-of-consciousness-of-self, and so on down the slippery slope of infinite regression. Moreover, doesn't this fiction too readily presume the universality of the reflexive self? Specifically, can the clear-sightedness of the generic individual in this asocialized example, clear-sightedness obtained by nothing but well-conducted introspection, really be attributed to everyone?

The second option operates on the understanding that intentionality is temporally longitudinal. It is important to distinguish this from phenomenological analysis, because what is really at issue here is teleological-type intentional causal explanation. The critique of teleological causation by proponents of mechanistic determinism caricatures on very principle the subtle differentiation of conceptual levels essential to a coherent teleological setup. The critics generally proceed by objecting to an intellectualist conception of omniscient consciousness, without taking into account either the temporalization offered by this approach or the way it distinguishes and gradates the three acts of deliberating, forming knowledge about the possibilities from which choices are to be made, and reflexively examining purposeful action as it unfolds.

It is worthwhile recalling with Charles Taylor that teleological explanation falls within the jurisdiction of causal system analysis—the system of

self-imposed order where an event occurs because the conditions that produced it were those required to produce that end—and that there is no
need to posit any prior or internal entity.[57]

Working in the tradition of analytic philosophy, Davidson sought to do
away with those mysterious entities known as volitions. In order to firmly
maintain the deterministic causal analysis program, he explains action by
describing it as caused by a reason the agent had for doing what he did: The
reality of the action consisted in a bodily movement that can be described
as an intentional gesture motivated by a mental state (belief, desire) of the
"mover." Determinism here is not psychological but physiological: The
intention-as-mental-event that occupies the place of causal antecedent in
this argument is a cerebral or neuronal event subject to natural laws in
a way consistent with physicalist, neurophysiological analysis. In fact, as
Ricoeur remarks in his reading of Davidson and Anscombe,[58] this analytic
schema presupposes an evaluative component in intention formation. This
is the role of judgment, either in its primary form as correlative of desire—
to judge is to take into consideration the desirability of what motivates the
action—or in its unconditional form, as a kind of supplementary judgment
affirming that the desirable character of the object aimed at suffices to set
the action in motion and govern it. Intention in Davidson's sense is the
equivalent of such unconditional judgment.

In fact, it is precisely through such judgment that temporal depth emerges,
in the form of a delay. In other words, this kind of temporality involves
projection and completion—precisely the temporality masked by the notion
of an act spontaneously equipped with adequate expectations in response
to information received from the environment. Recalling the Augustinian
dialectic of *intentio* and *distentio,* Ricoeur points out that compressing into
an instant the mental operations associated with action (regardless of the
type of causal analysis of those operations) masks the control and correction function of action, as it is essential to consider the longitudinal dimension of expectations. This is precisely the limitation of deterministic causal
thinking where the aim is to bring intentional causation and its complex
temporality "home" to an ontology of the event. An "intention-to," with
its teleological horizon, is not temporalized the same way as an "intention-
in-which," which represents a reduction to a grammar of reasons and,
ultimately, to a causation of events rather than actions.

Pleading for a structural analytic theory of action rather than a causal
one such as Davidson's, while distinguishing his position clearly from the
phenomenological option à la Ricoeur for conceiving of action temporality,[59] Descombes also underlines how meager temporal qualification of
events is in the causal scheme and opts for the idea of action as process:

> By process here [i.e., in the school Descombes calls "structural"] is meant not only an event—something happens—but a change in something oriented toward a *terminus ad quem*. We have a process if something proceeds gradually toward a final state and we have an action if the process in question is sufficiently controlled by the actor. . . . The notion of event, in contrast to that of change, does not encompass an internal completion or accomplishment criterion. There can be incomplete processes, but there are no incomplete events. An event takes place, period.[60]

Thinking of action outside the causal-continuist framework leads to reelaborating these two fundamental components of the relation between the ideas of action and temporality. First, in order for intentional action to be analytically conceivable, the actor has to be able to intervene in the course of things and that action has to be a process:

> It seems impossible to understand practical intentionality without an adequate definition of practical temporality. Clearly the notion of event does not exclude duration, as shown by several examples used in causal theory (a walk, an assassination, a medical operation). But in that theory, duration is thought of as a block and it is therefore not relevant to consider the difference between instantaneous changes (on the model of the lightning bolt or billiard balls colliding—events which occur at instant t) and gradual changes. The common notion of event—"something happens"—fails to cover the entire repertoire of what linguists call the aspects of a process. . . . That notion includes no grasp of the inchoative or terminative aspects of the process: Are we already engaged in it? Are we far from the goal?
>
> . . .
>
> The notion of intentionality implies not only that the event that occurs responds, in terms of one description of it, to the actor's intention, but also that the actor is a practical subject; i.e., endowed with a (finite) power to affect the course of things. To express this power, we have to specify the control a person exercises on the changes that occur around him. Some of the changes that occur correspond to the actor's desires; we can say he notes them with satisfaction. But this does not suffice to make him active. For the actor to be an actor and not merely a spectator with an interest in what happens, he has to be able to bring about changes (in cases where they would not occur without him) or facilitate changes, while making sure they are not disrupted. In sum, a change is due to a subject if he orders or permits it.
>
> We therefore have to take into account two types of actions: actions that consist in positive intervention and actions that consist in letting things evolve to the point where we desire to find them later on.[61]

Furthermore, when the schema is no longer one of immediately triggered and automatically adjusted action, the reflexivity that organizes ongoing oversight and control of the course of the action is no longer a self-founded solipsistic consciousness. The finite power of being oneself incorporates otherness—this is the point so strongly made by Ricoeur throughout his *Oneself as Another* and thematized above all in his conclusion, using several lines of argument that cannot be reproduced here; let it suffice to present a linchpin of that argument. Otherness pertains to the subject's passivity, to the twofold experience of the body exposed to the world (the subject is from the outset affected by the flow of information exchanged with her environment) and the self's relation to others as other-than-self (otherness being inherent in the relation of intersubjectivity, as noted above). But otherness is also the condition for apprehending self, for exercising self-control, and for exercising the power to act, namely the power to act on others that is due to role reversibility. This explains the ambivalent motive of self's incompleteness: Without others, whose presence enables me to draw myself together, assemble myself, consolidate myself, and maintain myself in my identity, my experience would never be totalizable. But it is also this incompleteness that gives meaning to acting and interacting. This is what grounds reflexivity, as it has been introduced in different ways by Mead, Mills, or Garfinkel: To motivate one's action by a justification that underlies and sustains the course of the action is to link up with the others in the action situation via reflexive oversight and control. As Descombes puts it in his commentary of Ricoeur's idea of the "complex capacity to be oneself," "the 'maintaining of self' [a characteristic manifestation of the power to be oneself] corresponds, for the subject, to the fact that others count on him and let him know this; the effect is that the subject ends up thinking of himself as accountable for what he does or says."[62]

If, in the causal-continuist schema, reflexivity can be exempted from intervening, this is because the world's temporality in that schema is calibrated by its stability and predictability. Conversely, it would be meaningless to bring intentionality and reflexive oversight and control into play if situations did not in fact provide actors with the very materials of the reflexivity-/expectation-formation dialectic by giving them wider experience of the possibilities for action. For this to happen, all types of action and interaction, from the most ritualized and routine to the most uncertain, have to be characterized by the knowledge and expectations that actors develop about the situation and its various participants (distribution of power to act, degree of control actors can exercise in the given situation, types of constraints they experience, and level and structure of the information they dispose of and the information they can obtain through observation or research). We now see how the process-like accomplishing of action is coordinated with actors' revisable hypotheses about others' actions and reactions, and with the reduction of uncertainty that follows on acquisition of information in the course of action or through observation of the course of recurrent situations.

To differentiate action situations outside of any probabilistic-frequentistic framework also involves equipping actors with a set of behavioral mechanisms whose specific characteristics cannot be merely aligned by using a genetic deductive construction, based on elementary perceptual imprints and associationist capacities linked to the experience of regularities. All studies of action intentionality distinguish at least three such mechanisms: (1) preferences and preference-based desires, (2) beliefs and representations constructed on the basis of information, and (3) operations (which can be ranked by degree of complexity) involved in handling information and assessing the behavioral solutions that organize action sequences.

If we require this set of mechanisms to depend on and be conditioned by perceptual filters and accumulation of regular experiences, we maximize actors' passivity and the explanatory power of initial behavioral programming conditions—thereby choosing, in fact, to abolish any analytic distinction between desires, preferences, beliefs and behavioral choices. Inversely, if we radically disconnect these active components from each other, we establish a static division between (1) what is exogenous and fixed for all time—preferences; (2) the "system postulate" of goodness of fit between representations and the situation according to each agent's amount of information; and (3) the "behavioral axiomatics" of optimizing rationality. In contrast to both of these ways of proceeding, an analysis that temporalizes action requires us to explore the relations between these different components of behavior (once they have been analytically identified and distinguished) and to coordinate the notion of the actor with hypotheses about the structure of interaction situations and the prevailing conception of time.

The historicity of time that will then prevail is not that of pure accumulation based on the regularity of events and configuration stability. It is much closer to the third type of time in Granger's three-part arrangement: stochastic time. In stochastic time, events do not follow one another in continually predictable fashion but are distributed by probabilities that lead actors to develop conjectures about their environment and the behavior of actors in it. The passing of a period of time is then "determined not so much by its pre- and post- boundaries as by the probabilistic characteristics of the events distributed in it."[63] It is this requalification of historicity that enables us to understand, for example, how Granger, in his examination of human science models, arrives at the conclusion that "a theory of decision-making stands opposed to a mere theory of causes—or determinations—in that it (1) brings into play both a complex of chance occurrences and an optimum, and (2) links an information apparatus to an action apparatus."[64]

In this kind of historicity, the interaction situation acquires properties that are not to be had in a causal-continuist model. It gets attributed a genuine "uncertainty coefficient," since uncertainty is both exogenous (that is, related to "nature's" behavior) and endogenous (related to the other actors' behavior). It leads actors to develop assessments (through probabilistic weighting of the characteristics of events to be judged) pertaining to the preferable evolution of things by degree of exercisable control, and to preferable strategic interaction outcomes. These probabilistic assessments are subject to learning, which, through emitting, receiving, acquiring, and reinterpreting information, moves the actor from initial subjective probability distributions to revised distributions via adjustment to newly acquired information. Bayesian behavior of this sort is what makes action-orienting judgment dialectical. In Bayesian behavior theory, as Granger underlines,[65] the postulated invariant is no longer "the world's property of being regular to some degree, but the coherence of our approach to handling uncertainty." The initial distribution of probabilities over uncertain outcomes in each case he forms beliefs in is, of course, exogenous, for the same reason that preferences in economic analysis are exogenous.

Rather than paying the "full" and indeed excessively heavy price of directly endogenizing preferences and beliefs—that is, nondifferentiation between preferences, beliefs, and representations, on the one hand, and, on the other, cognitive processing of information, nondifferentiation due to the necessary illusions of habitualist adjustment—it seems worthwhile to wager, as Granger does, that understanding knowledge as *work* rather than as the unveiling of a hidden being in itself is the way to represent the probabilistic activity of judgment linked to intentional acts and decisions that is "most likely to integrate [those probabilities] into the highly and increasingly complex structures that objectification of human behavior continues and will forever continue to demand."[66]

Conclusion

In the vision most often presented of it, the opposition between sociology and economics crystallizes around the two linchpins of any analytic model: actor and environment. In economics, the actor is understood as a generic being, differentiated only through the mathematical expression of a distribution of characteristics in continuous space, and the actor's environment amounts to a market made up of numerous, anonymous transactions with no depth and implying no memory. Each interaction situation is supposed to be analytically reducible to the confrontation between two entities (two individuals, businesses, countries) each of whom/which makes optimizing calculations on the basis of all available information in order to maximize his/her/its own advantage or profit. The standard economic model's rational actor seems readily contrastable, trait for trait, with the sociological undertaking in its very essence, as formulated by Pareto.[67] Sociologists' territory is heterogeneity and nonlogical action. The behavior and powers that economists endow actors with—individual gain maximization, optimizing rationality, capacity for strategic calculation—are understood in sociology to have reality or analytical validity only in certain highly particular situations and for the study of certain spheres of activity in society; they are susceptible of being modeled in a locally plausible way but can never be generalized or extrapolated from. One dimension of this opposition is the way time is handled: In economics the necessarily temporal dynamics of phenomena are reduced to stasis, while sociology, inversely, takes into account the historical depth of the action—this approach attaining an extreme in the radical historicization of social science objects theorized by Passeron in his non-Popperian epistemology.[68] I have tried to show that this opposition is changing by way of theoretical developments and competition within each discipline, developments and competition that crystallize around the relation between action temporality and actor differentiation. The division between deterministic and nondeterministic schemata runs through both sciences, and the terms of that division can now be systematically compared.

At this conclusive point in the analysis, let me bring to the forefront one dimension of the comparison practiced in it. How do the two sciences conceive of the relation between the individual's action and the overall aggregate of individual actions? Economics' key concept, the concept governing the entire architecture of its theories, is equilibrium. As D'Aspremont, Dos Santos Ferreira, and Gérard-Varet write, the aim is to "identify general coherence among actions in space as well as time" using the following three principles:

> a "Walrasian" principle of *mutual compatibility* between different agents' actions, . . . a "Cournotian" principle of *individual rationality,* or the internal coherence of each agent's individual action choices . . . and a "Marshallian" *expectation coordination principle* concerning consistency among the beliefs, conjectures and plans on the basis of which agents choose their actions.[69]

Economic analysis, particularly as influenced by game theory, has tried to determine more precisely how equilibria are constructed in the presence of all the "imperfections" of the real world and, above all, in strategic inter-action, which may be defined as the fruit of the differentiation provoked by otherness and asymmetry (unequal endowments and powers, information and knowledge asymmetry). This has moved economic researchers to contextualize their analyses more fully, namely by specifying interindividual relation dynamics. The proliferation of particular models then works to suspend or dissolve the reference to general equilibrium as the supreme guarantee of action efficiency and explanation consistency.

The three principles just mentioned can also be used to characterize the different levels at which sociologists are seeking to fit together micro- and macrosociology. In connection with at least one of the issues involved in renewing sociological theory—how to qualify individual differences—the movement under way in that discipline is not fundamentally different from the one just observed in economics. The question is how to qualify those differences in a way that will allow for analyzing interindividual adjustments dynamically—since the analytic space is that of conflict as well as negotiation and agreement construction—without actors' being weighed down from the outset by the deterministic model, and without situations being purged of elements of uncertainty, since uncertainty is what simultaneously gives substance to the acting other and to the course of action.

CHAPTER TWO

Is Working to Achieve
Self-Fulfillment Rational?

IN CLASSICAL economic analysis, labor is generally treated as a negative magnitude. It is described restrictively as a "disutility," an expense of individual energy in exchange for a salary and the consumer goods to which that salary provides access. Leisure and consumer goods are the only sources of satisfaction and individual well-being. Thus labor is reduced to "negative consumption." When labor is described this way, involvement in the labor market becomes a case of rational behavior and maximization under constraint: The choice to engage in a remunerated activity can be understood entirely as a choice balancing the sacrifice of well-being required by effort against the increased well-being provided by the goods and the leisure acquired as compensation for the productive effort.

However, the essential correlate of such an analysis is the extreme simplification of the reality of labor, which stands in the way of the most elementary observation: The disutility sensed in the completion of work varies a great deal depending on the occupation and the job. By enriching the analysis of work and of the employment relationship, it is possible to identify the various parameters that restore to the labor factor its real properties, in the diversity of its embodiments and realizations.

Each kind of work and each job can in fact be described as a particular combination of characteristics that leads to differentiating individuals correlatively to explain their choices and the constraints that weigh on their choices. The consequences on the collective level have to be deduced from the analysis of individual situations. If under certain conditions labor can become a factor of well-being and accomplishment, how can we be sure that everyone's pursuit of his own well-being in labor is compatible with the well-being of the collectivity as a whole?

The answers to this question vary according to the nature and distribution of factors affecting the individual performance of work roles, on the one hand, and to the organization of social relationships in labor, on the other hand. Theories that emphasize the value of the self-fulfillment included in the exercise of skilled labor can be divided into two main types. Theories of the first type postulate a high degree of equality among individual talents, or a strong complementarity of different talents possessed by individuals in a social community, in order to do away with the mechanism of interindividual competition and to correct the mutilating aspects of the specialization of productive skills through the division of labor. In this conception, the very unequal ability of jobs to provide well-being is connected with the excessive specialization and hierarchization of the tasks to be done.

Theories of the second type are based on the inverse reasoning: The argument from the gratifying nature of labor can be put in the service of an openly inegalitarian conception of the early selection of talented workers. The introduction of the vocabulary of talent into the world of business enterprises since the 1990s has in fact helped reorganize the management of personnel: The differentiation of the labor force seeks to select an elite amounting to 10 to 20 percent of the employees in order to put them on the fast track to promotion in the organization, and to create teams that are homogeneous in quality by using selective matching. Since these mechanisms of personnel management appeal to systems that are intended to increase the productivity of individuals and teams, the vocabulary of talent plays a twofold role: encouraging performance and labeling the skewed distribution of individual capacities. The argument from talent thus gives priority to a highly valorizing designation of the qualities and performances expected from the individual, but at the same time it brings out the conflict inherent in an ordinal definition of qualities: Qualities and performances are measured through relative comparisons, whereas the argument from talent always suggests that the qualities sought in individuals are also absolute qualities that support an intrinsic motivation.[1]

To grasp all the implications of the reversal of perspective that seeks to make labor a positive magnitude, I will develop here a twofold line of argumentation.

First, even if we can certainly use the vocabulary of consumption to describe certain elements of the choice and exercise of a job that are the object of monetary remuneration, the working individual cannot be directly assimilated to a consumer. On the one hand, he does not simply choose the level of investment in initial training that provides him with a diploma and certain skills; on the other hand, and above all, the exercise of a profession transforms the individual more profoundly than consumption changes the individual, his preferences, and his experiences. The temporal extension of the employment relationship allows skills and qualities that were not present at the outset to emerge and manifest themselves: The exercise of the job and the accumulation of work experience inform the individual regarding the abilities that he possessed in a virtual state, or else they give him supplementary skills that are added to those acquired during his initial training and that can make up for the latter's obsolescence.

Second, to understand in what way it has been possible to analyze labor as a positive condition of self-realization, I have to introduce the dimension of uncertainty. This is so for two reasons. The jobs traditionally considered as leading to self-realization are characterized by the not very routine nature of the tasks and work situations, and by a strong component of risk-taking. Correlatively, these activities appeal to talents and skills which the individual is not certain to possess at the outset, and that are revealed to him or procured by him only in the exercise itself of the work concerned. If these two conditions are met, it can be rational for an individual to choose jobs or sequences of jobs that inform him better regarding his abilities, knowing that these choices involve risks because they involve activities in which success and the quality of the job match are much more uncertain than in a situation in which the work would demand the foreseeable use of skills that are well defined *ab initio*. In this case, the description of the job and of the relationship of employment is enriched, but is not reduced to a simple principle of the segmentation of jobs in relation to their level of qualification. To be sure, it seems logical to associate the positive and expressive value of labor with the exercise of a superior profession that is complex and skilled. But once we have controlled for all the factors explaining access to a superior profession, there remain between individuals differences in success that designate the coefficient of uncertainty inherent in the practice of the activities considered the most fulfilling. The temporal horizon within which these activities are situated must be long, and is in no way comparable to an agenda that is easy to anticipate and to program rationally. The value of fulfillment that such activities harbor is ultimately associated with a great intensity of interindividual competition.

Labor: From Homogeneous to Heterogeneous

The Basic Postulates

Let us begin with the most schematic conception. In neoclassical economic analysis, the theory of competitive equilibrium postulates a "fictitious, abstract, homogeneous market in which permanent, instantaneous, and transparent adjustments allow optimizing agents to make their choices."[2]

In this basic model, labor is associated with an instrumental use of time, one that seeks to obtain remunerations that will be used to acquire consumer goods and services. Labor is a magnitude that is homogeneous, quantifiable, and perfectly divisible, an input that is required to produce goods and services: the individual who supplies his time for remunerated work sacrifices part of the other possible use of his time, leisure. Consumer goods and leisure are individual utility's sole arguments. Labor is part of the domain of necessity, and has only a negative value, a "disutility," because it forces the individual to give up leisure time: that is the price to be paid for the acquisition of goods. Let us remember this first characteristic: The more labor is reduced to a homogeneous quantity, the more it is assimilated to a disutility, with the sole purpose of determining how to optimize the choice between the level of effort to be accepted and the quantity of leisure desired. Further hypotheses seek to reduce the commitment made (by the worker) or the purchase of the labor factor (by the producer) to a problem of price and quantities, but these hypotheses depend logically on the initial reduction of labor to a homogeneous magnitude. The neoclassical theoretical model of a pure and perfect competitive market treats the market for the labor factor like that of any divisible good: The worker and the producer are assumed to act rationally, to continually adjust their respective utility maximization over labor and leisure (for the worker), and labor and capital (for the producer). They are also supposed to react with a complete flexibility to variations in the final demand for consumer goods. It is because labor is reduced to a homogeneous quantity whose price provides all the necessary information regarding jobs and employers that the labor market is considered transparent. If labor is homogeneous, then information about the salaries offered by the various employers, the nature of the jobs and the characteristics (abilities, skills, preferences, motivations) of the workers and the employers will be perfect. And under these conditions, transactions bearing on labor as merchandise are logically assimilable to exchanges of goods, thanks to this merchandise's perfect divisibility, to a permanent adjustment of the quantities in demand and the supplies offered, and to the perfect variability of prices.

This framework of hypotheses serves to make the behavior of the employer and that of the employee symmetrical, and to organize the play of supply and demand in the labor market as a sum of individual decisions independent of any strategic interaction. The employer has to determine what combination of factors will make it possible to produce at the lowest cost the quantity that maximizes his profit. The worker, on the other hand, has to determine, in relation to his preferences, what combination of income and leisure will allow him to maximize his well-being. Thus the current designation of labor as negative consumption symbolizes the homogenizing treatment given the labor factor in the dominant theory of competitive economics.

Labor, Training, and Job Differentiation

An initial enrichment of the analysis occurs with the introduction of the variable chiefly responsible for differences in remuneration, the level of training and qualification of the individual involved. The hierarchy of jobs and the hierarchy of salaries are mainly linked to differences in qualification. Two essential forms of investment in human capital procure qualifications. Training is initially acquired through study, and then accumulated through work experience and in vocational training programs. The resulting skills are transferable from one firm to another, in the event that the worker is mobile. The other component of human capital possessed by the individual is specific to the firm in which he is employed, and it produces in him skills that are more difficult to transfer from one firm to another.[3] According to most investigations, the sum total of this capital consisting of skills explains from 30 to 50 percent of the variations in salaries.

Thus analysis in terms of investment allows us to differentiate jobs according to the type of general training they initially require, and to the types of general and specific capital that they develop in the course of work experience. It brings out a first dimension of heterogeneity that offers material for analysis, as Mincer points out:

> The processes by which people develop their skills at school, at work, and through geographic mobility and job search are basic to an understanding not only of why their earnings differ, but to an understanding of a country's economic and social development as well. To be sure, other factors also influence earnings, for example, discrimination, trade union membership, inherited ability—or, simply, luck. But the importance of all these factors can be better assessed if the individual's skill development process and its consequences are understood. . . . The basic merit of human capital theory for labour economics

is its ability to handle analytically the heterogeneity of labour and the time-bound investment processes that play a role in creating heterogeneity.[4]

Bringing out the composite character of the accumulation of human capital leads us to stress an essential point. For an individual, the management of his time can no longer be considered simply the product of a labor/leisure decision, but derives from a utility function over labor, training, and leisure. The most skilled occupations have required a long initial period of training, but they are also those that procure for individuals the best chances of accumulating skills in the exercise of the job itself, and in a long-term horizon of individual development.

What is the precise value of the accumulation of human capital that is posterior to the initial training? The question is raised by the study of the relation between the development of the individual salary over time (seniority) and the curve of individual productivity. Why does salary rise with age? Is it really because the increase in remuneration reflects an increase in the worker's productivity?[5]

According to the theory of human capital, individual productivity varies with the quantity of human capital possessed by the worker, recognizing that an individual accumulates human capital at different rates during his initial training and all through his active life. This human capital is exposed to two contrary effects: The increase in transferable experience and the value of the capital specific to the firm that employs the individual have a positive effect on individual productivity, but the knowledge and skills possessed by the individual also depreciate at a rate that varies under the influence of numerous factors responsible for an absolute depreciation (for example, under the impact of technological change) and for a relative depreciation (for example, under the impact of more intense interindividual competition and management techniques that break with the organization of internal labor markets and introduce forced rankings of performance). If the combination of the two effects produces a positive result, the salary should increase with seniority, at least on the hypothesis that the salary is adjusted to the individual's productivity.

In reality, salarial practices frequently depart from this theoretical model: The practices observed in the labor market show how young workers who have just emerged from the training system and have the most up-to-date knowledge are substituted for more experienced workers who are at the high point of their salary curves. Consequently, various theoretical arguments have been developed to account for the gap, at any given moment, between a worker's productivity and the level of his remuneration. The theory of the salary based on efficiency makes the worker's productivity depend on the level of his salary itself: It states that the employer's monitoring of the worker's productivity is imperfect, and that a salary higher than the competitive one (that is, one that is continually adjusted to productivity) allows the employer to encourage the worker to provide the desired level of effort, to attract the best workers, or to manage equitably the situations of different workers.[6] On the other hand, the theory of the contract for deferred payment[7] plays a central role in determining the duration of the contractual relation of employment: Productivity is assumed to be constant, but the price the salaried employee asks for his work should rise with age to compensate for the increasing difficulty of the effort made, and over time the enterprise will make the salary equal to the value of the marginal product by underpaying the worker during the first period of the contractual relation, and overpaying him during the second period. On the whole, over the duration of his cycle of active life, the worker will be paid the equivalent of the competitive salary. This second model thus assumes long-term employment relations within an internal labor market: The salaried employee's contract functions as a kind of insurance.

However, in these last two theories, the homogeneity of the labor factor remains an essential postulate. In the deferred payment model, it is admitted, of course, that the individual experiences the disutility of labor differently over time, but the worker's productivity is assumed to be a constant, which amounts to saying that work experience supplies the worker with no additional qualification or information: The temporality of the employment relationship is expressed in the mathematical duration of a negotiation that bears, at the beginning of a period, on the whole work career of a self-identical individual. In the efficiency wage model, productivity naturally varies depending on the individuals concerned, but the differences that are treated with incentives are initially considered from the point of view of the employer who is imperfectly informed, and who cannot adjust his offer to the value of the competitive salary.

Among the explanations that have been advanced to account for differences in the remuneration of labor, that of equalizing wage differences formulated by Adam Smith[8] has been very influential. In a competitive labor market, differences in salary serve to equalize the net advantages of the various jobs. Smith established an initial list of job characteristics that gave rise to equalizing wage differences: "the ease or hardship" of the work, "the difficulty and expense of learning the business," "the constancy or inconstancy of employment," "the small or great trust which must be reposed in the workmen," and "the probability or improbability of success in the trade." The model of investment in human capital corresponds well to this framework, since the differences in remuneration among individuals with different levels of training are meant to compensate for the costs of acquiring the necessary training. But the interest of the argument of equalizing differences is also that it introduces a more complex characterization of jobs and of the relation of employment. First of all, we have to answer the commonsense objection that occupations in which work is unpleasant and precarious are also those that are in general the least well remunerated. It is therefore appropriate to identify and control for the factors responsible for differences in remuneration: The argument of equalizing and compensating differences applies for a given level of qualification and training costs. It is relatively easy to control for certain factors, and the compensating wage differences can be integrated into a rational behavior of labor supply; thus, at the level of a given qualification, a job that includes physical dangers must be better paid than one that is safe. But other characteristics of jobs and the relation between the individual, his job, and his employer are less easy to define right off and to observe, because they are revealed only in the exercise of the occupation itself: This holds for the probability of success or relations of trust, to remain with Adam Smith's list, but also for the prospects of accumulating human capital through on-the-job training offered by an employment. The same goes for the rapidity with which occupational skills can become obsolete if the activity is temporarily interrupted or if it is exercised part-time.[9]

One of the sources of equalizing differences deserves particular attention here: a job or an occupation's nonmonetary advantages. Authors like Smith, Marshall, or Friedman are fond of using artistic occupations to illustrate this point. These occupations seem to be situated at the top of the scale for almost all the factors that are traditionally taken into account by psychosociological studies of the satisfaction taken in work—the variety and complexity of the tasks, their ability to exploit all the worker's individual skills, the worker's feeling of responsibility, the recognition of individual merit, the role of technical competence in the definition and way of exercising hierarchical authority, the degree of autonomy in the organization of tasks,[10] the structure of relations with superiors, with colleagues, and with subordinates, the profession's social prestige, and the status accorded to those who succeed in it. After all, isn't the freedom to organize one's own work the condition par excellence of authentic artistic achievement?[11]

As I will show in Chapter 3, the argument of nonmonetary advantages is so strong that it has traditionally provided the foundation for the ideological enchantment of creative work. The median level of gains in the creative professions is in fact weaker than in comparable professions:

Intrinsic, not pecuniary, motivations must play an essential role, at least at the beginning of a career. The choice of such occupations thus depends as much on personal tastes as on investment in human capital. The general conclusion to be drawn from this example is that individuals' preferences and abilities, and the information at their disposal, leads each person to evaluate differently the relative advantages of the various occupations. The approach in terms of compensating differentials offers a way of making progress in the analysis of the heterogeneity of labor as soon as a profession and a job are considered as complex sets of characteristics on which individual preferences can be exercised in their diversity and lead to diverse evaluations. But this analysis also collides with the biases of endogeneity, as is pointed out by Killingsworth and Heckman:

> Despite its potential importance for labor supply analysis, surprisingly little has been done to allow explicitly for the heterogeneity of work in formal labor supply models. For the most part, studies in which job heterogeneity *has* been considered have been concerned with compensating wage differentials, i.e. with wages rather than labor supply per se. Such studies have typically been concerned with regressing wage rates on "job variables"—e.g. continuous variables measuring job characteristics, or dummy variables denoting "job held"—and on other variables, such as schooling, work experiences and the like. Studies of this kind usually provide little or no information about preferences (which might be useful for understanding labor supply to heterogeneous jobs); for the most part, they estimate the compensating wage differential required by the *marginal* individual in order to change the amount of a particular job characteristic or in order to change jobs per se. Moreover, such studies usually ignore the fact that the "job variables" included in such regressions are endogenous. Ironically (in view of the neglect of labor supply in such studies), analyzing labor supply in a model of job heterogeneity can also provide useful information on the forces that generate compensating wage differentials. By using information on labor supply as well as wages, one can estimate the supply (e.g. utility function) parameters that underlie compensating wage differentials while allowing explicitly for the endogeneity of individuals' "job variables." ... The reason for this is that data on labor supply within different jobs are generated by the same preference structure that generates job choice and compensating wage differentials.[12]

The Matching Model

Another theoretical model, that of "job matching,"[13] has the advantage of enriching the analysis of the employment relation and its temporal extension on three decisive points: (1) The individuals are unequally productive; (2) the jobs differ from one another in the skills and abilities they require; (3) neither the employers nor the employees know *a priori* whether the match between the worker and the job will be of good quality. On the basis of the first two points, the relation of employment is defined as a more or less successful matching: A good match guarantees good productivity, which increases with seniority (in conformity with the model of investment in human capital), and makes it possible to explain the positive correlation between salary and seniority. The third point allows us to conceive the relation of employment as a mutual adjustment between the employer and the employee that gradually reveals to each of the two actors the value of his choices. The dynamics of matching makes impossible the instantaneous optimization of choices, because it is based on research and on the accumulation of information. The characterization of the actors and the situations of labor are thus enriched without the paradigm of rationality being abandoned. Finally, one of the implications of the model is the emergence of a variable that has been absent up to this point, namely individual differences in ability and talent, which I will study in the following section.

In the matching model, transactions in the labor market can be assimilated to more or less lasting marriages. The optimal employment situation corresponds, in a system of equilibrium, to a successful matching:

> Getting the most out of the resources that are available requires matching the proper type of worker with the proper type of firm: the labor market must solve a type of marriage problem of slotting workers in their proper niches within and between firms. . . . A labor market transaction is viewed as a tied sale in which the worker simultaneously sells (rents) the services of his labor and buys the attributes of his job. These attributes are fixed for any one job, but may vary from job to job. Hence, the worker exercises choice over preferred job attributes by choosing the appropriate type of job and employer. On the other hand, employers simultaneously buy the services and characteristics of workers and sell the attributes of jobs offered to the market. The characteristics of a particular worker are fixed, but may differ among workers. An acceptable match occurs when the preferred choices of an employer and an employee are mutually consistent; when the worker finds the employer's job attributes to be the most desirable and the employer finds the worker's productive characteristics to be the most desirable, both among all feasible choices.[14]

The explanation of the dispersion of remunerations highlights the combined action of three main categories of factors distinguished by Rosen. Some factors correspond to job characteristics. The latter have a positive or a negative price that is added or subtracted from the remuneration, the worker making his choice, like a consumer, between goods whose total value is equivalent. Other factors characterize the function of investment in the acquisition of skills that extends over the whole duration of the cycle of active life, and belong to the theoretical model of human capital presented above. Finally, there are factors specific to the work environment within the organization that provides employment.

The dynamic analysis of the composition and development of individual human capital thus allows us to complete the description of the employment relationship. The employer seeks to obtain from the worker a growing productivity on the basis of specific skills that increase his productivity in the particular context of the job. For his part, the worker seeks in a job not only the best salary for a given quantity of labor and qualification, but also the best opportunities to augment his capital in the form of experience. An asymmetry emerges in the employment relationship thus conceived when the worker has the ability to transfer the gains in specific human capital to a job in another firm where he or she will obtain a better salary, and in certain cases to carry out what the firm may consider a hold-up,[15] and not simply as the cost of losing its personnel development investment by failing to retain its employees.

By placing general training and specific apprenticeship in a dynamic relationship, we can define the job as a "tied package of work and learning":

> A worker simultaneously sells the services of his skills and jointly buys the opportunity to augment those skills. Learning potential is viewed as a by-product of the work environment, tied to a specific work activity, but varying from activity to activity and from job to job. Some jobs provide more learning opportunities and some provide less. Therein lies a margin of choice for both workers and firms. . . . The firm is viewed as jointly producing both marketable output and training output, summarized by a production possibilities frontier between the two.[16]

If the capital in skills results from the two types of investment, on-the-job learning is a factor differentiating the labor force all the more powerfully to the extent that jobs procure more experience capital. In other words, the more that specific investment enters into the definition of qualification and is correlated with individual productivity, the more the price and the productivity of labor vary as a function of nonstandardized characteristics connected with the organizational environment of the job and the contingent quality of the relationship between an employer and an employee.

Interindividual Heterogeneity and
Factors of Inegalitarian Differentiation

The principle of my analysis is to differentiate jobs and individuals simultaneously, without taking into consideration the characteristics of either as independent realities. The stratification of the labor market in accord with the levels of competence required in the different job categories thus reveals that a magnitude that is apparently as easily measurable as qualification is in fact very complex. The study of the employment relationship and its organizational environment restores to human capital its twofold character and its temporal profile as a composite accumulation.

The more we enrich the characterization of jobs, the more each worker's preferences and abilities, and also the inequalities of opportunity in the acquisition of human capital, play an active role in the analysis. If all workers had equal abilities and equal capacities for educational investment, as well as tastes ordered in accord with a univocal hierarchy, and if jobs differed only in the level of qualification required and in the corresponding salary, the inequalities in salaries would represent the compensations offered for the direct and indirect expenses that are incurred by individuals to acquire a level of qualification. This hypothesis reduces to a simple dimension the observed heterogeneity of the labor force and of occupations, and leads us to affirm that the long-term labor supply for each occupation is perfectly elastic, thanks to a salary rate that equalizes, for all occupations, the present value of the earnings expected by each individual over the whole of his or her active life. As Robert Willis emphasizes, this version of the theory of human capital is the strongest one, and holds only under conditions of equality of opportunity and equality of ability:

> The assumption of homogeneous human capital regards workers as bringing to the labor market a number of homogeneous "efficiency" units of labor which is proportional to their stock of accumulated human capital. Thus, all workers are perfect substitutes in production at ratios proportional to their endowment of efficiency units. Equivalently, the efficiency unit view assumes that a given investment in human capital increases an individual's physical productivity in all production activities by the same amount. . . .
>
> While this assumption is patently counterfactual, it is usually justified as a fairly innocuous simplification which enables the analyst to abstract from the details of occupational skills in order to focus on the major forces determining the distribution of earnings by schooling and age. However, human capital theory encompasses optimization on both sides of the market and assumes equilibration of the supply and demand for labor. If all types of labor are perfect substitutes, the demand for efficiency units of labor is perfectly elastic so that the relative wages of workers who differ in human capital stocks are fixed by technology. In order to generate variation in the amount of investment across workers, it is necessary to emphasize interpersonal differences in ability and opportunity which cause variation in the supply of human capital.[17]

If we take into account these differences in ability and opportunity, the strongest version of the theory can be considered a particular case of a more general model that abandons the hypothesis of the homogeneity of human capital. On the one hand, the ability to finance investment in human capital varies depending on the individuals and their familial resources. On the other hand, individuals are not all endowed with the same abilities. These abilities designate, not without a certain ambiguity, the intrinsic differences between workers that exist prior to acquisition of skills in a school environment and ultimately in the occupational environment, and that act simultaneously on the chances of accumulating human capital and on the rapidity of the latter's acquisition. Some individuals get more out of their investment in human capital than others: Their abilities procure a higher yield on their investment in general and specific training.

What is the value of the separation of inequalities into two classes, opportunity and ability? It is easier to observe and measure inequalities of opportunity—the variations in the capacity for investment in academic training depending on the economic situation of the student's family and on the existence of loans and scholarships—than to gauge inequalities of ability, and it is easier to reduce the former by appropriate political measures. Moreover, sociological research has shown that a number of inequalities usually attributed to differences in ability go back to social and cultural factors connected with the individual's social origin and his family environment: These factors act on academic performances, on the choice of the most advantageous lines of work, and on the chances of being able to enter the different occupations. More generally, sociological theories of the inequality of opportunities criticize, for the most part, the naturalist conception of abilities, seeing in differences of ability and in differences in economic investment in education two closely connected manifestations of a single social causality that explains the intergenerational reproduction of inequalities in the agents' social and economic positions.

In explaining differences in remuneration, economic analyses also encounter problems connected with the interaction of the two dimensions of inequality. Is there a pure effect of inequalities of ability, or do the latter act essentially on the level of investment in human capital? In the second case, the function of compensatory equalization that adjusts salary depending on the level of the investment in training is not modified, and we remain within the framework of the theory of human capital: Individuals differ in their demands for training according to their acknowledged abilities, and the choices made by professionals are hierarchized accordingly. The difficulty that complicates the estimate of the yields on individual educational investment arises from the problems of self-selection produced by interactions between opportunities and abilities: If it is above all the individuals with the greatest ability who choose an elevated level of academic training, then these individuals will also have a higher yield on their academic investment, and on average the gains to be expected from additional training will consequently be overestimated.

If the first explanation is adopted, differences in ability play a much more radical role in explaining differences in individual productivity. Econometric analyses of the yields on investment in education and the explanations of the differences in salaries by reference to the accumulation of different types of human capital over the course of occupational life show that initial training and work experience account for only 30 to 50 percent of the variance in salaries, as I noted above. Part of the remaining variance is the net product of differences in ability. Spence's theory of signaling[18] is based on the hypothesis that people are endowed with different abilities resulting from their genetic capital and their initial socialization. Employers seek to discover which candidates for a job will be the most productive: They observe their level of education and the quality of their diplomas, and try to discern abilities not connected with the educational investment. The theory of signaling postulates that an individual who has great abilities can easily acquire a high level of training and that, by paying him well, the employer is betting on his talents as much as on his training to obtain a high productivity: Differences in ability are then a factor that determines individual productivity more than the investment in human capital, since they control the latter's magnitude and its quality. Pursuing long and selective higher education will be rational even if the educational investment has a sharply decreasing marginal yield, provided that the diploma obtained is interpreted by the employer as a signal of its holder's high productivity. This seeks to explain, for example, why an individual holding a diploma from a very selective university can obtain a high salary without being qualified for the job concerned—for example, someone holding a diploma in chemistry will be hired at a high salary as a bank official.

The hypothesis of differences in ability takes on particular prominence when the relation between training and work is considered in its complexity. Multiple sources of interindividual differentiation appear as a result of complex, dynamic interactions between the knowledge acquired by individuals and the aptitude the latter may have for converting, more or less rapidly and effectively, opportunities for learning into skills that can be capitalized and sold on the job market. These differences do not result simply from rational investment in human capital, even if it is granted that workers who learn more effectively accumulate more human capital and are assigned to jobs with greater opportunities for learning.

The essential interest of this kind of reasoning is that it enables us to understand how interindividual differences are constituted and gradually reveal themselves in a given work environment. Reasoning based on differences in ability and their effect on differences in productivity allows us to understand why, given an equal level of initial qualification, the sequence of matchings that makes up each individual's career can give rise to very different trajectories and spectacular inequalities in careers, under the impact of interactions among initial gifts, abilities, investment in education, and opportunities for learning in various work settings.

In sum, the distinctions made on the basis of the diverse components of human capital and on the basis of the diverse factors of the individualization of behaviors give rise to two kinds of heterogeneity in the labor factor: an interindividual heterogeneity and a temporal differentiation. On the one hand, workers differ from each other at every moment, and they evolve differently: They do not have the same resources or the same opportunities to increase the volume of their human capital in the course of their employment trajectory. On the other hand, the temporality of the employment relationship and of the cycle of occupational life is a complex temporality of accumulation, but also of the depreciation of skills: Time does not generate either learning or remuneration equally in accord with job characteristics. And it is impossible to anticipate it at the beginning. It is only in a temporality where everything is completely predictable that all the information necessary for realizing rational anticipations is available at the outset. That would be the case, after all, if the work to be done was entirely or very largely definable *ab initio*. Inversely, a kind of work whose course of completion is uncertain is one that forms and transforms the person who carries it out: In it, the individual experiences his abilities and, more profoundly, his identity, quite differently than he would if the work situation required implementing a range of preexisting skills in accord with a well-established repertory of diagnostics, choices, decisions, and actions.

Collective Rationality, Division of Labor, and Inequalities

I have gradually developed the list of the factors of the differentiation of jobs and workers: investment in human capital that makes it possible to characterize individuals' behavior as a function of utility with three arguments (leisure, training, work); equalizing differences that appear when jobs and occupations are seen as combinations of characteristics; and the dynamics of matching between employer and employee.

The theory of human capital allows us not only to explore the temporal dimension of the investment that determines the productivity of labor, but also to show how labor is, in a variable way, generative of knowledge and skills that can be capitalized. This theory is situated in the neoclassical framework of individual optimizing rationality because the worker is endowed with a function of making choices that takes into account the whole of the life cycle, and because he determines his level of total gain by fixing the volume of time devoted to augmenting his stock of human capital. This in turn leads to a differentiation of activities that does not involve preferences and abilities reflecting individual heterogeneity.

The theory of equalizing differences in salaries arrives at a multidimensional differentiation, but seeks to contain the diversity of jobs and occupations within the framework of optimizing rationality by preserving an essential point of contact with standard economic theory, namely the role of prices in the establishment of market's equilibrium. The principle of this approach is in fact to produce a measurable heterogeneity by constructing two orders of prices for the labor factor: prices observed through the scale of remunerations in the various categories of labor, and fictitious prices (nonmonetary magnitudes), to which the monetary equivalent is to be added or from which it is to be subtracted in order to obtain a theoretical total price that equalizes employment situations once workers' individual characteristics are factored in. Thus it is a matter of simulating the behavior of agents who, by hypothesis, incorporate these magnitudes into their optimizing calculation: The individual values accorded to these magnitudes are made commensurable by reducing them to a monetary equivalent.[19] By including the nonmonetary components of occupational choice, this theory broadens the basis for defining arguments from individual utility, and thus suggests not only that labor includes positive aspects as well as negative ones, but also that individual well-being may proceed to a significant degree from labor itself and not solely from the earnings it provides.

Let us examine the consequences of this reorientation of the analysis of labor. Jobs require implementing a plurality of qualifications and abilities and provide varying opportunities for acquiring new skills. Individuals differ in the qualifications and abilities they possess, their level of effort, their potential for learning, and their preferences. What matters for determining which individual employment situation is optimal is not only to identify the qualifications possessed by each worker and to be sure that these qualifications provide access to the corresponding job and to a given combination of income and leisure, but also to know how the qualifications possessed are used, and how the employment relationship can cause these individual resources to develop. As Rosen indicates,[20] this involves departing from the standard paradigm, because the peculiar identity of the actors in a situation of exchange becomes the condition of efficiency in the allocation of jobs. That is what reasoning in terms of matching requires. It is a question of pairing up in the best way possible the choices made by an employer and an employee, in order to optimize productivity and avoid squandering the available resources (human capital, salaries to be paid) involved on both sides of the market.

Differences in Talents, the Organization of the Market, and the Social Optimum

How should the right organization of the labor market be defined? Can the competitive and decentralized market achieve, at every moment, a sum of optimal matchings? In other words, on what conditions is what is good for an individual a valid criterion for defining and realizing the well-being of the collectivity? And does the well-being procured by labor match with the well-being procured by consumption?

Theories that take into account labor's dimension of well-being suggest a twofold response to these questions when labor is recognized as a heterogeneous reality and when the market has to carry out a process of selection and matching in order to attain equilibrium. These theories can be understood as positions taken with regard to what constitutes the ultimate factor of interindividual differentiation, namely the diversity of abilities and its relation to differences in individual productivity. The diversity of abilities has always been considered the bearer of richness, since it expresses the unfolding of individual singularities, and because it stimulates an increase in the productivity of labor through interaction, exchange, collaboration, and competition. But when it is no longer considered on a horizontal plane of complementarity but on a vertical plane of competition and classification, this diversity is considered a threat to the realization of the ideals of equality and social justice. The role played by individual abilities in the definition of the positive value of labor can thus give rise to divergent conceptions of the division of labor and of the specialization of tasks.

In a functional conception of the matching between individuals and jobs, the division of labor should ideally provide each individual with the best possible match with an available job, taking into account his level of training and experience as well as his preferences. That is the road taken by the economist Kelvin Lancaster, who is known primarily for his new approach to consumer theory. He has applied to the production and labor side his approach to goods in terms of a constellation of characteristics.[21] In his analysis of the variety of production, Lancaster situates labor in the perspective of the economics of well-being and tries to determine whether the well-being drawn individually from labor can be maximized collectively:

> The job itself carries positive and negative aspects which are independent of the time consumed or the pay received, and these enter in an important way into the individual's total well-being. Economists have not doubted this, and have even tried to make some allowance for it in certain contexts (as in the traditional idea of "non-monetary advantage" used to explain why an individual works in one occupation when he or she could earn more in another), but have never integrated it fully into a welfare setting. This has been primarily because of the lack of a suitable analytical framework within which to make such an integration. . . . A welfare analysis of work requires that the job be regarded as multidimensional, as requiring "plural" skills rather than a singular abstract "skill," with different jobs requiring these skills in different proportions. These skills required in a job are then exactly analogous to the characteristics associated with a good. Indeed, the term "characteristics" could be used also for the attributes of a job, but there is some advantage in keeping to the term "skills."
>
> Just as jobs vary in the combination of skills they require, individuals vary in the skills they possess and the combinations in which they prefer to have them employed. This last point is crucial. It is not just which skills are possessed by the individual, but in what proportion they are used, that determines that individual's welfare from work. A physically strong person who is also a very good problem solver may prefer a job which uses both skills (a football quarterback, perhaps) to one that uses only one, even if all other considerations, including pay, were the same.[22]

Next, Lancaster formulates two propositions in order to define his welfare economics of work. The first proposition, which asserts the existence of an optimal matching, postulates that:

> Among all the allocations of persons to jobs which satisfy the requirement that every person holding a job has the skills needed to perform it, there is an optimal allocation.[23]

Lancaster's model starts from the hypothesis that the set of jobs and the set of possible matchings between individuals and jobs are fixed. If we adopt the opposite hypothesis, that of an economy that may vary in the number and type of jobs, and in the qualifications required to fill these jobs, the level of production associated with these changing configurations of jobs becomes variable, and the two types of individual well-being, the one drawn from consumption and the one drawn from work, may diverge. That is what Lancaster's second proposition regarding the economy of the well-being of work, that of the optimal division of labor, seeks to establish:

If the number and specification of jobs can be varied, there is an output-maximizing division of labor which gives the greatest output from the skills available in the population and an optimal division of labor which gives the greatest overall welfare from work and consumption. The output-maximizing and optimal divisions of labor need not be the same. . . .

The problem could be investigated along the general lines of analysis of optimal product variety given earlier. A spectrum of job specifications analogous to the spectrum of goods specifications seems to provide a basic structure into which can be fitted the preferences of individuals over jobs of different kinds. If it can be assumed that costs of management (and perhaps costs of capital) are lower when many workers are performing standardized jobs than when different workers are doing their tasks in different ways, there is an effect analogous to economies of scale in the goods case. Greater variations in jobs enables more workers to be performing the kind of job they prefer but increases organization costs, so that there is a solution to the optimal degree of job variety which is analogous to the optimal degree of product variety.[24]

One of the conditions on which this model of the optimal organization of labor operates is its static character, which creates an important difficulty and marks the limit of Lancaster's reasoning. The matching that maximizes well-being presupposes that the variety of jobs or tasks corresponding to the characteristics of each job is sufficiently great to allow workers having diverse skills and preferences to make, once and for all, complementary choices, that is, ones that are individually satisfying and mutually compatible.

The second condition is that each worker is supposed to know himself perfectly and to have at his disposal perfect information about the variety of jobs among which he has to choose; the practice of the occupation does not provide the individual with any unforeseen information regarding his talents and skills. The variety of tasks and the variety of qualifications, mutually matched in a market in equilibrium that achieves an optimal division of labor, contain from the outset all the potential for differentiation necessary for producing the maximum of well-being. The development of differences over time is absorbed into the variety of coexisting situations.

The Ambivalences of Labor in Complex Societies

The quest for an optimal matching greatly increases the organization costs of the labor market: This argument given by Lancaster is analogous to the one that Durkheim developed in his *Division du travail social*,[25] in an entirely different vocabulary, but in response to the same question. Can we, Durkheim asks, divide and specialize labor in order to augment its productivity, while at the same time avoiding the danger that it will generally deteriorate into a parceling-out of tasks that assigns to labor a simply instrumental value sold on a market like any ordinary good? In modern societies, the organization of the division of labor is complex, and promotes a differentiation of behaviors. Durkheim reminds us that this development, which guarantees progress and individual emancipation, also brings with it dangers of social disorder. As the frequency and intensity of interindividual exchanges increases, the envious comparison that arises among individuals results from the specialization of each person's abilities and skills, a specialization that succeeds to varying degrees and is unequally gratifying. The differentiation of trajectories increases the costs of coordination for matching abilities, skills, and jobs. The demand for personal autonomy and the broadest possible range of individual choices intensifies the search for particular advantages that may not be mutually compatible. We are confronted by the complexity of the organization of a society with an organic solidarity: Durkheim tells us that without the establishment of institutions and collective regulatory mechanisms, the division and specialization of labor promote the unlimited differentiation of individual situations, to be sure, but they also exacerbate struggles and conflicts, and will lead to situations of anomie, that is, of disorder and social violence. One of these regulatory institutions is none other than the organization of activities into trades, into occupations and career structures, which makes it possible to contain the effects of individual heterogeneity and to reduce the costs of organizing the labor market.[26]

Durkheim's demonstration acquires particular relief when he discusses the arts. *A priori,* artistic activities should figure among the categories of specialized labor to which those who have the required talents wish to devote themselves. They may even be considered the embodiment par excellence of the irresistible movement toward individualism in complex societies. The progress of individualism is, after all, the correlate of artistic activity, since the deliberate expression of individual singularity constitutes the vector of the search for creative originality. Durkheim repeatedly reminds us that without the power of the creative faculty constituted by the imagination, individuals would not be led to constantly invent, to seek new solutions to meet new needs, in short, to progress. But art also embodies, and with a very particular vividness, the constitutive ambivalence of individualism. The growing differentiation of social activities makes each social actor an ever more autonomous individual, and artistic activity merely exacerbates the tendency toward interindividual differentiation that corrupts the mechanisms integrating individuals into the collectivity constituting society.

Why does art concentrate the ambivalences of the development toward complex societies? Durkheim's argument on this point is twofold. Art increases, in several ways, the risk of disordering individual passions worked upon by the illimitation of desires. For what defines art and the activities of cultural creation and consumption is the rejection of limits and constraints, that is, the negation of the mechanism that is the pivot of the social equilibrium, according to Durkheim:

> Art remains entirely resistant to anything resembling an obligation, since its domain is one where freedom reigns. It is a luxury and an ornament that it may well be fine to possess, but that one cannot be compelled to acquire: what is a superfluity cannot be imposed upon people. By contrast, morality is the indispensable minimum, that which is strictly necessary, the daily bread without which societies cannot live. Art corresponds to the need we have to widen those of our activities that lack purpose, for the pleasure of doing so, whilst morality constrains us to follow a path laid down, one which leads towards a definite goal. He who speaks of obligation speaks at the same time of constraint. Thus, although art can draw inspiration from moral ideas or is to be found intermingled with the evolution of strictly moral phenomena, it is not moral in itself. Observation might even establish perhaps that, with individuals as with societies, from the moral viewpoint the inordinate development of the aesthetic faculties is a grave symptom.[27]

Is this desire for free self-determination that each artist professes within reach of everyone? It is, in the act of consumption: Individuals are supposed to find, in the universe of artistic goods, consumer products with a high content of innovation, the symbolic nourishment par excellence for the imaginary satisfaction of their needs, which expand constantly and without limit, and feed their individualist immoderation. But how can individuals' attitudes of rejecting limits and constraints be made compatible with each other, how can we act in such a way that each person contains his desires and his envies without being haunted by the difference between his situation and that of others? Durkheim emphasizes that cultural and artistic consumption is a terrain that is particularly propitious for the exercise of envious comparison, the kind that poisons interindividual relations, when the inequalities of condition arising from class differences are expressed in it. And what is true of the consumption of artistic goods is no less true of the exercise of creative talents.

The analysis of art leads to the ultimate foundations of interindividual differentiation. The latter is notoriously based on inequalities of ability and talent: Some of these inequalities are irreducible and have their origin in what Durkheim calls "natural gifts" (intelligence, taste, aptitude for invention, courage, manual dexterity, physical strength), and he compares them to inherited capital. The meritocratic essence of the social regulation Durkheim imagines has as its fundamental principle that "the external conditions of competition should be equal"[28] without inhibiting interindividual differences in ability and talent:

> The workman is not in harmony with his social position if he is not convinced that he has his desserts. If he feels justified in occupying another, what he has would not satisfy him. So it is not enough for the average level of needs for each social condition to be regulated by public opinion, but another, more precise rule, must fix the way in which these conditions are open to individuals. There is no society in which such regulation does not exist. It varies with times and places. Once it regarded birth as the almost exclusive principle of social classification; today it recognizes no other inherent inequality than hereditary fortune and merit. But in all these various forms its object is unchanged. It is also only possible, everywhere, as a restriction upon individuals imposed by superior authority, that is, by collective authority. For it can be established only by requiring of one or another group of men, usually of all, sacrifices and concessions in the name of the public interest.
>
> Some, to be sure, have thought that this moral pressure would become unnecessary if men's economic circumstances were only no longer determined by heredity. If inheritance were abolished, the argument runs, if everyone began life with equal resources and if the competitive struggle were fought out on a basis of perfect equality, no one could think its results unjust. Each would instinctively feel that things are as they should be.
>
> Truly, the more nearly this ideal equality is approached, the less social restraint will be necessary. But it is only a matter of degree. One sort of heredity will always exist, that of natural talent. Intelligence, taste, scientific, artistic, literary or industrial ability, courage and manual dexterity are gifts received by each of us at birth, as the heir to wealth receives his capital or as the nobleman formerly received his title and function. A moral discipline will therefore still be required to make those less favored by nature accept the lesser advantages which they owe to the chance of birth. Shall it be demanded that all have an equal share and that no advantage be given those more useful and deserving? But then there would have to be a discipline far stronger to make these accept a treatment merely equal to that of the mediocre and incapable.[29]

The "moral discipline" invoked by Durkheim to promote organic solidarity among the members of a society dominated by the growing differentiation of situations and individual aspirations is supposed to do away with an essential problem, that of the inequality of the chances of gaining access to the exercise of activities in which the opportunities for self-expression in work are completely opened up. One puzzle has to be solved: How can we explain the admiration we may accord the most striking successes in these activities, even though individuals have such unequal chances of realizing themselves in them? If it is envious comparison that dominates interindividual passions, we are in a society of pure competition, in which the collective game being played is a zero-sum game: Anything that is obtained by some people is lost by others. But Durkheim also wants to see in creative activities the ferments of a civilizing progress that engenders admirable accomplishments. Can labor and success embody the creative power of individuals without triggering envious comparisons?

Individual Self-Fulfillment and Communal Well-Being: Rawls and the Aristotelian Principle

John Rawls's book *A Theory of Justice* can be read as an attempt to synthesize the conception that asserts the inequalities of talent and the necessity of a division of labor, on the one hand, and the conception that invites each individual to realize himself through the greatest possible development of his talents in work, on the other hand.

Rawls bases the rationality of self-fulfillment in productive activity on the Aristotelian principle of the full development of one's talents. Referring to long-term individual projects such as the choice of a profession or a job, he formulates the following argument:

> In accordance with the Aristotelian Principle . . . , I assume that human beings have a higher-order desire to follow the principle of inclusiveness.
> They prefer the more comprehensive long-term plan because its execution presumably involves a more complex combination of abilities. The Aristotelian Principle states that, other things equal, human beings enjoy the exercise of their realized capacities (their innate or trained abilities), and that this enjoyment increases the more the capacity is realized, or the greater its complexity. A person takes pleasure in doing something as he becomes more proficient at it, and of two activities which he performs equally well, he prefers the one that calls upon the greater number of more subtle and intricate discriminations. Thus the desire to carry out the larger pattern of ends which brings into play the more finely developed talents is an aspect of the Aristotelian Principle.[30]

Rawls sees in this principle a superior form of the rationality of action:

> One long-term plan is better than another for any given period (or number of periods) if it allows for the encouragement and satisfaction of all the aims and interests of the other plan and for the encouragement and satisfaction of some further aim or interest in addition. The more inclusive plan, if there is one, is to be preferred: it comprehends all the ends of the first plan and at least one other end as well. If this principle is combined with that of effective means, then together they define rationality as preferring, other things equal, the greater means for realizing our aims, and the development

of wider and more varied interests assuming that these aspirations can be carried through.[31]

How can we arrive at an equilibrium of collective well-being on the basis of this Aristotelian principle of self-fulfillment? Rawls's solution consists in the transformation of the excellences that result from differences in talent into common goods benefiting everyone. In other words, Rawls "collectivizes" the goods that are constituted by the qualities and talents of each individual and contrasts them with consumer goods and services that essentially satisfy selfish preferences:

> Let us distinguish between things that are good primarily for us (for the one who possesses them) and attributes of our person that are good both for us and for others as well. These two classes are not exhaustive but they indicate the relevant contrast. Thus commodities and items of property (exclusive goods) are goods mainly for those who own them and have use of them, and for others only indirectly. On the other hand, imagination and wit, beauty and grace, and other natural assets and abilities of the person are goods for others too: they are enjoyed by our associates as well as ourselves when properly displayed and rightly exercised. They form the human means for complementary activities in which persons join together and take pleasure in their own and one another's realization of their nature. This class of goods constitutes the excellences: they are the characteristics and abilities of the person that it is rational for everyone (including ourselves) to want us to have. From our standpoint, the excellences are goods since they enable us to carry out a more satisfying plan of life enhancing our sense of mastery. At the same time these attributes are appreciated by those with whom we associate, and the pleasure they take in our person and in what we do supports our self-esteem. Thus the excellences are a condition of human flourishing; they are goods from everyone's point of view. These facts relate them to the conditions of self-respect, and account for their connection with our confidence in our own value.[32]

The transfiguration of individual talents into goods that are collective and mutually beneficial extends to all members of society the Aristotelian imperative of developing talents by providing it with a social constraint. A purely individualistic and egocentric behavior of self-fulfillment would be self-destructive, since the irreducible singularity of the talents buried in each individual can be actualized only through the stimulating display of other people's talents:

> There is also a companion effect to the Aristotelian Principle. As we witness the exercise of well-trained abilities by others, these displays are enjoyed by us and arouse a desire that we should be able to do the same things ourselves. We want to be like those persons who can exercise the abilities that we find latent in our nature.[33]

A collective rationality emerges from the admiration of the most intrinsically personal qualities:

> A rational plan—constrained as always by the principles of right—allows a
> person to flourish, so far as circumstances permit, and to exercise his realized
> abilities as much as he can. Moreover, his fellow associates are likely to sup-
> port these activities as promoting the common interest and also to take plea-
> sure in them as displays of human excellence. To the degree, then, that the
> esteem and admiration of others is desired, the activities favored by the Aris-
> totelian Principle are good for other persons as well.[34]

How can that be? Difference is an essential principle because it is founded
on the variety of talents and skills, and on the fact that no one can realize
the totality of his talents and skills. The question then becomes: Do all individuals have, potentially, identically varied abilities which they actualize
incompletely because they have different projects and objectives? Or are
they really different from one another, some having skills that others will
never have?

Rawls's answer to this question is ambiguous. On the one hand, the
horizon for the actualization of individual potentialities is limited by the
finite nature of human life:

> Human beings have various talents and abilities the totality of which is unre-
> alizable by any one person or group of persons. Thus we not only benefit
> from the complementary nature of our developed inclinations but we take
> pleasure in one another's activities. It is as if others were bringing forth a part
> of ourselves that we have not been able to cultivate. We have had to devote
> ourselves to other things, to only a small part of what we might have done.[35]
>
>   In the account of goodness as rationality we came to the familiar conclusion
> that rational plans of life normally provide for the development of at least
> some of a person's powers. The Aristotelian Principle points in this direction.
> Yet one basic characteristic of human beings is that no one person can do
> everything that he might do; nor a fortiori can he do everything that any other
> person can do. The potentialities of each individual are greater than those he
> can hope to realize; and they fall far short of the powers among men gener-
> ally. Thus everyone must select which of his abilities and possible interests he
> wishes to encourage; he must plan their training and exercise, and schedule
> their pursuit in an orderly way.[36]

On the other hand, the principle of difference incontestably designates
irreducible natural and social inequalities that lead to differences in individual productivity. But Rawls seeks to affirm the differences without
transforming them into competitive advantages that generate illegitimate
inequalities. The differences can be fully and harmoniously deployed only
when they are put in the service of all:

Different persons with similar or complementary capacities may cooperate so to speak in realizing their common or matching nature. When men are secure in the enjoyment of the exercise of their own powers, they are disposed to appreciate the perfections of others, especially when their several excellences have an agreed place in a form of life the aims of which all accept.[37]

This is a manifestation of what Jean-Pierre Dupuy[38] has well described as the ambivalence of Rawls's system: Rawls seeks to ground in reason the concept of just inequality, which causes him to be caught in the crossfire of two kinds of criticism, the criticism of his egalitarianism and the criticism of his legitimation of inequalities. The principle of difference is supposed to find its expression and at the same time its equilibrium in a communitarian society in which each person realizes himself only in contact with and in relation to others. In other words, the talents each person seeks to develop in order to attain self-esteem and a feeling of mastery are a common heritage of excellences, and if individuals are unequally endowed, their differing endowments are worth nothing unless the use of them is supported by a generalized exchange of esteem and mutual admiration:

> The conditions for persons respecting themselves and one another would seem to require that their common plans be both rational and complementary: they call upon their educated endowments and arouse in each a sense of mastery, and they fit together into one scheme of activity that all can appreciate and enjoy.[39]

Does the specializing division of labor offer an appropriate framework in which the optimum of well-being is compatible with the optimum of productivity? Rawls's analysis reformulates the imperative of the division of labor to ensure that all individual work will be enriched, fulfilling, and complementary to that of others, provided that it is exercised within a collectivity that becomes the receptacle for fragmentary and complementary individual excellences:

> A well-ordered society does not do away with the division of labor in the most general sense. To be sure, the worst aspects of this division can be surmounted: no one need be servilely dependent on others and made to choose between monotonous and routine occupations which are deadening to human thought and sensibility. Each can be offered a variety of tasks so that the different elements of his nature find a suitable expression. But even when work is meaningful for all, we cannot overcome, nor should we wish to, our dependence on others. . . . It is tempting to suppose that everyone might fully realize his powers and that some at least can become complete exemplars of humanity. But this is impossible. It is a feature of human sociability that we are by ourselves but parts of what we might be. We must look to others to attain the excellences that we must leave aside, or lack altogether. The collective

activity of society, the many associations and the public life of the largest
community that regulates them, sustains our efforts and elicits our contribution. Yet the good attained from the common culture far exceeds our work in
the sense that we cease to be mere fragments: that part of ourselves that we
directly realize is joined to a wider and just arrangement the aims of which
we affirm. The division of labor is overcome not by each becoming complete
in himself, but by willing and meaningful work within a just social union of
social unions in which all can freely participate as they so incline.[40]

Uncertainty, Risk-Taking, and the Individualization
of Self-Fulfillment

Rawlsian theory seeks to neutralize the factor that generates irreducible
inequalities—differences in talent—by collectivizing excellences. Thus each
individual's talent becomes a public good endowed with a positive exter-
nality, and each individual succeeds in fulfilling himself only by participating in a community in which "the self is realized in the activities of many
selves."[41] However, there remains a fundamental ambiguity with regard to
the conditions of realizing a "justly inegalitarian society" that would allow
the individual to fulfill himself totally in his singularity without arousing the envy of others. As soon as it tries to combine the universality of the
Aristotelian principle of rational self-fulfillment in work with the recognition of irreducible differences in talent and the requirement of justice, the
Rawlsian conception becomes unstable, as Dupuy points out:

> The problem with the "Moderns," as they are understood by Benjamin Con-
> stant and de Tocqueville, is, as Rawls perceived very clearly, that they are trou-
> bled by a knowledge that prevents them from having recourse to the traditional
> solutions: the knowledge that there is no order that transcends the social order,
> and that humans alone are responsible for the organization of the city. The
> problem of a society emancipated from any control with regard to any exterior,
> is that those who found themselves in a condition of inferiority would have no
> way of attributing their misfortune to a cause situated outside their personal
> sphere. Moreover, this society would be the height of individualism in the sense
> that the individual, "disembedded," freed from all kinds of subordination and
> all the connections that constitute the traditional world, would be the sole
> receptacle of values. Henceforth, people's value would be discernible in their
> condition, without any attenuating circumstance. Envy would have free rein,
> and nothing would provide shelter from it.
>
> The characteristics of a well-ordered society compose precisely this kind of
> picture. Since this theory of envy is the one Rawls adopts, he cannot avoid the
> conclusion that his edifice is extremely fragile with regard to the undermining
> work of envy. The good Rawlsian society is a society that everyone agrees to

publicly recognize as just, and that pushes as far as possible the conditions for a genuine equity in the equality of chances. It is, moreover, an inegalitarian society in which inequalities are correlated with differences in abilities, talents, and skills, and thus make these differences visible. How could those at the bottom of the ladder blame their inferiority on anyone but themselves? . . . Thus to do away with envy it would be necessary to do away with merit—that is, difference in individual value.[42]

The Rawlsian conception neglects one of the principles of the expressivist model of praxis for which Aristotle provided the matrix. Of the three principles that in Aristotle's work justify the valorization of human labor— the principle of self-realization in a productive activity that has itself as its own end, the principle of individuation, and the principle of contingency— Rawls retains only the first two. But the third principle, the principle of contingency, which connects creative individualism with risk, is no less essential, as I will show after having briefly reconstituted Aristotle's argumentation, following in particular the interpretation of it given by Pierre Aubenque.[43]

In the *Nicomachean Ethics*,[44] Aristotle elaborates a philosophy of action *(praxis)* and production *(poēsis)* based on the principle of contingency and the indeterminacy of the future. The sublunary world in which humans exist is an incomplete world. Human action can modify its course: Change is a possibility that always remains open, and human action is situated in the gap between potential and actual being that is opened up by the "power of being different." The domain of contingency makes it possible to invent and produce something new because humans, in their productive activity, shape a matter that was previously indeterminate. The distinction between potential being and actual being would cancel the principle of contingency if there were no possibility of a gap between cause and effect, no obstacle to the actualization of the potential, in other words, if the sublunary world obeyed laws of causal determination like those that prevail in the cosmos and that govern the movement of the planets and the stars. We have to understand in passing that it is this cancellation of the principle of contingency that is implied by the argument according to which the individual can express the totality of his potentialities provided that he has enough time to actualize them: Individual failure or incompletion would exist only for lack of time.

Now, if I interpret the principle of contingency correctly, uncertainty is the bearer of the success as well as the failure of action. It is the test of uncertainty that gives creative work its human depth and its greatest satisfactions. Uncertainty about the course of the action and the existence of differences in ability between individuals, even if minimal, are essentially linked: That is what explains the social prestige of occupations whose success is uncertain.

How should we analyze the project of pursuing a career in occupations that are attractive and thus in conformity with the Aristotelian principle, but in which success is very uncertain? The classical explanation combines two arguments.

First, risk-taking is encouraged by the hope of high gains and, as is indicated by the argument of compensatory differences examined earlier, there are nonmonetary gratifications that can compensate temporarily or permanently for the loss of income. Risk-taking is thus related both to the characteristics of the activity and to individuals' personal characteristics. So far as individuals are concerned, the hypothesis is that the sources of risk-taking are never so active as when people are young and show "the contempt of risk and the presumptuous hope of success," as Adam Smith put it. Let us be sure we understand his argument: What is universal is each person's overestimation of his chances of gain and his symmetrical underestimation of his chances of loss, as is shown by the existence of lotteries, where "the vain hope of gaining some of the great prizes is the sole cause of this demand." But the strength of this overestimation is greater among young people. Does youth reflect a state of inexperience and unawareness that aggravates a defect in the rational evaluation of the probabilities of success? Or is it because the cost of error is easier to bear for young people, at a time when their vocational life has hardly begun, but becomes more important as the possibilities of decisive vocational reorientation become narrower with age, because the value of their human capital decreases on the job market? I leave this question unanswered here; it will be answered in the two following chapters by showing how the two hypotheses, which seem to be radically opposed, are in fact compatible: The overestimation of the chances of success is not antirational, provided that the career is organized with the help of sufficiently effective mechanisms of selection.

Second, the chance of success has to do with the intrinsic characteristics of the activity. The categorization of jobs isolates occupations that are risky, not so much in the sense that they endanger the individual's health and life, as in the sense that they provide only a weak guarantee of success or even of simply being able to continue in the vocational activity. This is especially true for independent, liberal professions, entrepreneurial activities, and athletic and artistic activities.

We can combine the two sides of the analysis, that of the individual's behavior under conditions of uncertainty and that of job characteristics, based on the matching model. The theory of matching suggests, in fact, that some of the characteristics of the mobility of the labor force are explained if the exercise itself of different occupations is conceived as a tentative accumulation of information that informs the individual regarding the occupation in which his chances are best. It is because the course of the activity is uncertain that the degree of matching between the qualities of a candidate for such occupations and the conditions for success in the exercise of them is revealed to the individual only gradually. In other words, the choice is all the more rational to the extent to which the qualities required for success in an occupation are only incompletely revealed in the course of initial training, as I will show in Chapter 4.

This model of occupational choice also presupposes, in order to define an equilibrium, that the lack of a specific talent is revealed soon enough to prevent an individual from getting caught up in a spiral of failure. But this hypothesis is not trivial: What is the optimal period for the revelation of an individual's abilities? In activities with high learning potential, which are often carried out in project-based work systems, the problem of knowing what quantity of experience is necessary before judging the quality of the job match is raised by the variability of the situations. Each work experience has specific characteristics, and the relations of collaboration are changing: This explains the feeling that the evaluation of one's skills by oneself and by others is eminently variable. Thus it is logical to conceive behavior with regard to risk as an element entering into the accumulation of human capital for individuals operating long-term in these occupations.

In conclusion, by examining the case of occupations in which success is very uncertain, I have arrived at the category of activities that accumulate to the highest degree the factors of the individualization of work situations: These factors are the fundamental role of abilities, individuals' imperfect information regarding their abilities, and the very frequently independent or quasi-independent exercise of these professions.[45] Strong autonomy or statutory independence brings to bear directly the interactions between abilities, investment in human capital, preferences, and dispositions with respect to risk.

The marriage of individualism with risk has a crucial organizational consequence: Professionals who set store by their work do not identify themselves primarily with an enterprise, but with a professional community, less on the basis of an integration of each person into a homogeneous group than on that of an organization of work connections into a network. That is what allows us to explain a strong tolerance for inequalities in success, which is the signature of risk, and a demand for the right to self-fulfillment in labor, which is the signature of the potential for unlimited differentiation of activity that is oriented toward a goal, but not determined by a foreseeable end.

The characteristics of salaried employment exercised within a firm are situated in a different temporal perspective, since a contract for salaried employment that links an employee to his employer has a temporal extension, unlike the services provided by independent professions that organize activity into a series of contractual bonds whose duration and recurrence are very variable. But in the case of salaried employment in an organization, as in that of independent activity, the argument regarding the career prospect applies as soon as the worker has enough discretionary power to reduce his dependency on his employer and to have an elevated market power. The argument regarding the job prospect was advanced by James Thompson[46] to distinguish between jobs and occupations, occupations that are "early ceiling" or "late ceiling" (or "high ceiling"). Three dimensions are crucial for determining this prospect: "the opportunity to learn," "the opportunity for visibility," and "the types of assessment levied by significant others on the individual's performance." Each job is a "sphere of action" whose characteristics vary according to the power exercised by the organization on the careers of individuals and according to individuals' ability to handle organizational dependency. In order for a career's prospects to continue and rise, the jobs that compose it must provide chances to learn and a potential for interaction sufficient to increase the individual's negotiating power. Jobs with short horizons (early ceiling jobs) have a weak potential for learning and are situated far from the zones where the organization contacts its environment. The chances of realizing occupational prospects increase when the job or the occupation offers more variability in tasks and in work interactions. The upper limit of this process is the bilateral monopoly: The salaried worker has an elevated negotiating power in proportion to the favorable exit options with which his reputation provides him. Then competition between organizations to attract the most talented employees exercises its pressure on each organization.

Thus these three dimensions combine to characterize a job with elevated opportunities for fulfillment: the unequal potential for personal development offered by different jobs and occupations, the functional localization of jobs in the organization, which provides unequal opportunities for learning and reputational visibility, and the competitive environment of other organizations. One of the recent innovations in human resource management results from the dilemma confronting enterprises: attracting the best employees by resorting to poaching outside talent while at the same time earning their most productive employees' loyalty.[47]

Thus whether it is realized within firms or operates in independent careers by basing itself on a mechanism of reputation controlled by judgment and peer evaluation, as in occupations practiced with a high degree of autonomy, matching individuals with jobs that have a great potential for personal fulfillment increases the intensity of competition and interpersonal comparison and leads to ordinal classifications of talents. A career can be understood, then, as an individual development based on a comparison between the successive realizations of an individual who accumulates human capital and information about his abilities gained via the trials of interindividual competition.

Only a deeper exploration of the heterogeneity of jobs and their attributes allows us to discern the positive characteristics of spending one's time and effort on an activity, above and beyond simple monetary compensation. It comes to this conclusion: The relation between individualism, the formative value of labor, and the test of uncertainty constitutes the equation of self-fulfillment in work, and it presupposes the social approval of individual value, not the denial of evaluation. In Chapter 4 I will show, by reasoning contrafactually, what the consequences of a complete denial of the evaluation of individual achievements would be.

CHAPTER THREE

Rationality and Uncertainty in the Artist's Life

T HE ARTIST'S LIFE has long been the subject of fables and legends. If we explore, as Ernst Kris and Otto Kurz have done, the literature on artists from classical antiquity to the present, we can assess the recurrence of such themes as the innate gift, precocity, self-teaching, and the role of chance in the discovery and consecration of talent.[1] These themes all transform artistic engagement into a vocation and the artist himself into a charismatic figure who, assuming luck comes his way, is driven exclusively by an inner need to realize himself through self-expression. The power of this stereotype derives from the way *a posteriori* rationalization acts to conjure away uncertainty: The dimension of choice is negated by the notion of an irresistible vocation; the vagaries of success are obscured by the predestination motif (embodied in the image of precocious talent); and the trials involved in acquiring skills are masked by glowing evidence of the artist's gift. This reconstruction by way of rationalization may be understood as a psychological and ideological response to a complex problem—that of the rationality of individual behavior and action under uncertainty. Indeed, while the uncertainty of success contributes to the social prestige of the artistic professions and grants a magical quality to a type of activity that has become the paradigm of unconstrained, nonroutine, and ideally fulfilling labor, it also generates considerable disparities between the conditions of artists who succeed and those of individuals who are relegated to the lower ranks of the celebrity pyramid.

In the sociology of art, deterministic approaches tend to ignore the dimension of uncertainty when, in order to outline the factors associated with artistic engagement and success, they examine the social recruitment of artists and the structural affinities between actors' professional positions and their individual dispositions. In economic analysis, the question is whether one can account for professional commitments that are, on average, notoriously risky and poorly remunerated, by deploying an axiomatics of rational, utility-maximizing behavior. My aim here is to show that the value of uncertainty can constitute a pivotal argument for integrating sociological and economic approaches, provided this integration involves (1) restoring actors' ability to take initiatives; (2) interpreting their behavior on the job market in dynamic terms; and (3) studying how, in the organization of the different art markets, the mechanisms responsible for discrepancies between the supply of goods and labor and the demand for them affect the choices of individual actors.

Monetary and Nonmonetary Arguments for Career Choice

One of the tasks the empirical sociology of art has set for itself is to study the conditions under which artistic professions are practiced, and, in particular, the conditions of remuneration for artistic labor.

The income gaps among artists and the varying degrees of success they achieve throughout their careers are so strongly apparent that, very often, researchers have been led to dispense with assessing the exact extent of these disparities, and to settle instead for unverifiable approximations. Given the numerous difficulties involved in collecting reliable and controllable data on artists' living conditions, the economic dimension of their social status is generally apprehended through partial indexes that are often more evocative than precise; for instance, the probability of artists actually making a living from their art. Moreover, the more the criteria for selecting the reference population are based on a broad definition of the "artist" category, the more the choice to represent artists' conditions via the "realistic" image of their modal situation (the one that, in view of the distribution of income levels into statistical classes, includes the greatest number of individuals) will lead to a grim picture of the artist as socioeconomically accursed. Nevertheless, there exist many ways of assessing the situation of artists and of utilizing the income indicator: Though they are complementary, the sets of data generated through these various approaches provide different answers to the question of why one chooses art as a career.

The first approach, which is the most traditional and comprehensive, measures the average or median income level of artists, as identified and classified in national censuses, surveys from major statistical institutions on income trends in the active population, and *ad hoc* studies of presumably representative sample populations. In an analysis based on the 1980 U.S. census data, Randall Filer estimated the gap between the average income of artists and that of the active population as a whole to be −6 percent.[2] The value of this gap—which calls for revising the myth of the economically accursed artist—varies depending on national contexts and survey methods. Nonetheless, when more specific bases for comparison are selected, all economic estimates converge. In the category wherein socioprofessional nomenclatures rank the majority of artists today—"Professional, Technical, and Managerial Workers" in the United States and "Higher Managerial and Professional Occupations" (*cadres et professions intellectuelles supérieures*) in France—artists are situated on the lower portion of the income scale.[3] Thus, the 1982 French census, which covered the same time period as Filer's calculations for the United States, showed that the average wage index for professionals in the news media, the arts, and the performing arts reached 143. This figure was nearly equidistant from the average wage index for employees as a whole—base 100—and from the average wage index for the entire category of "Higher Managerial and Professional Occupations" to which these professionals belonged—200. Moreover, artists were the lowest-ranking group in this category. Those gaps evolved slightly afterward: In the 1990 French census, the figures were, respectively, 146 and 187.

Such figures, however, can mask differences in the composition of the professions and professional groups under comparison. The analysis becomes more accurate when a series of characteristics of individual workers are taken into account, including sex, age, place of residence, family situation, nationality, and, above all, the two characteristics most strongly predictive of expected earnings: education or qualification level, and professional experience. We can thus attempt a second approach to explaining the reasons for choosing art as a career by constructing a second indicator of artists' economic situation: the estimation of opportunity cost. The latter represents the negative gap between the average income an individual can expect to earn in an artistic profession and the income he could earn from the best alternative solution available to him in the labor market, given his personal characteristics. According to Filer's calculations, the "penalty" for choosing art is approximately 10 percent. Aggregating the sacrifices made by individual artists throughout their careers, Glenn Withers estimated that the sum of "hidden subsidies" that artists pay by accepting this "penalized" income is three times the total sum of public subsidies for the arts in Australia.[4]

The evaluation of this opportunity cost varies depending on whether it is constructed according to a static or a dynamic model for estimating expected income. The dynamic model represents a third approach to measuring the economic destiny of individuals in artistic professions. It is not only average earnings that are taken into consideration here, but also the age-profile of earnings. Various statistical studies have in fact revealed an identical bell curve profile.[5] The latter shows that artists' maximum earnings are reached on average around age 50, and display very steep slopes of growth and decline on either side of this peak; this contrasts sharply with the traditional age-profile of earnings, which is concave when examined as a cross-section of the wages of all age groups.[6] In other words, the earnings of artists in the early stages of their careers are lower than the average earnings of the active population as a whole, yet they increase faster and surpass the average general level, before declining between the ages of 50 and 55. Artists' low average income can be imputed in part to the composition effects of this age-profile of earnings.

Comparisons based on consecutive population censuses reveal two major patterns. First, from 1970 to 1980, the fall in real income in the United States was greater for artists than for other professional categories. Second, the number of professional artists surveyed increased sharply over the same period, at an annual rate of more than 4 percent.[7] The same demographic trend was observed in Canada[8] and in France.[9] This divergent evolution can be explained by at least two factors: the feminization of artistic professions, which occurred at a faster rate than that of the active population as a whole; and a broadening of the statistical definition of the "artist" category, which led either to the inclusion of related professional specialties or to the softening of the criteria for professional identification.[10] The income profile of artists offers an additional explanation: Given that artists' income is particularly low in the early stages of their career, the influx of numerous young people into artistic professions lowered the average income for the entire period that immediately followed the sudden swelling in the number of artists.[11]

In working to show that choosing an artistic profession amounts to rational, utility-maximizing behavior, the economic calculations above base themselves on the average income of artistic professionals as a whole. Yet, in doing so, they also erase important differences in average income between the various professions. The data they use reveal that while there is only a gap of −6 percent between the average income of artists as a whole and that of the active population at large, this gap varies greatly by artistic profession, ranging from +58 percent for actors and theater and film directors to −69.5 percent for dancers and choreographers. These differences would widen even further if we took into account all the elements that determine the living conditions of artists.

Indeed, the above analysis of the sheer monetary arguments of utility ignores a whole set of factors that affect monetary returns in the various artistic professions, and hence impact the calculation of opportunity cost: training costs, direct expenses associated with professional practice, career length, seasonal employment variability, the more or less irregular evolution of earnings over the course of a career, the conditions of taxation on income (possibilities for income averaging or for tax evasion, and so forth). One should also include in the evaluation of expected earnings the various types of employee benefits that supplement income (health and unemployment insurance, retirement, paid vacations, paid expenses, and so on), part of which may be financed by the state, depending on the scope of its cultural policy. The impact of such factors on the economic situation of artists and on the financial desirability of artistic activities introduces marked disparities among artistic professions and among the different types of jobs available in these—as shown by the rare studies that take into account one or several of these factors.[12]

Economic explanations for the observed differences between average pay rates in the various professions usually bring into play the following series of factors:[13]

- The size and cost of human capital investments (education, self-teaching, health expenses) made by individuals prior to entering the job market, or financed by enterprises requiring highly specific skills;
- The institutional factors that create barriers to entry into a whole series of artistic professions, accessible only to members of "noncompeting groups" (to use Cairnes's formula[14]) endowed with the necessary assets: social stratification responsible for sharp inequalities in opportunities for accessing higher occupations; formal restrictions on entry into a given profession (imposed, for instance, by a professional association with a monopoly on professional practice—as in the liberal professions—or by a union's monopoly on hiring); lack of workforce mobility; racial discrimination;
- Delays in labor-market adjustment to short-term variations in supply and demand, which are responsible for the transitory portion of wage differences;
- Lastly, the set of factors that, in addition to determining wages per se, determine the attractiveness of the various professions and

generate differences in remuneration among these that are reputed to be equalizing. These include: the factors that affect the net returns expected from a job (as I evoked above); the variability and dispersion of income, which express the uncertainty of success in a given profession (as I will discuss below); and nonmonetary advantages and disadvantages.

Economic studies of artistic professions assign determinant weight to non-monetary advantages, for such benefits can altogether constitute the equalizing complement invariably invoked to uphold the rationality of choosing professions that offer mediocre expected earnings—as I indicated in Chapter 2. Sociological analysis is more likely to cite, among the determinants of artistic careers' desirability, the status and social prestige associated with artistic professions. Thus, in the French social space outlined by the INSEE (Institut National de la Statistique et des Études Économiques) in its new professional nomenclature, artists are assigned a high social position, among the "Higher Managerial and Professional Occupations." Michel Gollac and Baudoin Seys's analysis of the results from the 1982 census—the first to use and test the new classificatory grid—shows that, in view of their sociodemographic characteristics (sex, age, educational level, and, one should add, income), "artists are close to the mid-level administrative and business professionals found in firms."[15] The authors justify the position assigned to artists in the public statistical nomenclature by emphasizing the weakness of the educational level criterion (which does not take into account the importance of professional experience or on-the-job learning) and, above all, the social origin of artists, which ". . . nonetheless, can be used to assess [their] social position. . . . As 35% of artists are children of those who belong to the category of 'Higher Managerial and Professional Occupations,' they rank among individuals with the highest social origins. Only the members of liberal professions surpass them."[16]

The benefits drawn from nonmonetary advantages, however, are variable. According to the theory of equalizing differences, their magnitude must be adjusted for type of employment, level of professional recognition, and possibility of remaining in the profession while waiting for success (such as through resorting to subsistence jobs). Comparative studies reveal, for instance, that although independent artists obtain greater nonmonetary satisfactions than do artists employed in organizations, the average income of the former is below that of the latter due to greater job insecurity, a higher rate of unemployment, and wider dispersion around average income.[17] Some of the descriptions of labor among certain categories of salaried artists go so far as to discount a significant portion of the compensatory "psychic income." The emblematic case of orchestra musicians well illustrates the counter-mythology of the artist; in this case, musicians are subjected to the constraints of an organization, and are willing to make the latter pay for the disillusions of a highly specialized, routine job—a far cry from the expectations developed over several years of training oriented toward individual self-fulfillment in a soloist career.[18]

Conversely, the ideology of creative freedom can offer inexhaustible resources for justifying or self-justifying the choice of a life of limited material means—as demonstrated, for instance, in Dominique Schnapper's study of unemployment among artists.[19] It is as if artists inverted the values attached to, on the one hand, social integration by means of a regular and decently paid activity, and, on the other, personal autonomy in the typically painful experience of unemployment. Thus, they can celebrate the benefits of art, a peculiar type of labor that is ideally fulfilling, yet socially risky, and refuse the drawbacks of professions that are economically more reliable, yet more routine and utilitarian.

The nonmonetary argument can lead economists, via the principle of equalizing differences, to embrace the convenient solution of ad hoc justification. Nevertheless, it also constitutes the bedrock of ideological enchantment with artistic labor. Let us examine where this argument fails. Economic analysis considers that preferences, abilities, and access to information vary from one individual to another, causing each one to assess differently the relative advantages of the various professions. Yet what happens when we take into account not the average profile of expected earnings over the course of a professional career, but the reality of income distribution observed in a given population of artists? Since their situation appears to be quite mediocre overall, this relative majority of artists must be construed as having preferences and abilities that make them seem motivated almost exclusively by nonpecuniary considerations. In other words, they must be viewed as agreeing to sacrifice everything to practice their art, and to experience the sovereign satisfactions that such practice is reputed to provide.

Such a representation of the artist's life illustrates a limit case in the job market—one in which supply curves are completely inelastic and relative salary rates are determined solely by the conditions of demand.[20] The better-off artists benefit from an economic rent: Their more or less prolonged wait for success, at the cost of what can sometimes be considerable material sacrifice, demonstrates *a posteriori* that they would have agreed to remain in the profession even with a much lower income. In order to rationalize their career choice, the poorest-paid artists, who endure their condition rather than change profession, are logically led to attribute their mediocre situation largely, if not exclusively, to an endemic crisis of cultural underconsumption. As they see it, their economic marginalization is explained by an excessively low overall demand or—another manifestation of the same societal dysfunction—by the fact that consumer preferences, shaped by market forces and by the foundational inequalities of class society, become fixated on a desperately limited number of artworks and artists. This diagnosis has all the virtues of a "defense mechanism against disenchantment," to use Bourdieu's expression.[21] It relies cavalierly on history in order to transform the failure of talented artists into an eternal and eternally consoling law.

Raised to the level of doctrine, this diagnosis has produced the principle whereby the meanings attached to success and failure become inverted—following the "loser takes all" formula. This is the solipsistic purity of creative intention, which is absolutely indifferent to success, yet provides the best guarantee of success. In other words, success is all the easier to achieve when it is not pursued; or, according to a more imperative prescription, success is achieved only on the condition that it is not pursued. One need only add to this imperative a temporal condition to invent a schema of compensatory justice: The most rapid successes are the most ephemeral, and inversely, the longer it is in coming, the more enduring and ample the consecration will be. We can hear echoes of the evangelical principle of the reward of virtue, which is based on the subversion of all simplistic calculating schemes: The first shall be last; the least cynical shall be the most celebrated. This principle merely projects that which pertains to the ruses of reason—the logic of which Jon Elster deciphered in his work[22]—into the realm of ethics or, in Max Weber's words,[23] into an economy of charisma.

The redistribution of the meanings attached to success and failure has been, since the Romantic period, one of the means by which artists, and especially writers, have tried to render creative risk heroic without linking it to interindividual competition, and this to preserve an aristocratic ethics of individualism. In his unfinished book on Flaubert, Jean-Paul Sartre outlined the history of these conceptions of artistic failure—a history that remains to be written:

> For it is Romanticism—and not its bourgeois successors—that has for the first time put failure at the heart of literature as its innermost substance. Their sort of failure, however, does not contain the desperate darkness of the Postromantic shipwreck. They deck themselves out in sacrificial robes. . . . And so opting for the nobility within themselves and outside them, in society, they assume an ethic and a fate. Devotion to a lost cause, accepting its doom for oneself—this is precisely what is called generosity, an extravagant virtue denied on principle to the bourgeoisie.[24]

The rationalization of failure as a protest against bourgeois utilitarianism has had a long career in Postromanticism and in the doctrine of art for art's sake. It relies on a definition of the artwork as the opposite of the commodity, and assumes the intrinsic motivation of the creator "writing *for nothing* and *no one*, . . . for art, for God, for the self, for nothing, against everyone."[25] Yet it does so at the cost of what becomes a radical contradiction, for the act of writing leads to publication, reading, and evaluation, and thereby inscribes itself in the literary enterprise. Sartre, with dazzling analytic virtuosity, could thus draw up an inventory of the contradictions in which this negative theology of art becomes enmeshed when it presents the artwork's failure and impossibility as the supreme manifestation of the truth of art, and as the condition for the realization of "Absolute Art."[26]

The intrinsic motivation of each artist, which renders the absence of instrumental calculation rational in the context of creative activity, must compromise with that of all the others. Yet competition through the unlimited differentiation of artistic projects and artworks forbids the artist from seeing the other simply as a competitor against whom he must measure himself by comparing easily calibrated qualities that would help determine who possesses them in greater quantity. In order to render such competition acceptable, the artist must invent a peculiar conception of his relationship to the audience for which he designates his work, and of the action of market intermediaries: He must relativize or negate the sanctions produced by the orientation of audience preferences, and crudely divide the art markets between sectors of production for a vast audience, on the one hand, and sectors geared toward limited consumption, on the other.[27] Such partitioning of the art markets largely contributes to inscribing the mechanism of competition between artists of the same sector into the more striking vision of a mechanism of hyper-competition that radicalizes the opposition between the ways of doing art: one oriented toward profit and the other toward free and authentic invention. Thus, the conception of success and failure simultaneously incorporates elements of aesthetic, ethical, political, and, as in the case of Romanticism, religious doctrines—such as the ones explored by Sartre[28] and Bénichou[29]—along with elements of a professional rhetoric intended to equip artists with collective rationalizations in the face of competitive tests. The deformation of the statistical reality of success and failure, as well as the recourse to salient counter-examples, are among the cognitive mechanisms by which artists invent the illusions necessary to provide long-term motivation for their professional commitment. These mechanisms have been well analyzed by Daniel Kahneman.[30]

To be sure, the history of the various forms of art presents a series of illustrious and compelling examples of artists whose genius was recognized only late in life, or even posthumously, and whose material life seems to have been as difficult as their creative elation was great. Nevertheless, historical studies all show that reality is infinitely more complex than the legend built around exceptional cases would have us believe.

Competition and its sanctions ensure the scarcity of the most prized qualities. Yet when this essential factor in the professionalization of artists is reinterpreted following the Romantic logic just outlined, it shifts the argument concerning the compensatory benefit of artistic labor's nonmonetary rewards in a direction rigorously opposed to that of economic analysis. The negation or deformation of that factor has resulted in idealist or materialist philosophical interpretations of art that have provided the theoretical grounding for the exclusive valorization of nonmonetary arguments for choosing the artist's life.

Whereas economists deploy the "psychic income" argument to keep the adventurous choice of an artistic career within the bounds of rationality,[31] an entire tradition analyzes the specificity of artistic labor by emphasizing instead the extra-economic reality of genuinely creative activity. This tradition, which essentially coincides with the history of the expressivist model of *praxis*,[32] is at the root of Marx's distinction between nonalienated and alienated labor. Indeed, artistic creation occupies an exceptional position in the early writings of Marx, and notably in the *Economic and Philosophic Manuscripts of 1844*,[33] in which he developed a general rather than specific aesthetics of praxis—one whose normative content made artistic activity the standard against which wage labor could be judged and critiqued. Artistic labor is conceived here as the model of nonalienated labor, as that of the concrete activity through which the subject realizes himself in the plenitude of his freedom by externalizing and objectifying the powers that constitute the essence of his humanity. The subject's alienation is caused not by the objectification of his powers in free activity, for such objectification is the very condition of self-fulfillment; it is caused, rather, by the intromission of this objectification into capitalist social relations that reduce art to a commodity and artistic labor to wage labor.[34]

Two paths open onto the utopian invention of nonalienated labor. On the one hand, artistic labor can be situated in the private sphere of individual creativity, beyond social relations of exchange and the mutilating equivalence established between artistic products and the values constituted in the public marketplace. This path leads quite rapidly to the celebration of artistic amateurism, whereby vocation no longer coincides with professional exigencies, and to the ancient opposition between labor and leisure, the latter being the necessary condition for a form of creative activity that is subject solely to the imperative of self-expression, under the pressure of a freely oriented, internal exigency. On the other hand, artistic activity can be granted a form of social and economic existence through invoking the artisanal mode of production. For the young Marx, artisanal labor was exemplary because it preserved the undividable or weakly divided character of activity, and because the social relations of production that organized this form of labor seemed more egalitarian and more respectful of the personality of each of the individuals who cooperate in producing the artwork.[35]

The expressivist conception of artistic labor is, in fact, aporetic: How can artists be guaranteed better and more egalitarian social conditions *while also* operating in a regime of artistic invention wherein each creator is called upon to differentiate himself and individualize his artistic production? When it does not lead to unilaterally contesting the market system as the modern form of organization of artistic activities, the ideal contained in the expressivist model sparks a concrete demand, which is then taken up by artists and their professional organizations: the guarantee of full employment in the arts. This ideal is utopian in that it calls for reconciling via the first exigency—for egalitarian social conditions—two mutually exclusive modes of professionalization.

Full employment in the arts would, in fact, require (1) selective regulation upon entry into the profession; and (2) a supply so homogeneous or a demand so insensitive to differences in quality that the substitutability of artists and artistic goods in the various segments of production would preclude the emergence of competition-induced imbalances. Moreover, the ideal of full employment presupposes mechanisms of constant adjustment between supply and demand; that is, a perfectly mobile labor force and a production system capable of adapting itself flawlessly to changes in demand. Other mechanisms include the regulation of professional demographics; the homogeneity of the skills acquired from a long and highly specialized training process; and the self-limitation of competition within the professional group. These latter are some of the features that define the artisanal mode of production and the corporative organization of professions.[36]

But what does the second exigency—for the free expression of individual creativity—actually rest upon? Unless we conceive of the artist as radically desocialized, living and working outside of a community of peers, and fully ignorant of the past and present states of the artistic discipline, we have to construe artistic individualism as the product of a historical movement of gradual autonomization and internal differentiation of the sphere of artistic activities (following the Weberian analysis), and as the driving force behind competition among artists. The essentially Romantic origin of the expressivist model leaves no doubt as to its individualistic content: The deployment of idiosyncrasy is the very essence of unhindered production, and the artist's creative labor is the purest and loftiest embodiment of that idiosyncrasy. Approaches that simultaneously promote the full social integration of the artist and the complete recognition of his freedom of invention display the characteristics of the utopia Raymonde Moulin observed among innovative painters: "The problem is that artists tend to focus exclusively on the best in every system and fail to consider the social context. Esoteric modern artists profess to want to work for 'the people' like the artisans of the Middle Ages; or they wish they could enjoy the glory reserved for artists in the age of aristocracy, forgetting the constraints imposed by necessary commissions; or they dream of the freedom of the outcast artist, forgetting the insecurity that went with it."[37]

Isolating the nonmonetary and nontransactional dimensions of artistic labor amounts to ignoring two interdependent principles in the evolution of artistic life. Market-driven professionalization is the form of organization of artistic activities that has ensured the triumph of creative individualism. However, it is also that which fully activates the mechanism of risk involved in choosing and practicing professions wherein those who feel that they have a calling are infinitely more numerous than those who are actually chosen. The interdependence of individualism and risk has been acknowledged in economic analysis as much as in the Weberian sociology of professions. The risks associated with professional engagement in the arts constitute indeed one of the remarkable characteristics of artistic professions that have accorded them special treatment in economic theory. In turn, Weber used probabilistic analysis extensively in his sociology of the economic world to describe the economic orientation of action, with its expected utility and earnings calculations.[38] As I will now show, the present approach to analyzing career choice is of interest for two reasons: (1) It preserves the dimension of uncertainty inherent in artistic labor; and (2) it combines the sociology of action and social interactions with economic analysis in order to describe the organization of the art markets and the systems of artistic professionalization as modes of managing uncertainty.

The Seduction of Uncertainty and Incentives for Risk-Taking

There is a kind of uncertainty that lies at the heart of the satisfactions obtained from the practice of an artistic activity, so long as this activity offers all the psychic benefits of nonroutine work. In a highly astute analysis, Arthur Stinchcombe[39] ranked the structures of activity according to the degree of variability of the factors that directly determine their constituent properties. For instance, the stability or instability of an industrial market determines the properties of the system of labor organization required to continuously adapt production to changing environmental conditions (I will later show how this analysis can be applied fruitfully to artistic production). The outcome of an activity is uncertain when "(a) causal variables affecting the outcome of action have high variance; (b) we cannot ... predict the value of the causal variable which will have influence; and (c) we cannot cut the causal connection between this variable and the outcome."[40] By characterizing determining factors in terms of their variance, we can map activities along an axis running from the most standardized and repetitive to the least routine, based on whether the determinants of action have low or high variance. Artistic creation and scientific research, but also less prestigious activities such as advertising, gambling, fighting, sports, and the stock market, figure among the least routine of human enterprises, and their outcome is imperfectly predictable. As Stinchcombe observes, this explains the very frequent recourse to superstition, divining practices, or magic—all presumed to force the hand of chance and to reduce uncertainty. The values of inspiration, giftedness, genius, intuition, and creativity, which are more acceptable in the culturally sophisticated spheres of artistic and intellectual creation, actually do no more than transpose onto the individual and his intrinsic qualities this faith in magical and supernatural powers for the control of uncertainty.

As I indicated above, it is through the celebration of those values and the invention of a religion of art that artistic individualism triumphed in the Romantic period. Such individualism can be viewed both as the principle and outcome of competition among artists in their systematic quest for aesthetic originality, and as the product of the expressivist ideology whereby the artist is the individual par excellence—the person who realizes himself in the essence of his humanity. Yet the analysis differs depending on whether it construes the quasi-divine attributes with which Romantic ideology has bedecked the artist as various means for averting uncertainty, or whether it transforms, as Marx does, individual accomplishment through creative activity into an ideal that a de-alienated society will render accessible to all. The latter understanding ignores the possibility of failure, and, with it, everything that in the course of artistic activity and, more generally, of an artist's career, makes creative labor an arduous, disquieting undertaking, shot through with doubts about the value of the product, and uncertain about its own future even when success has been attained.[41]

Risk thus defined will hardly be idealized here. Artistic labor would be impossible if there were no conventions or routines for the creation and social existence of artworks, not only in traditional or conservative modes of artistic creation, in the different forms of collaborative activities or in less prestigious jobs, but also in the most individual and freest forms of creative invention. For without conventions, rules of interaction, and more or less stable procedures for dividing tasks and mutually adjusting expectations and exchanged meanings, there could be no cooperation among all those who take part in the production, diffusion, consumption, evaluation, and preservation of artworks.[42] The fact remains, however, that the seductive power and the very prestige of artistic professions are measured by their degree of unpredictability of outcome and success. As Albert Hirschman suggests, the less an activity is routine and utilitarian, the more uncertainty surrounding its accomplishment places the individual in an ambivalent situation. Here, the tensions and difficulties inherent in a venture for which chances of success are partially or wholly unpredictable are counterbalanced by the elating moments that punctuate and sustain the activity: moments of anticipated pleasure in future accomplishment, and fleeting convictions of attaining success.

> Certain activities, typically of a routine character, have perfectly predictable outcomes. With regard to such tasks, there is no doubt in the individual's mind that effort will yield the anticipated outcome—an hour of labor will yield the well-known, fully visualized result as well as entitle the worker, if he has been contracted for the job, to a wage that can be used for the purchase of desired (and usually also well-known) goods. Under these conditions, the separation of the process into means and ends, or into costs and benefits, occurs almost spontaneously and work appears to assume a wholly instrumental character.

> But there are many kinds of activities, from that of a research and development scientist to that of a composer or an advocate of some public policy, whose intended outcome cannot be relied upon to materialize with certainty. . . . These activities have sometimes been referred to, in contrast to the instrumental ones, as "affective" or "expressive." But labeling them does not contribute a great deal to understanding them, for the question is really why such activities should be taken up at all, as long as their successful outcome is so wholly uncertain. It is important to note that by no means are these activities always pleasant in themselves; in fact, some of them are sure to be quite strenuous or highly dangerous. . . . [F]rom the point of view of instrumental reason, noninstrumental action is bound to be something of a mystery. But I have proposed an at least semirational explanation: these noninstrumental activities whose outcome is so uncertain are strangely characterized by a certain fusion of (and confusion between) striving and attaining.

> According to conventional economic thinking, utility accrues to an individual primarily upon reaching the goal of consumption, that is, in the process of actually consuming a good or enjoying its use. But given our lively imagination, things are really rather more complicated. When we become sure that some

desired good is actually going to be ours or that some desired event is definitely going to happen . . . we experience the well-known pleasure of *savoring* that future event in advance (the term *savoring* was suggested to me by George Loewenstein). Moreover, this premature hauling in of utility is not limited to situations where the future event is near and certain, or is believed to be so. When the goal is distant and its attainment quite problematic, something very much like the savoring experience can occur, provided a determined personal quest is undertaken. He who strives after truth (or beauty) frequently experiences the conviction, fleeting though it may be, that he has found (or achieved) it. . . .

This savoring, this fusion of striving and attaining, is a fact of experience that goes far in accounting for the existence and importance of noninstrumental activities. As though in compensation for the uncertainty about the outcome, and for the strenuousness or dangerousness of the activity, the striving effort is colored by the goal and in this fashion makes for an experience that is very different from merely agreeable, pleasurable, or even stimulating: in spite of its frequently painful character it has a well-known, intoxicating quality.[43]

It is in this kind of experience, Hirschman remarks, that the subject can attain the powerful feeling of self-fulfillment and personal autonomy. Let us note in passing, however, that although Hirschman's analysis concords here with the expressivist theory of artistic creation, it starts from opposite premises, and proceeds by linking satisfaction to uncertainty.[44]

Uncertainty, as I have considered it thus far, merely characterizes the gap between efforts invested and the goal to be reached in the realization of a project. Given all the pleasures and anxieties uncertainty provokes, this definition of behavior in an uncertain horizon possesses a quasi-anthropological quality. One might deduce from this conception a social and community ideal: Far from a disutility, labor may well be the individual's only means of realizing himself in the fullness of his talents and resources, so long as he engages in the kind of nonroutine tasks that promise to offer the rewards of behaving under uncertainty.

However, if we consider the sum of these individual behaviors, a second dimension of uncertainty emerges: that of the strategic and the social. This is because the value of creative labor and the recognition of talent are indissociable from comparative evaluation, and hence from competitive tests between artworks and artists. Yet, this is precisely that which is negated by Marxist critique when it puts capitalist society on trial for reducing creative labor to wage labor and the artwork to an exchange value. In such a view, comparative and hierarchizing assessments of artworks and talents have no universal objectivity; they merely express the conditions under which the elites of a given society, in a specific historical period, proceed to define and valorize Beauty. Nevertheless, Marx himself was not so reductive since he emphasized that aesthetic appreciation could be more robust than this, and that the artworks considered the most beautiful by generations of our different ancestors could traverse time with remarkable longevity.

Be that as it may, no one can enter a game regulated in this manner with the certainty of triumphing, because talent is not directly measured with absolute values, but through gradual comparisons, and because initial training does not suffice to guarantee high chances of success. The social objectification of value, therefore, must be construed as a complex mechanism of selection, which reveals only *a posteriori* the risks entailed in artistic competition.

The two dimensions of uncertainty—intrinsic and strategic—are indissociable from one another. In order for the talent and the chances for success of aspiring artists to be measurable *a priori*, creative and professional artistic practice should be evaluated against a fixed, stable, and unanimously accepted model. Clearly, this condition can be met only in situations wherein artistic labor resembles an ordinary, routine, and predictable activity, or in periods when a classical aesthetics, based on the imitation of models and the respect of a constraining system of norms, prevails over an aesthetics of rupture and perpetual renewal. In the opposite case, uncertainty is lifted only *ex post*—and often only temporarily in moments of success, due to how ephemeral these moments can be. This renders competition sufficiently indeterminate for the number of aspiring artists to far exceed what it would be if candidates were capable of making perfectly rational estimates of their probabilities of success.

Economic analysis can provide an exact measure of the risks involved in pursuing a career in professions characterized by fierce internal competition, few monopolies of practice, low status security, and high "psychic income." Economists have acknowledged that, with regard to the artistic professions, the study of choices made under uncertainty poses a challenge to the classic model of rationality, according to which actors are perfectly informed of the states of the world in which they act. In the analyses of artists' income presented above, the attempt to reintegrate artistic professions into the conventional theoretical framework of rational, utility-maximizing behavior is not only unconvincing when it presents monetary rewards as the main argument of the artist's utility function; it also fails to provide a thorough interpretation of an essential datum—income variance—which reveals the risks involved in pursuing an artistic career. The average age-profile of earnings characteristic of artistic professions does, indeed, preclude citing low, fluctuating earnings in early career stages to invalidate the rational behavior hypothesis; yet the information obtained through studying averages remains incomplete, because a same average can be produced by two highly different distribution profiles.

Income variance in artistic professions is higher both globally and within each age group than it is in professions that require a comparable level of training.[45] This observation leads to a conundrum in classical economic theory. So long as the latter posits risk aversion as a norm of individual behavior, how can it explain commitment to professional careers that are so uncertain, in which the modal condition of artists is so mediocre, and in which the chances of obtaining high earnings (which might compensate for the risks taken) are especially low? The first answer to this question was provided by the founder of economic theory himself, Adam Smith (in book I, chapter 10 of *The Wealth of Nations*),[46] and then taken up and developed further by Alfred Marshall[47] and, more recently, by Milton Friedman.[48] It was developed through the study of earnings differences that use job characteristics as explanatory variables. For Marshall as for Smith before him, in order for individuals to enter professions wherein their future is so uncertain (the majority preferring secure jobs with a narrower earnings range), the principal earnings derived from what Smith compared to a lottery must be very high: It is the hope of obtaining such remuneration that, in some sense, dispels inhibition surrounding risk. In fact, as Marshall emphasized (for the early twentieth century), income dispersion was never so strong in the professions of writer, opera singer, actor, lawyer, or jockey, wherein the "exceptional ability" of the most talented was remunerated at levels never before observed.

Imperfect substitutability between artists, as revealed by consumer preferences, effectively gives rise to differences in demand that favor the most talented among them. Yet such an explanation of income inequality is not sufficient to account for the most unique economic characteristic of the "superstar" phenomenon, as analyzed by Sherwin Rosen:[49] the extreme concentration of professionals' attention and audience preferences on artists reputed to have the most talent or the greatest talent potential. Extreme inequalities are effectively explained by the fact that contemporary communications and transport technologies enable sellers of goods and services to supply a considerably wider market without seeing production costs increase in proportion to market size, and without experiencing an intolerable decrease in the quality of the goods or services supplied (for instance, listening to a CD rather than directly seeing an artist in concert). Reproducible goods (books, CDs, films, and such) and technologies for the diffusion and reproduction of images and sound are the purest illustration of this: Joint consumption of the same good by a very high number of buyers generates important economies of scale, causing the real price of entertainment services to fall, even as sellers can obtain extremely high profits owing to the widening of their markets. This analysis can be extended to other types of artistic goods and services whose markets are being internationalized due to the increased speed of information transmission and the quasi-ubiquity of the main actors involved. It should come as no surprise, then, that the most speculative segment of the contemporary painting market presents so many similarities with the cultural industries, notably due to the ongoing internationalization of this market and the speed at which its new products are being exploited.[50]

As Rosen demonstrates, the twofold effect of increased demand—which occurs either through a rise in the number of buyers or through the intensification of consumption—is to attract new artists into the artistic sector and to simultaneously widen income gaps in favor of the most talented. This is precisely what Adam Smith's lottery model suggested, albeit in a different manner: In order for the prizes that motivate aspiring artists to take risks to be truly sizeable, a sufficient number of candidates must enter the game so that those who actually succeed may collect the totality of that which their competitors have lost by failing in their professional wager—that is, by accepting mediocre remuneration or remuneration far below that which originally incited them to enter the game. We now see the process by which the vicious circle of artists' risk-taking is created: It is the very scarcity of a talent that brings, over the relatively long term, significant profits for the individual who possesses that talent; yet no individual can correctly estimate *ex ante* the value of his own skills or his chances of having them recognized and appreciated as manifestations of an exceptional talent.

The ambiguity of the lottery comparison now comes into focus. The parallel is plausible if it describes the structure of the distribution of gains and losses for a situation in which players compete for a minuscule number of very high positions in the hierarchy of professional success. It is deceptive, however, if it suggests that such success is unrelated to the distinctive characteristics of actors.[51] Marshall clearly separated the correlation between success and talent from the multiplication effect that the aura of success might have on the number of artistic vocations. Thus, he wrote: "The humdrum business man, who has inherited a good business and has just sufficient force to keep it together, may reap an income of many thousands a year, which contains very little rent of rare natural qualities. And, on the other hand, the greater part of incomes earned by exceptionally successful barristers, and writers, and painters, and singers, and jockeys may be classed as the rent of rare natural abilities—so long at least as we regard them as individuals, and are not considering the dependence of the normal supply of labour in their several occupations on the prospects of brilliant success which they hold out to aspiring youth."[52] This antirelativist description of talent tends toward the naturalization of genius. For Marshall, exceptional capacities are neither the result of human effort, nor the product of educational investments aimed at obtaining future benefits; they are, rather, a reflection of the vastly unequal distribution of the highest aptitudes in the general population. Yet the conditions under which talent is evaluated, recognized, and socially admired are not independent from the form and intensity of the competition among candidates for success. It may indeed be that antirelativist sentiments are strengthened by the existence of a lengthier process for achieving success and consecration, which grants greater stability to the consensus upon which these latter are founded. Conversely, success seems more arbitrary, and even often fabricated, when it is obtained rapidly and lasts only a short while—jostled by a flow of successive innovations that emerge at the pace of trends, and by the volatility of an even more unpredictable demand. In all cases, however, it is through interindividual competition and selective comparison that the value of an artist or artwork is initially established. Only after this can an acquired reputation act—with a strength and duration that vary sharply according to the type of market and production under consideration—as a guarantee that reduces uncertainty surrounding the quality of an artist's subsequent artworks or performances,[53] thus becoming akin to an economic rent.

The scarcity of talent imputed to those who succeed is the keystone of Marshall's analysis of risk-taking, and this, on two counts. First, scarcity determines the important variability in income, which in turn can attract aspiring artists. Second, scarcity is that which confers high social prestige on the entire artistic profession.

This point is important for discerning the individuals who show a preference for risk. In the portrait Smith and Marshall draw of audacious individuals, they highlight such characteristics as a desire for the social prestige associated with risky professions (which refers back to the nonmonetary arguments for career choice), and the adventurous spirit of young people, confident in their capacities and easily inclined to overestimate their probabilities of success. Yet numerous studies on the psychology of judgment and behavior under uncertainty[54] have shown that, regardless of the age of the subject, there are many ways in which individual choices and decisions can diverge from a correct assessment of the objective probabilities that a fact will occur or that an action will produce a given outcome. This is so because choices and decisions are based on different heuristic principles that skew the subject's perception of reality. Although young age does play a part in risk-taking, this factor must be taken into consideration for reasons other than its influence on the psychology of the subject. In reality, youth is important because it characterizes the state of inexperience of an individual whose only method of evaluating the extent to which a profession matches his aptitudes is actually to enter it.

Economic analyses of career choice based on the "job matching" model rely on two hypotheses.[55] First, the practice of a profession provides a capital of experience that varies according to the characteristics of the job and jobholder. Second, in order to decide whether he will pursue a lasting career in a given profession, the individual combines information he previously acquired on each of the characteristics of that profession with the sum of partial information he is able to accumulate in the course of his professional practice. Like the decision-maker in the Bayesian theory of choice under uncertainty, this individual can correct his initial anticipation and progressively reestimate his expected (monetary and nonmonetary) gains precisely because the degree to which his aptitudes match the conditions for succeeding in a potential profession is revealed to him only gradually—that is, on the job. Some of the features of labor-force mobility can be explained by viewing the very practice of different professions as a means for the individual to accumulate, through trial and error, information concerning the profession in which his chances for success are highest. In fact, since only practice can reveal to the individual, *a posteriori,* the value of his aptitudes, the professions that provide this type of information in the greatest quantity are also those in which success is highly uncertain.

As Robert Miller argues,[56] the desire for risk prevalent among youth can be interpreted as a demand for information: Inexperience pushes young people toward professions in which success is less likely to depend on factors that are easily identifiable *a priori.* As any pursuit or acquisition of information necessarily entails a cost, such professions are, on average, poorly remunerated (in accordance with the principle of equalizing differences), even though they offer important information benefits. High earnings variance in the artistic professions is thus explained by (1) the presence of a high proportion of inexperienced, novice artistic professionals who accept mediocre earnings in return for the information they acquire (and among whom an important number will quickly renounce the idea of making a career in the arts or, at the very least, of earning a living in this way); and (2) the success of a small minority of artists who profit from the accumulated experience.

Professionalization and Risk Reduction

By successively examining the expected earnings, nonmonetary benefits, and wide income dispersion in the artistic professions, I have reasoned exclusively on the basis of data that aggregate all income sources for individuals identified as artists in surveys and censuses. Yet the risks associated with the artistic professions—for example, mediocre income and underemployment—have as their correlate the obligation to lead a double professional life or to engage in multiple jobholding. Studies on the different populations of artists have shown that, as a general rule, less than 10 percent of artists in each category were able to live exclusively from their art at the time of research.[57] This suggests that, for the vast majority of artists who do not hold a stable job in an artistic organization wherein the practice of their art is remunerated as such, resorting to other resources and to one or several other jobs—stable, intermittent, or temporary—is necessary. This economic obligation coexists, more or less easily, with the vocation-related artistic activity.

Using an analytic indicator such as the income composition of artists raises several intertwined questions concerning the criteria to be used when determining who counts as an artist. At what threshold must we set the economic criterion? Is it the capacity to earn more than 50 percent of one's income from an artistic profession, or can the ceiling be lowered—as in the French legislation concerning the social protection of artists? Considering that the practice of an artistic profession is often irregular, what periods should be the focus of our observations? Should we refer to the week preceding the survey when determining the profession of a respondent, as is done in the U.S. census? And how should we delineate the artistic activity used to evaluate a respondent's share of earnings coming from art? Further broadening our field of interrogation, we can inquire into the exact role played by the income criterion, knowing that its uncertain meaning often leads to considering a wider range of criteria for defining the "artist" category.[58] These questions have obvious practical consequences: The proportion of artists earning a living from secondary activities increases when the criteria are loosened, thereby enlarging the reference population to include an increasingly composite set of practitioners—that is, all sorts of debutants, artists who have been relegated following a period of success, creators who practice their art intermittently, strictly occasional authors, and others.

In any case, the income sources to which artists resort are more diverse than is suggested by the key distinction between products of creative activity and monetary supplements obtained from side activities. Thus, spouses' contributions to household resources are an important factor in artistic survival, though their role remains relatively invisible. When total household resources are taken into account, it appears that artists' domestic partners often play, over the short or long term, the role of primary patron, owing to their important monetary contributions[59] and their performing numerous services linked to the artist's professional career (maintaining the network of relations, typing, secretarial work, and the like).[60] In the performing arts, unemployment benefits may, as is the case in France, be virtually included among the resources obtained from artistic labor, due to their strategic use by both employers and employees to soften the impact of extremely sharp fluctuations in economic activity.[61] More generally, the welfare state's management of the risks associated with artistic professions can provide artists with an entire panoply of direct and indirect support, which, in some sectors, exceed market-determined levels of remuneration for creative activities. Thus, the level of state support is particularly high in the field of contemporary art music, wherein a full-fledged, administered market for goods and labor has been established. Nevertheless, the defining feature of state intervention in cultural policy is the extension of the benefits and techniques of risk management to all artistic sectors and professions—heading toward the creation of a unique social status for artists.[62]

In sum, artists' different sources of income, as identified in monographic studies, can be classified into six categories: remuneration for primary artistic activities; remuneration for secondary artistic or para-artistic activities; income derived from nonartistic jobs; unemployment benefits; domestic partner's income and other types of resources such as material support from family and friends or personal wealth; resources obtained from public or private patronage.

How do artists combine these resources? Drawing on portfolio choice theory and its applications to the labor market,[63] I consider the range of earnings and employment situations that artists are made to combine to be equivalent to a stock portfolio. The (relatively constrained) composition of this portfolio enables artists to lower their career risks by diversifying the investments they can afford to make. According to the economics of financial markets, the fluctuations in asset returns can be disaggregated into two components. These fluctuations are due, in part, to the influence of the market as a whole, and, in part, to the specific characteristics of a given asset; the former corresponds to the systematic, nondiversifiable risks (or "market risks"), and the latter to the specific risks that express the particular value volatility of a stock. The analysis shows that as the portfolio is increasingly diversified, the ratio of specific risk to total risk decreases. In other words, the variance in return is much lower for the entire portfolio than it is for each investment considered separately. This is the well-known advantage of diversification: The overall risk of investment decisions is reduced when a portfolio is adequately composed of investments that involve different degrees of risk.[64]

This comparison is of interest for two reasons. First, it allows us to replace the rigid ideological opposition between nonalienated and alienated labor—the ideal of the full pursuit of one's artistic vocation versus the curse of a professional life divided among multiple jobholdings—with a differentiated analysis of the resource and employment combinations that depend on the specific organization of the labor markets in the various art worlds. Second, it helps us restore the dynamics of the artistic career—with its irregular and uncertain course—by conferring on the actor the ability to take initiatives (that is, to manage his career risks based on the various human capital assets and resources he can secure), which is denied to him by the static model of conflict between the creative project and the constraints of social life.

Central to the sociography of art worlds is the study of artistic or para-artistic side activities and nonartistic subsistence jobs. Eliot Freidson highlighted that, although they resemble licensed professions and academic research careers in terms of the motivation and commitment of their members, artistic professions remain singular in their accumulation of economic disadvantages.[65] In contrast to licensed professions, artistic professions have no formal system for the certification of skills and for the statutory protection of titles that would ensure their members both a monopoly on practice and control over professional demographics and internal competition. Moreover, unlike research and teaching careers in the university, they offer no reliable employment that would provide individuals with economic security and guaranteed social status. The lack of such means for reducing dependency on a complex and unstable demand explains why the majority of artists resort to highly varied employments in order to make ends meet.

Nevertheless, portraits of artistic life are doubly deceptive when, in order to accentuate artists' social dereliction, they depict the most peculiar associations between an artistic practice and different subsistence jobs: (1) They efface all the nuanced transitions and evolutions that can, over the course of a career, reduce the gap between different professional activities (which are then collapsed in the biography of artists); and (2) they generalize to all artistic professions specific employment situations whose frequency varies according to the constituent properties of the artistic field under consideration.

By attending art schools,[66] and above all by accumulating professional experience in the art worlds in which they began their careers, artists acquire information on the web of less prestigious artistic and para-artistic activities that surround the core of the most coveted positions and employment situations. Based on this information (the cost of which we now know), artists alter their method for managing risk—that is, their asset portfolio: The choice to remain in the profession and the ambition to succeed lead them to seek the optimal scheme for accumulating resources under existing constraints. This explains why studies show that multiple jobholding can also be correlated positively with the level of income obtained from the primary artistic activity. While holding several jobs is a constraint at the beginning of a career, it is also one of the levers for professional success—as demonstrated by the fact that the frequency of multiple jobholding does not drop when we move up the income scale for artists, and that it remains high for the age at which the income curve reaches its peak (that is, between the ages of forty and fifty-five). The major distinction between the different sequences of professional life lies, of course, in the composition of the portfolio. Career progression usually entails a shift from a random dispersion of activities to a concentration around key hubs, wherein the artistic vocation is associated with similar or related supplementary activities.

Critical analyses of the artist's alienation by the market[67] negate this dynamic when they contrast the ideal of the free practice of an art (inaccessible to most), recognized and remunerated as such by society at large, with its complete opposite, the splitting of the self into a series of unrelated activities. These analyses are normative in that they prescribe the following maximin strategy (that is, the choice of the best among an array of bad solutions): In order to safeguard the portion of artistic creation that is to remain free and pure from all external constraints, artists must give preference to all sorts of subsistence jobs over the fatal choice of submitting to market demand. Beyond the practice of commercial art, which can only contaminate and degrade the activity of free creation, what is called into question here is the artist's very ambition to live from his art. As Paul Claudel wrote: "There is no worse career than that of a writer seeking to live by his pen. There you are, forced to produce with an eye fixed on the boss or the public; forced to give them not what *you* like but what *they* like—and God knows what fine taste they've got."[68]

It may be worth recalling that hierarchical distinctions between pure, applied, and commercial art are socially constructed and historically shifting. The profile of these distinctions and the necessity with which they impose themselves in the competition among artists and artistic movements vary depending on the art world considered. The radical opposition between a free, fulfilling activity and a mercenary one is, in turn, the ideological expression of such distinctions. Nevertheless, one might ask: On what grounds can pure art be associated with disinterestedness? How is one to classify the invisible pursuit of profit constituted by the long-term artistic wager? How can self-interested motivation be reduced to the mere expectation of monetary gains? Should an artist's conscious exploitation of an innovation that he first developed through trial and error be interpreted as self-loyalty in the quest of a personal style, or rather as the manifestation of self-interested expectations of gain and fame? Conversely, is it so difficult to imagine that a commercial artist might realize himself within the framework of the constraints being imposed on him? Does his success reflect nothing but pure cynicism—which is considered to offer poor counsel, even by the most rudimentary psychology of professional motivation? In reality, interactionist sociology teaches us to view the choices that guide creative labor as projections of the artist onto others (colleagues, critics, publishers, spectators, and such), as anticipations of others' reactions, and as reactions to what is learned from such anticipations.[69] From this derives the idea that an artist can adopt different behaviors in the practice of a single activity—depending on the nature of the project, and on the constraints and resources of the situation—and that he has the capacity to split himself without this being a shattering experience.[70]

The management of career risks varies greatly depending on the organization of labor and the strength of the barriers to entry in the various art worlds. Varying the weight of the factors that determine the rate of professionalization in a given artistic profession leads to changing the combination of concurrently held jobs. The frequency of leading a double professional life that combines a vocation-related activity with a primary nonartistic activity is greater in professions in which there is little or no need for specific training, capital expenses for the practice of one's art, or a complex division of labor for the production and diffusion of artworks. This is particularly true in the case of writers and, to a lesser degree, visual artists. By contrast, in the fields of acting and singing, the combination of disparate activities, while common at the beginning of a career, actually works contrary to building a lasting one. There is, in fact, significant variation in the economic nature and organization of activities (that is, the production of goods or the provision of services), as well as in the possible career profiles. In the case of writers and visual artists, a slow or irregular pace of production does not preclude market success or peer esteem, whereas for performing artists, the system of activities is such that the artist's continuous presence in the job market is necessary to guarantee him both employment opportunities and a reputation.

The conventional depiction of the artist as virtually obligated to lead a double professional life likely owes much of its power to the justifications it provides for the phenomena of failure and abandonment. The recourse to subsistence jobs is, in fact, necessary for nearly all artists, but only at the beginning of their careers. As we shall later see, such recourse is more easily blamed for failure in artistic sectors in which artists achieve success at an increasingly young age, which are also those that contain the greatest number of aspiring artists. Actually, in sectors wherein success is precocious—but also, on average, short-lived—and in which a high number of young or very young artists, after achieving a momentary success, have only intermittent or marginal careers (for example, in the literature, painting, or song market), the recourse to resource combination decreases as artists become increasingly confronted with the question of pursuing or abandoning their artistic activity. Studies such as those of Karla Fohrbeck and Andreas Wiesand[71] show that the range of resource combinations is greatest at the beginning of a career, when the artist must rely, simultaneously or successively, on his family, his social circle, social benefits, and subsistence jobs to compensate for low initial earnings and to accumulate the experiences needed to evaluate his chances of success.

Nevertheless, since the emergence of bohemian culture in the nineteenth century, one of the peculiar characteristics of the artist's life has been the prolongation of this initial period of uncertainty and trial. There now exist schemes for combining resources and stringing together a series of living situations that amalgamate, over prolonged sequences, most forms of patronage (from family members, domestic partners, friends, or the state). These enable artists to nurture a lasting vocation, construct a subjective career (to use Erving Goffman's notion)[72] based on lifestyles that invert the values of social integration and marginalization, and view the wait for success as the price they must pay for preserving the purity of a creative project, rather than as a painful and interminable probationary period.

The most professionalized fields of activity (that is, those in which one finds the highest proportion of artists deriving most of their income from the practice of their specific skills) display two characteristics: (1) a requirement of strong technical skills; and (2) a strong interdependence of the professional milieu, linked to an extensive division of labor. The risks involved in choosing these professions can be evaluated in two steps: Monetary sacrifices accepted early in the artist's career only represent part of the price to pay; beyond this is the added potential cost of retraining for those who, upon encountering failure, are forced to leave the profession. Economic studies show, unsurprisingly, that the higher the artist's level of general education, the easier his retraining will be. Conversely, it is in professions that require specific skills, and thus call for precocious engagement in specialized artistic training (for example, classical music and ballet), that the penalties associated with retraining outside of the arts are the highest.[73] Nevertheless, the high rate of professionalization and the profile of multiple jobholding also indicate that the vast majority of artists in these latter professions derive most of their income from a homogeneous constellation of artistic or para-artistic activities. The specialized skills barrier acts as a filter for selective entry and as a factor of integration into the professional milieu: The extensive division of artistic labor in these sectors, together with the existence of a well-developed educational system providing artists with jobs, offer the resources needed to play different professional roles simultaneously.

The musical professions offer the best illustration of this mechanism of resource combination. In a study of serious music composers, Alan Peacock and Ronald Weir[74] calculated that, on average, a third of composers' income was derived from the creative activity per se, half from other professional musical activities (teaching, performing, conducting an orchestra, and the like), and only 13.4 percent from nonartistic employments or activities. However, playing multiple roles simultaneously does more than improve the economic position of composers. As Dennison Nash indicated[75] in his study of American composers' role versatility, by simultaneously or consecutively fulfilling the functions of performer, conductor, teacher, critic, music entrepreneur, or cultural administrator, composers help set the conditions for the circulation of their artworks and for the diffusion of their aesthetic ideas, as well as broaden their control over the chain of cooperation which is vital to their work and reputation. At the center of this configuration of concurrently held roles, teaching activities constitute, in statistical terms, the safest and most accessible professional refuge. They have become so important for the socioprofessional integration of composers that they now play a role similar to that which Freidson attributed to the teaching professions associated with scientific research. The analogy is, in fact, rigorous: The increasingly frequent association of the activity of composer with the host profession of teacher explains in part why composers in France identify themselves as researchers.[76]

The case of musical professions helps underscore the fact that the more the production, diffusion, consumption, and management of the arts are conceived as part of a cultural public service, the more cultural policy contributes to expanding the artistic labor market; and this, not only by providing direct support for individual creation and for the diffusion and commercialization of artistic goods, but also by widening the spectrum of publicly funded jobs and services linked organically to artistic creation (for example, cultural coordination, teaching, management of cultural innovation assistance programs, consulting activities, among others). Depending on the degree of public intervention in the various types of art markets (markets for unique objects, industries of reproducible goods, the performing arts), the state grants a greater or smaller proportion of artists the possibility of being less scattered among activities that are overly incompatible with their art, as well as the possibility of gaining greater control over the environment in which their artworks circulate and compete for success.[77] These are benefits that the market normally provides to artists in proportion to their level of success.

Uncertainty Management and Imbalances in the Artistic Labor Market

The analysis of risk-taking I have presented thus far calls for examining the relationship between the conditions of professionalization and the organization of the art markets. The demand for information expressed in risk-taking is less important when the practice of an artistic profession requires strong technical skills. In that case, individual qualities are evaluated in the course of a selective and hierarchically ordered learning process, which informs aspiring artists about their aptitudes before they enter the labor market. In fully accessible artistic professions that require no prior training—or, at the very least, no homogeneous, selective, and controlled training—the opposite is true. Here, the disparity between the condition of consumer and that of practitioner of a given art appears to be much smaller, even null, as every reader or spectator may be thought of as a potential novelist, singer, or actor. Moreover, demand is higher in these professions than in the more esoteric arts, which require costlier investments (in terms of training, time, and money) from both practitioners and audiences; it is also more heterogeneous and unstable, and thus drives a greater production volume and a faster pace of product turnover. In the resulting organization of the art market, both artist overpopulation and career risk appear as the correlates of industrial and entrepreneurial strategies for managing uncertainty.

Literary production is the purest example of a world of artistic creation and practice wherein there are no entry barriers and learning takes place "on the job," that is, through the accumulation of experience provided by the very practice of the artistic activity. The reason that all the themes which compose the mythology or critical sociology of the accursed artist in bourgeois society took on their most striking form in nineteenth-century literature is doubtlessly because the functioning of the capitalist system of production revealed during that period, for the first time and with exceptional clarity, the dilemmas of artistic professionalization by way of the market. The gap between the influx of candidates for a writing career and the limited chances of success, as well as that between the abundance of literary production and the selection mechanism operated by audience preferences, conferred on the activity of the French literary market all the hallmarks of a crisis of overpopulation and overproduction as early as the first quarter of the nineteenth century.[78]

The Romantic mythology of the bohemian, starving artist was first forged in the world of literary production because that world offered the first example of a developed cultural industry. All the cultural industries that have emerged since then likewise base their activities on the overproduction of goods and on the permanent, excess supply of talented candidates. This is notably the case in the most speculative segments of these industries, wherein the phenomena I have been describing are particularly obvious: an extremely high number of candidates for an artistic career, statistically low chances for success, a rapid obsolescence rate for artistic goods, and a very wide dispersion of artists' income.

Studies in the sociology and economics of organizations have traced the means by which firms manage the specific uncertainties of the environments in which they operate. Applying the same analysis to the cultural industries, Paul Hirsch described how, from the creation of artistic products (such as novels, songs, and films) all the way to their final consumption, a series of consecutive filters operate a gradual selection among the entire set of products that are destined for the market, limiting to a small portion those that will reach the public via the main channels of diffusion and information.[79] The primary areas of uncertainty in this process are the behavior of gatekeepers—who act as mediators between firms and publics (critics, radio programmers, and so on)—and the reactions of final consumer demand. If the preferences of gatekeepers and consumers were relatively stable and easily determined, firms would concentrate their production and their promotional and advertising efforts on a limited number of goods, which would be carefully selected or even developed in function of previously collected data. Yet the opposite prevails: Final demand is highly volatile and unpredictable, and gatekeepers use fluctuating criteria that follow the logic of trends as they select among available products.

Among the strategies used by firms to reduce the vagaries of success and lessen potential risks, I am particularly interested in overproduction. The trial-and-error quest for success is, in effect, accompanied by a rise in the number of different products that enter the filtering process I have described above. This response on the part of firms is rational only if the capital investments required by a given type of production remain fairly low. In that case, the cost of overproduction remains inferior to all attempts at reducing uncertainty that would seek to provide better guarantees of success to a more limited range of artistic goods produced on the basis of the results obtained from continuous tests and surveys on determinants of taste and changes in demand. A low level of capital investments at the stage of artistic production is one of the factors that contribute to intensifying competition among a multitude of entrepreneurs with market access, and hence to consolidating this collectively maintained regime of overproduction.

Solicited in excessive numbers, artists cherish the illusion that they somehow enjoy equal opportunities before the unpredictability of success. Yet one of the filters for gradually selecting artworks destined for the public is, in fact, implemented within the firm itself. Initial overproduction prevents the firm from equally supporting all the products it creates. Thus, heads of advertising make selections based on their anticipation of a given artistic product's chances for success; their decisions to focus commercial and promotional support on this limited set of goods act, in turn, as a signal for all those who control the crucial selection process (beyond the direct influence of the firm) by informing and advising final consumers. In this way, the firm seeks to maximize the chances for success of the products it has chosen to heavily support, while also creating a reserve of goods to be put into circulation should it fail to persuade external mediators to comply with its expectations.[80]

Let us note in passing that the reliance on the star system as well as the commercial imitation of winning formulas are secondary strategies for reducing uncertainty. Though these strategies are precisely what prompt all the imprecations against the cynicism of cultural entrepreneurs busy exploiting alienated consumers, they are effectively dependent on the phenomenon of overproduction just described, and cannot be viewed as a perfectly autonomous and guaranteed means of making profit. Cultural entrepreneurs are thus constantly tempted to exploit innovations obtained through trial and error, and to reiterate prior successes via diverse techniques that select and combine their various ingredients in the exact same way. However, although the market perfectly informs producers about the outcome of their initiatives through the reactions of demand, it offers no guarantees to strategies of imitation. The uncertainty of success and the unpredictability of demand render obsolete, more or less rapidly, the information that a success generates concerning consumer preferences, at least in the most speculative segments of the market.

The star system is assuredly the keystone of this organization built on artistic overproduction and artist overpopulation, insofar as the spectacle of success and its accompanying prestige largely contribute to artistic professions' capacity to attract a labor force whose employment and career prospects are, in fact, statistically mediocre. Yet although employing a star does increase the probabilities of success of a film, play, or CD, this wager also implies a heavy financial burden. The high salaries of stars sharply increase production costs. Moreover, they raise the threshold of investment profitability to the point where it becomes imperative to exploit such productions in the international market, and to have artists involved, to varying degrees, in the financing process—for instance, through the production of films or CDs, or through partnerships established between a highly reputed artist and the gallery or network of galleries that sell his paintings.

The processes described above characterize foremost the organization of markets for reproducible goods. However, this type of market organization has been exerting increasing influence on other cultural sectors. Transformations in the market for contemporary art have caused the practices of its most speculative segments to converge with those of cultural industries. In both sectors, the goal is to produce a series of hits bolstered by massive advertising campaigns, and to take advantage, in the very short term, of key successes through feverish speculation. These practices rely on having access, all at once, to a large and active internal market (the American cultural market being the most important, both in terms of the size of demand and the power of cultural entrepreneurs) and to an international, even global arena in which to exploit artistic values. The shorter the life of the innovation, the more the market must expand in order to increase speculation profits.

The consequences for the careers of artists operating in such segments are twofold: Success, when it arrives, is important and very rewarding financially; yet it is most often as fleeting as it is intense. The peak of the income curve is reached in the first years of regular professional activity, and the probability of being downgraded increases as the artist's capital of youth is depleted. This is because innovations (whose production is linked to the capital conferred by youth in this system) follow the cyclical rhythm of trend renewal, and further detach the new forms of creative labor from the classic model of creation based on the artist's intensifying pursuit of a personal aesthetic and on the invention of values that define his originality and personal style.

The accelerated pace of training and talent depletion changes the behavior of art entrepreneurs. The probationary period of candidates is ever shorter and occurs at an increasingly younger age, because art dealers, publishers, and music producers are no longer truly willing to build careers over the course of time—with the trials and errors and the relatively lengthy periods of investment amortization this implies. This probationary period is particularly brief when the pursuit of success takes the form of a highly speculative wager, and when there is an abundance of candidates who are too young to have already been subjected to the process of selection through failure. These candidates, moreover, make no exorbitant financial demands and can more easily bear the economic constraints of the wait for success. They can also better cope with the exigencies of the market if success comes, and if it must be intensely exploited through swiftly abundant production and an extravagant lifestyle—as demanded by the aggressive marketing and hyperbolic commercial promotion that feverishly orchestrate the success of the innovation.[81]

The organization of the art markets based on the above strategies for managing uncertainty is facilitated, if not conditioned, by the specific legal and professional ties that exist between firms or entrepreneurs and artists. What Stinchcombe[82] described as the craft administration of production—as opposed to its bureaucratic administration—can also be applied to the organization of labor in the arts. Relations between employers and artists (writers, painters, musicians, actors, and so on) generally take the form of temporary contracts and allow artists varying degrees of autonomy; this autonomy is sufficiently broad, however, to be only rarely limited by strict bureaucratic control over an artist's ability to perform tasks and hold commitments. Remuneration arrangements come in response to the exigency to lower fixed production costs and to share risks that I have described above. For example, publishing contracts most often stipulate that the remuneration of the beneficiary will be proportional to the commercial success of his artwork, and will hence be determined *a posteriori*—even though the terms of the contract are usually adjusted according to the reputation of the artist, and may lead to substantial advances on payment and other assurances for anticipated earnings. In all cases, risks taken conjointly are limited by the temporary duration of the contractual engagement.

The craft administration of cultural production imposes itself notably in sectors wherein the realization of artworks calls on an entire set of artistic personnel to partake in collaborative work. The performing arts (such as theater, dance, music, and cinema) rely on an extensive division of labor, along a chain of production whose length greatly varies depending on economic developments and on the conditions for aesthetic innovation specific to the art under consideration (the production of a film, for instance, may be contrasted with a solo recital).

In order to mobilize the artistic personnel needed to realize an artwork or perform a new show, an art world must have access to a supply of human resources that is far superior to the volume of labor demand expressed at any given moment. Though I recognize, as does Howard Becker,[83] that the reality of employment in the artistic labor market generally involves all sorts of intermediary situations, I nevertheless distinguish two fundamental mechanisms in the hiring of artistic workers. First, orchestras, opera houses, theaters, and ballets that have permanent troupes and employ stable and full-time personnel on the basis of multiyear contracts provide planned and relatively secure careers (though often supplemented with partial or occasional engagements) to a proportion of artists which varies by sector—a relatively high proportion in the case of classical musicians, and a minimal one in the case of actors. This proportion nonetheless represents a minority of the artist population overall. Second, human resources can be mobilized through hiring individuals on a case-by-case basis; that is, for the amount of time it takes to realize an artwork or perform a show. This second employment mechanism, which ensures the viability of the greater part of the production system, has a high social cost since it relies on the existence of a permanent, excess supply of artists. The very flexibility of this mechanism can lead every job applicant to believe individually in his chances for success in the absence of any real barriers to entry and any formally established hiring programs. Yet the combination of individual wagers on a potential acting career (to take, as an example, this profession with the highest number of candidates and the highest rates of unemployment and underemployment) contributes, through a composition effect, to the creation of a vast, endemically underemployed reserve of labor.

This system is, in fact, maintained collectively. Artists individually believe that the system guarantees sufficient flexibility in the labor market and in hiring procedures to preserve the randomness of success. Artists' unions draw strength and resources from the size of the unionized population; hence they have more to lose from a Malthusian adjustment of the number of artists (which might improve the average condition of all) than they do from fighting traditional battles to improve the salary and working conditions of those who do find employment. Lastly, employers derive advantages from having access to a vast reserve army of artistic workers: They can pay the lowest possible price for artistic labor, and they have the freedom to continuously seek and promote new talents.[84]

The advantages enjoyed by employers cannot be interpreted merely as the product of an unbalanced power struggle and an unequal distribution of benefits among the different partners of a given art world. The existence of an overabundant labor force concentrated in large urban centers wherein job opportunities and cultural demand are greatest has, of course, long enabled cultural entrepreneurs to resist the demands of artistic workers. It has allowed them, moreover, to maintain the better part of their power in negotiations with individual authors or creators by taking advantage of individualized contract relations in a highly unstable labor market. Nevertheless, the conditions under which the music, film, and performing arts industries hire and employ artists are also a function of the flexibility requirements specific to the organization of production in sectors that are confronted with a shifting environment, a volatile demand, unpredictable discontinuities in the pace of activity, and uncertainty surrounding the probable duration of employment (for example, a successful show will be readily extended, whereas one that fails will rapidly be brought to a close).

In the above analysis by Stinchcombe, the rapid and continual reorganization of the structure of production in order to cope with market instability necessitates: (1) a system of contract employment that calls upon artistic workers who are able to adapt immediately to the tasks at hand; (2) an efficient system for transmitting information about the performance capacities of the available personnel; and (3) a minimization of fixed overhead costs (especially administrative and capital costs) through recourse to subcontracting, equipment rental rather than purchase, and such. These first two characteristics are particularly important in that all the activities I have been discussing here are highly labor-intensive; they are, in fact, the properties of the freelance system of artistic labor described by Becker. Artistic workers must be relatively interchangeable (at least for the tasks deemed less essential; otherwise, there would not be such a high number of applicants to the same category of jobs), ready to work on a case-by-case basis, and willing to replace one another at the whim of available opportunities. In addition to direct evaluation—via the auditioning of actors or musicians, the reading of manuscripts, the examination of artists' earlier artworks—employers have at their disposal a tool for rapidly gaining information on artists' competencies: reputation.[85]

While this informational device preserves the relative fluidity of the labor market, it does not prevent the formation of veritable economic rents. Certainly, no freelancer is protected in the event of failure: Every professional encounter can be the occasion for assessing an artist's skills, and the employer is entirely free not to rehire an artist who has not performed to his satisfaction. Conversely, since the fastest and most economical tool for evaluating skills is the exchange of information through personal networks, the trust that an artist inspires in his employers or in colleagues willing to recommend him will become a reputation collectively guaranteed by the members of the constituted network. In a professional world in which the usual institutional indicators of qualifications and skills—educational degrees—are not operative, or have only secondary value as compared with experience accumulated on the job, an artist's reputation can earn him a virtual economic rent. This is so either because the talent of the artist is scarce, or because the guarantees offered to the employer suffice, and even incite him to restrict his recruitment pool to a small circle of artists with whom he has developed collaborative ties. As Robert Faulkner[86] and René Bonnell,[87] respectively, observed for Hollywood film score composers and French film actors and technicians, this explains why, in such a hiring system, a small minority can work with great regularity and combine the advantages of freelancing with those of a virtual salaried employment.

The organization of artistic production and labor that I have just described characterizes foremost the functioning of very specific segments of the art markets, in which the specific skills demanded of both artists and consumers can be acquired at low cost. Creators often perceive the segmentation of the art markets as the mere expression of pure inequalities in volume (production volume, market size, remuneration level) that generate relatively important constraints in the adjustment of supply to demand. Yet those inequalities are also closely related to differences in the mode of organization. One of the errors of Frankfurt School critical theory was to view success as foreseeable and the consumers of industrial culture as manipulable at will; another mistake was to attribute the uncertainty of success strictly to the allegedly autonomous sphere of high creation and to innovations within that sphere. In fact, in the production segments of classical music, art-house cinema, high literary creation, avant-garde painting, and others, demand may be lower, but it is also more stable. In those segments, the cultural and commercial value of artists and artistic goods develops more slowly and imposes longer investment amortization periods; moreover, the fluctuations of this value are more predictable. Lastly, the profile of success displays the gently rising curves that distinguish the destiny of artworks raised to the ranks of the "classics" from the infinitely briefer trajectory of best sellers.[88] The strategies for managing uncertainty adopted by publishers, art dealers, and other cultural entrepreneurs reflect this profile: They let time do its work, thereby rendering more invisible the link between the economic and aesthetic dimensions of artistic value and more incomprehensible the socioeconomic mechanisms that underpin its gradual construction.

The requirements for advanced specific training or for wide-ranging knowledge of a given discipline, the test of time, and the role of peer as-

sessment in determining the outcome of competitive struggles are all factors that significantly reduce the number of candidates—though they do
not eliminate the vagaries of success. In a certain number of art worlds, the
possession of strong and duly certified specific skills is a virtually necessary
(though insufficient) selective condition for professional success; the probability of acceding to the most highly coveted jobs and positions will
hereby depend on these. However, the skill factor has no direct regulatory
power over professional demographics when the labor market is open,
and hence not subjected to a *numerus clausus:* The disparity between the
evolution of supply and that of demand can remain high in the most accessible professions that do not offer any selective training to control the
influx of entrants.

The relative efficacy of systems of artistic professionalization such as those
instituted in the guilds and the academies depended on the control they
sought to establish over both training and labor market openings—though
without ever fully achieving such control.[89] In a market regime, adjusting
the supply of and demand for professional artists is an even more complex
and imperfect process. In the arts wherein specific training is required, the
organization of the educational system and the time needed to adapt to
conjectural variations in the demand for artistic goods and services can generate spectacular disjunctions, and even total opposition between the movements of the labor market and the demographic influx of aspiring artists.[90]
I will cite as an example the evolution of the architectural profession in
France in the last quarter of the twentieth century.

The organization of the architectural academy remained in place longer
than that of painting largely because, in the second half of the nineteenth
century, architects were faced with competition from increasingly ener-
getic and well-equipped civil engineers, and thus sought to close and consolidate their profession by instituting specialized training and degrees and
by equipping themselves with professional associations and a professional
code of ethics. This evolution culminated in the law of 1940, which created the French Order of Architects and reserved the title of architect for
graduates of state-accredited schools alone. The only significant problem
with this was the absence of a monopoly on professional practice for title-
holders, which gave rise to intense competition for acquiring project management contracts *(maîtrise d'oeuvre).*[91] Be that as it may, the number of
professional architects increased little from World War II to the mid-1970s—a
period that saw the extensive development of the construction market in
France. The profession's protectionist organization guaranteed almost full
employment to its members, but also, according to some, deprived architectural creation of the spark of competition, which, in such a favorable

context, might have stimulated original and audacious architectural works.[92] In 1977, a new law opened up the profession to licensed project managers (maîtres d'oeuvres). From 1975 to 1985, both this loosening of the conditions for entering the profession and an influx of new students led to a rapid increase in the number of architecture professionals; yet, over the same period, the construction market evolved in the opposite direction and began to shrink.[93]

The educational system can adapt to such discordant trends in one of two ways. On the one hand, barriers to entry can be raised through the highly selective regulation of student influx, the redefinition of professional skills, and the consolidation of specific expertise, and this in order to increase the power of professionals over a more restricted field and to better equip them for the competition. In the case of architecture in France, competition intensified as the number of new professionals grew, due to the rationalization of the construction process and the increased division of labor.[94] On the other hand, the content of training programs can be diversified. Thus, the 1984 reform in France officialized the diversification of architectural training, thereby validating the increase in the number of candidates and prompting, under the pressure of the search for new professional prospects, the relative despecialization of the profession.[95]

Despecialization processes (via the lessening importance of specific training) and, conversely, professionalization strategies, which are designed to make training more selective and to homogenize professional practice, show that the variability of creative practices renders even more fluid and uncertain the distinction between, on the one hand, the artistic fields in which careers and professional success presuppose highly specialized training and, on the other, those that are immediately accessible to aspiring artists. Differential requirements for specific training do not merely reflect the diversity of semiological properties that characterize each artistic discipline. The content of training and the weight assigned to technical skills in the assessment of talent are, in effect, strategic variables in the competition among artists and among artistic movements, insofar as they help determine both professional stratification in a given art world and the chances for success of innovations which, in order to last, must call into question some of the conventions that training has transmitted as legitimate.

The populations of artists and scientific researchers, as well as the number of aesthetic innovations and scientific discoveries, would be low if *only* those candidates who could correctly estimate their chances for success actually entered these professions.[96] Hence the following contradiction: The sum total of the risks taken by each individual—who will pay dearly for his decision should he encounter failure or a mediocre professional life—is beneficial to the collectivity because the prevailing risk equation guarantees the art and science worlds an optimal level of development, in accordance with the pace of societal change. This contradiction is more or less acute depending on the modes of selection at entry into the various art worlds, the risk-aversion mechanisms that prevail in the respective systems of organization within each of those worlds, and the level of direct and indirect support granted to artists by the collectivity. It is, moreover, sustained by the very conditions in which individuals experience their professional engagement in the arts—as revealed by the argument concerning the nonmonetary benefits of artistic labor. Artistic labor has a dual resonance: individual, in that it designates the flow of psychological gratifications that each artist may receive; and collective, since evident social prestige is attached to this form of nonutilitarian activity whose variable and uncertain course allows for the constant renewal of production and for the perpetual regeneration of the power of signification and seduction of artworks.

These two forms of compensation are differentially invoked depending on the importance of the monetary sacrifice to which the artist has consented; they cannot, however, be dissociated. They designate the two facets of a single ideological transfiguration of the artist's life. On the one hand, hedonistic individualism turns the artist into a social type—the pioneer of a lifestyle whose diffusion in contemporary society has notably expanded the notion of creation nearly infinitely. On the other hand, self-sacrifice (or the renunciation of material security) makes the artist a social hero committed to serving the superior interests of Art—namely, the general interest of the collectivity, and even that of humanity itself—provided he contributes to that sublimated form of enjoyment which is a deferred and perennial pleasure: the well-being of future generations.[97]

CHAPTER FOUR

Talent and Reputation

Social Science Explanations for Varying Degrees of Success

IN THIS CHAPTER, I will examine how differences in remuneration and reputation are analyzed in the social sciences, and investigate why artists attain such widely varying degrees of success. The commonsense view is that the main cause of differences in artists' success levels is talent. But how can talent be defined and to what source can it be traced? Theoretical frameworks surrounding giftedness and vocation provide a stereotypical answer: Talent is the expression of abilities that seem to originate in the genetic lottery (especially if they manifest themselves early in the artist's life) as well as in the interaction between this genetic capital and a family and social environment that can bring it to fruition. One need only inventory the unique traits of exceptional talent and the reactions elicited by its products to determine whether the creative activity of genius is supported, ignored, or thwarted by the artist's contemporaries, or at least, by the most influential among them. The biographical account thus becomes entirely that of the fortunes and misfortunes of the expression of pure talent in a more or less favorable environment.

But if "talent" is the point of origin to which all other factors that account for success must be related (in accordance with a deterministic approach centered on the notion of causal force, as presented in Chapter 1), then what of importance remains to be explained? The social sciences know how to inventory artists' social and economic resources and to describe the various forms of organization of artistic labor. In view of this, I will examine how far one might take the analysis of artists' careers and remuneration by relying on the classic variables used in the social sciences—specifically, the training variable, which is usually granted the greatest explanatory power in the analysis of individual trajectories in the labor market. We will see, however, that this factor does not go far in explaining the phenomena in question. Indeed, we must go further to ask: Are varying degrees of success primarily determined by inequalities in ability?

If abilities were readily definable and observable, there would be no uncertainty about success. Yet it is precisely such uncertainty that fuels creative labor, innovation, and competition within the various art worlds. These latter proceed by constant comparison because it is impossible to fully determine the sources of artistic invention and originality. But what is the value of the evaluation procedures used in the competitions that compare, rank, select, and eliminate—a process that shapes the professional careers of creative artists? There would seem to be innumerable potential biases.

One way to answer this question is to proceed in a counterfactual fashion. Let us hypothesize that differences in ability, or what is called talent, may be minimal or negligible at the beginning of a career. Models of cumulative advantage, developed notably in the sociology of science and in career analysis, show that these minimal or indeterminate differences may engender considerable gaps in success and remuneration levels. Would this not account for the ubiquity of competitions of relative comparison in the arts and explain how these constitute a dynamic amplification mechanism?

There are several ways of specifying these models of cumulative advantage. It would be tempting to go even further and radically negate the existence of substantial differences in talent: We might invoke chance factors to explain success, or more radically still, impute success to processes of pure social construction. But as I will demonstrate, these arguments contain logical incoherences. I will gradually bring to light four components of an explanatory model that I will present in its entirety at the end of this chapter. In Chapter 5, I will recall certain essential points in order to apply this model to the controversies generated by the sociological interpretations of Beethoven's early career.

Artists' Training and Income

Regularly conducted surveys on the structure of the active population allow us to sketch the following portrait of artistic professionals among the principal developed countries. The average age of the artists surveyed is lower than that of the active population, and their level of education is above average. Artists are more likely to live in metropolitan areas; they have higher rates of self-employment; and they show a continual trend toward feminization. The number of artists is increasing faster than the active population as a whole.[1] The same surveys converge to show that, given their level of education and the social status of their activity, artists' earnings are lower on average than those of the professional category in which public statistics rank them—that is, "Higher Managerial and Professional Occupations" (*cadres et professions intellectuelles supérieures*) in France and "Professional, Managerial, and Technical Workers" in the United States. The strong growth in the number of artists, which affects the age composition of the group, as well as growing feminization (correlated with women artists' persistent income disadvantage) are two factors that have a negative influence on income distribution and reduce average earnings.[2] But the pay gap remains high even when these factors are controlled. When the estimate of artists' expected income is compared with that of a representative individual of the larger professional category (calculated by means of an earnings equation),[3] the "penalty" for artists lessens but persists, varying widely according to the artistic profession under consideration.[4]

What Is the Value of Professional Art Training?

The poor adjustability of the earnings equation signals one reason for this income gap. Whereas training (measured by the length and type of educational degree or certification) is usually a crucial factor in the analysis of earnings gaps among individuals and professional categories, its explanatory power for artists' income is low.[5] Why?

The first challenge is the heterogeneity of the art sector. Not all artistic disciplines demand the same degree of specialized training. The most obvious contrast is between the profession of writing, on the one hand, and those of instrumentalist, art music composer, or ballet dancer, on the other: The former requires no training at all, while the latter necessitate early, long, demanding, and highly selective training. This, however, is not to present the dichotomy as invariable. The existence and content of artistic training varies across space; for example, creative writing courses are offered to apprentice writers in the English-speaking world but hardly at all in France. Artistic training, too, varies across time; thus, numerous experiments in the visual arts over the twentieth century were characterized by the rejection of the artistic languages and techniques traditionally acquired and transmitted through specialized training.

Moreover, such variations cut across artistic disciplines. For a long time, art music training has strictly followed a pyramidal structure, and it now offers the most developed model of competition-based talent selection. Attending one or more of the music conservatories located at the highest point of the training pyramid in each of the great musical nations and being awarded a prize that recognizes this training constitutes one of the only examples wherein obtaining an artistic diploma offers a significant competitive advantage in the labor market. Furthermore, music is the only artistic discipline that makes such significant use of national and international competitions. Success in the latter increases a musician's chances of attaining professional success on an international level, despite the risk of imperfection in the selection and ranking of competing talents, as we shall later see. By contrast, in the popular music sector, musicians vary greatly in terms of their type of training and level of technical skills. Were we to assess these musicians' training by measure of the art music model, we would present a long litany of deficiencies and compensatory *bricolages*. These are, in fact, true training trajectories that merit description and that range from active music listening to the mimetic acquisition of routines and gestures, to interpersonal learning, to collective labor and skills specialization.[6]

Training and Unlearning

Studies on professional careers in the arts confront us with a familiar paradox: Once they have attained professional status, a large number of artists claim to be engaged in a process of unlearning or, at least, they openly relativize the importance of their initial training. Is this a simple *a posteriori* rationalization, or a denial of school learning, explained by the fact that art does not mix well with inculcated rules of any sort now that originality has become the norm in artistic production? Or rather, should this be viewed as pointing to realities not easily apprehended by the sociology of professions, a discipline traditionally concerned with more simple and direct relations between skills training, professional insertion, and the probability of professional fulfillment?

Training as such occupies a thoroughly ambivalent position in artists' lives. Understood as essential in revealing and shaping the talents of the apprentice artist, it is considered negligible when it comes to measuring its exact influence on the artist's personality. The following excerpt, taken from the text accompanying a recording by one of the great twentieth-century violinists, Nathan Milstein, offers one example among thousands of this ambivalence.[7] A brief biographical sketch specifies that ". . . little Nathan started playing violin at the age of 4"; he ". . . demonstrated his mastery and exceptional ease by playing Glazunov's *Violin Concerto* at the age of 10 under the composer's direction"; and at age 12, he ". . . received training from Leopold Auer, who was, in some way, the high-priest of Russian pedagogues of the time." The following is Milstein's own commentary on this period of his life:

> It is difficult to say with certainty how one has learned what one knows— from one's professor, one's fellow students, what one has heard? Auer had considerable influence on me, but he never imposed his conception of music on me. And surely it is essential for a professor not to be too directive. Violin technique is not so difficult; I mastered it by age 7. The real difficulty is music itself—the years of a man's life are necessary to master it! And you don't learn music from a professor: It's all about listening, playing, and attaining ever-greater understanding.

Milstein's remarks evoke the key themes which are a source of wonder and perplexity for the layperson contemplating the artist: precocity; the radical distinction between technical mastery, acquired quickly by talented individuals, and artistic mastery, the result of an unending maturation process; the ambivalent role of the professor, a key figure whose importance and intelligence are nonetheless also measured in terms of his ability to consciously self-limit his influence on his pupil; lastly, the impossibility of breaking down the artist's accumulated knowledge into its various components. Rather than understand this as a variant of the "denial of learning" theme—which, nuances aside, would reinforce the ideology of giftedness on which the cult of genius is based[8]—we can read it as expressing a genuinely complex phenomenon, wherein the supreme value of artistic self-determination is balanced out by the artist's obvious debt toward all those who share and transmit formative knowledge. The artist does indeed become the container of this knowledge, though he transfigures it through his own art.

Thus, the teacher paradoxically embodies both a model and a counter-model: He is at once the possessor of desirable skills and the person whose authority the student must learn to challenge. Herein lies artists' frequent ambivalence toward teaching. Sociologists have described the ambivalence of this type of pedagogical relationship, noting that it brings about a psychological double bind due to competition between master and pupil. Discussing the teacher-student relationship in the sciences, Robert Merton emphasizes the structural constraint created by competition for employment and prestige. When students are made to compete for the same positions as their teachers, the ambivalence is maximized: The better the student's training, the more effectively he will be able to compete with his teacher.[9] Yet, I must highlight another dimension of this paradoxical learning relationship, which is more readily apparent in the arts. As the value of personal accomplishments is indexed to the law of creative originality, training must engender the creation of unique artworks, as opposed to producing, as in the sciences, results and knowledge that will be discussed and absorbed as intermediate goods in the collective advancement of research. Consider the following remarks by Pierre Boulez, in which he first adopts the point of view of the apprentice and then that of the master—in this case, Olivier Messiaen, to whom Boulez is paying tribute. Here, he conveys the same paradoxical message as Milstein: The artist is, in fact, an autodidact who learns through the intermediary of a master.

> Once a certain level has been reached, education has no further use, and this is what I later reiterated to my pupils during my three years at Basle. For all practical purposes you can learn all there is to be learnt from someone in the space of six months, and even that would be slow: Sometimes, a week is enough. After that, what counts most in the long run is hard work and personal preferences. When you have learnt certain skills of your craft, you have to build on them and this education can only be done by yourself. I like people who are *deliberately self-taught*—that is, those who have the strength of will to have done with models that existed before them. But people who are *accidentally self-taught*, who have no knowledge of things, are of no interest to me at all, because they will never be rid of their predecessors.[10]
>
> I should like to recall an experience that must have been shared by many others, both before and after me—that sudden feeling of attraction to a master of whom one knows, with an inexplicable sense of certainty, that it is he, and only he, that is going to reveal you to yourself. . . . This chosen master acts as a stimulus by his very presence, his behaviour, his very existence and the glimpses that he gives of what he demands of himself. He sees and listens, understands the clash in the pupil's personality as he tries to discover himself in a fog of contradictions and resentments. The master is prepared to accept ingratitude and injustice, rebuffs and rebelliousness, if the reactions mean the momentary loss of the pupil in order to establish him firmly as an original, independent personality. Attention and detachment are needed for this, and a sense of the adventure of preparing all the details of a long voyage without knowing its destination, a desire to set out for goals that are never clearly defined. Giving an example is as necessary as learning to forget it: "Throw away the book I have taught you to read and add a new, wholly unexpected page!"[11]

We begin to understand the contradiction in which the creator-pedagogue chooses to engage, as he teaches his pupil to show insubordination toward the master's authority. When it comes to transmitting rules and technique, teachers are readily interchangeable (assuming they have similar levels of technical mastery) and play a limited role. If, in addition, or even exclusively,

the teacher aims to communicate an aesthetic program, his pedagogy becomes authoritative mastership. The doctrine of that mastership, though,
is bound to fade, since the key to recognizing apprentice artists' talent is
the principle of originality and aesthetic differentiation. This is summed up
in what Paul Watzlawick refers to as a paradoxical injunction: "Do as I
do: Reject all models!"[12] Likewise, according to art historian Bernard Berenson: "Genius is the capacity to react productively against one's training."[13] The argument could be understood as a formula for dialectical
transcendence. After an initial phase spent fully appropriating the contents
and techniques taught to him, the artist takes critical distance from his
training and transcends it by simultaneously negating and preserving that
which he has learned. Such thinking may also have led to the simple rejection of conventional learning on the grounds that it hinders the free development of an individual's *ingenium*.

But the logical structure of both the argument and the situation it describes is even more complex. Kant's concept of genius provides an insight
into that complexity. Without entering into a detailed analysis of this notion,[14] it is worth noting how clearly its various components resonate with
the remarks above and help to clarify the double bind that confronts pedagogical transmission when it must conform to the law of creative originality. According to Kant, genius is the capacity to produce without reference
to determined rules. The product of genius, therefore, cannot be the fruit
of learning: "Originality must be its primary characteristic." Secondly, in
order to distinguish the products of genius from creations that, though
original, remain absurd, genius must be viewed as having the capacity to
produce artworks that "must at the same time be models, i.e., exemplary,
hence while not themselves the result of imitation, they must serve others
in that way, i.e., as a standard or a rule for judging." And which rules does
the artist's natural gift establish so that he may produce an artwork that
will become an exemplary model? "He does not know himself how the
ideas for it come to him, and also does not have in his power to think up
such things at will or according to plan, and to communicate to others
precepts that would put them in a position to produce similar products. . . .
Rather must the rule be gathered from the performance, i.e., from the
product, which others may use to put their own talent to the test, so as to
let it serve as a model, not for imitation, but for following." The main-
spring of this paradoxical situation, then, is the personality of the creator—
his *genius,* to borrow Kant's term. By measuring himself against the personality and artworks of the genius, the apprentice artist comes to understand
how the rules dictated to the genius by his innate dispositions[15] are impos-

sible to articulate and transmit, but also how those rules serve as an example. This is precisely what Milstein and Boulez were saying.

Learning the Artist's Life: Training as Socialization

Knowledge and technical skills are the conventional, codifiable content of transmission. But training, which requires the artist to create original work, must help the apprentice artist forge a unique personality. For among the conventions that the student internalizes is the reinterpretation of choices and technical constraints in terms of intention, self-expression, and emotional commitment—what Barbara Rosenblum calls learning to cultivate the Self.[16] The socializing quality of training allows the artist to find a balance between reference to others, on the one hand, and resistance to external influences, on the other: The former confers social depth on artistic activity and endows self-expression with an intersubjective dimension, while the latter safeguards the artist from elements that may negatively impact his self-esteem, and would thereby render unsustainable the ambition of artistic originality. The quest for this kind of balance extends far beyond the training years, and certainly constitutes one of the less visible mechanisms in the selection of candidates for an artistic career.

The training period provides for the initial socialization of the future artist in two ways. First, it enables him to construct an individual identity with reference to others, namely through the experience of an ambivalent relationship with teachers. Second, it allows him to acquire his first professional experiences in the course of his studies.

In effect, one function of attending advanced art training institutions is to familiarize apprentice artists with the art worlds that they hope to one day join, and to enable them to obtain some work experience before the completion of their studies. For example, many apprentice musicians studying in higher conservatories give concerts, substitute in orchestras, land occasional contracts, and teach classes—if only to pay for their studies and for the often costly private lessons they take alongside their collective training. A classic question in the sociology of professions deals with the exact role played by training institutions, not only in students' acquisition of knowledge, but also in the formation of their future professional identity or "self-concept," to borrow Charles Kadushin's term. In a study of students in two New York conservatories, Kadushin analyzes the formation of this self-concept, showing that landing professional contracts during institutionalized training and integrating into networks of activity play a significant part in learning the role of a musician.[17] My study of acting careers in France likewise shows that students who attended advanced theater schools obtained their first jobs while studying.[18]

These learning experiences serve not only to connect theoretical study with practical training, but also to equip the student with the skills necessary for overcoming the numerous competitive challenges on the path to a career, and throughout the career itself. These include managing self-esteem; being able to show resilience in the face of failure; building interpersonal skills; negotiating professional relationships; networking; discovering the range of behavioral idiosyncrasies that characterize professional culture in art worlds; and adjusting rapidly to teamwork in collective projects.

Raymonde Moulin's analysis of the position of the École Supérieure des Beaux-Arts de Paris in the 1950s and 1960s offers an eloquent demonstration of this process. The academic art training epitomized by the École des Beaux-Arts came under fire for staying frozen in time amidst a whirlwind of innovations that intensified the opposition between tradition and modernity. Furthermore, the École could no longer guarantee its graduates high chances for professional success. Nonetheless, it remained a key instrument in the professionalization of visual artists, primarily through its socializing function. The painters interviewed in the study primarily recall memories from their learning years that have little to do with explicit pedagogical transmission—the discussions they had, the bistros they frequented, the friendships they built in the studio, and the advantages of a dilettante existence, of a relatively protected bohemian life. Far from simple artist folklore or a denial of the gains of education, these attitudes reveal that, as Raymonde Moulin phrases it, "the inculcation of the artist's way" entails "a long process of adjusting the product of the educational system to labor market demand, [a process during which] aspirations are set either higher or lower; that is, toward pure creation or toward teaching and 'commercial' art."[19]

In fact, it is even tempting to see this as the primary function of advanced art training institutions, since, as Moulin shows, having information on the latest developments in artistic creation and in the market has become more important than technical training, and since the institution no longer plays a central role in the professionalization of artists.

In her study of the California Institute of the Arts, Judith Adler underlines all the contradictions that arise in teaching when artistic disciplines undergo rapid evolution, breaking with all traditions.

> To be a teacher in a field in which the only reliable tradition appears to be the tradition of breaking with tradition is, in a sense, to be a teacher without a

field, without any unified body of theory, without any guiding standards of practice which do not erode as fast as they can be established. . . .

Furthermore, given the rapidity with which fashions in art change, even those teachers who have themselves been successful are likely to be perceived as inadequate role models. A man of thirty-five can be honored nostalgically as a master of an earlier generation, a period-piece which, however worthy for its own vintage, would be utterly useless to emulate. Even if he has successfully established himself at thirty-five or forty, he appears to have done so in a world which no longer exists—a fleeting, evanescent world which his students will not be able to enter. The rules, the shibboleths, the routes, the very gateways to full occupational participation will have so changed since his own occupational entrance.[20]

These contradictions affect student behavior:

Nor, pressed to establish themselves early, are young artists likely to feel inclined to invest their own time in the development of skills which mature only slowly and with years of practice. Eager for cues to the latest developments, knowing that they have limited time in which to make a name for themselves, they will never find their teachers young enough, close enough to the bustling scene to convey the latest professional information. In fact, in their eyes, their teachers threaten to age as quickly as gossip or yesterday's newspaper. The less a professional segment bases its art on a slowly acquired skill and the greater its reliance upon the mystique of the most advanced technology, the less its protection against a dizzying rate of obsolescence. (pp. 136–137)[21]

The Composition of Artists' Income

Apprentice artists' investment in specialized training yields returns that are not easily apprehended through a standard analysis of income factors. In fact, the relationship between training and income can be broken down into two causal sequences: The relation between training and the probability of obtaining paid employment, and the relation between type of labor and level of income. I will examine them both in turn. The relation between educational degree and employment prospects for artists is radically different than that of what is known as the classic labor market, in which employment involves a stable and long-term contract with one employer. The employment situation of artists is generally composed of numerous, often brief, and intermittent transactions with different employers. Once the artist has surmounted the initial obstacles of market insertion—generally facilitated for graduates of reputable art schools—the construction of one's career unfolds as a stochastic process: The probability of obtaining employment at any given moment is determined by the value of the artist's most recent performances or artworks, which carry far more weight than any diploma.

Not only is an artist's activity discontinuous, but it is also divided between multiple employments that fall both within and outside of the art sector. The employment survey data used to estimate earnings equations do not distinguish between income from artistic activities and income from employment outside of the art sector. Yet, international studies concur that when occupations are ranked based on the rate at which their practitioners resort to multiple jobholding, artists figure at the top of the list. Moreover, the rate of multiple jobholding has risen faster in artistic professions than in the active population at large, and faster than in the categories of "Managerial and Professional Workers" and "Professional, Technical, and Managerial Workers," in which artists are categorized. Once multiple jobholding has been taken into account, earnings functions show that investment in training has a positive effect on the portion of expected earnings derived from nonartistic activities, but hardly any influence on art-related earnings.

The second factor affecting returns on initial training concerns the importance of learning by doing and the value of professional experience. As indicated in Chapter 2, according to Sherwin Rosen, all employments can be thought of as "tied packages of work and learning" ranked according to their variable learning potential—a potential realized as they are performed.[22] In the arts, therefore, practice itself provides experience but also forms of knowledge that together constitute a determinant element of professionalization. These include new skills acquired through diverse work experiences and environments; practical knowledge; information on the latest trends in artistic creation; familiarity with the rules of the professional game; and a sense of the disparity between one's creative intentions and their public perception. But we must go further than this: Artistic professions figure among the activities that provide, mainly through practice, what are considered to be the most essential skills. At the individual level, learning by doing does not follow any explicit formula for the appropriation of skills held by others: The artist must discern how best to grasp the information available in the labor context and convert it into knowledge and know-how capital. At the collective level, learning by doing involves organized skills transmission, as experienced professionals train beginners on the task to be accomplished. This is the trade guild formula, of greatest importance in the arts wherein labor is to a large extent collective. For instance, cinema and the performing arts are structured according to an explicit hierarchy of artistic and technical-artistic functions. Here, frequent and prolonged contact between apprentice artists and professionals with skills acquired through experience can ensure effective, complete transmission of the knowledge and know-how required in the profession.[23]

Artists themselves have discerned in the particular nature of their work the essential link between the trial-and-error character of creative activity and its training value. Paul Valéry, in commenting on an artist's sculpting of his own bust (Valéry's), describes the labor of creative invention in these terms:

> By *hardships* and *problems* [in the advanced practice of an art], I am not referring only to the difficulties that are evident, foremost, and almost natural, and that all accomplishment and all creation make us readily and vaguely imagine. For these are *finite*, almost innumerable difficulties that we manage to resolve, once and for all; and the means of resolving them can be fairly well transmitted, from one mind to another, in school or in the studio. I am thinking, in fact, of those other difficulties, of those problems of a higher order, incomprehensible to most people (and even to more than one in the trade), which the true artist *invents* and imposes on himself. Just as one invents a form, an idea, or an experience, so the artist invents hidden conditions and restrictions, invisible obstacles, that complicate his design, run counter to his acquired talents, delay his contentment, and finally draw out of him that for which he was searching—that which he did not know he possessed. I say that this imperceptible invention of desires and misgivings is an artwork perhaps more profound and important within him, than the visible artwork to which he extends his effort. And I say that this secret effort against oneself shapes and modifies he who engages in it, even more so than his hands modify the very matter they take on.[24]

The following hypothesis directly ensues: In the arts, the return on experience is greater than the return on initial training. To test this hypothesis, we can again reason counterfactually. The impact of training on income would be much greater if the value of artistic labor were based on well-defined criteria of professional performance, and if the result of creative activity could be evaluated in absolute terms. If this were the case, the art training system could be optimized to more effectively identify candidates with high abilities and to teach them the most profitable skills. Thus, the quality of initial training would have a more direct impact on a candidate's chances for success. To be sure, the above description carries more relevance for certain historical conjunctures and for certain modes of practice in given artistic disciplines. For instance, the technical learning central to the training of instrumental musicians and ballet dancers acts as an early selection mechanism and as a factor for predicting a candidate's chances for professionalization.

However, as we have learned from the aforementioned surveys of visual artists and actors, artists readily declare themselves autodidacts, even when they have been thoroughly trained. While expressing satisfaction with the technical aspects of their training, they also willingly complain of not having been sufficiently "prepared" for professional activity. This assessment must be understood as indicating the high value attributed to experience that is accumulated through artistic practice.

Learning by doing provides the student with a better appreciation of the disparity between the motivations for pursuing artistic studies and the actual conditions that shape professional careers. Richard Caves explains:

> A vital feature of the training regimens for visual artists and musicians is that they treat the highest career aspirations—dreams of being an artist of renowned originality, or a musician of the highest caliber—as the sole focus of training and attitudes. Lost from the calculus is the very low probability that any randomly selected "talented" student will indeed pass through successive gates and come even within sight of the avowed career goal. In terms of its economic implications, the training-supported attitudes of artists are in effect highly risk-loving. This may be partly a matter of limited information: everybody knows about the big successes and the glory rained upon them, while the failures and disappointments—and the opportunity cost that they exact—are far less evident. Teachers reinforce this attitude for its motivational value; in the words of one voice teacher, "without the fantasy of being great you could not even begin." Neither the student's motivation nor the teacher's employment prospects will benefit from harping on the student's low chances for big-time success. In the visual arts the process is further reinforced by the artist's thralldom to an inner truth, which devalues the relevance of others' opinions about the work.[25]

In sum, professional commitment in the arts follows a logic of absolute accomplishment, whereas evaluations of artworks are always conducted in relative terms. This is another way of explaining why overconfidence—based on self-aggrandizement, the minimization of others' opinions, and the denial of one's low chances for success—is necessary for entering artistic professions, in which competition always proceeds through innumerable comparisons.[26]

A strong desire for risk, combined with the concern for one's "inner truth"—in other words, with *intrinsic* motivation in labor—brings to light the last element affecting the relationship between training and expected gains: The nonmonetary component of remuneration for artistic labor, whose importance I discussed in Chapters 2 and 3. The value attributed to artistic labor, as to other activities characterized by a strong expressive component, can be understood and measured as a form of consent to sacrificing monetary gains. Engaging in an artistic activity provides the artist with essential gratifications that derive from the variety and degree of autonomy it offers, the training potential it contains, and the benefits it provides in terms of deeper self-knowledge. The qualities of artistic labor thus conceived constitute one of the dimensions that come into play in the ranking of professions according to their level of prestige.[27]

The weak statistical correlation between training and remuneration in the arts has led me to perform a twofold disaggregation. First, I have broken down training into two categories: initial training and learning by doing. Second, I have disaggregated artistic labor into several components: the artistic activity that corresponds to the desired professional engagement, with its high risks and intrinsic motivations; supplementary artistic or para-artistic activities such as teaching, cultural project coordination, or journalism; and extra-artistic activities—either "day jobs" or stable employment—that help support one's artistic vocation. Remuneration for artistic labor is composed of monetary income and nonmonetary rewards. The gains from supplementary artistic or extra-artistic activities are primarily or exclusively monetary; they supplement income from the primary artistic activity or substitute for it over a short or long period of time, should this income prove low or irregular.

How are these two disaggregated elements—training and paid labor—related? David Throsby shows that the level of initial training has a significant positive effect on the probability of engaging in para-artistic activities (such as teaching one's art) as a means of financing the "vocational" portion of one's professional engagement.[28] Having obtained a high level of training also raises the probability of earning income through side jobs, should the artist need to resort to this to develop a resource portfolio.[29] David Throsby's economic analysis of the careers of Australian artists, as well as that of Neil Alper and Ann Galligan for American artists, enables us to measure the nonmonetary rewards of artistic activity.[30] One method of isolating the intrinsic (nonmonetary) satisfaction component is to examine at what point artists relinquish better-paying side jobs. The aforementioned analyses show that artists perform extra-artistic activities only insofar as to reach the level of income necessary to maintain their involvement in the creative activity: Rather than maximizing their income, they allot time to their art as soon as they meet the resource threshold they have set for themselves.

Disaggregating income enables us to locate the main source of interindividual inequalities. Artists' earnings levels, the variability of those levels over time, and their skewed distribution are an overall monetary expression of the risks they take, but also of how they manage those risks. A closer look at income distribution for side jobs show that income gaps are significantly narrower for secondary employment than for the "vocational" activity. Intrinsic motivations for creative labor ensure that the opportunity cost of time is high. Devoting a large amount of time to realizing one's art—rather than investing that time in more lucrative artistic, para-artistic, or extra-artistic activities—entails a crucial decision for all artists, so long as their preference for risk-taking, another feature of intrinsic motivation, remains high. This condition is necessary, though not sufficient, to sustain their hopes for success and to enable them to obtain the monetary, social, and psychological rewards that may accompany it.

The composition of artists' income sources, as well as the variable strength of the links between each component and the level of general and specialized training artists have received, provides a nearly perfect illustration of what the sociology of social stratification and the economics of organization have taught us about the functional importance of employment, and about the breadth of earnings inequalities specific to the different types of employment. I am interested here in the sociological and economic theories of labor that are primarily concerned with activities in an organization or team. These start from the point of inquiry that I have just identified: Why does the social and economic value attributed to labor in some professions not vary according to the degree of professional qualification and to the span of control exercised by some professionals over others in the organization of labor? The point is to show that the value attributed to these activities is a function of the relative importance of good, excellent, or disastrous performance in the production of the final result, as well as a function of the scarcity of the talents needed to succeed.

Arthur Stinchcombe has proposed to distinguish between two categories of industries.[31] The first category includes activities in which a talented professional's contribution to the success of a given project or enterprise is more than proportional to that which distinguishes him from his colleagues; that is, his unique personal qualities contribute greatly to the success of the team or organization. These are the professions in which there is the fiercest competition to attract and remunerate individuals deemed exceptionally talented, and it is here that the concentration of earnings creates situations of winner-take-all or winner-take-the-most. In this category, Stinchcombe cites scientific research, the entertainment industry (for example, cinema, radio and television broadcasting, concerts, shows and performances for a wide audience), and sports. Talent in these sectors or professions is a "complementary" or "multiplicative" factor of production. For example, the exceptional value attributed to a researcher will help his team or university obtain significant research resources, just as the reputation of an opera singer may considerably increase a given show's chances for success. In the second category, individual contributions—even spectacular ones—cannot considerably increase the organization or team's reputation or profit. In these activities, the required skills constitute an "additive" factor of production, and they are more homogeneously distributed among the individuals concerned. Teaching at the high school and middle school levels, manufacturing, and artisanal production constitute professions wherein the presence of professionals who display exceptional (or deplorable) performance does not add considerable prestige to (or discredit) the profession in question.

In a later version of the model above (which I adopt here), David Jacobs, followed by James Baron and David Kreps,[32] offer a three-term typology, while stressing the asymmetries between good and poor performance in a given activity. "Star jobs" are those in which knowledge and innovation play an important role; for example, the job of scientific researcher. In this case, even a poor performance does not considerably hurt the organization or firm, while a good performance (a good idea, expertly assessed as such) can generate substantial gains. In such professions, the probability of obtaining a very good result is low and most performances produce average results. The cost to the company of hiring an average professional is low in comparison to the profits it stands to gain from hiring someone exceptional. This leads to a policy of employment or contractual relations that brings in a great number of different individuals—the aim being to find the "real gem."

In other types of employment, a good performance has only a slightly above average value for the organization, whereas a poor performance is disastrous. A pilot who keeps to his flight schedule and lands his aircraft gently is certainly valuable; but if he misses his landing, the negative result of his poor performance will be incomparably more damaging than the good performance will be profitable. These are "guardian jobs," and they are generally found in complex systems of production, in which great interdependencies between workers prevail and overall performance is primarily determined by the worst individual contribution. The hiring process for these jobs involves a very careful screening of applicants as well as long periods of apprenticeship.

Lastly, in the case of "foot-soldier jobs," variations in individual performance have but a limited impact, and the range of individual differences is small. Here, the success of the organization depends on the aggregation of all individual performances. Recruitment is undertaken on the basis of a simple wage negotiation: Whoever accepts the proposed wage gets hired.

Artistic production within an organization (a theater, orchestra, opera house, film crew, or publishing house), with all the different occupations and functions it requires (creation, editing, technical and artistic occupations, administration, commercialization, promotion, and so forth), provides a simple illustration of the relevance of this categorization. Let us focus our analysis on the example of artistic and technical jobs required for the interpretation of an opera. Such a production mobilizes solo opera singers, a choir, an orchestra, a conductor, a director, set and stage designers, and a technical crew. In order to maintain their jobs, the solo singers must be at a high enough level so that, show after show, their performances are—at least—of the normally expected caliber. A particularly successful performance by a young singer, however, may help the show make quite a splash. For their part, the orchestra, choir, and conductor risk rendering the show a disaster if they perform very poorly; but if they perform successfully, this will have less of an influence on the final result than will the performance of the singers. Lastly, the work of stagehands (but also that of ushers and receptionists) is usually up to par and has little influence on the value of performances.

Here, we are speaking of work executed within a team, either in a stable organization or in one centered on specific projects (for example, an opera as part of a festival). It is not difficult to extend this analysis to the individual work of an artist outside of an organization. In fact, in managing and diversifying his activity, the artist behaves similarly to a micro-organization. In the cases of multiple jobholding that I have examined, I came across the two or three types of employment that are discussed in functional analysis. The job of the artist (creator or solo performer) is obviously a "star job." The supplementary artistic or intellectual activity (such as teaching associated with a career as a painter or composer, or journalism associated with a writing career) belongs to Stinchcombe's second category, and could be either a "guardian job" or a "foot-soldier job" in Baron and Kreps's typology. Lastly, extra-artistic activities are usually the equivalent of "foot-soldier jobs." In many arts, one rarely sees the association of an artistic career with a permanent job that is functionally essential to a company—Charles Ives, who worked both as an insurance agent and as a composer, was a rare example of this combination. This is, however, more frequent in literature, especially if the creative profession is associated with a career in the civil service (for example, the famous cases of writers who were also ambassadors or members of the diplomatic corps, such as Paul Claudel and Saint-John Perse).

Further in this chapter, I will show how, for "star jobs" that constitute the primary artistic activity, cultural enterprises (for example, publishers, gallery owners, recording and film companies) operate by searching precisely for what Baron and Kreps refer to as the "real gem." Yet they do so by contracting on a project-by-project basis, via artists' freelance status or via equivalent positions in the French system of atypical salaried employment, in order to minimize the fixed costs of productive activity. Strategies for managing uncertainty surrounding quality and commercial success—which rely on the overproduction of goods—depend precisely on this organizational mechanism based on contract labor. As I will later demonstrate, production in the arts is, in many respects, akin to a skein of contracts that favor mechanisms of selection through elimination tournaments.

Spectacular Inequalities: From Critique to Analysis

I have examined the relationship between training and remuneration in order to find the key explanation for the poor adjustability of earnings equations in the case of artists. As compared with the other higher professions, artistic professions present a complex picture of income derived from diverse activities and job decisions that depend on both the artist's handling of his career risks and the amount of nonmonetary satisfaction he derives from the accomplishment of his principal artistic activity.

By contrast, the result of this complex combination of sources of income and allocations of effort to multiple activities is quite simple. All national studies show that earnings inequality, income variability over time, and rates of unemployment and underemployment are higher among artists than in nearly all the other occupations included in the same statistical category. Neil Alper and Greg Wassall have calculated that, in the United States, inequalities in professional income among artists have increased at a faster rate in the last sixty years than among the other categories of "Professional, Technical, and Managerial Workers." Out of a total of 123 higher occupations studied, nine of the eleven artistic professions rank in the top fifteen professions with the strongest internal income inequalities; among these nine professions, actors and musicians score the highest in terms of inequality.[33]

The distribution of income in artistic professions generally follows a Pareto curve: One-tenth of professionals in the given field earn half of all annually distributed income and one-fifth of professionals concentrate 80 percent of earnings.[34] Once expenses for exercising their professions are deducted, there are more individuals making zero or even negative income in the arts than in any other higher occupation. At the other extreme, the highly elongated peak in the distribution signals the presence of artists with astronomically high remuneration levels, bringing to mind the lottery pay-off matrices discussed in Chapter 3. Thus, whereas the distribution of human capital factors included in earnings equations follows a typical bell curve—with a rather symmetrical distribution of individuals from the study population around mean values, and a concentration of the majority of individuals in the middle of the distribution—we are dealing, here, with a very asymmetrical curve. To what mechanisms of the artistic labor market should we attribute both this discrepancy and the extreme inequalities that result from it?

A few of the most important social science analyses dedicated to the causes and mechanisms of growth in social inequalities originate in studies of the arts and sciences. Among these, I will first consider the normative and critical approaches. I will show why we arrive at a complete impasse when we settle for imputing Pareto-type inequalities to the mere fact that artistic production is organized according to competition mechanisms that fuel the market economy's incessant quest for innovation. The critique of the competitive, market-oriented organization of the arts is aimed at demonstrating that competition can exhaust or curb creativity; it substitutes a normative approach to inequalities for a detailed explanatory one. By asking what would happen if art functioned according to a law other than that of interindividual competition—which is reflected in the varying degrees of success among artists—the critical approach reasons in terms analogous to those of experimental reasoning. Yet it begins from a thought experiment only to transform one of the most fundamental properties of art worlds—that is, the attribution of value and the hierarchical ordering of values—into a contingent and arbitrary mechanism that could be radically altered in a different organizational system. Identifying the contradictions that result from the Marxian variant of the (longed-for) abolition of comparison and interindividual competition will allow me to seek out why it is that art worlds proceed by incessant rankings and hierarchical orderings.

Why Rank? The Antinomies of Evaluation

In the arts, the imputation of value and talent operates through quality ratings and transforms the latter into carefully ranked hierarchies (celebrity rankings, multiple awards and accolades, halls of fame, hit parades, best-seller lists, quality and originality ratings such as music critics' scoring of classical music interpretations), or into rougher rankings (major/minor artists; major literary works/good-quality books/third-rate novels; quality films/B-movies, and so on). What we are dealing with are in fact sharply differentiated artistic goods and performances, created and put into circulation under the law of originality. Artworks must differentiate themselves by their degree of originality, which, in theory, renders them poorly comparable.

How can the evaluation process, which is central to the system of competition in the arts, claim to effectively sort and rank so many different artworks put into circulation by so many poorly substitutable artists? Let us accomplish a drastic simplification by considering the two principal antinomies of evaluation. Two theses may be put in opposition. The first thesis defends the efficacy of systems of competition and ranking in art worlds by recognizing their capacity to identify talents and allocate reputations based on the intrinsic merits of each artist and artwork designated for an audience. The second thesis holds that evaluation processes are highly imperfect and excessively Malthusian, and that a different organization of art worlds would render competition less harsh and, ultimately, less necessary. The content of these antinomic theses will reappear below as I examine the mechanisms by which gaps in quality are disproportionately amplified. First, though, I will examine the arguments used to support these two claims.

The first antinomy concerns the judgment of actors in art worlds. Reputation is founded on these actors' perceptions of the qualitative differences between artworks and between artists, as well as on the choices they make based on their personal preferences. How are these perceptions formed? The argument that explains differences in reputation by invoking intrinsic differences in quality between artists relies on two postulates. First, each person's judgment—be it that of a professional evaluator or that of a lay art-consumer—is based on complete information about the entire set of artists and artworks that are put in competition to attract attention; without such information, quality comparisons would be imperfect and could not correctly identify intrinsic differences in quality. Second, the information must be acquired and processed and judgments made independently by each person, in order to prevent strategic games of influence from affecting the evaluations. These two conditions would prevail if we were situated in a world in which artists could make the unlimited differentiation of their artworks coincide with the unlimited attention given to their respective qualities. Are these two conditions actually met? It is easy to object, as does Howard Becker,[35] that no selection system can fairly handle the multitude of artworks contending for judgment, or require that publics know the entirety of that which is being compared in order to formulate their own evaluations. Moreover, there exist innumerable violations of the principle of independent evaluation: collusive moves in which the interests of evaluators converge with those of producers and market intermediaries; interdependencies between critical evaluations due to mimetic behavior or games of influence; and officially illegal practices such as payola.[36]

The second antinomy is grounded in a remarkable property of artworks. According to Hannah Arendt's classic analysis, within the realm of the products of human work, artworks possess the unique characteristic of durability. They thus have the ability to generate lasting admiration, to the point of attaining a level of success that can become universal and indefinite. The durability of artworks must, however, be acquired. It is important to distinguish between the short, medium, and long term in the development of reputations and the convergence of evaluations. In the short term, there is a high level of uncertainty concerning the aesthetic quality of artworks and the relative importance of artists. It is in the short term that the dispersion of evaluations is greatest, speculations most feverishly take advantage of information asymmetries, and competition is fiercest among all those involved in judging and ranking artists. In the medium term, the range of interventions affecting the price and value attributed to artworks becomes more limited. Art dealers impact the supply of artworks by controlling the number of goods placed on the market so as to influence prices (so long as they retain a monopoly on this supply), or they attempt to renew the careers of artists who have been overshadowed by competition from newcomers. These actions occur at the same time as the selection process narrows in on a small number of artists with the potential to last. In the long term, evaluations benefit from a reduction in the uncertainty surrounding the identity and importance of artworks. The supply by artists who have reached the end of their career or have passed away is exhausted, and the most renowned artists have become the object of scholarly analysis as well as conservation and patrimonialization in museums and repertoires.[37] The durability of artworks is that which renders possible the convergence between evaluations and the removal of uncertainty, wherein, as in the case of high art, such works pretend to be able to deliver an indefinite flow of aesthetic pleasures. This flow will persist so long as artworks remain seen, read, listened to, commentated on, discussed, diversely interpreted, and made into enigmas and controversies, and so long as, like stars, they continue to emit light as they cross time and space—to use George Kubler's evocative comparison.[38]

Thus, it is possible to state the principle of stability of universally ratified rankings. An overselection is set in motion among the creators and artworks recognized as the best at a given moment, supplying rankings with the most lasting values and allowing a few artists from each period to enter a pantheon of universally and indefinitely celebrated values. Humanity does not have a better definition for the objectivity of artistic values than that of their enduring universality. The latter is precisely what enables us to qualify artworks as public goods: Their value is not confined to the immediate context of their production and reception. This is what pushed Marx, though a staunch theorist of historical determinism, to experience perplexity when faced with the beauty of Greek art. In asking himself why the artworks produced in a given society (such as slaveholding Greece) could continue to elicit such artistic pleasure to the point of serving as a norm—as an inaccessible model—he suggested that the dialectic of production and consumption must reckon with the autonomous historical career of artworks and with a nondialectical history of artistic evaluation.

One might, however, question the process through which durability is effectively acquired. Is the selection process so perfect that it allows us to go from uncertainty regarding artistic quality to certainty about that which should produce consensus and inspire a general, even universal, admiration? The opposing thesis would hold that this would be to neglect the cases of error or omission in the attribution of value, as well as all the examples of fluctuation of values and reputations over the long term. It is indeed false to think that evaluations proceed in a linear fashion. In reality, there are multiple reasons why certain artworks and artists enjoy a lasting reputation, reasons that intertwine historico-aesthetic and economic considerations. This entanglement is itself unstable, as proven by the phenomena of rediscovery or demotion, or by the attribution of historical importance to certain artworks regardless of their aesthetic value.[39] This is what leads Howard Becker, in the last chapter of *Art Worlds,* to claim that the reasons for the convergence on artists who are the winners of increasingly selective eliminatory competitions are, in fact, too blurred and too general to provide a truly convincing explanation in terms of perceptible and indisputable differences in quality. He adds that these selective competitions fail to take into account whole genres of artistic production, such as naïve or popular art, which are too distant from dominant aesthetic norms to be included in the selection process with any reasonable chances of success. Lastly, what is seen as an objectification of artistic value is also the product of institutional and social mechanisms responsible for the rigidity and inertia of rankings, in the context of the proliferation of museums and other forms of cultural patrimonialization. The life span of the most renowned artworks transforms itself into an uncontested index of artistic quality through a mechanism of self-reinforcement and self-perpetuation of reputations. Artworks' durability, indeed, is not merely sustained by an intrinsic quality that would shine endlessly on its own and remain convincing solely through its self-evident power.

How can we escape the grasp of these antinomies? Rife with imperfections and yet generative of lasting convergences of opinions and preferences, the evaluation mechanism—which subjects artists and artworks to multiple comparisons—gives rise to a simple interrogation that may, nonetheless, rapidly become devastating. Is talent truly a significant intrinsic advantage possessed by an individual, one that remains, once all other possible factors of success have been calibrated, like an unexplained residue, designating what economic analysis calls a coefficient of interindividual heterogeneity and what common sense refers to as a gift or rare ability? Or, should talent be considered an attribute whose definition and very existence depend on and vary along with the forms of competition and market selection procedures? Why should interindividual differences, which are the levers of originality, become interindividual inequalities, which are the products of competition?

Selective Competition: Revelation or Construction of Value?

In the concluding chapter of *Art Worlds,* Howard Becker examines the selection procedures that produce rankings and hierarchies. He calls into question the very principle of selectivity prevailing in art worlds on the grounds that it produces socially constructed, changing, and reviewable procedures.

First, he writes, the selection could always be different: "[T]he process of selection through which art worlds operate and art reputations are made, leaves out most of the works which might be, under other procedures of definition and selection, included in the corpus of what is recognized as art, good or competent art, and great art."[40] Second, the rate of elimination is much too high: "[F]or everyone we eventually hear of, hundreds never come to anyone's attention and never get counted in."[41] Lastly comes the counterfactual objection, which sums up the critical distance effected by constructionist relativization:

> Theories which find evidence of a society's values and cultural emphases in its art, then, really find that evidence in the art which survives a complicated and historically variable process of selection and reputation making. Would such theories find the same result if they considered all the art made in a society?[42]

In an exchange with me, Becker reacted to my analysis of his positions by articulating the following arguments:

1. I do think it's perfectly possible to arrive at "valid" consensual judgments about the value of this or that art object or performance—

IF everyone has learned the same standards and ways of applying them. So it's common enough for jazz players to agree that this player "swings" and that one doesn't—they've all grown up in the same world and learned to apply that criterion in the same way (even though no one can really explain how they do it, the judgments are usually very reliable).

2. But sometimes and some places that preliminary consensus doesn't exist (Barbara Herrnstein Smith's essay that I quote, about her judgments of Shakespeare's sonnets, is relevant here), and then you can't achieve similar judgments. People are starting from different premises and necessarily arriving at different conclusions.

3. It's also common for well-socialized members of the same artistic community to use a variety of (non necessarily or non-contradictory) standards of judgment. So that they can say that this player really swings and that one has great melodic ideas and a third one puts together a solo that has great coherence. These things may not go together, often don't, and these folks recognize that your judgment of the worth of the player will depend on which standard you use and there's no reason for everyone to always use the same one. So some days I like Glenn Gould's *Goldberg Variations* and some days I like Charles Rosen's.

4. Where I come down hardest on the side of "democratization" is where you emphasize it, when whole genres are just left out by "cultivated people" as not worthy of notice or judgment.

5. There is an aesthetic behind the way I think and I've thought about writing this up, but who would care? Certainly not the aestheticians. My basic idea is that, as I say in the book, aesthetics is typically a negative enterprise, which tries to sort out the deserving "good art" from undeserving "bad art." The whole idea is to prevent people from liking and enjoying things they shouldn't. This approach thus diminishes the amount of possible pleasure in the world. My idea is just the opposite—to discover ways to maximize the amount of pleasure by finding ways to like things that one "shouldn't like." So, if I can find a way to like something that is really trashy, that's good. (I'm reminded that Charles Rosen wrote a great essay in the *New York Review of Books* on trashy music, Liszt being his major example, in which he talked about how it was possible to really enjoy musical trash.)[43]

These different arguments can be ranked on an ascending scale of constructionist commitment, based on the principle formulated by Ian Hacking.[44]

Is Becker merely considering the amelioration of evaluation procedures to correct the imperfections of competition that do not ensure the election of the best under the best conditions (Hacking's grade 1)? Is he being ironic and anarchistic, as he loses patience with the excessive celebrations that, after all, praise an infinitely small number of artists? Given the infinite diversity of creative practices, can the choice of "winners" appear objective or grounded in reason at such levels of scarcity (grade 2)? Or is Becker envisioning a possible world in which everything that is produced would have equal chances for recognition and esteem (grade 3)?

Grades 1 and 2 call into question the conditions under which competition operates within art worlds, but they do not challenge the principle of competitive selection itself. Other modes of organization, other systems of evaluation, and other structures of consumer preferences would simply produce different results, as demonstrated by the history and variability of cultural systems.

The grade 1 argument may be illustrated by an example taken from Becker's own work, in which he examines the speculative whirlwinds of the contemporary art market and the manipulative advertising techniques aimed at inflating the reputations and ratings of new artists in New York. Becker suggests that excesses in reputational volatility were rendered possible by the disappearance of the "community of taste," which once established stable, consensus-generating rules for artistic competition and rivalry among art lovers less influenced than today by the economic operators of the art market.[45]

The grade 2 argument is stronger and may be formalized as follows. Suppose that the qualities necessary for attaining professional success in the arts or sciences are distributed continuously among individuals, in the same way that the Scholastic Aptitude Test scores rank American students seeking university admission. In this distribution, individuals are ranked by their abilities and intrinsic qualities (regardless of their origin and nature); yet for each distribution segment, two individuals with very similar measurements of their desired qualities (their score) are only separated by a minimal gap. At the higher end of the distribution, where the most talented individuals are concentrated, market-based competition spectacularly widens the material and symbolic earnings gaps between the winner(s) and everybody else. The earnings matrix is similar to that of a lottery, with one or few substantial prizes—except that the winners are not chosen at random. The competition, rather, is entirely based on the deployment of the highest qualities of personal accomplishment: inventiveness, creativity, and the most valued intellectual resources. The competition very often takes the form of a tournament, epitomized by literary and scientific prizes, hit parades, best-seller lists, and critics' rankings. The most radical type of tournament—that is, the most inegalitarian—is the one that gives visibility to and honors one or two winners in a "winner-take-all" scenario, as is the case with several prestigious international prizes like the Goncourt prize, the Pulitzer prize, the Pritzker prize, the Nobel prize, and the Fields Medal. The same is true for the election of a new member to an elite circle whose composition is restricted by a *numerus clausus*. For instance, there are forty seats in the Académie Française and, as Harriet Zuckerman points out,[46] were it to exist, the forty-first chair would be attributed to someone whose merits were equivalent to those of the other *académiciens*.

The twentieth century nevertheless produced, in the arts as in the sciences, an ever-growing number of prizes, rankings, awards, and distinctive signs of celebrity. The very development of competitive markets in these two fields may have increased the level of admiration shown toward the best professionals. But what has been the result? Has success become less scarce, has there been a proliferation of success categories, or have persisting hierarchies been weakened? Overall, are the symbolic and material gains from success less concentrated than before? Do winners now hold a smaller share of the market? In the United States, approximately twenty literary prizes were awarded in the late 1920s; in the early twenty-first century, there exist more than a thousand such prizes. James English has devised an index for the number of literary prizes awarded in the United States and Great Britain, which he defines as the ratio between the number of prizes awarded each year and the number of new books published annually, expressed as multiples of one thousand.[47] The value of this index has risen to ten times what it was in the 1920s. In other words, the competitive value of writers and their books, as signaled by the attribution of prizes, has increased ten times as fast as the diversity of literary production. There would seem to exist, then, enough room for more competitors to gain visibility and acquire readerships. This is Tyler Cowen's argument, according to which volatility in reputations has increased and the domination of the markets by superstars has weakened.[48] In Cowen's view, inflationist allocation of ephemeral fame, which can only be converted into lasting glory once it is identified with a particular merit, is a positive-sum game in that it leads the public to become passionate about a greater number of artists, while inciting professionals to invent distinctions and celebrations for all sorts of talent. But is the weakening of the once-durable link between celebrity and artistic merit good or bad news? One who favors a "democracy of admiration" would find it to be good news, provided the mobility of reputations prohibits any one artist from dominating a given art scene for too long and from enjoying an exorbitant reputational rent. However, we would still have to verify if, in a more perfectly competitive market, more equal opportunities might be offered to artists to develop a career, or if only short-term success would prevail, thus favoring a type of production that best corresponds to the demands of mass cultural markets (without abolishing cross-sectional inequalities in the Pareto-style earnings distribution). If this last hypothesis is correct, Cowen's findings would be bad news for advocates of merit-based success, because it would mean that markets with a high potential for immediate profit would tend to impose their model and to standardize artistic production to make it a more easily consumable form of entertainment.

The data measuring the concentration of success contain no ambiguity: Pareto's law is still very much in effect.[49] In reality, the set of prizes is distributed in accordance with a hierarchy of influence and prestige that has the same profile as that of inequalities in reputation among artists. Moreover, the accumulation of prizes by certain creators, of which James English provides a series of examples, distances us from Cowen's utopian notion of wide-scale "fame decentralization."[50]

What is the essential point here? Under the hypothesis of a continuous distribution of the qualities required by professional practice in the arts or sciences, the following critical argument may be formulated: There is an unfair, radical split between those who fall to one side or the other of the barriers raised by competition, it being rare to find oneself in a winning position. Yet this hypothesis of a continuous distribution is easier to formulate than to specify rigorously. The sociology of science offers fertile ground for examining both this question and its normative significance.

Scientometric studies developed in the 1960s supplied the sociology of science with empirical material that made it possible to isolate the factors of scientific productivity and competitiveness. One decisive issue, whose political significance is evident, concerns the estimation of the causal relationship between the size of the scientific population and the degree of advancement in scientific research.[51] In the case of a linear correlation, the argument is direct: Numbers determine quality. The efficiency argument, in turn, may be formulated as follows: Numbers play an even more important role when they are correlated to an optimal mode of organization of scientific research. For example, Joseph Ben-David showed how, in the late nineteenth century, scientific research was stronger in Germany than in France or England, and this for two reasons. First, German higher education was decentralized and included a great number of competing universities (approximately twenty German universities competed for leadership, against two highly dominant ones in the two other countries). Second, many scientific jobs had been created due to the expansion and competitive dynamics generated by such an organization.[52]

This argument of "power in numbers" nonetheless came as a surprise to researchers who had shown the extent to which productivity is unequally distributed among scientists (supply-side inequality), and, above all, how much the recognition and esteem given by the professional community to its members (through citations of their work) are ruthlessly reserved for an elite.

The calculations and estimates that were performed in the 1960s by Derek de Solla Price confirmed Lotka's law: The number of scientists producing N articles is approximately proportionate to $1/N^2$, meaning that out of one hundred authors who publish one article, twenty-five publish two, eleven publish three, and so on.[53] Price went further to explain that if we rank one thousand articles or one thousand scientists in descending order by colleagues' citations of them, half of the total number of citations concern some thirty-two articles or authors—a number equivalent to the square root of the total population of articles or individuals considered. From this, Price derived the following argument: Increasing the population of scientists would create a far-less-than-proportionate increase in the total value of research produced, since doubling the number of scientists would only create a 5 percent increase in the production of valuable research.

These pyramidal inequalities immediately raise the question of a dysfunctional allocation of means and abilities. Is it not an incredible waste of human and social resources to allow the development of systems of activity wherein the exceptional success of a few fuels the foolish hopes for success of all those who enter the competition—the vast majority of whom will end up rank-and-file soldiers, rather than recognized and well-esteemed producers?

We may wonder, then, whether research would suffer if the number of scientists were reduced. If so, this would confirm what Jonathan and Stephen Cole call the "Ortega hypothesis": José Ortega y Gasset's argument, according to which the scientific advances and breakthroughs of leading scientists would be impossible without the minor discoveries and productions of the great mass of lesser-known scientists.[54] Though science is highly inegalitarian and structured throughout by competition, it nevertheless seems to function according to community-oriented and collective properties. Interdependencies between the activities of differently reputed scientists are so strong that they together make science advance; in other words, whether great or small, no individual is irreplaceable. Evidence of this appears to be found in the phenomena of simultaneous or nearly simultaneous discoveries examined by Robert Merton.[55] Science, it would seem, progresses regardless of which researcher makes the discoveries. Nonetheless, Merton also observes that exceptional scientists are not simply those who make a discovery that could just as well be made by another, but are those who are implicated in multiple discoveries: "The individual man of scientific genius is the functional equivalent of a considerable array of other scientists of varying degrees of talent."[56]

For the Coles, however, Ortega's hypothesis does not stand up under scrutiny: Certain scientists are, indeed, more irreplaceable than others. The formidable conclusion they draw is that, "it may not be necessary to have 80 percent of the scientific community occupied in producing 15 or 20 percent of the work used in scientific discoveries of significance, when perhaps only half their number could produce the same."[57] Such diagnoses of "social waste" can be as devastating as the following is naïve: the argument that a linear relation exists between the level of a country's spending on scientific research and the value of its scientific production. This argument does not take into consideration the organization of scientific careers and scientific work, the concentration of resources, competition, stratification, monetary and symbolic incentives, or the conditions under which research is performed, both by researchers and their students.

Price highlights the problem with the Coles' conclusion, as he warns against the devastating conclusions which could be drawn from his own calculations: "The only snag is that one can never know in advance that any particular people or papers or books or concepts will become part of the core or the elite."[58] Here, the principle of uncertainty is a central argument. It applies as much to the sciences as it does to the arts and to the cultural industries: This is the "nobody knows principle," so well evoked by Richard Caves.[59]

Is a World without Competition or Differences in Talent Possible?

To show the cost of negating this principle of uncertainty, we will consider the most radical scenario (which falls under Hacking's grade 3 argument), as well as the conclusions that can be drawn from this examination. Can artists work without being forced into rivalry by comparative evaluations by critics, experts, professionals, and audiences?

Some thinkers maintain that the current technological revolution gives us a glimpse into what a world of totally atomized production might look like.[60] Innumerable producers of cultural goods, with access to technologies that would be ever more powerful and ever less costly to acquire and exploit, would produce at lower cost artworks made instantly available for diffusion and appropriation. There would emerge, in sum, a community of producers with no need for any of the intermediaries responsible for preparing artworks and artists for presentation, competition, comparison, and evaluation. In this scenario, the free access to goods diffused on the Internet, transported and exchanged from one terminal (computer, cell phone, iPod, Kindle, and the like) to all the others, would impose its law, thereby creating symmetry between those taking part in the exchange. Every beneficiary of an exchange could become the producer of a good to be delivered for free. The chain of gifts and counter-gifts would organize a universe of production without friction (that of envious comparisons and exploitable differences in talent) and without monetarization—with the obvious exception of monetary investments in the initial purchase, upkeep, and replacement of the necessary equipment. This scenario would reinvent what has often been presented as the supreme love of art—that of the amateur practitioner finally rid of the delicate (and reputedly alienating) conversion of his creative act into a creation of value.

Thus, in this scenario, technologies and their convergences would have the quasi-magical property of simultaneously resolving the three aporias of cultural markets. First, they would increase and modify consumption by providing more complete information on artworks, thanks to unlimited sampling that would let consumers test all that might interest them before according their preference to a certain artist or artwork. Consumption would therefore cease to be influenced by the advertising that surrounds star artists, as the return on promotional marketing would have significantly decreased or become nonexistent. Second, the number of artists would rise, as production costs would fall continuously and creative practices would offer ever greater possibilities for recombining, mixing, collaging, and hybridizing the existing production—thereby lowering the cost of invention.[61] Technologies would thus have the capacity to reestablish a Gaussian distribution of abilities and reputations, since the intensely inegalitarian competition orchestrated by large firms would be replaced by slight variations around an average reputational value. Third, social well-being would increase, in that production and consumption would become more abundant and diverse, the cost of accessing artworks would diminish or become nil (and this for units of consumption that would be more easily dividable—a title rather than an album, thirty seconds of music for one's ringtone rather than an entire song, for example), and, logically, inequalities in success would be radically reduced just as reputational rents would die out.

The major firms would rapidly decline, and the star system with them. This is at once the vision of a community of independent entrepreneurial creators, and that of a community of strongly interconnected consumers exchanging just about everything among themselves. Better still, the barrier separating the consumer from the artist (as creator-producer who places his artworks into circulation) would be lowered to almost nothing. This is, in fact, precisely what Marx had imagined: a community of artists as creators, no longer made to compete by consumers' evaluative comparisons, because the disjunction between producer and consumer would gradually disappear.

In the *Manuscripts of 1844*, and later in his conceptualization of non-alienated labor in *Capital*, Marx postulated an essential link between the competitive organization of production and the valorization of talent. In his analysis, the division of labor is the main source of human alienation, notably because it causes the specialization of individual abilities that leads to mental mutilation. Instead, labor should be the means for each person to realize himself in the fullness of his individual essence, in accordance with an Aristotelian ideal in which Jon Elster sees the essence of Marxian communism.[62] According to Marx, it is the capitalist economy of exchange and production for consumption purposes that has turned labor into a commodity. As stated by Elster, "The alienation from the means of production is the crucial structural fact that underlies the alienation from the means of consumption, since it deprives the worker of his claim on the whole net product. Also, the dispossession from the means of production excludes the worker from full control of the work process and prevents him, therefore, from fully exercising his creative capacities."[63] Marx's project is to reach a point where labor ceases to be a simple means, a negative value, or mere energy expended to obtain the goods that provide satisfaction. In a good society (which, for Marx, is one that has successively moved beyond capitalism and socialism), labor will manifest itself in the fullness of its positivity as the instrument par excellence of individual well-being. What is the decisive condition for attaining this desirable society? It could be the neutralization of all mechanisms of interindividual competition, which prompt the selection of certain abilities, favor individuals with greater abilities than the average person, and set in motion a process of specialization of individuals and activities. The Marxian solution is even more simple and radical than this, though it is also anthropologically and socially illogical.

There is, indeed, a key postulate in Marx's scenario, which is that all individuals are equally endowed with similar abilities. Acknowledged and exploited inequalities in ability are, according to Marx, simply the product of the institutional structure of capitalist and precapitalist societies, and are in no way a natural fact. But how might this premise be reconciled with the power of individuation that is inherent in labor and released through free and creative labor in the process of self-fulfillment?

In the Marxian conception, every individual is endowed with a set of abilities that are sufficiently numerous and diverse for any form of division of labor—even one that allows for organized mobility among various jobs—to appear as a form of mutilation. It follows, then, that in order to consider these abilities as being evenly distributed among all members of a given society, one must accept that they exist as potential in every individual, but that the opportunities for actualizing them are not equally available. Moreover, this actualization must be allowed to take place over an indefinite time span. In other words, in the course of his social existence, an individual must encounter enough opportunities to actualize, one after another, the entirety of his abilities, and not limit their development to the initial training period wherein a precocious selection of certain abilities acts to the detriment of all the rest. Lastly, the exchange society composed of producers and consumers must be replaced by a community of creators in which the productive act manifests itself, following a typically Hegelian logic, as a never-ending process of learning and self-discovery. The rejection of the division of labor and the negation of differences in ability thus require an indefinite horizon of actualization of the qualities unique to each individual. As Luc Boltanski remarks:

> Marx's critique of the division of labor . . . is tied more fundamentally to his rejection, already expressed in *The German Ideology,* of difference in natural talents. The refusal to recognize any inequality of talents is inscribed in Marx in the framework of the relation he establishes between power and act. This relation is determined by his insistence on maintaining a radical uncertainty about the powers invested in persons: since these powers become apparent only when they are realized through acts, they are never completely revealed, because the possibility of acting is never foreclosed. Yet the division of labor, which rests on a differentiation and a hierarchization of competencies, implies predetermination and stabilization, which support the reciprocal expectations of persons established in different positions.[64]

Here, we are led to a temporality of activity that is peculiar in nature. An uncertain future and indeterminate individual abilities must exist simultaneously so that time may be replete with novel opportunities for the actualization of potentialities. These factors are also necessary to preclude individuals from knowing themselves or each other enough to speculate about the particular abilities they might possess, and to thereby activate all the mechanisms of interpersonal competition. In brief, the future is uncertain, but it does not generate uncertain situations—be this an uncertainty about the future states of the world, or a strategic uncertainty engendered by the behavior of others and its effects on the ego's decisions.

Gerald Cohen and Jon Elster have highlighted the logical inconsistencies in Marx's theory. Cohen distinguishes four sets of ideas: (1) a philosophical anthropology whereby "humans are essentially creative beings . . . most at home with themselves when they are developing and exercising their talents and powers"; (2) a theory of history, according to which "growth in productive power is the force underlying social change"; (3) an economic theory that attributes to every activity and product a value commensurate with the quantity of labor it requires (that is, muscular, neural, and cognitive energy expended), and that rejects the factors of scarcity and desire as ultimate determinants of value; (4) a vision of a future society that indicts capitalism foremost for crushing people's creative potentials, and that seeks a way to organize society so that "the free expression of the powers inside each person harmonizes with the free expression of the powers of all."[65] The logical inconsistencies in Marx's theory stem essentially from the tension between his philosophical anthropology and his economic theory.

Let us begin with an example. Referring to a painting as the classic embodiment of creative labor, Marx raises the following objection to his own theory of value: The value of a painting is measured more as a function of the intensity of demand for it than as a function of the quantity of labor congealed in it. However, Marx argues, this objection could be dispelled if society were organized based on relations other than those of market competition. To arrive at this, according to the hopes of Marxian eschatology, one would have to overcome the constraints of physical resource scarcity in a differently organized economy. The question then becomes: Do the scarcity and desirability of the qualities admired in a painting constitute residues from an outmoded social system, and hence anthropological values to be superseded? Here, we encounter one of the aporias in Marx's theory, which resides in the hypothesis that individuals might be able to realize themselves in creative activities without ever relating to others as models or counter-models, and without ever comparing themselves to their past or future selves—and this, in order to verify whether or not they have made progress, and to consider what might incite them to renounce a certain activity or choose a specialization in which they believe they will more readily realize themselves. But what can one learn and know about oneself without reference to others and to the different selves one embodies over the course of time? How can an individual realize himself in the fullness of his humanity if the latter is an abstraction indifferent both to the deployment of real differences between individuals and to the benefits that can be drawn from every interindividual exchange (as I have shown in Chapters 1 and 2)?

The Marxian solution amounts to inventing a sort of individualism that is both undifferentiated and indifferent to itself. Here, individuals must never be allowed to interact with each other, in order to avoid bringing to the surface differences, and along with them, situations of exchange and transaction based on the comparative advantages that each person could exploit by doing what the other would not do as well or as willingly. In short, the specialization and commodification of the productive act must be thoroughly prevented. Each worker-creator must be indifferent to any appreciation of the result of his labor by others, because this evaluation would unmistakably carry the seeds of hierarchical comparison—those of admiration, like those of envy. This clause, in fact, boils down to abolishing the strategic uncertainty introduced by both interindividual appreciation and rivalry. Yet intrinsic uncertainty would disappear as well: The possibility of failure would be erased, and every creative enterprise would be sure to end in success. Talent itself and differences in talent would then vanish, for there would no longer be any relative performances—more or less successful, more or less admirable—as each act of creative labor would fully attain its goal. As Marx writes, "Milton produced *Paradise Lost* for the same reason that a silk worm produces silk. It was an activity of *his* nature."[66] Herein lies a vision totally opposed to the most elementary determination of that which is fulfilling in creative activity—its obstacles, its difficulties, its surprises, its unexpected trajectory, the excitement of discovery, and the lessons to be learned from failure—as I have shown earlier in this chapter, and as I will again demonstrate in Chapter 6.

The Marxian vision leads to the ideal of a community of creators whose activity remains undisturbed by any competitive relationships. As Elster notes, such a model presupposes that the worker-creator does not expose the results of his labor to consumers, so as to deter the negative consequences of competition. This conception of well-being has as its horizon the establishment of a monadic society wherein each person can deploy his talents freely without fearing that they will be subjected to social demand—otherwise put, a society devoid of interactions and intersubjectivity. The need for self-identification and the necessity of relating to others, however, are the conditions that make possible the social organization of a community; the denial of these conditions constitutes a major weakness in Marx's philosophical anthropology. As Elster highlights, the search for recognition from others—even beyond market-based operations—is inevitable:

Marx conceived communism as a synthesis of capitalist and pre-capitalist societies, reconciling the individualism of the former and the communitarian character of the latter. Individual self-realization should take place in creative work for the sake of the community. Yet an extreme emphasis on creative self-realization comes into conflict with the value of community. If production is to be for the sake of the community, at least some of the members, at least some of the time, must indulge in the passive pleasures of consumption—of consuming the products that are the outcome of self-realization through work. The only form of community which is fully compatible with extreme emphasis on creation is the community of creators. A novelist might know that there is no reaction to expect from the public, but he might eagerly wait for the reaction of his fellow novelists. Science is one domain in which there are no customers, only colleagues. It is also a domain in which altruism takes second place to emulation, competition and self-assertion. In Hegel's phrase, it is *"das geistige Tierreich."* To some extent, this is unavoidable. Self-realization is closely linked to recognition by competent others.[67]

As I have discussed in Chapter 2, Rawls made a similar point when writing that certain "individuals display skills and abilities, and virtues of character and temperament, that attract our fancy and arouse in us the desire that we should be like them, and able to do the same things."[68] The Rawlsian argument is also an attempt to ward off the dangers of envious comparison, which can transform differences in ability for one activity or another into a devastating zero-sum game. Whereas Marx equalizes excellence by endowing every individual with the same abilities, Rawls transforms differences in ability into a collective good: "It is as if others [through their remarkable accomplishments] were bringing forth a part of ourselves that we have not been able to cultivate. We have had to devote ourselves to other things, to only a small part of what we might have done."[69]

It is worth comparing Rawls's argument with that of Ronald Dworkin.[70] According to Dworkin, talents (and handicaps) ought to figure among the resources that must be equalized in a socially desirable world—in other words, one that is fundamentally egalitarian. At the same time, basing his argument in the Aristotelian conception of the good life as the ideal of individual realization, Dworkin would like to define the "critical wellbeing" of each individual through a model of challenge. This model "holds that living a life is *itself* a performance that demands skill, that it is the most comprehensive and important challenge we face, and that our critical interests consist in the achievements, events, and experiences that mean that we have met the challenge well."[71] Here, each person is faced with circumstances (physical abilities, health, resources, life environment, language and culture, and so forth) that shape his evaluation of the challenge at hand: Some of these circumstances are limitations or obstacles, while others are parameters that help define his making of an ideal life. In his critical discussion of Dworkin's work,[72] Kwame Anthony Appiah raises the question of whether an individual's innate talents might intrinsically constitute the parameters that define his ideal life and lie beyond the reach of an equalizing framework, lest we abolish the individual's project of the good life as a challenge to be met. Equalization would, in effect, entail the redistributive transfer—via income taxation—of a more or less significant portion of the surplus earnings that exceptional talents bring to those who possess them. Alternatively, it would mean that talents constitute resources to be redistributed in such a fashion that no one manages to achieve the full expression of his abilities, thus preventing situations of comparative selection that give a cumulative advantage to the best; or, that the fiscal policy of redistribution acts as a considerable disincentive for all investments in training and professional projects that would favor the full development of individual excellence. Once again the key point is to determine whether interindividual differentiation and comparison enrich the collectivity or, rather, essentially engender a conflict of envious rivalry.

The history of the arts and their different modes of organization teach us that the fundamental values of creative activity—the qualities of invention and perfection, and the originality and individuality of creative labor—would neither exist nor have purpose without comparison among artists and artworks. Comparison renders possible the progression of creative labor, the training and self-training it requires, the attention it solicits from audiences, and the investments it demands. Success or failure in creation and invention cannot depend solely on the creator's personal assessment of the degree to which he has accomplished his work, independent of all reference to aesthetic judgments. Originality (or lack thereof) in individual invention, as well as the value of self-realization, can only have meaning in a world of interindividual comparison. It is the forms of competition that vary and characterize the historically changing sources of value formation.

In actuality, comparison and competition are inseparable from the dimension of uncertainty, which is the seat of creative activity. Competition certainly characterizes the system that organizes the transaction and determination of values and prices; however, we can just as assuredly say that competition structures uncertainty in interactions and in interdependencies with others (such as peers, personnel in a given professional world, audiences). This is the strategic dimension of uncertainty. The intrinsic dimension of uncertainty, by contrast, pertains to the process of creative activity itself. The fact that this activity is never certain to reach its end is precisely what renders creative labor so desirable. Intrinsic uncertainty is a necessary, if feared, condition: It is what renders artistic labor inventive, expressive, and nonroutine; however, it is also what makes artistic labor a constantly grueling challenge, always accommodating to trial and error—oriented toward completion, but without a clearly and readily definable end. In this sense, regimes of artistic invention are coupled with regimes for managing uncertainty, as I have been working to demonstrate throughout this book.

What is the value of the argument whereby each individual should be able to develop and utilize all of his faculties? If the Marxian solution were possible, it would resolve at once the twofold problem that lies at the heart of the critique of the division of labor. The development of productive forces through self-fulfillment in creative labor would increase labor productivity and accelerate the accumulation of wealth to be shared; at the same time, there would be a transfer of well-being from the satisfactions sought through consumption toward those obtained through labor, which would become the "primary need in life." Is this ideal any more plausible than that of creative labor without competition? The collectivity can only turn itself into a community of creators on two exorbitant conditions. The first is that each individual's desire for self-fulfillment must not hinder that of anyone else. As Elster notes, this would require freedom from all constraints for each individual to maximize his utility: a condition known as "the society of abundance," which constitutes a perfect image of utopia. The second condition is absolute indifference toward others. Can an individual be moved to create and experience the type of satisfaction offered by the practice of a creative activity if that activity is not put in relation with others? In this scenario, the individual would relate to another neither in actuality—by showing him the result of his activity, discussing it with him, or, *a fortiori*, exposing it to his judgment—nor in the abstract—through internal dialogue with an imaginary other. This is impossible, unless we are to consider creative activity as a pure and simple form of rudimentary, natural need for production—one that characterizes the labor of a silkworm occupied in producing its thread (recall the aforementioned comparison). If Marx were right, the quality of genius—defined by Kant as "the inborn predisposition of the mind *(ingenium)* through which nature gives the rule to art"—would have to be extended to every individual, by virtue of one's belonging to the nature of living species. But this, precisely, was not the Kantian position: He saw a difference in nature (a "specific difference") between those who are gifted for the fine arts and those who do nothing but imitate rather than invent.[73]

Ultimately, in order to abolish competition without eradicating the expressive and fulfilling value of creative labor, Marx must erase from his model the principle of uncertainty, attention from others, communication with others, and all other external constraints. Here, however, the creative act becomes a natural impulse: It no longer emanates from a socialized individual working to relate self-grounded invention to interindividual exchange (such as with peers or audiences) and cooperation with professional worlds.

Exploiting Uncertainty: Overproduction, Tournaments, and Careers

It would be easy to evaluate artists and their artworks and to perceive qualitative differences among them if the assessment were made in absolute terms, and if it entailed using an unequivocal scale of measurement and a stable set of unambiguous criteria to determine both the qualities of artists and the characteristics of their artworks. This, however, can never be the case. As I have already noted, the fundamental property of artistic activity is the unlimited differentiation of artistic goods and artists' qualities, which is driven by competition for originality. Thus, in contrast to a timed sports performance or the solving of a problem, aesthetic originality and artistic value can only be measured in relative terms.

But how does a relative measurement of quality operate? In order to respond, I must first recall the main characteristics of artistic careers that were uncovered in the preceding analyses. I will then lay out the procedures for managing uncertainty that have been conceived by cultural entrepreneurs—in particular, the solicitation of a great number of artists (an inflated number, given the chances for success). From these two starting points, the mechanism of selection and the dynamics of careers will be readily deduced.

First, the careers of artists (and artworks) unfold outside of the stable organizational structure provided by a firm that enters into a long-term contract with its employees—in which they are remunerated for the acts of labor that the firm imposes and seeks to control and whose productivity it aims to measure. On the contrary, an artist's career generally follows a trajectory of projects realized through a string of contractual transactions, and for which there exist none of the guarantees associated with ordinary wage labor.

Second, it is competition in a given market that determines the value of artists' accomplishments. It does so through the intensity of immediate preferential demand, and through a flow in demand that is linked to the durability of the artwork and to the interdependencies between the artworks that are successively produced over the course of an artist's career (since the success of one artwork can trigger enthusiasm for the artist's previous works, and bring heightened attention to those that follow). The quality of each artistic good supplied is uncertain: It is impossible to directly assess the abilities of artists and the value of artworks through skills measurements or standardized tests. Since it is impossible to assess performances or products in absolute terms, the rankings, remuneration schemes, and career advancement profiles must take the form of tournaments (competitive tournaments in music, recruitment through auditions, awarding of prizes, hit parade rankings, critics' evaluations and scorings, and such) in which evaluations are based on incessant comparison. Artists work to differentiate themselves from one another on multiple levels so as to make their mark in the competition. However, critics, art world professionals, market intermediaries (producers, employers, organizers, and agents), and consumers never cease their rankings. The cultural knowledge required to appreciate and assess artworks can be defined as the sum of significant comparisons an individual is capable of making, explicitly or implicitly, for the purpose of attributing meaning and value to an artwork. Thus, artworks initially juxtaposed through the law of originality become hierarchically ordered by audiences and art world professionals, through a series of competitive and comparative tests, according to their preferences and investments. What is called "talent" can be defined as the quality gradient attributed to the individual artist through these relative comparisons. The difficulty in defining talent rests, in that it is not an arbitrary value, but rather a purely differential quality.

Third, careers distribute artistic professionals according to a reputation hierarchy that is based on their past accomplishments.

Taken together, these three characteristics are reflected in the twofold, operational strategy of cultural entrepreneurs: the exploitation of uncertainty, which is a condition for entrepreneurial profit,[74] and the reduction of uncertainty. Very little is known about the ingredients for success. Uncertainty about the market potential of each artwork and innovation therefore pushes each firm to hedge its bets across a broad range of artists; this drives cultural industry entrepreneurs as a whole to feed, through a composition effect, a structural excess supply characterized by seasonal peaks and short-term fluctuations. For example, the literary seasons *(rentrées littéraires)* in France are accompanied by media statistics on the skyrocketing growth, year after year, in the number of published books contending for literary awards.[75] Yet, as soon as cultural entrepreneurs manage to identify an artist with "high potential," they set about overexposing him and activating the mechanisms of contagious imitation in the general public. They do this by exploiting the self-reinforcing dynamic that transforms an artist's success into both an effect and a cause of the quality attributed to him by consumers. They may then seek to "develop" the artist who has enjoyed his first successes, just as is done in research and development with scientific inventions or technical innovations. Thus, after having taken advantage of the uncertainty about who will emerge as winners by exploiting competition through differentiation, cultural entrepreneurs endeavor to reduce uncertainty about a promising artist's chances of future success by seeking to transform his instant value into a lasting one—a sure asset in which it is possible to invest.

Should the problem of artistic overproduction simply be regarded as the modern phenomenon of the industrialization of culture—or, as Charles Lalo put it, the Americanization of culture?[76] In fact, nearly every sociologist, economist, and historian who has ever studied artistic labor markets has underscored the excess supply of artists.[77] Each time, analysts have put forward a similar range of factors: increasing demand for art (stimulated by such factors as urbanization, rising educational and income levels, increasing leisure time, public subsidies); changes in the commercialization of art; and the impact of technological innovation on artistic production, distribution and consumption.

The argument of overproduction—which is often accompanied by lamentations over the devastating effects of Pareto's law—should thus be specified according to artistic discipline, market segment, and time period. Nevertheless, if overproduction is so frequently invoked as a disease caused by the industrialization of culture, it is because cultural industries are constantly organizing and reorganizing themselves in order to turn overproduction into an advanced technique for managing uncertainty and into a mechanism for increasing profitability. The wide range of influences exerted by cultural entrepreneurs over consumer choice and over the evaluation of competing artists is illustrated here with the greatest clarity.

In effect, the entire architecture of the cultural industries (music, book, cinema, and audiovisual production) has been built on organized relations between the production, distribution, promotion, and consumption of artistic goods and services—thereby generating competition through tournaments (hit parades) to identify profitable talents. The basic economic principles at work here are well known.[78] The form of competition in this sector is that of oligopolistic concentration. In the music industry, for example, a few big firms realize three-quarters of the worldwide turnover for the sector, and a nebula of so-called independent producers maintain relations of "co-opetition" with these major labels.[79] Concentration is explained by the cost structure: In the music and book industries, the cost of producing a good (the acquisition and payment of the raw material—creative labor) and the cost of material production are proportionately low and variable, whereas the costs of distribution and promotion are high and fixed (accounting for three-quarters of total costs). Industrial concentration is, consequently, motivated by economies of scale linked to the distribution and commercial exploitation of a raw material—artists' creativity—that can be obtained and controlled at low cost, even though its market value is difficult to predict.

The structure of competition reflects this way of proceeding. Large firms find it more profitable to let independent producers act as adventurous explorers—as risk-takers and fine connoisseurs of market niches and emerging trends—and to engage in cooperative competition with them, via the distribution of their products and financial participation in their capital. This is the classic figure of "oligopoly with a competitive fringe." Small firms devote most of their resources to scouting talents and to financing their own productions. The major firms, meanwhile, extract rent via the distribution of independent productions, buy up the contracts of independent producers with successful artists, develop the most promising careers, ally themselves with stars, and work on triggering and reinforcing the dynamics of success amplification through investments in advertising and promotion. The picture should, however, not be painted in such binary terms: The major firms themselves are in reality entire galaxies in which labels behave like autonomous centers of production and profit while also acting as talent scouts. Nonetheless, the distinction according to size continues to hold; it imparts its characteristics on the demographics of firm population, resulting in a high mortality rate for small firms, growth for more skillful or fortunate ones, buy-outs, mergers, and firm concentration. Furthermore, the pattern of concentration has changed: In continuity with past practice, vast multimedia groups have been formed that produce and distribute their own products along with those of other producers, and that control publishing companies (with copyrights protected for ever-longer periods of time). However, these groups currently have much greater control than before over radio and television stations and over commercial operation networks (for example, retail sales, on-line sales, and payable downloads), enabling them to directly activate the levers of success amplification.

Under conditions of flexible specialization, the number of independent producers grows, even as the rate of sector concentration increases. What is also on the rise, in fact, is the density of independent producers' interdependencies with both other firms and dominant companies.[80] Thus, the "openness" of the system of co-opetitive production explains why, despite the fact that the rate of oligopolistic concentration in the recording industry has increased since the early 1970s, rates of innovation and diversity in musical production (as calculated on the basis of hit parades) either remained stable or increased throughout the 1980s (depending on the indicator chosen).[81]

If we now consider careers and markets together, we see that there are two causes for the excess supply of artistic goods and candidates for an artistic career. First, the number of artists and the variety of artistic production increase faster than demand, because overproduction is a rational response of firms to an uncertain environment. Second, the organization of artistic production on a project-by-project basis, which helps minimize the fixed costs incurred by the schema of rational overproduction, relies heavily on temporary contractual relations with the diverse categories of professionals involved in key operations (from the creation to the distribution of artistic goods). One characteristic of this mode of organization is that it generates an excess supply of labor, available for any project that might solicit it.

How can one identify, from within this stream of candidates, the individuals who will make lasting careers in the artistic professions? The difficulties are many: Quality cannot be measured directly or in absolute terms; uncertainty reigns, surrounding the potential value of artists; essential qualities can only be revealed through a series of professional experiences; and it is difficult to assemble and update information on the characteristics of each individual artist in the context of competition through differentiation. The answer, in fact, lies in the mechanism of competition through relative comparison and evaluation tournaments, which is ubiquitous in art worlds for the ranking of artists and artworks.

What does a career modeled on a competitive tournament look like? According to James Rosenbaum,[82] the conditions required for implementing a tournament mechanism are as follows: (1) substantial interindividual differences, as these justify the fact that the most deserving win out over others; (2) imperfect information on individual abilities that prompts the need for repetitive competitions, in contrast to activities in which abilities seem unambiguously measurable; (3) the importance of past accomplishments, which influences the chances for success of current ones (in contrast to Rosenbaum's example of the door-to-door salesman, whose previous success rate will have no real influence on his chances of succeeding with his next customer); and (4) an efficient system for interpreting information on the past accomplishments of the individual under evaluation. These hypotheses derive from two simple observations. First, it is difficult or impossible to specify and directly measure the exact quantity and nature of the resources deployed by an individual (abilities, effort, acquired skills). Second, the value of the labor outcome can only be assessed through ordinal rankings. Both hypotheses correspond closely to the observations at hand.

If, for example, we postulate that there do indeed exist differences in ability and productivity among artists, then how can we characterize those differences? What do we know about these unevenly distributed abilities? The answer applies to the analysis of success not only in the arts, but also in sciences, sports, political action, and business. Certain qualities are measurable capacities (intellectual capacities, physical and psychological qualities) that function as necessary, readily detected conditions. This is especially the case when competition is oriented early in life by success in competitive tests at the primary, secondary, or university level—with the accompanying cumulative advantages offered by achieving speedy success in one's studies, attending the best institutions, and entering into contact with high-level teachers and students. Other qualities have been documented in biographical explorations: amount of work invested, tenacity,[83] fertility of the imagination, and aptitude for divergent thinking (which constitutes one of the wellsprings of creative invention). Also important is the capacity to concentrate on activities that stimulate one's interest to the point where intrinsic motivation effectively drives a quasi-obsessional behavior that combines the values of work and play.[84] The hierarchy of these qualities varies according to the nature of the activity under consideration. Superior endowment with the most important qualities in a specific sphere of activity provides candidates with the means for passing to the next stage of the competitive selection process. However, from this point onward, reasoning in terms of success factors is misleading because, beyond a certain threshold, the advantage gained from possessing a greater quantity of one or another of these qualities—for example, significantly greater intellectual capacities than one's competitors—no longer truly increases one's chances of achieving significant success in the activity in question. It is, of course, the combination of various types of qualities and capacities that matters, but there is no detectable formula for the exact dosage that might produce an optimal combination.[85] We simply know that the distribution of these qualities and their indecipherable combinations creates pronounced inequalities in chances of success, and that it is impossible to estimate these qualities *a priori;* hence, the recourse to practices of relative comparison.

It is now possible to provide a more complete explanation of why art worlds proceed by comparative rankings and processes of eliminatory selection. Competition for originality, the valorization of novelty as an emergent and unpredictable value, and the poor capacity to anticipate consumer preferences all contribute to defining the uncertainty surrounding the relative quality of artistic goods and artists. This uncertainty is revealed by the marked indeterminacy of the combination of qualities necessary to succeed in the competition.

In this context, artists' careers can be analyzed as a stochastic process:[86] Young artists are uncertain about the quality of their work, and their professional engagements constitute a series of evaluative tests (exhibitions, publications, performances, or concerts). If initial evaluations by peers, critics, and members of their reference group are favorable, they will choose to pursue the profession. Artists who achieve lesser or very little success in this first career phase are exposed to a mechanism of cumulative disadvantage. Whether artists remain in the profession with hopes of overcoming the negative effects of a mediocre debut depends on the resources available to them for managing career risks (such as multiple jobholding, unemployment benefits, entrepreneurial initiatives, public subsidies, and diversification of activities in order to acquire visibility), as well as on the value artists attribute to the nonmonetary rewards they obtain from their activity, as compared with alternative activities that may offer greater chances for success.

A cohort of artists who have simultaneously entered the market therefore includes a majority of individuals who earn a low income and obtain only modest success or rapidly encounter failure, and a minority of professionals who emerge successfully from the competition in the first career phase. Income inequalities reflect the composition effects of the artistic population, the growth of which is driven by two mechanisms. First, the number of entrants hoping to make a career in the arts increases faster than the proportion of those who are relegated and eliminated by the competition. Second, artists in a given cohort who choose to pursue their careers are made to compete with artists from prior cohorts; their position in the competition does not depend on their employment status, as in an organization with seniority and hierarchical positions, but instead on the estimated value of what they produce and on their chances of maintaining their position or raising their status in the reputation hierarchy.

Interestingly, this same analysis can be applied to the population of evaluators themselves. Let us examine how artistic critique operates. In order to identify and assess the work of artists in the early stages of their careers, art worlds rely on a very heterogeneous population of actors for which there is rapid turnover: candidates for a career in the field of artistic organization and information. These candidates integrate themselves into networks of art world professionals, and then research and process information on promising talents and emerging trends in artistic creation. In doing so, they engage in a combination of the following activities: journalistic reporting, informed chronicling of art venues, importation of information from abroad, dissemination of a constant flow of predictions by market professionals, and production of critical assessments.

At this stage, the activity of professionals and apprentice-professionals in the domain of artistic information and evaluation has little to do with sound expertise: It is practiced by a great variety of agents, who research and diffuse information that will fuel artistic competition—with all the aesthetic and financial stakes this involves. It is impossible to define the value of a young artist by the stream of monetary and symbolic gains that his work is expected to yield. The best approximate estimation of an artist's uncertain value is the sum of information on his work and personality that is shared among actors in the market and in cultural institutions. This information entails little expert evaluation, even for the most promising artists, simply because the categories of evaluation must be partially remodeled through contact with what may prove to be a significant innovation, whose impact as of yet remains unknown. Predictably, evaluative discourse at this stage is likely to amalgamate journalistic information, blurbs, various forms of critical judgment in the service of promotional advertising, as well as attempts at aesthetic analysis whose relevance can only be verified over the longer term.[87]

When an artist's visibility increases, it is easier to engage in qualitative comparison; the evaluation is more often performed by gatekeeper critics and tastemakers who, like the artists whom they debate and showcase, have completed the first stages of integration into professional art circles. They have greater cultural knowledge because their criteria of evaluation have been forged within a more homogeneous space of comparison. The expertise of art historians and critics specialized in contemporary artistic creation acts as a third degree of evaluation, giving greater comparative substance and credibility to the judgments made. In the field of contemporary art, competence is difficult to define because it is exercised without the benefit of hindsight. As Raymonde Moulin writes, this competence largely amounts to experience and acquired familiarity with the history of art from the past few decades, and to empathy with the spirit of the times. Mastering a great amount of information and constantly keeping oneself up to date is, in fact, what defines the "erudite" knowledge of the influential critic or contemporary art curator. Moreover, this information is continually increased and updated thanks to the multiplicity of positions occupied by evaluators who act, all at once or each in turn, as critics, theorists, exhibition commissioners, curators, foundation administrators—and this, at the intersection between the artistic universe of creation and the economic universe of the market.[88]

When viewed in instantaneous cross-section, the hierarchy of artist reputations appears to express substantial differences in quality, as revealed by a series of comparisons and competitions. However, as James Rosenbaum has underlined,[89] comparative rankings do not merely reveal unequally distributed qualities and then select individuals on that basis. These competitions cause divergences in contenders' career paths, despite the fact that their abilities may have been similar. The concentration of earnings and reputations on a very small number of individuals could therefore correspond to gaps in success that are far greater than the gaps in abilities known as talents. The signal emitted by winning a competition helps trigger the process of reputation accumulation. But does this accumulation correspond to an advantage in intrinsic quality, which would have become apparent and amplified? Or does the reputation of a famous artist create a positive bias in the perception of his relative qualities as compared with those of his competitors?

The selection and ranking mechanisms utilized in art worlds reveal how actors in these worlds behave when faced with uncertainty concerning the fundamental value of an artist or artistic good. However, they tell us nothing of the breadth of differences in quality that underlie differences in earnings. This point has intrigued sociologists and economists alike. What exactly produces Pareto-type inequalities for a population of artists or scientists (the two most-studied populations in connection with this question), as well as the colossal earnings of stars? The analysis can take one of two different directions. On the one hand, we can suppose that inequalities are triggered by intrinsic differences in talent among artists or scientists engaged in competing careers—while also specifying the paradox that these gaps in talent are of indeterminate breadth, since we do not know how to measure these qualities directly, but only how to compare and rank them relative to each other. On the other hand, we can suppose that difference in talent is one hypothesis among many, and that considerable differences in individual trajectories can occur even in the absence of talent gaps: This is the Mertonian model of cumulative advantage. Examining each in turn, I will show that these two analytical approaches are not wholly incompatible, but can, in fact, intersect.

An Explanation for Inequalities in Success: Sherwin Rosen's Superstar Model

Remuneration for creative labor varies foremost according to the sensitivity of demand to differences in quality among artists; this is true whether income is obtained through a contractual relation based on the duration of the work performed and the reputation of the artist, from the sale of an artwork, or via an influx of copyright fees. This elasticity of demand for quality is reflected in the price that a consumer is willing to pay for a certain level of quality in artworks or performances, or for a wide and diversified range of artistic goods (when the unit price is fixed). The consumer's decisions will depend on the weight of cultural expenses in his budget and on his usage of art—either as a simple source of gratification, or in the case of unique artworks and collectible goods, as a store of value equivalent to a financial asset.

An essentialist conception of talent or genius would hold that gaps in material and symbolic recognition in the arts and sciences are due to proportional differences in ability. It would also postulate that the community of peers (in the sciences) and that of different audiences (in the arts)—even when imperfectly informed or poorly cultured—will sooner or later recognize the evidence of talent, thereby establishing a universal foundation for differences in value and value judgments. If this were indeed the case, the factorial breakdown of earnings inequalities would capture the determinant influence of abilities presumed to be very unevenly distributed among individuals. Yet this is precisely what wage equations fail to do, as I noted above. We must, therefore, find a different explanation.

The model Sherwin Rosen proposes is based on two assumptions: It posits that there do indeed exist differences in talent, and that demand is sensitive to those differences. His explanation thus comes close to the essentialist conception just described, which presents talent as an exogenous factor. However, Rosen's model also differs from this conception in that it shows how differences in artists' remuneration levels can be disproportionate to differences in talent among artists. This analysis is featured in a frequently cited article,[90] in which Rosen examines the phenomenon of superstars in the arts, sports, and liberal professions. In these sectors of activity, there typically exist "star jobs" whose principal characteristic is to make perceived talent appear to be a rare and coveted quality. Rosen's initial distinction is simple:

> Some tasks are so routine and so circumscribed by existing practice that nearly any competent person achieves about the same outcome. Others are more difficult, more uncertain, and, this being so, allow greater possibilities for alternative courses of action and decision. Such tasks offer greater scope for superior talent to stand out and make its mark. More capable physicians spend smaller fractions of their time on routine cases and larger fractions on difficult ones than do physicians of more modest ability.[91]

In these professions, goods and services are highly differentiated, expertise and originality are considerably valued, and perceived differences in quality have decisive importance in orienting consumer preferences. At a given price for a good or service, the utility to a consumer will be greater if he chooses the professional who is considered to be the most talented. For example, a surgeon whose ability to save lives is 10 percent greater than that of his colleagues can attract a very significant demand. His fees will exceed those of his colleagues by far more than 10 percent, and his total earnings will be much greater than the gap in quality that distinguishes him from his colleagues. The most talented professionals are thus in a position to reap the joint benefits of charging a higher price for their services and of increasing their level of activity in response to a strong demand—provided they find a means to satisfy the growing demand without lowering the quality of the goods or services they offer (as compared with their competitors). According to this model, the difference in the quality of a given service holds an intrinsic value, and can thus be detected without bias.

In the case of artistic goods, the mechanism that causes earnings to be concentrated in the hands of a professional elite is, of course, also activated by consumer perception of differences in quality. This perception orients demand toward the artists who are considered to be the most talented. When the artistic good in question is nonreproducible (such as a painting), or when the performance can only be presented "live" over an incompressible duration (such as a musical or theatrical performance), the artist who has won the public's favor will see an increase in demand for his labor. This is the case, provided that he has chosen a discipline that sparks stronger interest (for example, the piano or the violin over the double bass), and that he bases his activities in a major urban center wherein potential demand is high. Both the considerable development of information systems and the ease of travel enlarge artists' potential market to global proportions: The worldwide demand for fine arts and for interpretations of opera or instrumental classical music is concentrated on a small number of artists whose reputations and careers benefit from significant lever effects.

When the artistic good is reproducible (a book, CD, film, video, for example), both the artist and the firm will have the capacity to serve far greater markets simultaneously. Highly reputed artists make intensive use of joint consumption technology. By resorting to traditional means of audiovisual distribution and physical duplication of goods, and by taking advantage of the cascade of innovations that have resulted from signal digitization and from the development of networks (of all sizes) for the instantaneous sales and exchange of digital content, artists can rapidly serve the global market.

> The superstar is someone whose audience is enormous relative to the scale on which most of us operate. Personal markets of that magnitude are almost exclusively sustained by use of media as a cooperating resource. These markets represent technologies that, in effect, allow a person to clone himself at little cost. More precisely, costs do not increase nearly in proportion to market

size; . . . Once an author delivers a manuscript to a publisher, it can be duplicated at small expense practically indefinitely. A television or radio program
is communicated virtually costlessly and identically to whomever happens
to tune in. The performer or author puts out more or less the same effort
whether one thousand or one million people show up to listen to the concert or buy the book.[92]

Another essential element in Rosen's model is talent's capacity to attract
demand. While a surgeon's talent can be gauged by objective criteria, the
quality of artistic goods and services effectively represents a form of subjective utility. The difference in quality that yields greater subjective utility
is, in fact, precisely what the public is looking for in the arts. In order to
understand why artists compete with each other, we must make the hypothesis that differences in quality play a fundamental role in orienting
consumer preferences. This is because, as in the case of the expert surgeon
who saves more lives than his colleagues (though with less dramatic consequences), an artist deemed superior is much more desirable than an artist of inferior quality—even for consumers who are not subjected to any
kind of influence. Two concerts, exhibitions, or films of moderate quality
do not give a consumer as much satisfaction as one high-quality concert,
exhibition, or film. The comparative advantage of a quality perceived as
superior is powerful enough to trigger a concentration of demand, and
with it, fame and fortune for those artists reputed to have the greatest
talent.

But how much greater must talent be for it to attract demand? Referring
to classical musicians, Rosen notes: "Interestingly, income differences between first-rank and second-rank performers are substantial, even though,
in a blind hearing, an infinitesimal portion of the audience could detect
more than minor differences among them."[93] His model does not merely
affirm that returns on talent are multiplied by the various tools for enlarging markets—that is, media and communications technologies, the spatial
mobility of professionals and consumers, and the globalization of exchanges
and elite careers. What Rosen also claims, and seeks to explain, is that even
minimal differences in talent among professionals can suffice to concentrate
a more-than-proportionate increase in demand on those deemed (either
slightly or significantly) more talented, and to win them a reputation and
work opportunities that will greatly reinforce (in the short or long term) their
position in the competition.

The same argument can be found in the now-classic work by sociologist
William Goode, *The Celebration of Heroes*,[94] published a few years before
Rosen's article:

Though there are only a few who are outstanding at the upper levels of performance, in activities where competition is keen the highest achievements are usually close in rank. In sports, where quantitative measurement is taken for granted, the winning racer can be separated from the next man by a few tenths or even hundredths of a second. Only a handful of people can distinguish the minute differences in excellence that separate the ten, or more likely eighty, finest concert pianists in the world. Indeed, in perhaps most fields, including ditch digging, the most astute critics might argue that there is no "top" man or woman but rather a handful of first-rate people, each distinguished from the other by complex differences in quality rather than simple degrees of excellence. Although the differences in excellence among the top performers are small, the disparity in acclaim is large between a few leaders and those very close to them in accomplishment; or between the "winner" and those who fall short by microscopic differences. The most creative of scientists knows that at any given time the new idea that he or she is entertaining may well be approaching fruition in another person, perhaps as yet unknown.[95]

Rosen's argument offers a convincing explanation of the considerable market power held by highly reputed artists—a power they can use to exploit their fame on a large scale, and to gain income that is completely disproportionate to the gap in quality separating them from their slightly less famous competitors. However, like Goode, Rosen ignores one of the fundamental characteristics of the functioning of art markets: uncertainty about quality. There is, in fact, something enigmatic about Rosen's model.[96] He postulates, on the one hand, that differences in quality among artists and artworks are real and perceptible, and that the qualitative superiority of certain artists is exogenous to the competition and not—as constructionist hypotheses would suggest—purely fabricated (for example, by markets and their entrepreneurs, a coalition of interests, and the like). It is on this exogenous factor that the individual preferences of consumers converge. Likewise, consumer preferences constitute exogenous characteristics: They are fixed and independent from one another. The hypothesis follows that the consumer can perceive the gap in quality clearly enough to be in a position to choose unambiguously and obtain greater satisfaction from what he considers to be the better choice.

On the other hand, Rosen admits that qualitative differences can be minimal, or virtually negligible, to the extent that only a few people can perceive them. If such is the case, then the question is raised: How can these differences be perceived at all? And how can these differences acquire such power that they can orient consumer choices and cause artists' success trajectories to diverge, even when those artists' qualities may, hypothetically, have been very similar? In order for talent to constitute a fixed exogenous factor and offer a solid advantage in the competition, consumers must be able to recognize talent by exercising their judgment—provided they are the ultimate and sovereign deciders of that which suits their preferences.

Rosen and Goode invoke the "infinitesimal portion of the audience" and the "handful of people" that are capable of detecting minute differences in quality. These experts operate in situations that seem to constitute crucial tests of judgment—for example, blind listening in which the listener is deprived of the information provided by the name and reputation of the artist. Though they are only a handful, some individuals are thus capable of distinguishing superior quality without fail: They must be more cultured and sensitive to such differences than the lay audience, especially when evaluative assessment requires, as we may readily imagine, strong aesthetic expertise. But is this hypothesis really so obvious? For example, are strong aesthetic competencies in contemporary art (supposing these are easily definable) sufficient for discerning the promising talent of a young painter? The diverging opinions of critics and the antinomies of evaluation that I have established earlier remind us that expert judgment manifests itself not only in individuals who are endowed with uncommon acuity, or in those who are trained to conduct evaluations. Opinions are also the product of multiple exchanges, experimentations, and confrontations of ideas.

Moreover, the postulate that there exists a core of experts who are fine connoisseurs of talent suggests that the latter is attributed not solely by a population of consumers who freely and independently exercise their sovereign judgment; talent, rather, can be attributed by certain individuals and then ratified by others. Accordingly, the amplification of an artist's reputation is the result of a social process—that is, a mechanism for the diffusion of evaluations conducted by expert consumers or credible professionals. Such diffusion may manifest itself as a gradual widening of the circle in which talent is recognized: from the kernel of peers to critics, art dealers, informed consumers, collectors, and, ultimately, lay audiences for whom the information provided and certified by experts constitutes a sufficient and reliable quality signal.[97] Yet social influence over individual judgment and preferences may take other forms. As Françoise Benhamou writes: "The star-system collapses the stages [of increasing recognition] described by Alan Bowness and Raymond Boudon by reducing their duration; the media then intervene to consolidate or even short-circuit the effects of recognition [by peers, critics and informed audiences]."[98] In that case, all sorts of techniques for influencing consumers can be devised and implemented: advertising, spontaneous or orchestrated word-of-mouth (buzz), the emission of signals through various rankings, and so on. What remains, then, of talent's exogenous reality as the seat of convergence of evaluations? This question must now be examined.

Talent and Social Influence

Consumers are sensitive to differences in quality among artists. But how is their perception of difference—even a minimal one—actually formed? Does it derive from direct experience, from evaluations by critics and trendsetters, from informal assessments shared within social circles (by word-of-mouth), from imitative contagion, or else from information and persuasive pitches generated by cultural industries? Or are consumers' perceptions of differences in quality formed through varying combinations of these different sources?

According to the efficient market hypothesis, the reputation of artworks and artists is founded on the perception that actors in art worlds have of qualitative differences: Measurements of the fundamental value of artworks and artists are based on the totality of the relevant information exploited by professionals and consumer audiences alike. In a world of perfect competition, the lay consumer or professional evaluator would render independent judgments and have access to complete information on the entire set of artworks of possible interest to him.

The cost of obtaining complete information in order to exercise an independent choice and express an intrinsic preference is exorbitant, and this is for two interrelated reasons. First, consumers are confronted with a universe of unlimited variety in artistic production, just as entrepreneurs and professionals are faced with a vast population of artists who compete for originality through the diversification of their qualities; the different parties can thus focus only on a very limited fraction of artworks and artists. No selection system can equitably process the multitude of artworks contending for assessment, or demand that those who experience such works possess complete knowledge of all that is being compared in order to form their evaluation. Second, artistic goods are paradigmatic examples of experiential goods. The direct evaluation of artworks and performances is impossible without each person having had the experience of listening, viewing, and reading them before rendering a judgment. Even when the consumer resorts to various forms of sampling and zapping (which are widespread in cultural markets today), he merely obtains surrogate experiences with limited informative value.

Consumer knowledge, then, is often highly imperfect. If the consumer seeks out high-quality information, he must ensure that the costs of his pursuit are proportionate to the value of the good or service considered and to the flow of satisfaction he expects to achieve. If the information is too costly or impossible to obtain, the consumer can purchase the good or service, proceed to experience it directly, and then draw conclusions (in a sort of learning process) concerning his future spending decisions.[99] The search for information will be more limited for the selection of a performance or film than for the purchase of a durable cultural good whose potential for disappointment is greater—to echo Albert Hirschman's nuanced analysis of consumption goods in general.[100]

One way of accounting for differences in success among artists is to interpret these differences as the result of how consumers handle the search for information, and especially of whether or not they adopt mimetic behavior. The argument runs as follows: A consumer wants to choose a live performance, a book, a film, or an exhibition. He is faced with artists, artworks, or performances about which he knows nothing, or very little. One of the least costly methods for acquiring information is to observe the behavior of other consumers. For the consumer, choosing artists or performances that are already the preferred choices of others spectacularly reduces the costs of his search, assuming he interprets the expression of those preferences as a signal of probable quality.

The process of obtaining information on the underlying, unknown quality of goods through the observation of others' consumption behavior lends itself to a particular modeling of success phenomena: The probability that a new cultural goods consumer will choose an artist is proportionate to the number of consumers who are already familiar with this artist, buy his artworks, discuss him, and await his forthcoming works. Kee Chung and Raymond Cox studied the probability for artists to receive a gold record award in the United States from 1958 to 1989.[101] They modeled the consumption dynamics as a sequential purchasing process: "Suppose that each consumer buys the same number of records . . . and that the records are bought in the following order: All consumers first buy sequentially one record each. After the last consumer has bought her first record, the process repeats itself with the second record, and so on."[102] The choice of a record in each period obeys two hypotheses: (1) The probability that an additional consumer will buy a given record is a function proportional to the number of buyers who have already chosen it; and (2) the probability that the additional consumer will choose a different record is low and constant. The authors indicate that because the observed distribution of gold record awards coincides with the distribution of the stochastic process they modeled, the superstar phenomenon is simply a probabilistic mechanism predicting that artistic and financial success will be concentrated on a few lucky individuals. There is no need, they claim, to bring into consideration any difference in talent: An initial event suffices to trigger consumers' choice of a particular artist and to engender a phenomenon of contagion. But what is the nature of this initial event? Chung and Cox's model presents a purely probabilistic hypothesis: "If there were a slight majority of consumers that select an artist as their choice, that artist would snowball into a star because after each period the majority would increase."[103]

In a compelling experimental study, Matthew Salganik, Peter Dodds, and Duncan Watts[104] asked 14,000 Internet users to rank unknown songs by unknown bands according to their degree of preference (on a scale of 1 to 5). Participants were randomly distributed into two groups. The first group was asked to listen to forty-eight songs presented on a list that was ordered randomly for each listener. Each participant had to decide in which order to listen to the songs, on the sole basis of the name of the bands; after listening, he had to assign a quality rating to each song, and was offered the opportunity to download it—which he accepted or declined. The experiment revealed how the intrinsic characteristics of songs constitute the object of listeners' preference judgments; it thus provided a natural measure of the quality of songs based on their ranking (which is equivalent to their market share).

The second group of listeners was randomly broken down into eight subgroups acting independently of each other. The individuals in each subgroup were given a list of the same forty-eight songs (randomly ordered) and were asked to listen to and rank them, as in the first protocol. However, each Internet user in these eight subgroups was given an additional piece of information: Before submitting his evaluation, each individual was told how many times a song had been downloaded by the previous listeners in his subgroup—which constituted a weak but real signal informing the listener about others' preferences. This second protocol revealed the effect of social influence, brought about by obtaining information concerning the choices of others.

In a variant of this second protocol, the list of songs with their download counts was no longer ordered randomly, but presented in descending order of popularity (by the number of downloads); this arrangement increased the impact of the information signal on the songs' popularity at the moment the listener made his choices and evaluations. The comparison between the two protocols revealed that differences in perceived quality between songs (measured by the ratings assigned to them) are always greater when the listener's choice is informed by that of others, than when it is made independently. In other words, well-rated songs are significantly more popular, and poorly rated ones are far less so. Measured inequality in quality was even higher in the variant protocol, wherein information about the choice of other listeners was presented as a list ordered by song popularity (the equivalent of a hit parade).

Another important result of this study concerns the uncertainty of success. If we compare the popularity ratings of the songs, as attributed by each of the randomly constituted listener groups, we observe marked differences in ranking from one group to another; this, in spite of the songs being identical, and presented under the same conditions to groups of Internet users formed at random, and thus free of any identifiable differences. Moreover, unpredictability is stronger when choice is influenced by the knowledge of other listeners' choices, and it increases when the information is structured according to the format of the hit parade. A same song, of a given quality, thus obtains very different ratings from one group to another: "This type of unpredictability is inherent to the process and cannot be eliminated simply by knowing more about the songs or market participants."[105]

These results confirm the validity of some of the informational cascade models:

> On the one hand, the more information participants have regarding the decisions of others, the greater agreement they will seem to display regarding their musical preferences; thus, the characteristics of success will seem predictable in retrospect. On the other hand, looking across different realizations of the same process, we see that as social influence increases, . . . which particular products turn out to be regarded as good or bad becomes increasingly unpredictable. . . .[106]

The public information a consumer obtains from observing the behavior of others is a decidedly inexpensive signal, but it is also quite thin as compared with the private information provided by a consumer's detailed knowledge concerning an artist, genre, style, or artistic domain. The low cost of public information explains its strong potential for propagation, but its poor informational content is also what renders it fragile. Strong enthusiasm can be triggered by a simple piece of information on sales for a book or CD or on a film's box office receipts—a reaction that can be orchestrated, of course, by those who make predictions on a film's success. But the thinness of information on the value of a good renders it vulnerable to even minimal shocks, when consumers begin exchanging opinions and acquiring additional information. Word-of-mouth may elicit a flow of private evaluations that thwart the contagion process and reverse the dynamic toward snowballing discontent. Both success and sudden drops in esteem result from a process of imitative contagion, or informational cascade; their robustness, however, increases as individuals obtain more substantial information.[107]

The imitation of others' behavior must not be construed as a form of passivity or non-choice associated with incompetence. The following dichotomy would be overly simplistic: On the one hand, the informed consumer bequeathed with substantial cultural and monetary resources, who makes choices informed by full background knowledge and moves about easily in the universe of the most sophisticated goods, obtaining an optimal return on his investments; and, on the other, the consumer with low cultural and economic capital, who orients himself exclusively toward cultural domains that require little knowledge, and makes choices by adopting elementary herding behavior. In fact, such herding behavior also affects the most sophisticated universes of artistic consumption. Snobbery has long designated the disparity between aesthetic competence, which would seem to sustain the cultural choices of an individual, and the dynamics of interdependent preferences that unleash contagion in the more rarefied universe of the happy few.[108]

In reality, imitative contagion is rational in that it maximizes opportunities for exchanging opinions and information about artworks. And one of the essential features of aesthetic consumption lies in the dynamic of learning and exchange. The aesthetic satisfaction derived from reading a book or having a cultural experience is greater for those who can turn these activities into a topic of conversation. The benefit lies in what is called network effects or externalities: The value of an artwork also depends on the number of individuals who show an interest in it, and who can discuss it amongst themselves. One need only segment the consumer population according to the appropriate variables (such as social position, cultural capital, social capital) to render this mechanism of preference interdependence more realistic, and to grant it the capacity to yield social capital. In order to obtain or transmit information and exchange ideas with others, the consumer turns primarily to his reference group or circle of peers. Competitive differentiation between social groups—which sociology has long analyzed, from Simmel's analyses of fashion, to Tarde's and Simmel's works on imitation, all the way to Bourdieu's theoretical generalization of the same notion[109]—explains why consumers of symbolic goods can distinguish themselves by perpetually selecting new consumption goods and styles, about which they exchange and obtain information within their circle of peers.

The search for information via the observation of others, the exchange of opinions, and the delegation of judgment to evaluation professionals does not mean that consumption is solely guided by a quest for quality signals. In his contribution to the economic analysis of success and stardom from the perspective of consumer behavior,[110] Moshe Adler views the act of artistic consumption as both of the following: (1) a combination of direct personal experience and socialization of that experience through discussion with others; and (2) a learning process in which consumers are driven to deepen their knowledge of certain artworks, domains, and artists. Artistic consumption is also known to display the characteristics of addiction, with its increasing marginal utility that runs counter to the standard laws of ordinary goods consumption.[111] The pleasure the consumer obtains from engaging with artworks increases with the intensity of his consumption, for he accumulates knowledge that will offer him ever more refined pleasures and expand both his range of choices and his capacity to discriminate between the artworks available to him. The great diversity of artists' qualities, artworks, and artistic performances provides him with a boundless field of exploration, in which he may progress by increasing his ability to derive a growing variety of pleasures from what he consumes.[112] The aesthetic satisfaction the consumer seeks to obtain from an artist obeys the law of diminishing marginal utility: Though he may want to follow—novel upon novel—the work of a novelist he likes, he will grow weary of reading only one novelist.[113] Nevertheless, his investment in an artistic domain can rapidly take different directions and expand to encompass new artists, causing the return on addictive cultural investment to marginally increase. Depending on the extent and depth of his cultural knowledge, a consumer will thus tend to connect with discussion and exchange partners who at least match his profile. Through these exchanges with others, he will be able to benefit from experiences and knowledge that are complementary to his own.

Cultural goods seem to be exchange goods par excellence: Their characteristics are revealed in social exchanges, and their evaluation involves mechanisms of social influence by which they are consumed and judged at once privately and collectively.[114] From this, we can deduce a sociological interpretation that presents the penchant for rankings as compatible with the desire to freely exercise one's individual judgment. How can we define the point of convergence of the experiences about which consumers converse? The accumulation of knowledge contained in the addictive value of artistic consumption allows for the development of a preference group centered on famous artists: It is those artists who provoke the most frequent or most balanced exchanges among consumers. Excessive taste dispersion across an overly high number of artists would destroy the benefits associated with the exchange of information and the confrontation of opinions on a given artist or artwork. Conversely, an excessive concentration of admiration and enthusiasm on a handful of artists would exhaust the desire for a variety of experiences, which is one of the sources for the learning value contained in the discovery of novelty.

In light of this, it is possible to establish a gradation of consumer behavior. At one end of the spectrum is the consumer who lacks direct information on the presumed value of the good offered to him, and who allows himself to be guided by the choices of others in a process of weakly informative mimesis. At the other extremity is the expert consumer who invests in the knowledge of artistic production (for example, a given artist, period, genre, and so on) and exchanges with other cultured individuals. In between is a wide range of intermediary situations, as well as the variability of behaviors adopted by a single consumer.

Consumers express preferences that are situated within the following triangle of forces: (1) They take advantage of an extremely varied supply; (2) they reduce the variety of supply by extracting information from others' behavior and engaging in interindividual exchanges; (3) they convert experiences into investments that structure their field of choices. In this analytical scheme, the chances for success of artists and artworks generally follow what statisticians call a power law. The latter describes the stochastic processes that explain why the rich get richer, why city size distribution creates widening gaps that favor heavily populated areas, or why, in the scientific literature, one-fifth of articles account for four-fifths of all citations. In cultural markets, the power law follows a Yule distribution: The probability that an artist will be known and chosen by a new cultural goods consumer is proportional to the number of consumers who are already familiar with him, buy his artworks, discuss him, and await his forthcoming works. This process explains the formation of stable reputations, as well as the cyclical movements sparked by the waxing and waning of fads and fashions.

The Manufacturing of Talent and Success: High Culture versus Industrial Culture

The above analysis can be summed up as follows: If we treat difference in talent among artists as an exogenous datum, and if we view this difference as an essential determinant of differences in income and recognition, then it is logical to assume that the value of an artist's talent will be a function of the intensity of the demand for that artist. It is, however, more interesting to suppose that even a minimal difference in talent can suffice to generate enormous differences in rewards. This hypothesis has led me to investigate the extent to which the sensitivity of demand to quality may be formed otherwise than via each consumer's independent judgment of what he sees, reads, and hears. Might interindividual imitation and the contagion of preferences be signs that the sovereign consumer has abdicated—surrendered his own power of judgment—to the benefit of market intermediaries or experts capable of exerting unlimited influence on him? In fact, highlighting the indissociably private and collective aspects of artistic consumption, as well as the judgments that sustain it, allows us to rule out the dual abstraction of the sovereign rational consumer, on the one hand, and the passive and wholly influenced consumer, on the other.

One might ask, however, whether this reasoning can be applied indiscriminately to all the different arts, as well as to the two commonly distinguished spheres of high culture and mass culture. Is it not the case that the consumer of high culture is more sovereign than the (more common) consumer of popular culture? Is talent not manufactured for the latter, while the former actively seeks to detect it? And is it not possible to reduce or control uncertainty about quality—which is, nonetheless, a necessary condition of competition for originality?

When it comes to the question of talent, analyzing the amplification process of differences in quality that can initially be very slight constantly runs the risk of erasing the core argument of uncertainty about quality and success. This occurs in two opposite ways. On the one hand, the analysis can postulate that underlying, intrinsic differences in talent are easily perceived by the lay consumer, or, at the very least, by the expert consumer. On the other hand, it can assume that talent is a pure and simple social and commercial construction—the name given to the production and exploitation of profitable novelty by the industrial engineering of creativity.

Highlighting the mechanisms of social influence, as I have done above, does not automatically lead to erasing the dimension of uncertainty. In fact, the social influence exerted on consumer choices most often occurs through multiple channels: interindividual exchange within peer groups (word-of-mouth), fan activism, buzz, and the attention paid to the evaluations of critics and the prescriptions of tastemakers. Uncertainty is preserved when the sources that trigger a process of contagion are multiple, and when choices differ from one group to another in a random fashion.[115] This is precisely what Salganik, Dodds, and Watts indicate in the conclusion they draw from their experimental study:

We conjecture . . . that experts fail to predict success not because they are incompetent judges or misinformed about the preferences of others, but because when individual decisions are subject to social influence, markets do not simply aggregate pre-existing individual preferences. In such a world, there are inherent limits on the predictability of outcomes, irrespective of how much skill or information one has.[116]

The argument of social influence, however, can also be inverted, thus weakening the role of uncertainty. The quality attributed to the winners of the competition can be presented as the result of market strategies for constructing value and exploiting the oversupply of talented individuals crowding the competition. Talent then becomes a label through which the creativity industry signals the originality of the artists it fashions and promotes.

The Frankfurt School's inaugural research on cultural industries engaged in this type of critical analysis, attributing to entrepreneurs and markets the capacity to format cultural products and build success from scratch.[117] They applied this analysis to popular artistic genres, whose appreciation requires lower cultural investment. In this sector, markets are larger, exploitation cycles for artworks are shorter, and fashions change more rapidly. Moreover, competition is fiercer because it involves a higher number of artists in each of the popular genres, and because economic interests tied to market success engender a multitude of practices aimed at influencing preferences and choices. It is tempting, in view of this, to discard the hypothesis of intrinsic differences in talent, and to postulate instead the ingenious efficacy of cultural entrepreneurs as well as the weak resistance of audiences to the persuasion of advertising.

But why assume that this reduction in artists' inventiveness and in their publics' capacities for judgment is limited to the sphere of mass cultural markets? A social ontology that upholds talent in the world of high culture while denying its existence in the world of popular culture would seem to follow the all-too-common interpretive drift that opposes high art to popular art. According to this interpretation, high art is filled with the meaning of freely conceived artistic projects, just as its public is endowed with competencies and aptitudes for aesthetic judgment; by contrast, popular art lacks artistic substance, just as the lower classes that consume it are deprived of the capacity for such judgment.[118]

What is entailed in this standard division of the world of artistic creation into two hemispheres with diametrically opposed characteristics? In the domain of high culture, artistic production is understood to occur essentially *prior to* a demand that develops gradually. The structural gap between supply and demand reinforces the power of expert evaluators (such as critics, professionals, historians, curators), while competition generates selection procedures that are presumably sheltered from the corrupting effects of social and market influence (for example, the manipulation of juries and awards, direct or indirect control over critical judgments, artificially created fads). In an economy marked by the slow accumulation of reputation and the determination of artworks' value based on their staying power, meritocratic competition always prevails over maneuverings to achieve fame. Initially low public demand for high art grows as the time needed for an artist or artwork to attain consecration increases; this process follows a success equation which is the reverse of that prevailing in so-called popular artistic creation. Originally concentrated on a minuscule number of artists who have managed to endure, reputation diffuses out as the circles of recognition become increasingly wider.

Moreover, artistic production in this field resembles a simple organizational model, one in which the autonomy of the creative act is best understood as preceding—and hence as protected from—deliberate attempts at influencing the very nature of artistic invention. This rests upon the assumption that, from the stage of invention all the way to those of commercialization and evaluation, creative labor is inserted into a chain of successive interventions by professionals who play the different roles assigned to them in the division of labor (for example, publisher, proofreader, printer, distributor, bookseller, or critic). These professionals conduct their interventions without submitting the core of the activity—the content of creation—to negotiations or to an instability that the artist would be unable to control.

This autonomy—or relative autonomy—of creative activity is one of the characteristics traditionally associated with the sphere of high art production.[119] It should be understood, in fact, as an organizational characteristic. Such autonomy provides information on the degree of control the artist seeks to exercise over his production, but it does not indicate that creative labor is an activity masterfully removed from the network of interactions that render this activity possible and sustainable. This is precisely the lesson learned from the analysis of the interactions between the artist and his environment, as formulated in Howard Becker's theory of art worlds.

For their part, the various types of so-called popular artistic creations (popular novels, commercial music, Broadway shows, comedy theater, television dramas, and such) are said to compete essentially for rapid and brief success. Their mode of economic existence presupposes that consumers are immediately responsible for the destiny of artworks and the evolution of production. The fierce competition between firms and the rate of obsolescence of artworks require producers to exploit the signals of consumer preferences very rapidly.[120] The various procedures for measuring success provide professionals with ongoing information that guides their promotion and investment decisions concerning the artistic careers they will endorse or dismiss; these procedures, moreover, provide consumers with information on the behavior of others. Thus, they partly comprise the resources that cultural market entrepreneurs draw on when they engage in the particular structuration of demand, which consists of organizing the interdependence of evaluations and individual preferences by putting forth the guarantee of collective consumer behavior.[121]

Of course, we could significantly rectify this simplified partitioning of cultural production. Thus, we will account for "evergreen" songs (that is, perennial successes), and examine the procedures by which artistic forms and genres initially situated outside of high culture (for example, detective novels, comic strips, jazz) are canonized. Indeed, these latter often rise in the cultural hierarchy, as they acquire histories, pioneer creators, "classic" authors, artistic legacies, collectors, a repertoire of touchstone works, and so on. Conversely, immediate consecration in high culture always provokes turmoil in a universe wherein reputation has traditionally been acquired over a long cycle. This is true for "art biz" events, celebrity bubbles, and waves of speculation, which allow for the short-term realization of gains and losses in the contemporary art market that are markedly higher than those obtained in classified art or in artistic segments on the road to consecration—as Raymonde Moulin has shown.[122]

In the sphere of popular artistic creation and mass cultural consumption, commercial success is generally described as the product of coordinated intervention in the production, distribution, advertising, and critical acclaim of artistic goods. Interdependencies among key actors (authors, producers, artistic directors, marketing professionals, distributors, sellers, programmers) catch the contingent of "creative" actors in a web of feedback loops between the upstream and downstream of creative work. This takes place according to a system of negotiations, tests, revisions, and procedures that are intended to manage escalating engagement toward the final accomplishment. A project can be interrupted, redesigned, radically remodeled, or abandoned, either after its initial conception, after a first stage of preproduction, or at a more advanced stage. Once the project has reached a first level of completion, it can be tested with clients, programmers, and tastemakers, and then subsequently modified. These multiple negotiations and decisions contribute to revising expectations of the project's chances for success. Production is organized in such a way that the project's content can be modified until the advanced stages, adjusted to new information on its estimated value, subjected to explicit clashes of authority and expertise regarding its originality and profitability, and submitted to negotiations surrounding advertising and promotional investments that correspond to its estimated commercial potential.

Here, social influence becomes the deliberate result of procedures developed by firms and art market professionals aiming to efficiently control areas of market uncertainty. As I recalled earlier, exerting influence over consumer preferences entails ever-growing expenses and incessant innovations. The range of marketing tools, in effect, has been continuously expanding: from advertising campaigns to product overexposure in physical and virtual spaces of commercialization, buzz,[123] praise for sale, hit parades, best-seller lists, and purchase recommendations based on other buyers' complementary choices of the same good. These tools have been making use of the two functions of advertising—providing free information, on the one hand, and persuading and influencing consumers, on the other. The type of influence exerted over consumers by advertising technologies has changed with the development of multisided markets; in these, platforms can provide Internet users with free access to cultural content, while also allowing advertisers to purchase target audiences with increasingly specified characteristics.[124] Social influence technologies used in advertising are particularly effective when they operate within social networks of exchange developed via the Internet.

The question of control, however, has always been more acute concerning the other facet of cultural industries: the creation of cultural content. At the heart of studies on cultural industries is the debate over the optimal degree of control that firms must wield over artists in order to reduce uncertainty about success. Are there recipes for success? Can popular works and genres be broken down into a series of characteristics, the various assemblages of which would constitute so many parameters to be controlled when conducting multiple large-scale tests (with the overproduction of artworks serving as the raw material)—and this, through intense learning by trial and error? The answer lies, notably, in the efficacy of techniques for formatting cultural products. Cultural production is divided into a series of genres and categories, and the conventions specific to production in each of these can vary greatly. Reputation levels and appraisals of artistic quality also differ by genre; stylistic conventions, formal elaborations, and originality ratings can also show more or less variance. In fact, formulas for creation vary little wherever uncertainty has been reduced through the conventional formatting of content. After all, in the high arts as in the popular arts, artistic genres have long constituted a typical conventional resource that helps establish the horizon of publics' expectations, both in terms of the pleasures they can derive from these arts and the social uses they can attribute to them.

Genres and subgenres constitute markers around which expectations on both sides of the market can be coordinated. Cultural industry innovations for reducing uncertainty about demand behavior and for building regular ties with consistent audience segments largely consist of bringing forth new genres or converting successes into identifiable genres and categories. They do so at the cost of typifying artists and artworks in ways that endow each artistic good with a double identity: the identity of its singularity coefficient, and that of the category to which it belongs. The exploitation of a success in the form of a series of replicas or sequels as well as the serialization of production (for example, serial novels, comic strip series, television series, among others) constitute other modes of conventional formatting aimed at gaining audience loyalty.[125] David Hesmondhalgh highlights that the growing importance of marketing in cultural industries is reflected notably in the sophistication of operations for categorizing and formatting goods. These operations are aimed at obtaining an ever-more precise alignment between consumer segments, categories of preferences and expectations, and the typical contents of products offered to consumers.[126]

One classic hypothesis is that the genre hierarchy in each cultural domain reflects the relative degree of control exerted over artists in that genre. This is, however, too simplistic a hypothesis. The Beckerian argument surrounding artistic labor conventions holds that control is also a mechanism of self-control used by the artist and his colleagues to anticipate a series of constraints; it is only once these constraints have been taken into consideration that the originality of an artwork can be appreciated. In each sphere of artistic production—high and popular alike—as in each of these spheres' respective genres, innovation implies both intense competition for originality and the remuneration of originality.

Cultural industries offer a unique field of observation and analysis for exploring the central question of the autonomy of the creative act. The common argument is that there is a disconnect between flexible control over creation and strict control over the distribution process and marketing and sales operations. Without sufficient autonomy (or without sufficiently flexible control), the fuel of creativity evaporates. However, without downstream control in distribution through strategies for selectively promoting artworks and artists with the highest expected commercial potential, overproduction cannot be managed efficiently.[127] The history of vertical deconcentration in the film industry well illustrates the combination between flexible specialization of production, persistent oligopolistic domination by the major firms, and increased variety of artistic production.[128] Organizational innovations have contributed to the disintegration of large firms into independent units, to the externalization of functions and personnel that can be subcontracted to provide services on intermittent projects, and, ultimately, to the evolution of firms into nexuses of contracts immersed in networks of relationships and in an environment of "co-opetitors," partner service providers, and professionals hired on a project-by-project basis.[129]

In order to understand whether talent is constructed or discovered and then "developed" (as an industrial innovation would be), we might inquire into the tolerable or optimal degree of control that can be exerted over the creative sector by the other sectors—notably, by marketing professionals whose influence has been continually expanding. Such reasoning, however, contains a logical fallacy, for it posits that it is not the artist himself, but the cultural entrepreneur (publisher, art dealer, film producer, recording company artistic director, or marketing manager) who possesses a particularly desirable and sought-after talent—that of transforming a novice into a renowned artist. The same reasoning underpins the claim that it is the critic who has the power to shape reputations, or the sponsor who can control the entire process; yet this only pushes the logical problem one step back.

We can assume that the talent-maker has sufficient social and economic power to subject the market and others' opinions to his own will. In doing so, however, we fall back on limited explanations, which maintain that it is always possible to beat the market, provided one is stronger, bigger, and more dominant. The major firms of the cultural industries have long since discovered that success is attained and constructed otherwise. Alternatively, we can deny that the artist is endowed with an intrinsically superior talent, and ascribe that talent instead to the talent-maker. Thus, we would replace the remarkable quality of the artist with that of he who succeeds in hoisting a certain artist above the rest, attributing to that person a variety of possible talents that make him exceptionally efficacious in his function and career. He will be said to possess a superior understanding of markets, significant new knowledge on consumer behavior and consumption trends, a greater mastery of the dosage of ingredients necessary for profitable innovation, and a capacity for organizing promotional advertising ingeniously—all to persuade ever more finely targeted audiences that are connected to a growing variety of media in which he knows how to act in a coordinated fashion.

But then we would have to suppose, on the one hand, that these ingredients can neither be observed nor measured; otherwise, they would be quickly taught and transmitted, thereby destroying the competitive advantage of the talent-maker. On the other hand, we would have to posit that these ingredients are sufficient for the talent-maker to transform any candidate for success into a star. Cases of swift success that associate a skillful and innovative entrepreneur with a formerly unknown artist (who will quickly fall back into anonymity) do represent one type of success story. But if the talent-maker were so incredibly talented, he could easily reproduce this feat. In reality, he is himself engaged in a process of trial-and-error, and attains in a single instance what he fails to produce in the majority of others.

The analysis of career dynamics and inequalities of success can extricate the argumentation from this quagmire. From this perspective, talent cannot be construed merely as an artist's intrinsic difference in quality, one whose manifestation would be either thwarted or unleashed by an environment that would control its expression with more or less flexibility. Nor, for the reasons that I have just evoked, can talent be understood as the product of a simple marketing strategy. Reputation-based ratings are conducted not only for artists, but also for the professionals with whom they work. Creative intelligence must be understood as a distributed resource: The career of an artist is shaped by collaborations, sponsorships, and associations with professionals of comparable quality in their respective functions. I will return to this point in greater detail when discussing the significance of the two principal models I examine below.

The Mertonian Model of Cumulative Advantage

In Rosen's model, the entire analysis is focused on demand, for the behavior and growth of demand are assumed to explain why successes are disproportionate to relative differences in quality. Demand behavior is impossible to understand if one fails to see that consumers learn, seek out information, speak with, and imitate each other. But how can we characterize the behavior of artists? We cannot merely assume that they have passed the competitive tests enabling them to access the largest market because they are endowed since the start with a talent they need merely express to have hopes of succeeding. What do artists learn from the competitive tests punctuating their careers that may enable them to influence the course of events? What mechanism can provide us with a convincing explanation of such behavioral dynamics?

Merton's cumulative advantage model allows for analyzing social inequalities as the product of increasingly divergent trajectories that originate in a situation of near-equal opportunities. The argument runs as follows: An individual, group, or firm—whose characteristics are all very similar to those of their competitors—manages to gain a minimal advantage. This advantage may consist in a particular aptitude, an investment opportunity, the good fortune of an invention, or the pure and simple intervention of chance. While this advantage favors the individual, group, or firm only slightly at the outset, it is amplified to the point of creating considerable inequality in the distribution of the benefits it allows these actors to obtain (for example, income, profits, prestige, market power).

As Thomas DiPrete and Gregory Eirich highlight,[130] Merton's cumulative advantage model leaves open the question of differences in talent. Nothing prevents us from supposing that it is real differences in talent that are being revealed by professionals' respective careers. In contrast to Rosen, however, Merton posits that although the trajectories of two young professionals can diverge considerably, their intrinsic qualities may very well be equivalent at the outset. The cause of growing inequality could be a purely random factor. Let us examine Merton's argument and, in particular, his most radical hypothesis: the absence of differences in talent.

Let us take a set of scientists or artists who possess a high level of initial training and a comparable level of social capital, but whose levels of professional success vary greatly. Let us then suspend the argument of substantial differences in ability, since the latter are not easily observable and since success depends on multiple qualities, the right combination of which is extremely difficult to determine. This group, after all, enjoys a high level of training that may have played the role of selective filter by demanding important qualities at the outset. Defined in hypothetical terms, the group is sufficiently homogenous for the study of inequalities in success to seem unaffected by uncontrolled initial factors. How are spectacularly divergent success trajectories generated? Answering this question is central to this second explanatory model of significant inequalities in income and reputation. This model, in brief, seeks to trace the sources of reputation formation so as to determine whether the rating of qualities and their conversion into reputations might constitute a system sensitive to slight initial disturbances in the conditions of the competition.

This model, also known as the Matthew Effect, comes from the sociology of science. Merton began with the hypothesis that considerable inequality in success and reputation in scientific careers (as measured by the impact factor, monetary income, high status position, symbolic remuneration in the form of prestige and social recognition) can perfectly result from an initially negligible difference in the intrinsic quality of individuals.[131] The hypothesis does not involve placing all possible candidates for a career in the sciences (or in the arts, or in any world that strongly values individual creativity) on the same starting line; rather, it entails comparing the respective professional trajectories of individuals endowed with equivalent training, skills, and economic and social resources.

Merton's model is founded on the following postulates. Resources in the world of sciences (for example, scholarships, credits, honors, and jobs) are limited; this is the constraint of scarcity. These resources are allocated through competitive tests that allow for measuring talent in relative terms, since the latter is difficult to observe directly. Moreover, they are granted to reward past performances while also encouraging future productivity. In the scientific community, peers have limited capacity for evaluating the considerable mass of current scientific studies and for estimating researchers' future productivity. Their decisions are myopic: They give their attention, respect, esteem (that is, citations of others' research), and resources principally to researchers who have already acquired a reputation—and this, due to reputation's signal value. Their expectations are thus essentially extrapolations: Based on the observation of past performances, they must predict what is likely to be produced, and they must stimulate the productivity of scientists selected on that basis.

Specifying the action system and actors' behavior in this way leads to the following explanation of how the gap between two scientists tends to increase over time. A researcher known for having produced high-quality work early in his career obtains jobs and publishes more easily; he is also cited more often. Overall, his work benefits from a halo effect brought on by the reputation he has acquired from his most significant productions.[132] The advantages are gained directly. For research of a given quality, the chances of obtaining rewards (for example, additional resources, a more competitive research team, stronger market power in the competition for the best academic positions) are superior for the researcher of higher status, including when his research does not surpass the average work produced by his colleagues. Even if the work of a lesser-known colleague is of comparable quality, as we might readily imagine in the case of a co-signed article, greater recognition is awarded to the more prestigious author. In sum, as Joel Podolny notes in his commentary on Merton's model, it is easier—that is, less costly—for a high-status researcher to produce work of a given quality. He is more likely to receive invitations to present his work at high-level institutions, and can thus expect to engage in more fruitful exchanges that will enable him to improve his work. In the stratified world of academia, his value allows him to increase his productivity. He will be in a position to negotiate his recruitment into a powerful and renowned university, and to achieve, here more than elsewhere, the right balance between his teaching responsibilities and the time he can devote to his research. He is more likely to develop collaborative ties with scientists of equivalent or superior caliber, and to attract brilliant students who are strongly invested in their doctoral studies, leading to collaborative projects on whose benefits he will partly capitalize.[133] In short, he will accumulate human capital.

Let us examine the beginning of the process of reputation accumulation. Can reputation be entirely disconnected from talent? The mechanism of cumulative advantage is activated as soon as a performance gap appears among a set of candidates for success, and as soon as one of the young scientists obtains an advantage over others. The explanation lies in the process of self-reinforcement: Recognized for a remarkable performance early in his career, the scientist attracts the attention of his peers and receives support from mentors and colleagues who are more advanced in their careers. This allows him to reduce the costs of producing quality research and to increase his chances of enlarging his audience.

It is thus understood that what causally determines the early attainment of a strong reputation and a high status is the difference in value between the accomplishments of competing scientists in the same age group. And it is also clear that this causal link reinforces itself as advantages accumulate—to the point where what may have been a slight gap in quality at the outset comes to appear as a significant, intrinsic difference in quality. Merton's reasoning does not identify the source of differences in performance: This causal origin might be an intrinsic difference in ability or quality (however one defines quality or the combination of superior qualities possessed by the most brilliant competitor), or simply a random factor. By lowering the initial difference to nothing or nearly nothing, Merton aims to dismiss the argument that would reduce the analysis of cumulative advantage to a simple tautology: If competition were strongly unequal from the outset, and if differences in quality were thereby easily observable and predictive of future accomplishments, success would follow a simple causal mechanism. By postulating that this gap may have a random origin, the Mertonian model shifts attention toward the social dynamic that causes disproportionate gaps in career trajectories: "[E]minent scientists get disproportionately great credit for their contributions to science while relatively unknown scientists tend to get disproportionately little credit for comparable contributions."[134]

Merton mentions two situations in which disproportionate differences in prestige rewards can be easily observed: co-signed articles and simultaneous discoveries. In the first case, two or more researchers who have worked together receive unequal attention and benefits. The most renowned among them gains greater visibility, despite the fact that the work has been shared equally. In the second case, two or more researchers have the same idea independently of each other at approximately the same moment, but one of them publishes his work slightly before the other(s). In these examples, the reasoning is consistent with the constructionist argument: Individuals' initial qualities are considered equal, and the system of prestige allocation is said to create spectacularly different levels of reputation. The key hypothesis is, of course, that the contributions of the different researchers were of equal value. This prompts in turn a counterfactual argument: Things might have occurred very differently if the allocation of reputation were less exclusionary than it is in a "winner takes most" or "winner takes all" system, and if the reputation hierarchy did not have such an impact on the attention that researchers receive from their peers.

What, ultimately, generates the early divergence of trajectories and allows the mechanism of cumulative advantage to enter into action? The specificity of the cumulative advantage argument is that it places at the heart of the analysis a mechanism triggered by differences that may be either minute or indeterminate in size, but nevertheless grow rapidly. It is highly tempting to identify this mechanism with the factors typically cited to explain inequalities in school performances. Scientific research is an activity in which the quality of initial training has a considerable impact on one's chances of professional success. In her study of the scientific elite of Nobel laureates, Harriet Zuckerman has shown that the majority of exceptionally productive scientists studied in the best universities and developed their careers in the best university departments.[135] The training and research system imposes its competitive logic every step of the way—from a scientist's early studies through to the peak of his career—so as to match the best scientists with the best research and teaching institutions. This operates by way of career mobility, competitive recruitment bids, and advantages offered by the presence of a critical mass of high-value scientists in the most coveted universities. All of this is measurable and produces well-documented results.

The observation of scientific elites reveals the power of selection mechanisms that operate at every stage to progressively concentrate promising talents in the most fertile environments. Among the easily documented causal factors of such exceptional success are social origin, religious culture and affiliation (attested in particular by the overrepresentation of laureates of Jewish origin), and the identity of one's mentors. Thus, Nobel laureates are twice as likely as other scientists to have parents classified in the upper category of "Professional Workers." Furthermore, among these laureates, most had scientific professionals for fathers. Lastly, more than half of them had worked with Nobel laureates during their studies and in their very first collaborations as junior scientists.

The selective power of initial training is so strong in certain professions (such as those in scientific research) that, in the advanced stages of professional competition, competitive tests can be restricted to a limited set of individuals whose school performances are very similar.[136] In order to isolate the factors that produce both divergent career trajectories and peak achievements, we would need to compare the careers of Nobel laureates with those of scientists with comparable social origins, trained by similarly renowned mentors, and holding positions in equally prestigious universities. If we cannot statistically control for the factors that cause the initial advantage, however, doubt arises as to the direction of causality. Is it the prestigious teacher who immediately confers an advantage on his protégé by publishing with him, enabling him to progress in a highly stimulating environment, and ensuring that expectations of success will converge on him—thus increasing his self-confidence and placing him in an ideal position to receive job offers from top universities and research centers? Or rather, is it due to his own extraordinary capacities that the student can have access to an exceptional university environment and make the best of this early on, notably through receiving mentorship from a prestigious professor?

Several of the empirical studies elicited by Merton's cumulative advantage model have been applied to scientific research and its organizational apparatus.[137] When stratification in the world of scientific research is plagued with dysfunctional bias, both the efficacy and the equity of the system of professional competition in the sciences are called into question. Indeed, the ideal of universality at the heart of the model of meritocratic competition is broken when the scarcity of time and attention allotted to producing evaluations or seeking information on the quality of scientific works generates excessive reliance on reputational signals, as well as distortions in the competition in a context of imperfect information. Not to mention the strategic maneuvers that may be aimed at influencing the allocation of reputations, and that would seem to confirm the conception of the scientific world as a political arena and as a universe of transactions and negotiations surrounding appraisals of quality. The ideal of universality and fair competition is even more seriously fractured when the mechanism of cumulative advantage operates in a context wherein there is a marked scarcity of positions for the best candidates: Here, we return to the previously cited argument concerning the forty-first seat of the Académie Française, which, if attributed, would go to someone with the same obvious merits as the other forty academicians. It is this pairing between the scarcity of elite positions and the benefits offered by such positions that inspires Harriet Zuckerman to write: "The processes involved in the accumulation of advantage cast considerable doubt on the conclusion that marked differences in performance between the ultra-elite and other scientists reflect equally marked differences in their initial capacities to do scientific work."[138]

Jonathan and Stephen Cole conclude their study of social stratification in the sciences[139] by discussing the above points, as they aim to delimit the relevance and precise applicability of the cumulative advantage model. In their view, science comes fairly close to realizing its ideal of universality and of fair reputation allocation based on the quality of the work produced—as measured by the success of a scientist in his professional community (that is, by the number of citations received). However, they also point out that the process of cumulative advantage is the only mechanism that creates a significant gap between the real world of science and this functional ideal of stratification by quality: "In almost all cases where science departs from the ideal we find the process of accumulative advantage at work. People who have done well at time 1 have a better chance of doing well at time 2, independently of their objective role-performance; the initially successful are given advantage in subsequent competition for rewards."[140]

The mechanism of cumulative advantage relies on the existence of an initial difference. In this preliminary phase, competitive tests (for example, publications, applications for grants and jobs) lead to recurring assessments of who performs best, thereby enabling those selected to move at an accelerated pace and to attain greater opportunities for accumulating accomplishments in the stratified system of competition. What makes someone perform better from the outset? Answering this question requires a precise modeling of the cumulative advantage argument such as that put forward by Paul Allison, Scott Long, and Tad Krauze.[141] If we assume that, at the start of their careers, researchers in the same cohort have the same propensity for publishing, and that each article they publish increases this propensity by a coefficient which is the same for all, then the differences in productivity we obtain remain constant over time. Inequalities in the pace of publication of different researchers certainly appear early on: The hypothesis is that these differences are caused in large part by random processes beyond individuals' control. Under such conditions of initial homogeneity in researcher quality, the statistical modeling concludes that inequalities in productivity do not vary over time. Merton's model, however, predicts that inequalities in productivity among researchers of a same cohort actually do increase with time. To arrive at this result, one must introduce interindividual heterogeneity. All researchers do not start out with the same propensity to publish. Moreover, all researchers, after a first publication or series of publications, do not benefit from the same additional impetus to publish at an even faster pace: Those whose articles are deemed good or remarkable are encouraged to produce more. In sum, in order to explain increasing inequalities, one must abandon the hypothesis that all competitors have the same initial capacity to produce. A coefficient of heterogeneity or of qualitative difference must be introduced from the outset in order to account for inequalities in success; these begin, after all, with different capacities to produce high-quality results.

Chance: The Source of Divergent Trajectories

In Merton's argumentation, chance is a possible cause for the gaps in performance observed between two scientists. This chance coefficient merits closer examination, as it plays a distinctive role in the context of the arts.

The chance coefficient usually serves to characterize the unpredictability of both discovery and original novelty. The high value placed on creativity in the scientific and artistic professions directly corresponds to the element of chance located at the heart of creative labor, as indicated by descriptions of the discovery process in terms of a sequence of distinct phases: intensive labor, infraconscious rumination, unpredictable and unconscious association of previously disconnected ideas, emergence of discovery, scrupulous control over the value of the new idea, and public communication.[142]

The organization of labor may increase the coefficients of variability and uncertainty. As I mentioned above, in contrast to the situation in the sciences, competition and success in most artistic professions are only weakly correlated to initial training. The importance of receiving on-the-job training and accumulating work experience is notably explained by the heavy exposure of individual labor to the uncertainty of a highly turbulent environment—one characterized by the organization of labor on a project-by-project basis and by the variable degree of control the individual can exert over the result of teamwork. A successful career can be likened to a gradual increase in the control the artist can exercise over the most variable aspects of his activity and over his interactions with his environment; this occurs in a universe wherein stratification by reputation is not tied to stable organizations, as is the case in the sciences. It is therefore the very system of artistic labor that creates the conditions for the intervention of chance. An artistic career develops from one project to the next, and the chances for success vary depending on each project. Most often, individual labor is immersed in a collective undertaking whose chances for success are imperfectly correlated with the qualities of each individual team member. Thus, the skill or talent of an actress, evaluated in terms of her personal performance, are certainly not fundamentally different depending on whether the film in which she stars is a success or a failure; however, her visibility and chances of being associated with other relatively promising projects depend in part on the success of that film.[143] Organizing labor on a project-by-project basis introduces very high variability in a professional activity. It also increases the number of potential junctures: possessing the right information on upcoming projects or employment opportunities; being called in at a moment's notice to replace the star opera singer who has caught the flu; landing a role in which, against all expectations, one can demonstrate a real talent without having been cast in that category of roles before.[144] The complexity of projects increases the role of chance, and in some cases contributes to successive strokes of bad luck.[145] There are few professions, in fact, in which practitioners resort so frequently to superstitious practices and conjuring rituals. These latter are the correlate of another essential behavioral mechanism: the overvalorization of the self, which I evoked earlier.

Chance can also be characterized in simpler terms. In Merton's model, uncertainty surrounding the course of the competition can intervene at the very outset in the form of chance events capable of deflecting the trajectory of a career. These include the choice of a research topic that coincides with an unforeseen news item or a high social demand, or the designation of grant proposal reviewers who, due to their own interests and private concerns, may become enthusiastic about the work of a particular candidate, thereby having a decisive impact on his career, and so forth.

In the case of the arts, chance factors include the fortunate or unfortunate coincidence between, on the one hand, the publication of a novel, the release of a film, or the auction of a painting, and, on the other hand, a current event that either garners unexpected visibility for the artwork or entirely eclipses it (for example, a terrorist attack, a stock market crash, and more).[146] A research study on the evaluation of the quality of classical musicians in musical competitions provides a troubling example of the causal intervention of pure chance. In an analysis of eleven Queen Elizabeth piano competitions from 1952 to 1991, Victor Ginsburgh and Jan van Ours uncovered a relation between the final rankings of candidates and the order in which they performed in front of the jury, and this, at various stages of the contest. The order of appearance was decided at random, for reasons of *ex ante* equity, but revealed itself to have generated *ex post* inequity: Candidates who auditioned at the very beginning of the competition were at a disadvantage. The authors suggested several possible explanations for this.

First, judges may have had high expectations and shown themselves to be quite strict at the outset, only to revise their assessment criteria after the first auditions. Second, a concerto was specifically composed for each competition and was therefore unknown to pianists and jury members alike; once again, the judges seem to have engaged in a learning process whereby they revised their expectations as they became increasingly familiar with the piece and its successive interpretations.

The two economists' analysis is consistent with the cumulative advantage model: Ranking order does have a direct influence on competing pianists' chances for professional success. Yet classical music interpretation is a field of activity that involves brutal technical training and ruthless selection based on precocity; it would seem easier in this artistic field than in others to base judgments on objective quality criteria. The effect of the random order of appearance in the competition suggests that although selected candidates possessed similar abilities and were previously subjected to a merciless process of preliminary selection, the intervention of chance ultimately produced a result which the music market then amplified by interpreting the ranking as an irrefutable signal of objective quality—thereby triggering the spiral of accumulation of contracts and recordings, which in turn generates gains in reputation.[147] Merton would have concluded that the formation of gaps in quality and talent is governed in part by processes whose origin lies beyond the control of either researchers or artists.[148]

However, as in Allison's analysis cited above, one must acknowledge the inequalities in individuals' capacities to exploit the opportunities available to them—even those that happen upon them by chance. In his analysis of the extreme inequalities generated by the uncertainty of success in the film industry, Arthur De Vany[149] raises the following question: Which portion of success should be attributed to luck and which to talent? Suppose that a director is faced with only two possible outcomes for the film he is shooting: success or failure. If the film succeeds, he will continue; if it fails, he will cease his current activity and start a new one (for example, in a different film craft, television, or audiovisual production) or he will abandon the sector entirely. If chance governs the whole process, then the distribution must follow a binomial law B $(n, \frac{1}{2})$, as in a game of heads or tails: The probability of making two films is 0.5 (according to this hypothesis, half of novice directors will make no more than one film), that of making three films is 0.25, and that of making four is 0.125, and so on. What do we learn from De Vany's data on the distribution of the number of films by directors in North American cinema from 1982 to 2001? We see that the distribution follows the binomial law curve; in other words, the probability of making another film boils down to a simple game of heads or tails. A bending of the curve nonetheless appears in the data: For the seventh movie and beyond, the probability of continuing is higher than it is for a random draw with two possible outcomes. Other factors must therefore influence career chances. The study brings into focus a threshold effect that illustrates Pareto's law:

> The high odds ratios for the most prolific directors suggests there is something beyond luck in determining how many movies a director will make. In seeking to further draw the line between luck and talent, we rely on a remarkable property of the Paretian distribution. A merely lucky director would find that the probability of succeeding with her next film is 0.5. And this would be the same for each film, no matter how many the director made. That is to say, the probability of success is not altered with experience as measured by the number of successful films made.
>
> If talent, skill, or learning have anything to do with success, then the probability of success should not remain constant; it ought to increase with the number of successes realized. And this is just what the Pareto distribution implies.[150]

This leads to a different calculation of probability. Instead of distributing individuals by number of movies made, one can determine, at every point in a director's career, what chances he has of making one or more additional films: After a first movie, the probability of making one or several more is 0.35; after two films, 0.54; after three, 0.64; and after four, 0.71, and so on.[151] This increasing probability captures the influence of reputation or accumulated experience, and reveals the dynamic of cumulative advantage once it has been activated. The lesson to be learned from this is that a career involves completing the different stages of elimination tournaments (summarily represented here by a game of heads or tails), which amounts to beating chance. The development of a career acts as a revelator of underlying qualities that are unequally distributed among individuals, and that enable artists to complete those different stages. An individual who succeeds in developing his career in this project-by-project environment increases his skills and benefits from the advantages of a well-established reputation; the latter allows him to expand his social and professional networks, which supply him with information and job opportunities. This dynamic is particularly influential in professions wherein learning by doing plays an important role and the reputational signal constitutes a highly functional means of obtaining information, one that professionals share via their networks in order to organize labor on a project-by-project basis.

When an artist practices his activity as part of an employment relation in which he is remunerated per act of labor—as in the world of performing arts—income gaps are foremost generated by the impact of professional reputation on chances of employment and on remuneration. This analysis is easy to conduct because it is possible to measure the quantity of paid labor. Thus, in the performing arts—with the exception of orchestras and operas, which hire part of their personnel on a permanent basis—the system of recruitment and labor adjusts the duration of employment and the level of remuneration to the characteristics of each individual project. This flexible organization of production strongly individualizes the employment relation, and essentially draws on the information contained in the reputation of artists and technicians. Every professional engagement can be the occasion for evaluating an artist's qualities and skills, and the employer or intermediary (such as an artists agency, project liaison, or production company) is free not to rehire an artist who has not performed satisfactorily. The fastest and cheapest method for evaluating skills is to exploit the information contained in an artist's employment history (the frequency of his professional engagements, the value and success of the projects on which he has collaborated, his visibility within the professional community, his degree of specialization in certain types of employment, and so forth). Conversely, the employment and remuneration to which a freelance actor or musician can aspire are indexed on the reputational signals contained in this history, or at least in the listing of their most recent employment. A typical mechanism of cumulative advantage intervenes when the fact of having landed several contracts acts as a good quality signal, which increases one's chances of employment. On the contrary, having held few jobs constitutes a bad-quality signal that reduces these chances. The resulting distribution of labor quantities is highly asymmetrical, and that of earnings levels even more so.[152]

In his analysis of the careers of music composers for Hollywood movies, Robert Faulkner[153] showed that this self-reinforcing process was fueled by the very characteristics of the project-by-project organization of labor that are specific to the cultural industries. These include, in particular, the stratification of the different categories of professionals who are called upon to collaborate with project teams, based on their level of reputation and on the density of the professional networks to which they belong. De Vany likewise recalls how film producers are "the hubs of personal networks of contacts among a pool of freelance artists."[154] The reputation and employability of a successful artist increase as a result of the growing density of the ties he develops within professional networks centered around the producers and agents who assemble the crews for each project.

It should be noted here that it is impossible to determine or measure the quantity and price of artistic labor in the same way for all artistic disciplines. For artists who cede their rights to publishers, record producers, or gallery operators, earnings are indexed on the commercial career of the artwork itself. In the case of reproducible artworks, earnings are spread over a period that extends, by law, beyond the artist's death and lasts as long as is stipulated by the literary and artistic property legislation in effect. Revenue flows are thus a direct function of the market performance of the artwork.

The price of unique artworks is essentially determined as a function of both the intensity of demand and the (short- or long-term) actions that may be performed to raise the reputation of the artist and influence demand. A given quantity of labor may be paid at a price ranging from zero to infinity.[155] Furthermore, a single artist may observe extreme variations between the effort put into producing an artwork and the remuneration for that effort. An artwork produced in record time may achieve considerable success, whereas a project realized over an entire lifetime may prove incomplete and unexploitable. The pace of creation can also fluctuate considerably over the course of an artist's career—often alternating between demanding or exhausting works (in which he undertakes new experiments), and more ordinary activities (in which he applies a tested and immediately lucrative formula).[156]

In the arts wherein the physical uniqueness of the artwork (or the controlled scarcity of its reproductions, as in the case of bronze castings) is determinant, it is the price signal that acts as a mechanism of cumulative advantage or disadvantage. As Bruno Frey and Werner Pommerehne[157] have noted, when a visual artist encounters too little demand for his artworks and labor, he may consider two options to improve his situation: He may sell his existing artworks at a lower price in order to attract more buyers, or he may downgrade his production so as to sell more artworks at a lower unit price. These two solutions would be available to him if excess supply could be defined with reference to a theoretical equilibrium price. Yet the labor situation of visual artists disrupts the common reasoning that defines production equilibrium by relating price to quantity. This is so because in the art market, the price of artworks is held as a quality signal. As Olav Vethius has shown, an artist's rating cannot decrease without arousing suspicion that the quality of his artworks is insufficient or in decline.[158] Likewise, overtly abundant artistic production may trigger the suspicion that the artist is seeking to tap into a target market or into a temporary increase in demand, and hence that he is losing his quality of intrinsic motivation and joining the ranks of inauthentic and profit-driven creators.

Conversely, it is common for artists to exploit a new idea or major innovation—thereby revealing its full potential—in a series of artworks. A creator's ability to increase his production without degrading the value assigned to the multiple iterations of his innovation (which become embodiments of an easily identifiable style or brand) varies along with the strength of his reputation, and thus with the intensity of demand.[159] In effect, assessments of artists' behaviors and motivations can go in opposite directions. A recognized artist who exploits a success formula he has himself developed holds temporary market power and enjoys the economic rent of an innovator. The artist's exploitation of his own innovation in a series of highly similar artworks will be celebrated as a manifestation of creative fertility—so long as he and his art dealer can exploit demand by enlarging the circle of buyers, collectors, and institutions interested in his work. However, as the exploitation cycle of the innovation becomes exhausted, the assessment is reversed, and that which had been considered a commendable demonstration of creative fertility comes to be viewed as repetition, compulsion, or barren self-plagiarism.[160] Alternative career paths must then open, which place the artist in competition not only with his fellow colleagues, but also with himself (that is, with his own past). Cumulative advantage can thus transform itself into cumulative disadvantage.

The Variable Intensity of Cumulative Advantage

The intensity of a mechanism of cumulative advantage is variable. The parameters of this variability are numerous, and give unique substance to the history of art worlds (and science worlds) and to the changing organization of their activities. I will illustrate this variability via two opposite examples: (1) the convergence between the demand for aesthetic innovation and the advantage provided by an early professional start; and (2) the impact of the digital revolution on the cultural industry.

In his analyses of the Matthew Effect, Robert Merton emphasizes that the criterion of precocity plays a major role in the mechanism of cumulative advantage, and that it constitutes an institutional bias, characteristic of the entire American educational system.[161] He cites the arguments of Alan Gregg, who identified four profiles of emergent ability: (1) the "rampart" type, who manifests a precocious ability that reaches its peak very early on and then gradually declines; (2) the "plateau" type, whose performance emerges precociously and remains solid and steady over time; (3) the "slow crescendo" type, who begins slowly and improves over the course of his career—a reliable value that proves neither exceptional nor disappointing; and (4) the "late-blooming" type, whose success is startling because it manifests itself so late and unexpectedly that it sparks little envy. Careers may be governed by selection mechanisms that systematically advantage precocity, owing to the particular timeline for maturation and expression of ability. Researchers in physics and mathematics, for instance, attain their maximum creativity and productivity very early on—much earlier than those in the humanities and social sciences.[162] Similarly, aptitudes for ballet or for the practice of classical music are detected and developed—through highly selective technical training—at a very precocious age. The speed at which training and its certification are acquired is a good predictor of the probability of successful professionalization.[163]

Demand for the precocious manifestation of a creative potential can become an argument of market competition, and can draw on the excess supply of candidates to accelerate competitive tournaments (to the point of shortening the probationary period during which an artist is to learn by doing and to accumulate experience). In this situation, Gregg's "slow crescendo" and "late-blooming" types are unlikely to manifest themselves. One way of analyzing the social and economic determinants of artistic success is actually to examine career profiles by age.[164]

In a study focused on major painters from the second half of the nineteenth century through the twentieth, David Galenson[165] starts from the hypothesis that the painters consecrated by posterity were one of two types of innovators. First, "conceptual" innovators—such as Picasso—made an aesthetic breakthrough very early on (similar to a scientific discovery made at a precocious age); art historians as well as museum and art market professionals consider their early artworks to be their best, and it is these artworks that are priced the highest. Second, "experimental" innovators—such as Cézanne—developed a fundamental principle of creative research throughout their careers; it is their final artworks that are recognized as the most important and assigned the highest value. Galenson's data lead him to conclude that the value assigned to innovation has been constantly on the rise. It is true that the demand for innovation—from art dealers, collectors, and the growing number of museums, foundations, art fairs, and international exhibitions of contemporary art—is increasing. Painters conducting "conceptual" innovations develop their creative formula and make a breakthrough early in their careers. Moreover, they enjoy a competitive advantage because they adjust better (more rapidly) than others to the encompassing demand for innovation. As Galenson writes, "The probability that an artist would execute his most valuable work early in his career increased considerably over time."[166] But how should we read this observed tendency? Does the demand for aesthetic originality indicate that admiration becomes concentrated on the discovery of new methods and ideas, to the detriment of the slow, reflective maturation of the painter whose entire production is but the incessant resolution of a single problem? Does the market economy of the arts lead to the increasingly irresistible assimilation of desirable creative invention to a "conceptual" innovation? The valorization of "conceptual" innovation and precocity might, in fact, mean something other than the triumph of one type of creative personality over another. In his discussion of Galenson's work, Fabien Accominotti[167] brings to light the factors that shape the collective organization of artistic labor, as well as their evolution. He especially emphasizes the importance of the post-1850 structuration of innovation and artistic competition in aesthetic movements and collaborative networks, with their associated coalitions of actors (art dealers, critics, and now curators).

The evolution of cultural industries raises the question of how transformations in the art markets and in the various forms of artistic competition affect the temporal development of careers. The impact of these changes is as follows. Large firms—which continue to dominate this sector so long as they show a superior ability to develop innovation by funding the quest for success through overproduction—have gradually invested a growing proportion of their resources in promoting the most competitive artists and artworks.[168] Though production is increasingly diversified, the organization of distribution channels has reduced the chances for survival of this abundant supply by shortening the exploitation cycle of goods. Information systems have been developed that provide increasingly precise and rapid information on the market performance of goods. Competition through differentiation has adjusted to distribution constraints by overexposing a limited portion of the supply to the attention of consumers. Cultural entrepreneurs have reduced the cost of searching for consumers by increasing their promotional expenses and diversifying their advertising messages. Thus, the opportunities an artist has available to develop his qualities are linked to the speed at which evaluations that position him in the competition either promote or evict him based on the success he encounters in the first stages of his career. Lastly, races for fame (such as *Star Academy* in France and *American Idol* in the United States) have transformed short-term speculation about talent into genuine tournaments offered as entertainment and the audiences into effective decision-makers.

The variable intensity of cumulative advantage is also manifest in the changes introduced by contemporary digital technologies. One explanation for the power of the mechanism of cumulative advantage is resource scarcity—on the side of producers and entrepreneurs as much as on that of consumers and evaluators. I described earlier how consumers reduce the cost of their search for information on the identity and quality of goods by observing the behavior of others, or even how professional networks find in projected reputation a low-cost piece of information on the quality of individuals to be contracted for a given project. In his model, Merton highlights that peer evaluation is constrained by the scarcity of time and attention that can be devoted to the considerable mass of (incessantly produced) studies; under this constraint, evaluation and co-optation on the basis of reputation prove efficient at a lesser cost, and the reputation hierarchy exerts a lever effect on the accumulation of advantages.

The technological revolutions that came about with the digitization of contents and their exchange prompt us to verify whether it is possible to alter the mechanisms responsible for the disproportionate concentration of attention, reputation, and earnings on a minority of talented professionals, and whether excess supply can be lessened through increasing its diversity—in the form of niche markets that would prove more efficient than mass markets. The normative arguments (recalled above) that have been put forth to criticize artistic competition and its inegalitarian effects remain abstract and lead to irresolvable contradictions. Here, by contrast, we are facing real and rapid changes in the organization of activities: What do we know at present about the impact of these changes?

The scenario of a creative economy that would no longer obey Pareto's law has been put forward. Economic concentration in cultural industries, herding behavior, and the heavy concentration of demand on a narrow proportion of creators have been motivated notably by scarcity factors. Some of these factors have now been annulled or substantially modified: Digital channels have led to the dematerialization of content distribution; a greater diversity of non-dematerialized products can now be commercialized and physically sold via online sales tools such as Amazon; contents can now be legally or illegally obtained for free; and the number of information and exchange networks is on the rise. All of these innovations seem to be eliminating, one at a time, the obstacles that have hampered the diversification of consumption behavior and the viability of niche markets. Would this not create a more perfect competition, one in which the chances for success would be more equally distributed across a much larger number of artworks?[169] Such is the "long-tail scenario": the Pareto curve with a long distribution tail. We are now promised a realm of greater abundance wherein all products are continuously available, the range of choices offered to consumers is unlimited, and increasing demand can be spread across this infinitely growing supply.[170]

The credibility of this prediction may be assessed against empirical analyses that, even with little hindsight, seek to measure actual changes in the trade and consumption of cultural goods brought about by the digital revolution and the explosion of online sales. Anita Elberse has provided a good overview of the existing hypotheses and proposed to test them.[171] First, Chris Anderson predicts that the elimination of the costs associated with the physical presentation of goods in stores will considerably increase the variety of products available online. Research and recommendation tools, moreover, will keep consumers from feeling overwhelmed by the immensity of choice. The long tail phenomenon will thus correspond to an increase in consumption generated by the online sales and digital distribution of products that have been underexposed in traditional commerce due to their excessively weak or slow sales. The technological revolution in distribution will therefore ensure the commercial viability of a considerable variety of cultural products (video films, CDs, books, and so on), in spite of their low sales.

How viable is this hypothesis in light of available statistical data? Having collected data on online music and video sales in the United States and Australia, Elberse observes that online purchases are concentrated in the manner predicted by Pareto's law: 10 percent of song titles account for 78 percent of song sales, and 1 percent of titles accounts for 32 percent of sales. Yet Elberse also notes that sales, while highly concentrated, were tallied on the basis of a million available titles—a considerably greater supply than that in traditional physical distribution or even in radio broadcasting. Video rentals showed lower, but still significant, concentration of demand: Of the 16,000 titles available, 10 percent accounted for 48 percent of rentals, and 1 percent of titles (that is to say, the equivalent of Hollywood's annual film production) accounted for 18 percent of rentals. Another study coauthored by Elberse[172] indicates that the sales of products figuring in the long tail are indeed increasing: The number of videos sold online in small numbers doubled in five years. The number of available titles that were not purchased a single time, however, quadrupled over the same period. In other words, the growing variety of titles available for purchase is accompanied, at one end of the curve, by an increasing proportion of titles that sell little or not at all, and, at the other end, by a growing concentration of strong sales (in the last distribution decile) on an increasingly reduced number of titles.

Anderson's second prediction is that online distribution will alter the behavior of consumers, prompting them to pay greater attention to niche products (which correspond to their specific interests) than to mass-produced ones. The Internet will contribute to lengthening the long tail and will allow individuals to discover products that better suit their tastes. The market is therefore likely to fragment into a multitude of niches. Far from being a zero-sum game, this evolution will correspond to an expansion of markets and to an increase in consumption: Multiple niche sales will aggregate and eventually exceed the level of sales in the market dominated by products of mass consumption.

Elberse observes that consumers who are attracted by obscure products display high-intensity cultural consumption, and have more extensive cultural knowledge of music and films (measurable by the number of possible choices they can make). But while they are more likely to venture toward artworks destined for a limited audience, their critical assessment (collected via online surveys) is harsher for those products than it is for the most popular ones. In other words, cultural addiction is satisfied through the exploration of a greater variety of products made possible by e-commerce; yet it does not abolish the highly asymmetrical distribution of preferences and purchases. Niche markets do not replace the market of competitive tournaments and mimetic consumption.[173]

Assortative Matching

In the models I have discussed thus far, spectacular inequalities in success primarily concern the specific situation in which artists or professionals with valued expertise are competing to attract demand—each acting individually, through direct interaction with the market, and without any apparent partners. However, in order to work and to produce and diffuse their products, professionals usually join a permanent or temporary organization (for example, orchestra, theater company, film production crew, and such); alternatively, they enter into a contract with an organization that acts as an intermediary (such as a publishing house, recording company, or art gallery) in order to create material reproductions of a given good, place an artwork into circulation, and gain access to the market. It is here that another trigger of inequality comes into play: assortative matching. Introducing the model of assortative matching allows for the resolution of some of the difficulties encountered in the examination of Rosen's and Merton's models.

Assortative matching characterizes the multiplicative nature of the production function in artistic labor. Like a scientist in Merton's cumulative advantage model, an artist benefits from associating with professionals reputed to be of equal or superior quality in their respective careers. Indeed, in order for an artist to secure the best chances of developing his talent, it is important for him to associate with professionals of comparable value working in the other professions involved in the production and circulation of artworks. For example, a reputed director will seek to enlist top professionals in the key positions of a film production (such as cinematography, screenwriting, editing, costume design, and so forth), and the head of a publishing house will entrust his most seasoned literary director with the task of managing labor relations with the company's most talented and promising writers or with the latter's agents.[174] Furthermore, in the very early stages of artistic and scientific careers, formal learning trajectories followed by on-the-job learning (and even by apprenticeship, a persistent form of artisanal organization in certain artistic and technical-artistic trades) are heavily determined by an individual's association with experienced partners. These are the people who provide an artist on the path toward professionalization with better opportunities for developing his skills in demanding projects, through contact with fellow artists who have themselves been selected based on their potential.

Art worlds combine labile organizational architectures (for example, networks, projects, and/or vertical disintegration) with teams structured through the association of professionals of equivalent quality or reputation— that is, through assortative matching. Labor markets for the most highly qualified jobs are, in this way, hierarchically ordered by professional pairings. A successful career dynamic constitutes a movement of upward mobility in a world stratified by networks of acquaintances and recurring collaborations. In my above presentation of the existing analyses of job stratification by functional importance, I highlighted that, in the practice of an artistic profession, talent is a complementary rather than additive factor of production. Assembling talents of approximately equal level—each in their respective function (interpretation, organizational mediation, editing, fundraising, among others)—has a multiplicative effect on a given project's chances for success and on the project collaborators' chances of accumulating reputation.[175] The interdependence of performances renders the benefits of this relationship complementary: A publisher who attracts talented authors will increase his own chances of expanding his experience and renown in the editorial field, just as a talented author will benefit from collaborating with a publisher reputed for his professional qualities.

Robert Faulkner was first to demonstrate, in his study of Hollywood cinema, the power of assortative matching in the cultural industry.[176] Fabien Accominotti has since shown that the mobility of painters in the gallery networks he studied follows a similar mechanism.[177] Numerous studies dedicated to scientific careers, networks of collaboration and copublication among researchers, and upward mobility in the American academic labor market have likewise revealed how (1) stratification of the professor-researcher population by reputation level (in terms of productivity, visibility, and readership) regulates collaborative pairings; and (2) the recruitment and career mobility market is governed by the rule whereby the candidate's relative value must be matched to the institution's position in the hierarchy of excellence.

We can easily connect the assortative matching argument to the dynamic analysis of careers based on the mechanisms of competitive tournament and cumulative advantage. In the course of artists' early formative experiences, capacities manifest themselves differently and unequally according to each individual. What still remains undetermined, however, is the nature of the differences in talent that exist between the creators who, over the relatively long term, will achieve success—either lastingly or not—and those who will fare less well. Expressed in terms of probabilities of success, the advantage gained from demonstrating a potential talent early in one's career may indeed be weak; yet any (great or small) difference perceived in each test of competitive comparison suffices to polarize the investments and wagers of system actors (such as the artists themselves, trainers, professionals, patrons, entrepreneurs, critics, consumers). The learning content of different work situations relies on the same mechanism: There exists an optimal profile for expanding one's skills, which is a function of the number and variety of work experiences and of the quality of the collaborative networks mobilized by the artist as he or she moves from one project to the next.

The relative comparison of artworks and artistic performances conducted in competitive tests, together with the lasting indeterminacy of the course of creative activity, imbue artistic labor with a continual tension. It is on this basis that analyses of the gaps in reputation and success put forth the causal role of networks of interdependence and cooperation in artistic labor. For in order to create and diffuse their works, creators and artists enter into contractual relations with organizations, such as artist agencies, publishing houses, recording companies, painting galleries, production companies, and so on.

Selective tests, as well as information on the value of an artist's commitment to creative labor provided step by step to himself, his peers, his colleagues, and his supporters, allow us to understand the career dynamics of artists foremost as a learning trajectory within a segmented system of activity. Whether we focus on the professionals who sponsor the artist's debut, on his partners, or on the various other categories of art world actors with whom he establishes work relationships, it is through the development of collaborative networks that an artist organizes his activities. This is especially so given that he must mobilize diversified resources in order to develop his work capabilities.

Two remarkable consequences of assortative matching must be highlighted. First, the multiple and incessant evaluative judgments, on the basis of which reputation hierarchies are constructed, act as structuring forces that segment a professional milieu whose activities do not fit in a stable organizational mold. Second, gaps in talent that are initially small, or at the very least of uncertain importance with regard to future success, are rapidly increased by the game of assortative matching—and this, due to the multiplicative effect this game has on the expression of the individual qualities of collaborators, and to the authority it bestows on those who co-opt each other for their creative projects.

We are now in a better position to understand how a hierarchy develops. A hierarchy is founded on reputation, which has the functional property of an efficient vector of information and investment in a universe of sharply differentiated activities and goods. Neither art world professionals nor consumers can estimate through direct experience the value of every artist and artwork; nor can they continuously reestimate an artist's value in the shifting context of incessantly renewed competition. As Arthur Stinchcombe explains,[178] the vocabulary of talent, genius, brilliance, and creativity is a common means of attributing extraordinary qualities to individuals in sectors of activity wherein success is highly uncertain (for example, the arts, research, advertising). The primary semantic function of these terms is to draw a sharp distinction between these extraordinary qualities and all the other typically measurable qualities of an individual. Furthermore, these terms are essentially assigned *a posteriori,* as a means of domesticating and categorizing that which is unmeasurable—that which cannot be predicted but only "retrodicted." This vocabulary acts to convert an uncertainty dispelled *a posteriori* (in light of experience) into an expectation of success. To paraphrase the title of a work by Niklas Luhmann, the attribution of talent acts as a mechanism for reducing social complexity.[179]

The increase in artist reputation reveals the existence of a mechanism of cumulative advantage. The artistic career presents itself to a young professional as a succession of comparative tests in which each performance is judged individually. For an artist who has completed a series of such tests, reputation constitutes a form of capital that can be managed in various ways to protect him from the variability of instantaneous evaluations and to more rapidly increase the benefits derived from his fame. Ascribing talent leads to granting a more stable value to the favored artist and his works; insofar as it is equated with the substantial qualities evoked by the artist's name, this value becomes incorporated into the artist's identity.

Rather than defending only artworks, publishers and art dealers support artists themselves. They thus contribute to building artists' careers, and urge consumers to focus their interest and cultural investments on these specifically.[180]

An artist's reputation rating allows for his integration into a system of stratified relations: It is profitable for an artist to be associated with other artists and professionals of at least equivalent standing. The game of relations of exchange and collaboration defines a hierarchy of artist status. In a competitive system of this type, an artist's position in the hierarchy is associated with the reputation he has accumulated. This position becomes a "status": a hierarchical indicator of quality utilized in a system of relations and exchanges that is more stable than the sum of information contained in the value attributed to an individual's different accomplishments. According to Joel Podolny's analysis:

> Each knows that there exists uncertainty about her underlying qualities, and each knows that past enactments of those qualities will not entirely remove the uncertainty about whether those qualities exist today. Given this uncertainty, each knows that others will look to her status, as revealed through associations and relations, as a signal of that underlying quality.[181]

Thus, reputation reduces uncertainty, and status reduces uncertainty about the current informative value of reputational signals linked to past "enactments." The complete trajectory of reputation accumulation no longer matters when we assume that the value ascribed to an artist—his status, as Podolny puts it—sums up and guarantees all of the information produced and exchanged in the art world concerning that artist's relative quality.

Reputation, of course, can always be contested so long as it continues to be subjected to tests of interindividual competition. Nonetheless, through the mechanisms of self-reinforcement and assortative matching, reputation offers deeply unequal opportunities for the actualization of creative talent, no matter how small and indeterminate this talent's initial distinctive value may be.

Talent and Hierarchies: A Model

The picture formed by the different elements of the analytical puzzle that I have presented in this chapter to explore the question of talent and inequalities in the arts is, in fact, more simple than it appears. This picture can be likened to the model Roger Gould developed to explain the emergence of social hierarchies.[182] The four components of Gould's theoretical model, as highlighted by Thomas DiPrete and Gregory Eirich, are as follows.[183]

First, there exist intrinsic differences in quality between individuals' performance of activities that generate both hierarchical rankings and segmentation by status. These differences (or the distribution of qualities that they express) are an exogenous characteristic of the action system. It is impossible to determine with precision the magnitude of these differences, but their existence is revealed through relative comparisons. This point emerged from the above analysis, when I examined the relevance of two models of disproportionate reward amplification: Rosen's superstar model and Merton's model of cumulative advantage. Merton sought to strengthen the force of his argument by postulating that diverging trajectories in individual careers can be entirely due to chance, rather than to any intrinsic differences in quality. In doing so, however, he merely conferred a chance coefficient on the basic postulate according to which even a small initial difference is sufficient to trigger gaps in success, which are then considerably amplified. In support of the argument of intrinsic differences, I presented the following: Allison, Long, and Krauze's modeling of Merton's argument; De Vany's calculations, which bring into focus the inflection points at which the probability of making a career in cinema differentiates itself from a random game of chance; and the analysis of careers based on the model of competitive tournaments, in which stars emerge from a series of selective tests that gradually reduce the number of artists in a given cohort. In these models, the probability of completing, in a stochastic process, a great number of stages increases when, at every stage, the individual performs even slightly better than his competitors. Opposed to this is the postulate that differences simply do not exist. This postulate underlies analyses that attribute success entirely to processes of social influence (talent as a pure social and commercial construction), as well as counterfactual analyses that examine how society would look if there were no competition or differences in talent. We have seen that these analyses present insurmountable logical and anthropological incoherencies.

Second, the differences in quality that underlie gaps in success are not fully observable. The analysis I have conducted here is based on the following hypothesis: The mechanism of relative comparison draws its power from the fact that it is impossible to observe the personal factors implicated in success or the way these factors are combined. Does our ignorance on this point amount to epistemic uncertainty, which the progress of research will eventually reduce to a distribution of measurable probabilities? A more fruitful hypothesis is that we are facing a more fundamental uncertainty—one that relates to the interactions and retroactions present in the list of factors that determine success. This incomplete observability of differences in quality has a major function: It acts as a veil of ignorance that lets a great number of candidates nourish the hope of making a career in the professions of invention and creation, despite the harsh reality of a sharply asymmetrical, Pareto-type distribution of chances for success. Everyone can assume that success is the result of a combination of factors such as hard work, chance, and ability. However, the highly imperfect specification of those factors and of how they are combined leads each candidate to overestimate his chances for success. For the individual, the benefits of this indeterminacy lie in the experience he acquires through on-the-job learning. When persistence in the face of failure is facilitated by mechanisms that act as barriers preventing a candidate from exiting the field (for example, psychological predispositions, collective culture, deceptive socialization surrounding career risks), losses are measured in terms of wasted qualities that could be employed in other professions. Artistic and scientific careers must be bound to a constellation of secondary professional roles (teaching, entrepreneurship, management, for example) that offer resources for managing the uncertainty attached to the most attractive role—that of creator—which bestows outstanding reputations and rewards on a narrow minority of professionals.

Third, we infer the quality of an individual from the attention that others accord him. I have highlighted that artistic or scientific work would be unthinkable were it not oriented toward attracting others' attention. Moreover, as I showed in the first two chapters, winning the attention of others involves entering into a situation in which one is judged by and compared to others. This allows us to grasp how the dynamic of cumulative advantage is triggered by the selective attention accorded to individuals and artworks in a given public or professional community. This attention is an informational signal transmitted to others that can rapidly provoke rational contagion through networks of interpersonal relationships among an increasing number of individuals. As a result, the status conferred on the person that is most successful concentrates attention on him, and in turn provides him with a disproportionate advantage. Gould formulates the argument as such:

> According to the theory proposed here, the reason positions with greater and lesser advantage exist is that judgments about relative quality are socially influenced. Socially influenced judgments amplify underlying differences, so that actors who objectively rank above the mean on some abstract quality dimension are overvalued while those ranking below the mean are undervalued—relative to the baseline scenario, in which social influence does not operate. Amplification occurs because observable interactions expressing

judgments of quality are also cues to other actors seeking guidance for their own judgments.

As a result, even if judgments are ultimately shaped by the underlying qualities of individuals, the benefits those judgments determine are exaggerated on one end of the scale and diminished on the other. At the same time, the advantageous positions individuals on the high end occupy are not, in this theory, consciously created or defended by anyone: each individual contributes to the creation of structural positions simply by allowing the judgments of others to influence his or her own.

Note that the mechanism just sketched succinctly captures much of what sociologists mean by the term "status," which is to say the prestige accorded to individuals because of the abstract positions they occupy rather than because of immediately observable behavior. The opinions of a respected public figure, for instance, receive more attention and credence than those of ordinary folk even when the opinions themselves are quite mundane. The difference is no doubt due in part to the past achievements that made the public figure's reputation in the first place; but it is also, according to my argument, due to the recognition by observers that all other observers are prepared to give the opinion in question a great deal of attention.[184]

Fourth, I have emphasized the dynamic of assortative matching, which itself acts as a trigger in the mechanism of cumulative advantage. The unique characteristic of assortative matching is that it provides "matched" individuals with higher returns on their respective abilities than they would otherwise obtain in the case of random matching. A first-rate actor and a great director can hope to obtain benefits from their collaboration in the form of experience and rewards far superior than those presented by a simple additive function. One aspect of talent—and one of its benefits—is that it leads to higher gains through collaboration with such a partner over a less talented actor or director; this form of association, in other words, has a multiplicative effect. This is especially the case when work is organized on a project-by-project basis, as is so common in the arts. This type of organization assembles and disassembles teams from one project to the next, selecting and matching individuals based on their reputation and value. In turn, the analysis in terms of assortative matching reinforces the argument that individuals are stratified by status in the highly competitive worlds of the arts and sciences. Whenever individuals' qualities are incompletely observed, reputation reduces uncertainty about individual value. Moreover, as Podolny explains, the status obtained from a given position in the structure of the professional world reinforces the credibility of the information provided by reputation. Assortative matching does not, however, constitute an iron law of success. There are two contradictory forces in operation. On the one hand, competition mechanisms that exploit uncertainty as the fuel of innovation favor reputation rankings with little historical depth: An artist is worth the value of his latest art-works or performances. Furthermore, team composition must achieve a balance between the reputational value of matched members and the search for new talents that also match the project. On the other hand, ar-tistic labor is organized into careers, which reduces the excessive volatility of reputations: An artist has an intrinsic value, attested by the cumulative dynamic of his career, and this value affects how the quality of his new creations will be perceived.

The Romain Gary/Émile Ajar Affair

This four-point argument may be illustrated, in the form of a natural ex-periment,[185] by the career of the French writer Romain Gary, who won the prestigious Goncourt Prize literary award in 1956. Gary later published under the pen name of Émile Ajar and was once again a laureate of the Goncourt Prize under this fictitious identity. A detailed account of the affair may be found on the website of Émile Ajar's publisher, Mercure de France:

> In the early 1970s, Romain Gary was a very well-known author whose works were published by the renowned French publisher, Gallimard. His first novel, *Education européenne,* came out in 1945. In 1956, Gary was awarded the Goncourt Prize for *Les Racines du ciel.* But the writer soon yearned to start anew. By 1973, he had already written 19 novels and felt he could no longer surprise anyone. Thus began the adventure of Émile Ajar. After having fin-ished writing *Gros câlin*—a sort of fable on solitude in which a statistician falls in love with a python—Gary signed his book Émile Ajar and sent it to Gallimard, where the manuscript was refused. Without exposing himself as the real author, Gary then sent it to Simone Gallimard at Mercure de France, where it was immediately accepted for publishing. Taken for a first novel, the book was quite favorably received by critics, but doubt soon spread about the author's real identity. Who might have been behind the name Émile Ajar? Raymond Queneau? Perhaps Louis Aragon? *Gros Câlin* was expected to win the Renaudot Prize, but Gary's confidant Robert Gallimard convinced him to refuse the award in advance. In 1975, in order to put an end to all suspicion, Gary decided to give life to his pseudonym. This scenario played out in the publication of a text whose temporary working title was *La Tendresse des pierres,* before being released under the title *La vie devant soi.* Gary chose his young nephew Paul Pavlowitch, a rather gifted jack-of-all-trades, to incarnate the novelist Ajar. Then-literary director Michel Cournot met the young man in Geneva and Simone Gallimard met him in a Copenhagen suburb. Émile Ajar was awarded the Goncourt Prize for this novel in November of the same year. Since no single author could be awarded the prize more than once,

Gary—following advice from his lawyer Gisèle Halimi—tried to dissuade his nephew from accepting it, but Paul Pavlowitch was by then too caught up in the game. Soon identified as Gary's nephew, Pavlowitch admitted that he had had no part in writing the novel. However, this had no effect on its triumphant success: It sold more than a million copies and was translated into twenty-three languages. In 1979, a final novel—*L'Angoisse du roi Salomon*—was released under the name Émile Ajar. Romain Gary committed suicide on December 2, 1980. In a text written on March 21, 1979, and entitled *Vie et mort d'Emile Ajar,* he had concluded with these words: "I've had a lot of fun. Goodbye and thank you." On June 30, 1981, an AFP press release revealed Ajar's true identity.[186]

Romain Gary revealed his double identity only posthumously, in a book published after his suicide. In it, he explained his desire to perform a "creation of the self by the self":

> I was an author who was ranked, catalogued, taken for granted—which spared professionals from truly reading and knowing my work. . . . I was weary of being only myself. I was tired of the image of Romain Gary that people had fixed upon me once and for all for thirty years—since *Education européenne* brought sudden fame to a young aviator. . . . They'd turned me into this character. . . . To begin anew, to relive, to be someone else became the great temptation of my existence. . . . The truth is that I was profoundly overtaken by the oldest, protean temptation of man: multiplicity.[187]

This doubling of identity—twice crowned with success—is a natural experiment on the relationship between intrinsic quality and statutory identity. Owing to his intrinsic qualities, the author gained notable success with his first novel, published under the pen name Romain Gary (after having published under his legally registered birth name), and attained consecration with the Goncourt Prize. Then, displeased to find himself constrained by a reputation and status that, as he saw it, negatively biased evaluations of his work, he rid himself of the burden of being oneself and initiated a second, parallel literary career, winning the Goncourt Prize for his second novel published under his alias. In doing so, he sought to demonstrate that his success was entirely due to his intrinsic qualities, and that gains derived from the status he had acquired in his official career had become handicaps. On the one hand, the new identity freed him from the burden of his past and provided him with increased freedom of invention, sheltered from the predetermined expectations that shaped evaluations by the public and critics. On the other hand, he took the risk of seeing the experiment confirm the decline in the renown attached to his official career. Were these, then, the same intrinsic qualities of a talented writer that were exposed to the erosion of public attention *and* protected by a pseudonym that eliminated the statutory assignations produced by the machinery of competition and the pursuit of originality in the literary world?[188] And were these the only qualities at play in determining the success of the experiment? When we consider the intervention of some of the key Parisian publishers of the time, as well as the advantages offered by Gary's own expertise in negotiating demands with them, we understand that the engineering of Ajar also resided in the networks of assortative matching discussed above.

CHAPTER FIVE

How Can Artistic Greatness Be Analyzed?

Beethoven and His Genius

ANALYZING the career and the work of a great artist assumes that it is possible to describe a fragment of the history of the world subject to the laws of causality, and at the same time to endow the artist with the power to act: The artist's greatness can then be characterized by his ability to change the predictable course of things (in the artistic world and beyond it, directly or indirectly, in the world in general)—an ability to which causes and reasons must be assigned. That is why works on artistic greatness or genius hesitate between several formulas. One of these stresses the power of control that makes the artist dependent on social and economic forces, even in the enclosed space that is his professional world, where he is nonetheless supposed to enjoy a "relative autonomy." According to the common schema of the ruse of historical reason, brilliant invention, even and especially when it is reputed to break with the social order, in fact serves to consolidate that order. A second conception of artistic greatness makes the artist a rational strategist capable of seeking out the best way of organizing his activity in order to appropriate an artistic and social power equal to the talent he knows he has.

In the first case, the creator is merely a remarkable agent of history, the plaything of forces that pervasively determine his activity. In the second case, he is an actor who intervenes, deliberates, makes use of resources. Does he escape the laws of social gravity? Certainly not. But then how can we understand his power of action and his ability to make something radically new emerge, if his action is caught in the nets of social determinism? The solution that often used to be proposed consisted of explaining the great artist's behavior by means of analytical contortions that were more enigmatic than clarifying: If the creator is great, that is because he is the producer of the objective truth of society, like the thinkers, scientists or philosophers who are supposed to look down on the social or historical game from a privileged, superior position in order to conceive it. The great artist is one who succeeds in twisting historical determinisms back on themselves. This heroic construction, visible in the work of Adorno or Bourdieu, assumes in particular that a society's successive historical configurations can be described as structured totalities within which conflicts occur between "macro-actors" (classes or fractions of classes) with which the artist never identifies completely, and that precisely this confers on him the power of objectivizing their oppositions along with the whole sociohistorical arena of these competitive battles.

We still have to understand how a creator's reputation is established. The attributed greatness of his work is ratified only gradually, on the basis of evaluations that are at first divergent and competing. Historical analysis of the gradual convergence of evaluations arouses the suspicion that the attribution of value is historically and socially contingent: Things could have gone quite differently, and what we moderns—oddly committed to the conservative cult of heritages and to the destructive cult of perpetual innovations—count among the creations that are candidates for eternal admiration might be no more than the greatly magnified result of a contingent organization of social struggles. The price to be paid for our celebration of genius would be the disregard of social violence. In this case, given sufficient persistence and means, the act of invention could be wholly explained, and the author would be merely the plaything of forces that might have been organized in an entirely different way.

The creative career of Ludwig van Beethoven is not part of the Romantic legend of the misunderstood, suffering genius, because his importance was rapidly recognized on an international scale. It is the precocious success of a profoundly original creator that constitutes the puzzle: Was he the representative of social forces that backed him and were able to take advantage of his audacities and successes, a revolutionary who was able to mobilize unusually diverse sources of support, or the glorious embodiment of the development of art in a sphere that was henceforth to be much more autonomous, thanks to transformations in the musical system that Beethoven's work accelerated or even made possible?

In the usual way of presenting the evolution of composers' social condition, matters are clear: Beethoven's career provides the paradigm for a series of changes that transformed the composer's social status around the turn of the nineteenth century[1] on both sides of the organization of creative labor. On the side of employers, patrons, and individual or institutional sponsors, supervision lost its power of constraint, in accord with a conjunction of motives that entered sequentially into a self-reinforcing spiral of emancipation. The traditional power of the social groups that were the main investors in artistic "patronage"[2] was weakened by the social and political revolutions that hastened the decline of aristocracies or was subjected to increasingly effective competition by the growing power of the bourgeoisie, and, on the other hand, artistic individualism asserted itself, armed with the ideological apparatus that celebrates the incommensurable merits of exceptional talent, of genius. The notion of genius provided a new way of calibrating the originality embodied in the person of the artist when the aesthetics of the second half of the eighteenth century refounded the theory of the exceptional individual, a model defying imitation and mistrusting it, an unpredictable personality that is ideally creative in the ontological sense of the term.[3] The expressive counterpart of this historical pivoting toward a different embodiment of innovative accomplishment is the psychological framework of Beethovenian genius: the fierce will to independence, the spirit of rebellion always ready to resist an authority too quick to forget that it has only temporal power and can exercise no serious control in the intellectual order, which is the highest because it is more directly expressive of humanity's superior and universal interests.

But the composer also moves in a more complex environment in which his multiple and composite ties can no longer be reduced to the relationship of employment and patronage. The historical change operates in the system that organizes musical life: With Beethoven, the proofs of the decisive consolidation of market structures begin to multiply greatly. What does the term "market" refer to, in this case? On the supply side, it refers mainly to the conditions of the professionalization of musicians resulting from the multiplication of remunerated forms of activity intended to meet a stimulated demand. A massive rise in the number of public concerts with admission fees, revenues procured by publishing scores and their many different offshoots (transcriptions, abridgments, arrangements), a supply of new musical works for several distinct markets (on a continuum ranging from the most sophisticated and demanding forms of art music to music intended to entertain and to harmonizations of popular music), the development of music instruction, the multiplication of orchestral and instrumental performances that put works into circulation and provide new commissions for composers and work for performing artists—such is the virtuous circle in which the Beethovenian paradigm is inscribed. If these changes are cumulative and operate gradually, it remains that Beethoven's reputation and the style of control it guaranteed him to have over the means of providing for himself offer an example of a precocious emancipation.

Thus the Beethovenian paradigm is that of the intersection of the new social situation, which strengthened the power of the bourgeoisie in its battle against the aristocracy, the success of the norm of expressive individualism in art, and the development of the music market. In the works to which I will refer, these three dimensions are mentioned, but taken into account unequally. The resulting explanatory compromises provide an instructive yardstick for gauging the difficulty of conceiving the success of creative labor.

Confronted by this challenge, there are three possible solutions. The first consists in perpetuating the traditional diagnosis of the correlation between an artistic destiny and a given social configuration endowed with its distinctive structure. The empirical requirement will remain limited, the essential point residing in the modeling by the play of forces and the play of homologies between the social scene and the fabric of the artwork, via the position of the artist, whose activity and personality must remain summarizable in a determining equation, and stable during the time of his career. But an author like Theodor Adorno does not endorse the mechanistic simplicity of assimilation of Beethovenian genius to the dynamics of the emancipation of the bourgeoisie. Instead, he opts for a dialectical interpretation of artistic greatness as the production of social truth.[4] The result is a strange operation of turning social determination back on itself in order to preserve, under the name of autonomy, the emergent value of creative invention and its power to intervene in the course of history.

The second solution may initially seem to be an empiricist variant of the first. The goal is to base explanation in terms of determining causes and social structures on a sociohistorical investigation. Beethoven becomes the actor of an ambivalent historical configuration: According to an argument frequently employed in studies in historical sociology or the social history of art, there is a category of great artists whose careers can be analyzed on the basis of the overlapping of, and transition between, two very different systems for organizing artistic life. Norbert Elias applied this explanatory scheme to the study of the career and behavior of Mozart.[5] Tia DeNora situated her examination of Beethoven's career[6] in the transition and competition between classes and between modes of organizing musical life by increasing the empirical density of her study, and also by radicalizing the enterprise of reducing the greatness of genius to a pure matter of social construction and self-interested conflict between social classes. One of the

most spectacular procedures of this constructionist approach is the abolition of differences of talent: By assuming that competing composers are
equally endowed with creative inventiveness, DeNora thinks she can gauge
the importance and the efficacy of the social and economic resources invested more heavily in one creator than in another and thereby explain the
considerable differences in artistic success and social recognition that put
Beethoven at the top. Such a solution is unrealistic and leads to a mass of
contradictions in the argument.

I would suggest a third mode of analysis. The competitive organization
of professional activities and the persistent indetermination of the course
of innovative labor situate the course of the creator's career in a segmented,
but not fixed, world of networks of activity rather than under the control
of omnipotent entities ("the aristocracy," "the bourgeoisie"). In this framework, the question of talent and differences in talent can be approached in
a different way: Rather than hesitating between the reduction to zero ad-
vocated by an untenable egalitarianism and the age-old mythology of the
infinite gap that makes great creators the equals of the gods, it is easy to
take a different path, which brings out the mechanisms of the amplification of differences in talent that are initially indeterminate, and makes
room for the socially and economically structuring power of networks of
actors.

The Artist's Greatness: A Social Maximum?

A first conception sees in the great artist the representative of a class or a
fraction of a class as it is embodied in closely linked groups of patrons and
sponsors whose worldview or ideology guide (or even determine) the artist's production through and through. In the opening chapter of his book
Le Dieu Caché, Lucien Goldmann sets forth his materialist theory of artistic greatness this way:

> What I have called a "world vision" is a convenient term for the whole com-
> plex of ideas, aspirations and feelings which links together the members of a
> social group (a group which, in most cases, assumes the existence of a social
> class) and which opposes them to members of other social groups.
>
> This is certainly a highly schematic view, an extrapolation made by the
> historian for purposes of convenience; nevertheless, it does extrapolate a ten-
> dency which really exists among the members of a certain social group, who
> all attain this class consciousness in a more or less coherent manner. I say
> "more or less," because even though it is only rarely that an individual is
> completely and wholly aware of the whole meaning and direction of his aspi-

rations, behavior and emotions, he is nevertheless always relatively conscious of them. In a few cases—and it is these which interest us—there are exceptional individuals who either actually achieve or who come very near to achieving a completely integrated and coherent view of what they and the social class to which they belong are trying to do. The men who express this vision on an imaginative or conceptual plane are writers and philosophers, and the more closely their work expresses this vision in its complete and integrated form, the more important does it become. They then achieve the maximum possible awareness of the social group whose nature they are expressing.[7]

This characterization of artistic greatness, by simply linking determining variables with their maximum level, continues to confine the artist in the social net of the group he represents. On this account, the great artist should in all logic be deprived of any chance of acceding to a lasting or universal glory beyond the horizon of a generation. That is the argument used by those who reduce the significance of the artist's work to the point of view of the members of the upper class who commission and finance his work or are its principal consumers. The deduction is crude and reductive: The argument is that if these artworks were created in societies shaped by very profound social inequalities and were even made possible by the domination of the upper classes, they could not, in an ideally democratic world, be designated for public and universal admiration, as it is the case today when they are presented and preserved in museums, concert halls, theaters, operas, libraries, and all the places and manifestations financed by public funds, and beyond that, and incorporated into the powerful vector of the intergenerational transmission of reverence for masterpieces that is the content of educational programs in schools and universities. Marx was far more subtly perplexed when he asked why the artworks produced by a given society—Greek, slave-owning—could continue to give us artistic enjoyment to the point of serving as a norm, an inaccessible model. He suggested that the dialectic of production and consumption must therefore assume that the historical career of artworks is autonomous and that the history of artistic evaluation is nondialectical.

There is another possible way of linking the greatness of genius with a social maximum. Instead of examining an artist's relation to his contemporaries in order to see how the consciousness and worldview that the group cannot formulate is concentrated in him, we can consider the genealogical depth of exceptional figures by taking advantage of an essential characteristic of the artwork, its goal of becoming a durable good. The artwork contains time within itself, the time of the preservation of the past and its transformation into a heritage, and that of the transmission of knowledge and models from which creators must both take their inspiration and deviate: They have to avoid allowing themselves to be crushed by the weight of the past[8] while at the same time conferring on their work a historical "positional value,"[9] on pain of running the fatal risk to which originality exposes an artist, that of insignificant arbitrariness. As I will show in Chapter 6, the merging of the two principles of unpredictability and inevitability, of freedom and necessity, in the determination of the creative act and its result, is at the origin of all modern aesthetics.

This argument is used by Georg Simmel to entwine the exceptional artist in the strands of historical determinism. In *Philosophy of Money,* Simmel took his inspiration from Marxist theory, which reduces the value of any good or any performance to the quantity of labor necessary to produce it. The problem resides in the great difference in remuneration between activities that nonetheless "subjectively" demand equal levels of commitment."[10] The solution is provided by the transition from the subjective to the objective level: It consists in taking into account, for each activity, the "quantum of labor already accumulated in the objective, technical prerequisites" whose contributions are condensed in the activity of professionals occupying superior positions:

> Compared with "unqualified" labour, all qualified labour as such in no way rests solely upon the higher education of the worker but rests equally upon the higher and more complicated structure of the objective conditions of work, of materials and the historical-technical organization. Similarly, however mediocre the pianist may be, he requires such an old and broad tradition, such an immense supra-individual supply of technical and artistic labour products, that of course these, in their collective ennoblement of his work, extend far beyond the possibly subjectively much more considerable talents of the tightrope walker or the conjurer. The same is true more generally. What we treasure as the higher achievements—viewed solely according to the category of the occupation and without personal elements affecting their level— are those achievements that, in the development of culture, have been relatively conclusively and almost completely prepared over a long period of time. Within such achievements is included a maximum amount of work on the part of predecessors and contemporaries rather than of their technical pre-conditions, however unjust it may be to award a particularly high payment or estimation for the fortuitous holder of such talents that are derived from this emergent value in view of the completely supra-personal origins of the objective performance.[11]

Here Simmel transposes to the evaluation of artistic activity the Marxist labor theory of value (inspired by Ricardo), in which the price of goods is determined on the basis of the infinite series of all the labor inputs that have in the past served to produce what is currently necessary for the production of the merchandise in question.

In order to be generalizable, the Marxist labor theory of value had to radically homogenize the value of labor, that is, to transform every form of labor, right up to the most complex and most skilled activity, into a multiple of simple, unskilled work. Could this theory be applied to the determination of the value of artworks? Marx identified the case of unique artworks, such as paintings and sculptures, as one of the possible objections to his theory: According to him, the determination of the price of artworks is a function of the relation between the monopoly-holding vendor and the intensity of the demand by buyers, and not of the quantity of labor socially necessary for their production. The market for artworks is in fact based on mechanisms of monopolistic competition that situate them, with their character of uniqueness and thus intrinsic physical rarity, at a distance from the usual procedures of pricing goods.[12]

Marx denied the existence of competences that could not be produced, and thus could not be expressed in investments in training and apprenticeship: In other words, as I showed in Chapter 4, he rejected the existence of different talents and abilities unequally distributed from one individual to another. Simmel, for his part, reduces qualities to quantitative considerations, and thus the complex to a multiple of the simple, but he does not reject exceptional talent. In the manifestation of exceptional facilities and abilities accorded to certain individuals he sees the expression of a collective heredity. Genius is equivalent to an intense accumulation of labor carried out by several generations and condensed in one individual, and the rarity of artistic geniuses is due to the length of time necessary to achieve this accumulation:

> The fact that a genius needs to learn so much less than the average person for a similar achievement, that a genius knows things that they have not experienced—this wonder seems to indicate an exceptionally full and easy impressive co-ordination of inherited energies. If one traces this inheritance sequence far enough back and makes clear that all experiences and accomplishments within the same series can be gained and developed further only through real labours and through practising, then the individual distinctiveness of the genius's achievement also appears as the condensed result of the *work* of generations. The "well-endowed" person would, consequently, be the one in whom a maximum of his predecessors' work is accumulated in a latent form that is designed for further accumulation. Thus, the higher value that the labour of such a person possesses because of its quality also rests, in the last instance, upon a quantitatively larger amount of labour that of course he personally does not have to perform but rather that the quality of its organization makes possible further results. If we presuppose the same actual labour effort on the part of the individual, then the achievement would be distinctively higher in so far as the structure of its psychic-physical system embodied with noticeably greater ease a distinctively greater sum of experiences and abilities gained by the ancestors. And if one were to express the

amount of value of the achievements not through the amount of labour necessary but through the "socially necessary labour time" for their production, then this too would not avoid the same interpretation: that the higher value of achievements containing special endowments means that society must always live through and function for a specific longer period before it can again produce a genius. It requires the longer period of time, which determines the value of the achievement, not, in this case, for its immediate production but for the production of—though appearing only in relatively longer intervals— the producers of such achievements.[13]

Here *qualia,* the qualities that seem to designate the very essence of individuality, are no more than contractions of *quanta.* What is this argument worth? Either it falls into the strictest kind of determinism, and socializing heredity in this way is equivalent to identifying certain individuals' exceptional gifts with the advantages of a social position inherited from a family line. Or, as is clear in Simmel's other works devoted to great creators, the hypothesis is not at all so determinist, and simply says that the genius is never as individual and self-created as he may seem, and that it is good for society to recognize this. However, the hypothesis thereby loses all chance of being correctly specified. For how can we explain on this basis the fact that one artist's talent can attract a much greater demand than that of his competitor, and be rated at a much higher price, to the point that the difference in prices has no relation to the quantities of labor and training incorporated in the product or performance of these two artists?

The Torsions of the Determinist Explanation of Genius

The arguments that sociology has put forth against the mechanistic determinism that was so highly valued in the first studies on the social history of art were sufficiently well argued that a great artist's production is no longer considered to be a simple vehicle for spreading a dominant ideology. But so long as the deterministic framework is recognized, the characterization of the creator paradoxically becomes more problematic insofar as it seeks to become denser and more realistic. How, in fact, can the great creator be made a social being, a part of a whole subjected to laws determining behaviors no one can escape, and at the same time see in him the active principle, the motive force in a world of production organized according to its own laws?

Adorno's reply is based on the motif of the differentiation and autonomization of spheres of activity that had already been advanced by Durkheim and even more by Weber. But Adorno arrives at a paradoxical solution. The

relationship the artwork maintains with society is not in any way a classical causal relation: Like a Moebius strip, the artwork expresses the essence
of society all the more completely because it is the flipside of a depiction of
social realities or of a representation of social realities. To produce this
figure of the objectification of the world as it surges up from the creative
act, Adorno has to challenge any conscious and deliberate attempt to absorb social reality into art, and to state a law of the maximum autonomy
and distance as the condition of the maximum of truth. That is what is
suggested by the reference to Leibnizian monadology:

> The relation of works of art to society is comparable to Leibniz's monad.
> Windowless—that is to say, without being conscious of society, and in any
> event without being constantly and necessarily accompanied by this
> consciousness—the works of art, and notably of music which is far removed
> from concepts, represent society.[14]

How can creative activity, its success and its social anchoring, be described
on the basis of such a conception? The creator becomes great when he
takes up "objective tasks" in the Hegelian sense, that is, when he seeks to
do what the course of history tells him to do in order for society to realize
itself. This makes artistic experience a "contrary of the freedom connected
with the concept of the creative act." In accord with an explicitly Hegelian
schema, the individual is emptied of his particularity when he becomes the
operator of historical necessity:

> Successful works are those in which—as Hegel already knew—the individual
> effort, and indeed the accidental quality of an individual's being as it is, will
> vanish in the necessity of the matter. Its successful particularization recoils
> into the universal.[15]

If there is a creator that Adorno is thinking of, in elaborating this materialist theory anchored in the principle of the autonomy of art, it is precisely
Beethoven. The latter remains, in the part of Adorno's work devoted to
music, the central figure, the creator who obsessed him throughout his life,
and on whom he hoped to finish a great book indefinitely deferred, of
which we have only fragments.[16] For everything having to do with the sociological interpretation of Beethoven's case, Adorno provided the main
lines of approach in his *Introduction to the Sociology of Music,* in which
Beethoven is the composer most often cited and in many respects the heart
of the argument. In this book, Beethoven embodies a sort of Hegel-as-
composer, "since the categories of the philosophy of Hegel can be applied,
without forcing, to every detail of his music." In the artwork Adorno sees
the embodiment of the enigma of an art that is authentically the bearer of
a truth value, and yet socially determined:

If he is the musical prototype of the revolutionary bourgeoisie, he is at the same type the prototype of a music that has escaped from its social tutelage and is esthetically fully autonomous, a servant no longer. His work explodes the schema of a complaisant adequacy of music and society. In it, for all its idealism in tone and posture the essence of society, for which he speaks as the vicar of the total subject, becomes the essence of music itself.[17]

The subject Beethoven is a pure prototype of the bourgeoisie at the same time that he is an antibourgeois, whence the improbable equation of aristocratic support with a work which is that of bourgeois emancipation par excellence:

That this archbourgeois was a protégé of aristocrats fits as neatly into the social character of his oeuvre as the scene we know from Goethe's biography, when he snubbed the court. Reports on Beethoven's personality leave little doubt of his anticonventional nature, a combination of sansculottism with Fichtean braggadocio; it recurs in the plebeian habitus of his humanity. His humanity is suffering and protesting. It feels the fissure of its loneliness. Loneliness is what the emancipated individual is condemned to in a society retaining the mores of the absolutist age, and with them the style by which the self-positing subjectivity takes its own measure.[18]

According to Adorno, Beethoven is the one who has to resolve the problem of the form of the sonata that Haydn and Mozart bequeathed to him, that is, the problem of the production of the musical work as a totality unified deductively, as the systematic dialectic of the isolated parts and the coherence of the compositional whole and as a movement toward full formal autonomy. In so doing, Beethoven produces the essential truth of the society that surrounds him:

The central categories of artistic construction can be translated into social ones. The kinship with that bourgeois libertarianism which rings all through Beethoven's music is a kinship of the dynamically unfolding totality. It is in fitting together under their own law, as becoming, negating, confirming themselves and the whole without looking outward, that his movements come to resemble the world whose forces move them; they do not do it by imitating that world. In this respect Beethoven's attitude on social objectivity is more that of philosophy—the Kantian, in some points, and the Hegelian in decisive ones—than it is the ominous mirroring posture: in Beethoven's music society is conceptlessly known, not photographed.[19]

What is being opposed here is the false identification of the artist with triumphal singularity, a sort of epiphany of bizarreness or individualist idiosyncrasy that would exalt the artist as free self-determination, the pseudo-historical signature of the arbitrary or the gratuitousness of the inventive imagination, without historical depth. For Adorno, being an artist equal to the task means shedding the false individualism that is merely a pseudo-teleological advertisement for the bourgeois order of the world, by means of which artists, "by virtue of the objectivity of tasks, including the tasks they supposedly set themselves, the artists cease to be private individuals and become either a social subject or its vicar."[20]

But this initial qualification of the artist's greatness is not sufficient: It serves only to make him one of the historical figures of the accomplishment of a social order, and thus, if society is governed by the triumph of the bourgeoisie, a full-fledged representative of the latter's ideals. Beethoven's greatness, like Haydn's and Mozart's in their own ways, is to work on the fermentation of artistic leavening: Greatness is a function of a teleological dialectic, because no realization, no accomplishment, is self-contained, and the artist inherits from his predecessors a series of problems that have to be solved, which he re-elaborates and transmits, thus anticipating his own transcendence. The quality of art is measured by its duality, which for Adorno embodies its truth, which consists in expressing social totality from its point of view (this is the Leibnizian metaphor) and, simultaneously, dismantling the identification of the content of art with any social content whatever that can be deduced from the intelligible structure of society:

> As a matter of principle, instead of searching for the musical expression of class standpoints one will do better so to conceive the relation of music to the classes that any music will present the picture of antagonistic society as a whole—and will do it less in the language it speaks than in its inner structural composition. . . . Intramusical tensions are the unconscious phenomena of social tensions.[21]

In this sense, the authentic artwork, the great artwork, is one that constantly spews forth the violence, the resistance, the contradiction inherent in every social organization and, consequently, any inscription of an artist in a given society:

> What joins in the complexion of the work of art are society's *disjecta membra*, no matter how unrecognizable. Gathering in their truth content is all their power, all their contradictoriness, and all their misery. The social side of works of art, to which the cognitive effort is devoted, is not only their adjustment to extraneous desiderates of patrons or of the marketplace but precisely their autonomy and immanent logic. It is true that the problems and solutions of works of art do not arise beyond the systems of social norms. But they do not acquire social dignity until they remove themselves from these norms; the highest productions actually negate them. The esthetic quality of works, their truth content, has little to do with any truth that can be empirically pictured, not even with the life of the soul. But it converges with social truth.[22]

Despite appearances, the Durkheimians who have ventured into the analysis of art[23] have proposed a rather similar analytical framework, which was later systematized in Pierre Bourdieu's structuralist-constructivist theory.[24] A self-limiting mechanism of determination is invoked, that of "relative autonomy":[25] In the course of historical evolution, the sphere of artistic activity has gradually constituted and separated itself as a space of protective confinement in which the artist seeks shelter from the directly constraining influences that are supposed to be exercised on his work. But this professional space is only one part of the social totality, the determining action of the social structure and of the forces that animate it being retranslated into the internal logic of the system of activity concerned. The most valuable artworks and the greatest artists are qualified more or less in accord with the same analytical schema as in Adorno.

Flaubert, as Bourdieu studies him in his *Règles de l'art,* objectifies his social milieu through his work as a writer. How can the artist be made the revealer of the social forces that produce him and the greatness of the artwork be gauged by its truth value? Isn't art governed by the same forces that determine the organization and gravitation of other spheres of the social structure? Two conditions are put upon this surprising turning of social determinism against itself. On the one hand, the social forces that causally determine the great artist's behavior have contradictory properties. Bourdieu takes care to loosen the bonds that are supposed to imprison the great artist in the ideology of his class: The artist has every chance of dominating and objectifying correctly the social world, of which he is nonetheless a member, only if he does not have a set social identity, only if he is not dependent on his origins or a group. That is what allows the creator to produce an artwork endowed with truth value, that of the objectification of his social world:

> The great artistic revolutions are not the act either of the (temporally) dominant, who here as elsewhere have no quarrel with an order that consecrates them, or of the simply dominated, who are usually condemned by their conditions of existence and dispositions to a routine practice of literature and who may supply troops equally to the heretics or to the guardians of the symbolic order. Revolutions are incumbent on those hybrid and unclassifiable beings whose aristocratic dispositions, often associated with a privileged social origin and with the possession of large symbolic capital . . . , underpin a profound "impatience with limits," social but also aesthetic limits, and a lofty intolerance of all compromises with the times.[26]

On the other hand, this objectification is not in any way an enterprise that assimilates the artwork to a sociological essay deliberately undertaken, with his literary means, by a writer of superior lucidity. The operator of the torsion that has to turn determinism against itself, Bourdieu says as Adorno had before him, is work on the form. The same goes for Flaubert's novels, in this case *L'Éducation sentimentale*:

> This series of ruptures in all relationships that, like moorings, could attach the work to groups, to their interests and their habits of thought . . . are totally analogous with those accomplished by science, but are not willed as such and operate at the deepest level of the "unknowing poetics," that is to say, in the work of writing and the work of the social unconscious fostered by the work on form, the instrument of an anamnesis that is both favored and limited by the denegation involved in the imposition of form.[27]

Here, as in Adorno, it is through a kind of emptying out of the self as subject that the creator is produced as an instance of objectification: He frees himself from the laws of social gravity without leaving his world. The sociological equation of artistic genius amounts to making the value of the artist a function of this capacity of "self-determination": Through his work on forms, the great artist is able to attain knowledge of the laws that determine his world and his art. On these two conditions—the unusual composition of forces determining the artist's social identity, work on form—art can claim to be an activity unlike any other. But does the commutation that converts the determined subject into an actor, molding the history of his artistic world and the history of the world, really have the properties of a resource that preserves the determinist framework within which the authors just presented situate their whole analysis?[28] As we have seen, the answer they give is that of an unclassifiable social identity: The individual of genius is a statistically improbable figure because he combines in himself characteristics that are usually separate. But this causal resource might well have only the frail appearance of an argument ad hoc, which would upset the whole analytical edifice. For how can we be sure, for example, that the general principle explaining individual behaviors by social determinisms will hold good if the most eminent individuals strangely escape its law?

Thus, one of the contradictions easily discerned in sociological writings on great artists has to do with a frequent epistemological doubling of the explanation. On the one hand, according to determinist, and even ultradeterminist (in the most spectacular formulas of critical reduction) analytical schemas, the artist's career and success are presented as programmed or controlled, and the artist's behavioral oddities become one of the indices of his social unclassifiability. On the other hand, a strategic interpretation of the creator's behavior and psychology tends to make him an ambitious, calculating figure, determined and rational, who is capable of successful maneuvering.

Conflicting behavioral traits composing an unclassifiable being—this is something that belongs to the repertory of topoi describing the multiple personalities of great men to emphasize the paradoxical dimensions of genius: The great man manipulating great humanistic principles, completely engaged in devoting himself to the cause of art to the point of sacrificing his failing body and to suffering redemptively[29]—this is the Romantic part of the transfiguration—and yet a punctilious calculator of his interests who is capable of baseness and indignities—so much for the realism of the social embodiment. The characteristic under which these contradictory postulations have been summed up for a very long time, and with a marked symbolic prominence since the case of Michelangelo, is that of excess, of the hubris of the genius's temperament. The point would be of little interest did it not suggest that the genius thus appears to be endowed with a hypertrophied, exceptionally discordant humanity. The rhetoric of magnification can in fact also be applied to all the parameters of behavior—the great scientist, the great technician, the great worker, the great hypochondriac, the great fanatic, the great egoist, the great devourer of souls, the great strategist, and so on—and the legend can be woven from all the paradoxes; that is one of the matrices of artistic originality transposed from the artwork to biography.

But the treatment given the theme of the multiplication of the exceptional personality takes on a surprising profile in many sociological explanations of the genius's innovation. The conjunction of the determinist motifs explaining success with strategist notions can escape the most flagrant contradictions only if creative activity as a whole is conceived in terms of control, sometimes internal, sometimes external: The control exercised by patrons or mercantile entrepreneurs over the maturation of creative talent and over its activity, the control the famous creator gradually gains over his environment. Whence this geometry of the play of forces that leads to the conception of the successful artist's creative activity as a process of reversal: The artist turns against his patrons the weapons that initially served to control him. His passivity as a controlled subject, as an individual without particular qualities, over whom the social investment of the powerful or the merchants can deploy its limitless efficacy, is turned into a capacity for action or into activism thanks to the very success of the investment. The puzzle then moves a notch backward: What could drive this commutation?

To support an argument whose epistemological foundation and explanatory value are questionable, another argument, with a very different scope, can be brought in by authors caught in the trap of determinism: one has to seek in the spatial and temporal coordinates of creative activity characteristics that are in accord with the exceptional creator's atypical social identity; that is, the artist's invention has to be connected with an unusual historical situation. This is the case when a great artist or group of innovative artists seems to make the transition from one system of organizing artistic life to another, or when the artist's work is situated in the tension and competition between two systems, for instance between the patronage system and the market[30] or between the corporative and the academic organization of professional activities,[31] or again between academic control of careers and the competitive system of the market.[32] In such situations the forms of social control acting on the artistic sphere and the chances of strategic play increase.

Beethoven between Patronage and the Market, or How to Situate the Genius in His Social Setting

The social history of the arts has greatly cultivated the simplifying narrative when it has been a question of analyzing the means by which artists gradually emancipated themselves from direct control by the powerful. The power of constraint exercised up to the end of the eighteenth century by patrons acting as employers within princely cliques and court structures seemed to offer an example of art's pure relations of direct dependency on its social environment. The study of this power was supposed to provide the key, making it possible to move from the outside of creation— the conditions of production—to its inside—the structure of artworks. In these studies, the great artist is often seen as an innovator on both the aesthetic and social levels, whether he represents the rising power of social forces bearing new aspirations and new worldviews in agreement with the foundations of their power of challenging and socioeconomic revolution, or whether he marks the transition between an old and a new way of organizing artistic production and their respective aesthetic bases. This latter perspective seems to be able to combine analytic attractions in a very particular way: History is embodied in individuals who stand out, that is, who signal ruptures. Without these exceptional figures, history would not manage to provide itself with innovations and discoveries that shift the boundaries of human invention. But without social transformations that act on the probability of seeing these exceptional figures emerge, art, we are told, would not have the powers of invention and rupture provided by geniuses.

The description of the great artist engaged in a battle for a liberation that is indissociably aesthetic and social, who generally makes use of conflicts internal to the dominant classes to support his will to emancipation, that is typically the schema Norbert Elias adopts in his fragmentary analysis of the case of Mozart. However, Elias's view is distinguished from the most mechanistic versions of a certain Marxist determinism, such as the one that governed the historical sociologies of writers like Frederik Antal and Arnold Hauser,[33] for whom the rise of the bourgeoisie and the correlative decline of the aristocracy form a historical background drawn up in accord with a simple geometry that can be maintained for centuries in the same terms—the rise and fall just keep happening—so strangely static is this conception of social clockwork with its weights and counterweights.

Elias's argument is based chiefly on the hypothesis of a relation of constraint between the artist and those who "patronize" him. The only factor that might trigger an emancipatory energy is the ambivalence of the artist's personality, which is such that he can attune himself to the transformations of the society in which he seeks the resources to achieve his professional liberation. According to Elias, in the case of Mozart this ambivalence is the product of two determinisms, one psycho-affective and the other social, and of a high degree of self-consciousness on the part of the artist-genius: Mozart is described as a commoner who lacked the manners of the petite bourgeoisie, but whose spontaneity and frankness provided him with the shelter of a psychological acquiescence to domination as it was imposed by the univocal relations of patronal authority. Mozart's emancipatory power is in reality the product of the combination of two contrary forces—an external relation of dependency and inferiority, and an internal mechanism of reassurance based on implicit confidence in his exceptional talent and an unshakable sense of his superiority over his colleagues. Mozart thus appears transgressive and submissive, in revolt and eager for recognition on the part of the powerful, exceptionally conscious of his talent and of the means of struggling against the system that reined him in, and attached, by his musical imagination and artistic consciousness, to the taste of that traditional society. Aware of his value but caught in the nets of constraint, he seeks paths to emancipation through social and psychological insubordination with regard to the etiquette of court relations. The strong Oedipal flavor of his revolt, as Elias presents it, superimposes, in the explanation of Mozart's behavior and activity, a psychoanalytic determinism on a freedom with regard to his personal history that his acute awareness of his value confers on him. This is in fact the schema of the turning of determinism back on itself, made possible by the ambivalent characteristics of the individual and the situation in which he moves. The general law in which Elias ends up imprisoning and thus making insipid this suggestive analysis remains rather banally mechanistic and substitutes for the genius, the supreme incarnation of the worldview of a period or a class, the fertilizing power of periods of transition:

> On closer examination, however, it not uncommonly emerges that outstanding achievements occur most frequently at times which could at most be called transitional phases if static concepts of epochs are used. In other words, such achievements arise from the dynamics of the conflict between the canons of older declining classes and newer rising ones.[34]

To be sure, historical reality is easier to stylize than to explore in detail. In a brief, dryly critical, and rather condescending review of Elias's book, Tia DeNora[35] denounced the lightweight nature of the enterprise, which amounts to drawing from a very limited body of material—Mozart's correspondence, a biographical essay by Wolfgang Hildesheimer,[36] which is moreover very questionable, and a few not very reliable secondary sources— the substance required for an attempt to produce a bold or revolutionary interpretation. The result is presented sometimes as banal and scientifically outmoded, sometimes as false and naively (indeed, even sentimentally) hagiographic, because of the poorly monitored retrospective biases that pass off as contemporary data what is in fact only the work of historical construction carried out *post facto*—for example, the absolutizing of Mozart's genius on the same basis as that of Beethoven, or that simplify reality in order to make it fit into the seductive schema of a great, well-ordered narrative—for example, the legend of the successful emancipation of Beethoven, who is supposed to be the true beneficiary of a process begun, but not completed, by Mozart. This is a historical process far more chaotic and contradictory than Elias could suspect, because starting with Beethoven the history of the composer's situation can no longer be written simply as that of the irresistible advent of freelancing.[37]

DeNora herself, in her work on Beethoven,[38] seeks to show that Beethoven was able to take advantage, with a certain pragmatism, of the coexistence, in a period of transition, of several concurrent sources of income, sometimes perceived as incompatible: the musical salon and the concert hall. As I will show in the following section, the goal of DeNora's study of Beethoven's career is to demonstrate that his exceptional talent and the status of genius accorded him during his own lifetime can be analyzed as perfect social constructions. Thus it is important (for DeNora) to substitute or to add (for other authors, such as Bourdieu) to artistic greatness a greatness of another kind that provides the creator with the psychological equipment necessary to develop optimally during the "period of transition." Beethoven's practical sense, his eagerness for gain, his pragmatism or ability to maneuver, which many authors have described in a more or less picturesque fashion,[39] are transfigured into manifestations of talent as a "social entrepreneur," or even as "a pioneer in the use of commercial tactics in music," according to DeNora, or again, according to Bourdieu, as proof of the "economic genius" of Beethoven, who was "a great musical innovator because he was a great economic entrepreneur" and even a "political innovator."[40] In another context and for another art, the same argument has been used by Svetlana Alpers to make Rembrandt's career coincide with the emergence of the art market.[41] Alpers wants to show how Rembrandt went about liberating himself from patronage in order to impose his ideas and establish his autonomy. Thus the painter becomes the strategist for a new mercantile economy of cultural goods in which the artist lives on credit and pays his debts with artworks, so that neither the making nor the degree of completion of his artworks escape his control.

But how can we be sure that the matching of great creations with stylized transformations of the social and economic configuration concerned is not an artifact? Isn't the point to produce a convenient condensation of the gradual changes and temporal prolongation of emergent phenomena that set the pace for transformations of the social and economic organization of artistic labor? Isn't that the way to synchronize at little cost the transition chronicled and the coordinates of the career of a path-breaking artist, or even to make historical time and social and economic transformations coincide with the production of certain key works? It is true that the schema of the transition between two systems of organization of artistic life can be used to accredit the idea that artistic innovation develops simultaneously in a moving setting and in a very limited temporality. In her research on Beethoven and the economy of music in Vienna, Julia Moore emphasized that this double setting in which Beethoven is said to have acted as a virtuoso strategist and innovative entrepreneur was already in place before he arrived, and that the opportunities for playing a double game and getting double benefits had already been largely exploited by famous composers such as Haydn and Salieri.[42]

The superimposition, term for term, of two orders of innovation, the aesthetic and the socioeconomic, runs the risk of deforming the reality of the organization of artists' activity and their working relations. Those who acquire a strong reputation do not need to be innovative entrepreneurs in order to have a power of negotiation and action that extricates them from situations of pure dependence. The works that Christoph Wolff has devoted to Bach offer many examples of the tactical skill shown by the composer in order to increase his salary, to cope with excessively strict constraints on his contractual work as a musical director, to establish his musical superiority in everyone's eyes, and to do all this while playing generally on the rivalry between patrons' organizations or between courts that wanted to reserve for themselves the services of a composer whose reputation was growing.[43]

In her essay, DeNora seeks to carry out a double displacement: to re-anchor Beethoven's career in Viennese society at the end of the eighteenth century, with its division into classes and the impact of competition among the latter on the system of aesthetic values to be defended; and to deconstruct the myth of the genius propelled to the summit of history solely by the strength of his considerable talents, whose dazzling evidence is supposed to suffice to explain the success of the great man and the admiration, first of connoisseurs, and then of the masses.

The main actors in this narrative are, as in the work of Hauser, Elias, and Adorno, social classes and fractions of social classes, of which certain patron figures, no matter how individualizable they may be, are only the representatives. DeNora's theoretical framework is a determinist explanation similar to that of her predecessors, but this time nourished by far more extensive empirical material.[44] The works she draws on lead her to reject the argument for a Beethoven who was the instrument of the bourgeoisie's emancipation, and to underline that for everything that concerns the first part of the composer's career, which was the most decisive in establishing his reputation and position in Vienna, it was in reality the old aristocratic families that provided the main supports. The argument that makes Beethoven the genius a pure social construction begins from the following syllogism: (1) Music is a genuine stake in social competition and thus a powerful tool of social control; (2) whoever controls the hierarchy of values controls the musical sphere; (3) aristocrats found in Beethoven the composer ideally suited to impose the ideologically and aesthetically most favorable hierarchy, that of great music; (4) the celebration of Beethoven is an instrument of social control. The thesis thus summed up seems to fall into the classical errors of functionalism. The precautions DeNora takes to deflect this criticism actually only reinforce it.

There is no extant explicit testimony from the aristocrats themselves acknowledging that they perceived their traditional authority to be under threat. . . . But why should we expect there to be any? Moreover, even if this aristocratic enterprise were not strategic in its intent, the social consequences— the structuration of status groups—are not to be denied. To expect the nobility to declare or even to hold such an externalist view of their own situation may be to paint a far too rational portrait of aristocratic consciousness. At the same time, it is worth speculating on the cultural context of aristocratic sponsorship, and asking how strategic this form of aristocratic aesthetic entrepreneurship was.[45]

What does the aristocracy do, according to DeNora? In the long term, the decline of its authority over the cultural sphere became irresistible because of the twofold process of the strengthening of the middle classes and the professionalization of musicians, who sought in the expansion of the music market the means of gaining greater social and economic independence and a capacity for innovation in accord with the necessity of diversifying their activities. To prevent the erosion of their influence, aristocrats tried to modify the aesthetically and socially ranking categories of the production and consumption of music in order to preserve monopoly control over a sphere inaccessible to amateurs without culture; in short, in order to re-create a distance from competing classes by making them recognize and accept the new hierarchy of values that made Beethoven the paragon of serious music—complex, subtle, and powerfully expressive—in the tradition of Haydn and to a lesser extent that of Mozart. Which leads to this summary of the battles between strategic macro-actors:

> Admittedly, the court's withdrawal from instrumental musical support effectively diminished the relevance of attempts on the part of the higher aristocrats to symbolically usurp the court's position as the most lavish of music patrons. Simultaneously, however, the lower aristocratic and upper middle-class entry into musical life necessitated an increasing emphasis on musical forms of exclusion if aristocrats were to remain distinct as musical leaders.[46]

What happened to composers and musicians? The old structures of patronage (court orchestras employing permanent musicians) fell into disuse; musicians sought to develop a market for public and private concerts, performances and productions created to organize their activity and to finance their independence. They tried to base themselves on a new demand for music that was beginning to manifest itself in the ranks of the upper middle class and the recently ennobled aristocracy.

In the Viennese setting, what drives the plot of this narrative is a twofold dynamics of competition. This competition takes place first of all between social fractions seeking to retain or change leadership over musical life—being well aware (though this is a functionalist postulate that is by definition unverifiable) that music is a major stake involved in establishing the social domination of competing groups, in short, a weapon in social struggles. Secondly, for musicians it is a competition for success and the conquest of dominant and/or secure positions in a highly unbalanced market, the supply of talent being very much greater than what reliable demand could absorb, in terms not of punctual engagements but of careers made up of a series of such engagements—that is the new order of things involving independent careers. The outcome—provisional, for here we are talking about some twenty years of Viennese history—was that old aristocracy, which was not, moreover, declining economically, maintained its control over musical life by promoting the ideology of "serious music," "serious music in the high style," accessible to those who had the most solid and long-standing cultivation, and embodied in the demanding creative power of Beethoven. The bourgeois could, of course, seek to compete with the aristocracy on the terrain of acts of patronage—financing private concerts in connection with the organization of salons, arranging public concerts or subscriptions to public concerts—but they were defeated on the symbolic terrain, because the prestige of the loftiest music went solely to those who were able to understand it and support it the most vigorously: the aristocrats.

What becomes of Beethoven's talent in such an analytical framework? Far from being an isolated and spontaneous embodiment of the productive power of nature, as the Romantic definition would have it, or from appearing as the operator of historical necessity, as in Adorno's theory, the genius celebrated in Beethoven is constructed on the basis of the resources allocated to him primarily by patrons and secondarily by professionals in the music market, who expected a return on their investment. More precisely, the reduction of great genius to a process of pure social construction is based on two arguments. On the one hand, the composer best prepared to occupy the position directly connected with the ideology and expectation of the dominant class has the advantage. This is the argument proper to the Viennese context, in which the canonical value of serious music and the ideology of "serious music" are supposed to be dominant. On the other hand, given equal talents, the composer who has the greater social capital has the advantage (an argument that is supposed to hold for any context). I will begin by examining this second argument.

Is Genius Simply a Matter of Social Construction?

How does constructionist sociology operate when it wants to demonstrate that what common sense considers an essential reality is in fact only a product of contingent social arrangements? In his examination of constructionist procedures, Ian Hacking proposes to distinguish three degrees of radicalness.[47] At the first level, the claim is that result X, which is the object of an analysis of social construction and, in our example, a strong reputation attributable to great talent, was not inevitable. The second level pushes the argument to the conclusion that X turns out to be a bad thing. The third level is still more radical: The world would be better off without X. In terms of these three levels of radicalness, Hacking classifies constructionist positions according to a movement of increasing opposition to essentialism. The bracketing of the obvious can become, for example, an initiation to skeptical suspicion, but does not automatically lead to rapid movement toward a rebellion against the social realities to be demystified. Still more radical is the enterprise of unmasking and disassembly, whose most vigorous formula resides, according to Hacking, in the application of the Marxist theory of ideology to the whole domain of knowledge. In a pioneering article published in 1925,[48] Karl Mannheim had inaugurated such an enterprise, whose goal is to discern behind X the social, economic, and political functions that support its existence and that, once they have been revealed, suffice to destroy X's import.

The constructionist radicalism that takes the creative talent of the artist as its object is generally situated rather high on this scale, at the level necessary to overthrow idols and carry out a spectacular reversal. The latter consists in making talent no longer an explanatory variable but a variable to be explained. The argumentative resources mobilized to support such a position are diverse. To challenge the essentialist conception that makes scientific discoveries or artistic innovations the necessary product of their authors' genius, one might imagine deploying the various possible courses of creative activity and examining how other artworks and other evolutions might have appeared. In this case, is it necessary to deny the talent or genius of the scientist or artist who are the authors of the innovative work? Not necessarily. It will suffice, for example, to maintain that the talent of the creator in question is not limited to a considerable capital of competences in his discipline, and that this talent also includes abilities or capacities required by the conduct of creative labor—the capacities of a negotiator, strategist, politician, and so forth. The figure of the scientist or artist guided solely by his intrinsic motivation and his disinterestedness is then relegated to the storehouse of legends, but the creative power of the brilliant scientist or artist remains the origin to which we have to go back. More directly reductive is the argument that challenges any difference in aptitude that would give its possessor an insuperable advantage, and that thus denies any interindividual inequality in talent. But how can the factor of "talent" be neutralized in order to maintain this position? One of the favorite tools used in constructionist analyses is the thought experiment: The goal is to construct different possible scenarios by going back beyond observed reality by means of counterfactual hypotheses of the type: "What would have happened if . . . ?" This deployment of alternative scenarios is presented as experimentation by means of imaginary variations based on the real course of things: Given an event or a case to be explained, one has to find what cause, had it acted differently, would have contributed the most directly to changing the result. Applied to a single case, this procedure seems to be a matter of what Paul Ricoeur calls "singular causal imputation" ("l'imputation causale singulière"): The latter "presents a twofold similarity, on the one hand, with emplotment, which is itself a probable imaginary construction, and, on the other hand, with explanation in terms of laws."[49] It is this twofold affinity that explains the procedure's attraction: Half exercise of the imagination, half protocol for mental experimentation, it invites us to go back in time and in the causal chain to freely envelop the real in the possibilities from which it issued and from which another reality might have emerged.

In the present case, the point is to imagine what might have happened if the distribution of factors characterizing the artist's individual resources and the givens of his environment of activity had been different, and then to compare the probable consequences of this imaginary scenario with the real course of events. To vary the social conditions in which the artist's aptitudes and competences develop, it may be tempting to compare the careers of different artists who have unequal reputations even though nothing clearly indicates that they were endowed with significantly different talents at the outset or in the very first stages of their careers. The study of the social and professional trajectory of each of these artists should make it possible to discover the elements that are considered causally responsible for their observed differences in success and achievement. These mental experiments seem to provide an approximate transcription of the probabilistic reasoning that seeks to determine the respective weight of each factor by controlling the influence of all the others, but they do not contain the empirical substance of statistical operations of logistical regression that formalize the argument of the type "all other things being equal." By what means can one do away with the importance of differences in reputation that quite soon set Beethoven above his competitors and then made him the figure par excellence of creative genius in music? The first operation consists in challenging a distinction of kind between talent and genius. As Raymond Williams reminds us in his article "Genius" in his *Keywords*,[50] the notion of genius was originally constructed to mark a difference in kind between the artist of genius and the artist who is simply talented, before usage gradually transformed this difference in kind into a distinction in degree. So let us grant that an artist is great if he has a great deal of talent, and a genius if he has exceptional talents, in the statistical sense taken on by exceptional value. The second operation consists in asking the question that I began to explore in the preceding chapter: What precisely is talent? And what, then, is exceptionally talented about the genius?

Peter Kivy, in his book on different conceptions of the genius, defends a commonsense conception of the genius against the various attempts at skeptical reduction that he demolishes, and, first of all, that of the constructionist sociology illustrated by DeNora's essay on Beethoven, which he severely criticizes. The commonsense conception says simply that the proof of the existence of the genius or the exceptionally talented person is to be sought in what he has produced, in his artworks. This is the "dispositional" conception of genius:

> [M]usical genius is not something that can be read off someone, like the color of her hair or her blood pressure, or the strength of her biceps. It is a "dispositional" property, and, ordinarily, one knows that the disposition is present by its being "expressed." We discover that something is soluble in water by seeing it dissolve in water. And we know that Beethoven was a musical genius because we know that, during his lifetime, he created musical works upon which we place the highest possible musical value.[51]

The question thus becomes: How are the evaluations made that provide the basis for reputations and, in a few extreme cases, for the attribution of exceptional greatness to certain artists? Evaluation and the attribution of reputation to which it gives rise are imperfect processes: The actors involved in evaluation have to perceive qualitative differences among artworks and among artists, and consolidate them in the course of competitions that lead to eliminations, but there is a nonnegligible frequency of error or forgetting. The various evaluations have to converge, but this convergence does not have the value of a ratification founded on independent judgments that are fully informed regarding the variety of possible choices if the mechanisms of affiliation, imitation, or influence mar the process, and if the chief evaluators have only a limited or biased knowledge of all the artworks that are candidates for recognition. Selection competitions have the effect of conferring a growing value on the winners, but the mechanisms of this selection are not homogeneous in time, amalgamating aesthetic, historical, and institutional considerations.

Thus if the mechanism of evaluation is imperfect, must we not examine more closely the causal link between talent and the chances of success in evaluative competitions among artists? Different degrees of critical suspicion are conceivable to weaken the strength of this link. Does it not seem legitimate to point out that Beethoven's artistic greatness was not ratified as simply as our retrospective assessment of the productions of the composer and his competitors leads us to believe? Between the initial evaluations, which were divergent and not very stable, and the certainty arrived at by the test of time, was the road not more sinuous than we imagine it to have been? How exactly does one move from the dispersion of evaluations to their convergence, and to the classifications that are constructed through successive decanting and that oppose living artists to dead ones, dead artists to other dead ones, and dead artists to living ones, since art is patrimonialized, museumified, included in a musical repertory, preserved, transmitted, taught, celebrated, collected?

The usual constructionist argument, whose content I indicated in the preceding chapter, seeks to carry out a suspension of the obvious in the name of scenarios that could have taken place, but of which we have lost even the notion, so blinded are we by all the mythologies that make us believe in eternal and essential truths, where we ought instead to understand that we are dealing with socially constructed situations and values that are contingent and historically mutable. And to cease to believe in ideas as blinding as the one stated by Kivy, who claims that the quality of Beethoven's musical works was the decisive factor in his recognition and his glory, what could be simpler than to assume that these judgments are perennial only because we obliterate the genesis of the realities to be examined by relying on the false certitudes of retrospective interpretations?[52]

To correct this retrospective bias and make us cease believing that Beethoven's superiority was apparent and resounding very early on, De-Nora cites divergent opinions regarding the respective talents of Beethoven and other composers: "Within modern musicological circles, it is quite difficult to construct a convincing argument that the music of Wölffl, for instance, is "better" than Beethoven's, even though some of Beethoven's contemporaries suggested just that."[53] The argument is empirically thin in comparison to the goal, which is to shake up historiography. Nonetheless, proofs of Beethoven's exceptional reputation in the world of his contemporaries are superabundant: Historical research has long since provided concordant evidence showing the exceptional amplitude of Beethoven's success in Vienna, and then in all of Europe, starting in the years following 1800, and it has done so without having to violate the chronology of the recognition of the composer's talent.[54] In truth, the key point for getting the constructionist argument under way is not the verification of power relationships—how many people supported Beethoven, how many scorned his work, at the time in question. This kind of information is in any case not available. It is instead a matter of casting doubt on the very mechanism of the formation of evaluations, and invoking the effectiveness of advertising techniques in amplifying Beethoven's reputation.

A discrepancy existed between the reception of Beethoven's talent (which was clearly mixed and possibly polarized) and that reception as it was publicly dramatized by those who believed (or wanted to believe) in it and who helped to ensure that it would be represented in flattering ways. . . . The history of Beethoven's reputation and success among his contemporaries during the late eighteenth and early nineteenth century, therefore, is the history of the representation of reputation and not merely of reputation *per se.*[55]

What is a well-formed evaluation that can accredit the reality of differences in talent? Here I return to one of the main arguments in Chapter 4. Evaluation is based on comparisons and competitive testing whose mechanisms are imperfect, to be sure, but which remain effective so long as the uncertainty that makes the competitive game possible provides greater profits than if artistic production were subject to bureaucratic or monopolistic control. At the beginning of Beethoven's career in Vienna, was he in a sufficiently competitive world for the difference in reputation to result from well-formed evaluations produced by the whole group of actors in the art world concerned, regarding the quality of the competing artists and artworks?

All the authors who have made close studies of musical life in Vienna at the turn of the nineteenth century agree in diagnosing a situation of transition during which two forms of organization are superimposed or overlap: patronage and private dissemination in salons controlled by the powerful, on the one hand, and on the other hand the emergence of a competitive market of public concerts and positions as instrumentalists and teachers, allocated according to punctual engagements, in a context of a growing demand for performances, of amateur practice, which promoted the professionalization of artists and the growth of the musical publishing industry and musical instrument manufacturing.

How much influence did this overlap of two systems have on the formation of musicians' reputations and incomes? Julia Moore analyzes the new situation this way:

> A peculiar aspect of the new situation was that precisely those few musicians who were still protected by the security of the old patronage system, namely the Kapellmeister, were most likely to reap the financial rewards of the new musical free market, such as frequent access to theaters to give academies, larger publication fees, and so on. Haydn and Salieri are perhaps the clearest examples of artists who had the best of both worlds. The income inequalities outside of permanent positions extended beyond the infrequent opportunities to earn large sums via public concerts and publications, and even the single engagements that appealed to Mozart provided large fees for a few star performers, while the average musician was very badly paid.[56]

The growing gaps between the conditions of the musicians described here can be understood in two different ways. One comes to us from the sociology of inequalities and is based on the argument of the cumulative advantage that allows someone, who already has an enviable position and reputation, to benefit more than proportionally from the value his talent is recognized to have, particularly in a context of the growth of the activity, the development of the market, and the expansion of the arena in which his works are distributed. The question that remains unanswered, in this scenario of the concentration of gains to the benefit of a few creators who are already famous, is whether there are real differences in talent that lead to this increasing polarization of the chances of professional success. I will return to this later on. The other interpretation sees in the new situation a simple hardening of the earlier reality and reduces the change that is supposed to lead to the transitional situation to being no more than an augmentation of the degree of control exercised by the dominant. This is the formula of radical social pessimism that is dear to critical sociology and that undertakes the indispensable sociohistorical contextualization of the facts, only in order to find in it the proof of the power of mechanisms of control and constraint that ensure the reproduction of the social and artistic organization under consideration. It is the interpretation favored by DeNora:

> In Vienna during the 1790s, routes to independent commercial success in the musical field remained obstructed and individual aristocrats stayed secure in their role as gatekeepers for public exposure. Existing public forums were usually buttressed or underwritten with private means so that even the benefit concerts and sometimes music publications were not nearly as "public" or self-sustaining as they might appear to the casual observer."[57]

The thesis adopted is that of an ideally effective control exercised by aristocratic patrons capable of making the best use of the two systems of patronage and the market in order to retain in the latter, which was developing, the power that they had constructed in the former, which was in decline. The reasoning is paradoxical. The diversity of contemporaries' opinions concerning the respective artistic merits of Beethoven and one or another of his competitors was invoked by DeNora to reduce Beethoven's alleged superiority to a construction elaborated *a posteriori*. Now, the mere existence of diverse opinions and varied sources of evaluation that is characteristic of a system of competition that is mercantile, or mercantile and patronal, is itself reduced to its simplest expression, since it has no chance of having any effect on the formation of reputations: Everything is in the hands of those who have both a judgment and a social and economic power, the aristocratic patrons. In other words, the constructionist operation consists in leveling out the distribution of artistic talent and making the distribution of social and economic capitals as prominent as possible. The autonomy of the art world is reduced to nothing, and the field is left wide open for the exercise of power by the dominant social forces: The constructionist analysis can be focused on the power and the judgment of patrons regarding the ability to shape the success of this or that composer. The analysis of artistic success and innovation is, as it were, purged of its individual component, the one that made Beethoven an extraordinary person. But how can it be demonstrated that everything is social in Beethoven's success and innovative genius?

The Power of the Patron, the Ability of the Genius

Ideally, to measure the influence of the system of social relations on the respective career prospects of two composers, we would have to be able to place them on the same starting line and see whether, with equal artistic competences, the one better endowed with social resources went faster and farther in achieving success and/or innovation. The experiment is impossible, and thus rigorous proof is inaccessible, but the thought experiment still seems possible.

Where, then, can we seek the manifestation of an equality of talents that runs counter to what seems obvious? As close as possible to the beginning of the career, and particularly at the moment when Beethoven wants to complete his training with Haydn. During that period, Haydn was the most famous composer in Europe and an influential teacher who was able to sponsor promising young talents very effectively. Haydn's opinion of his students, as reported by his biographer Griesinger[58] and cited by DeNora, tends to diminish the intrinsic value of Beethoven's creative potential to the benefit of other composers such as Pleyel, Neukomm, or Lessel, whom Haydn considered better students. The relations that were established between Haydn and Beethoven were ambivalent, mixing mutual admiration, rivalry, and virtual adoption, as DeNora amply shows. The two great creators had considerable respect for each other at a point where the career of one of them had already reached its end and that of the other was taking off. All this does not prevent DeNora from thinking it plausible that in the situation of an apprenticeship with Haydn, Beethoven's superiority would not have been recognized. And yet the future creative careers of these various students were to be very different. Why? The factor mentioned is once again their unequal endowment with social capital.

Elsewhere, DeNora suggests that we compare Beethoven's career with Dussek's. This comparison of the artistic identities of the two composers, intended to equalize their chances of success in order to show that it was the contexts that made everything diverge, is a strong analytical move, but here it takes place in a completely anodyne way:

At a time when aristocratic connections were still crucial to a musician's economic survival, Beethoven was exceptionally well placed. The aristocrats with whom he was associated were already receptive to the notion of musical greatness. In terms of his connections and position within the musical field, Beethoven was perhaps unique among the composers of his day. The significant differences that social connections like Beethoven's made to the shape of his career (and to the content of his work) can be seen more clearly when he is compared with Jan Ladislav Dussek, a composer whose career and musical style during the 1790s and early 1800s resembled Beethoven's own.[59]

In making this comparison of two careers, DeNora enumerates the handicaps that Dussek had to overcome and discerns in the considerable praise that went to Beethoven the manifestation of all sorts of self-interested games. The accumulation of suspicions is such that DeNora seeks to protect herself against the excesses that threaten the exercise of suspicion and attribute to all the actors in the game an absolutely calculating and totally cynical behavior. But as soon as the concession is made, the exercise in decreasing the value of the "talent" factor and in increasing the "relationship capital" factor resumes, and the back-and-forth is incessant.

> It would be overly cynical (and sociologically questionable) to reduce Beethoven's success and the emergence of his talent to mere nepotism: of course Beethoven was musically competent and musically interesting. The point is rather that there were numerous other musicians who, under different circumstances, could also have ended up as celebrities. The importance of Beethoven's initial connections must not be underplayed, especially since by all accounts Beethoven, unlike Mozart was not recognized as exhibiting many signs of precocious talent early on.[60]

The "all other things being equal" argument, which is supposed to reveal the true effect of the artist's capital and social relations, is generalized elsewhere in a hypothetical form:

> One may wonder whether any composer, once "plugged into" the supportive patronage network that surrounded Beethoven, would have been able to achieve such historically unprecedented success. This view, however, overlooks the fact that Beethoven was not a passive object around which his patrons constituted a frame of greatness. Beethoven's initial and subsequent status during the early nineteenth century was inextricably linked to his own entrepreneurial contributions, both musical and social. This is not to say, however, that there were not composers who might have been capable of garnering a similar sort of reputation. Some, I think, were better suited for the part than others (Gelinek less so than Dussek or Wölffl, for instance). It is interesting to consider what our modern musical evaluative standards would look like if a different composer had been inserted into the supportive frame that surrounded Beethoven.[61]

Invariably, DeNora makes elementary corrections to her demonstrative excesses:

> To focus on the representation of Beethoven's talent is by no means to depict Beethoven and supporters as hyperrational managers of Beethoven's image, as if they set out from the start to market Beethoven's art. I have meant neither to imply such a cynical interpretation nor to imply that Beethoven and his patrons were marketing a "finished product." Such an account oversimplifies the complex social processes I have described; it also tends to evade the ways in which Beethoven's own artistic activities, his self-perception, and the elaboration of a supportive climate for his reception interacted over time.[62]

One can easily subscribe to a processual view of the dynamics of a career, and to the modest scientific observation that "in the making, it was accumulated gradually, practically, and unremarkably, in time and space, neither preordained nor planned in its entirety."[63] But how can we understand when, a few lines earlier, we read that "Beethoven succeeded because a complex network intended to call forth and recognize his talent had been constructed," or when elsewhere in the work DeNora explains, after the ritual concessions to antireductionism:

> Beethoven arrived in Vienna with a good deal of social and cultural capital in the form of connections and previous honors, which enabled him (to extend the metaphor) to establish "credit" with new and potential patrons in Vienna. . . . To be sure, Beethoven's success cannot be attributed to his social connections alone; at the same time, his career was underwritten from the start, and this security became a condition for his becoming known as a unique and particularly imposing kind of talent: because he could afford to do so socially, Beethoven took artistic risks.[64]

The retractions are incessant, but the project is basically rectilinear. Not the best student, and certainly not a new Mozart, nor probably a better composer per se than others, but better endowed socially, more ambitious, and plunged into a more favorable environment in which he exploited optimally his initial advantage—that is the equation adopted by DeNora to designate Beethoven's distinctive qualities and abilities. And to be sure that the social capital at Beethoven's disposition was not acquired because of his intrinsic value, on which all those who played a role in local musical life would gamble, DeNora transports us to the original scene, in Bonn, the city where Beethoven was born in 1770 and lived until he took up residence in Vienna in late 1792.

In order to claim to correct the bias of retrospective reconstruction that projects, over the whole of Beethoven's career, the image of the absolute musical genius, ideally human and ideally superhuman, the critical analysis has to be based entirely on the hypothesis that Beethoven obtained an advantage at the beginning, in Bonn, and that he later exploited it optimally in Vienna. This advantage is supposed to be essentially social: The Bonn aristocracy is alleged to have mobilized itself to have this young, promising talent defend the renown of the city, and, first of all, that of its social and cultural elite and its supposed values (that is, its engagement on behalf of "great" music). As DeNora interprets it, this is nothing less than an advertising technique, that of the self-fulfilling prophecy, which fabricates out of whole cloth the composer's reputation by predicting that he has the brightest future and by programming his social and artistic ascent: Posterity is supposed to have seized upon this prophecy to construct the legend of the irresistible power of Beethoven's genius.[65] The best-known slogan of this advertising machinery must be seen in the letter that Count Waldstein, an aristocrat from Bonn who knew and passionately admired Mozart and who was convinced of the value of Beethoven's future, addressed to the young composer just as the latter was leaving to study with Haydn in Vienna:

> Dear Beethoven! You are going to Vienna in fulfillment of a wish that has long been frustrated. Mozart's genius is still in mourning and weeps for the death of its pupil. It found a refuge with the inexhaustible Haydn, but no occupation; through him it wishes to form a union with another. With the help of unceasing diligence you will receive the spirit of Mozart from the hands of Haydn.[66]

In his biography of Beethoven, Lewis Lockwood examines the years during which Beethoven was studying in Bonn. We find here quite different ingredients for the analysis of Beethoven's promising talent. A small city, Bonn was nonetheless the seat of the Elector of Cologne and his court: As a result, musical patronage was very active there and provided employment for many musicians. The extent of aristocratic support for music varied with the economic situation, with the personality of the Elector and those of the members of his court, and with the intensity of the competition with nearby cities. The reputation of the orchestra and musical life in Mannheim, with which Bonn was competing for musical leadership in the provinces, declined at the end of the 1770s. Support for Bonn's municipal orchestra increased, and its main orchestra directors were musicians of great skill: the violinist Franz Anton Ries, whose son Ferdinand was Beethoven's schoolmate in his musical studies and remained very close to him throughout his life, as a copyist, agent, and biographer; the violinist Andreas Romberg, who later had a brilliant career as an instrumentalist and composer at Hamburg, and whose cousin Bernhard Romberg joined the orchestra for a few years before starting an international career as a soloist and becoming the most celebrated cellist of his time; the remarkable cellist Joseph Reicha, who directed the Court Opera of Bonn and whose nephew Anton Reicha was Neefe's student alongside Beethoven before becoming a professor and influential theorist in France, where he went to pursue his career; the French horn player Nikolaus Simrock, who founded a publishing house in Bonn in 1793, maintained close ties to Beethoven, and was the first publisher of some of his major works, such as the Kreutzer Sonata op. 47 for violin and piano, the sonata for piano *Les Adieux,* op. 81a, and two sonatas for cello and piano, op. 102.

> For a smaller musical center [like Bonn], the array of talent was remarkable and playing viola [as Beethoven did] in the orchestra with such performers offered Beethoven a first-class introduction to the major orchestral literature of the time, including symphonies by Haydn, Mozart, and many other composers.[67]

Beethoven's principal teacher in Bonn was Christian Gottlob Neefe, who had come from Leipzig. A mediocre composer, but cultivated, and a demanding, rigorous, and generous teacher, he had been in contact with poets and writers belonging to the literary and political movement of *Sturm und Drang,* and above all he transmitted to Beethoven his profound knowledge of Bach's work and his admiration for Mozart. Most of Bach's work was not well known in the 1780s, and the scores of his musical works were difficult to find outside the circles of his friends and admirers, his sons, his students, and some learned theorists. Beethoven the pianist learned and played *The Well-tempered Clavier* at a time when that musical work, which was still unpublished, was for many musicians incomprehensible and too difficult to perform. The knowledge and dissemination of Bach's published work underwent a real boom starting at the beginning of the nineteenth century, in the course of Beethoven's career. Beethoven's early contact with Bach's art, which combined in the highest degree the power of compositional science with the power of musical expression, came at about the time when Mozart was deepening his knowledge of Bach in Vienna in the salon of the Baron van Swieten, Beethoven's future great patron, by taking part in concerts devoted to Bach's and Handel's choral and instrumental works. But it was from Mozart that Beethoven drew his inspiration most directly in his first attempts at composition, and he played several of Mozart's concertos with the Bonn orchestra.

To define the advantages that Beethoven might have had during the period of his musical education, Lockwood emphasizes the artistic resources and expectations that characterized musical activity in Bonn, to the shap-

ing of which the new Elector, Archduke Maximilian Franz, made a decisive contribution from 1784 on. The brother of Emperor Joseph II, the
archduke was a passionate music lover and a great admirer of Mozart,
whom he had tried to engage as the director of his court orchestra, and he
surely wanted to see in Beethoven's precocious talent a possible new incarnation of the prodigious genius that Mozart had earlier symbolized to the
highest point. The triumph of Mozart and his family during their first tour
of Europe between 1763 and 1766 had marked people's minds because
of the young artist's stupefying precociousness as a pianist and composer.
Beethoven certainly belonged to the rather large number of very precocious child musicians who issued from musical milieus and became familiar with music very early on through the examples of their fathers and
grandfathers, who pressured them to engage in rigorous apprenticeships.
Seeing his son's remarkable dispositions, Beethoven's father, his first
teacher, organized a concert in Cologne in 1778 in which he presented
Ludwig, falsifying his age to make him a year younger than he actually
was. Neefe also claimed that Beethoven was younger than he was when he
presented the young composer's first musical work in 1783, writing:

> Louis van Beethoven [*sic*], son of the tenor singer mentioned, a boy of eleven
> years, and of most promising talent. He plays the clavier very skillfully and
> with power, reads at sight very well, and—to put it as simply possible—, he
> plays chiefly *The Well-Tempered Clavier* of Sebastian Bach, which Herr Neefe
> put into his hands. Whoever knows the collection of preludes and fugues in
> all the keys—which might almost be called the *non plus ultra* of our art—will
> know what this means. . . . This youthful genius is deserving of help to enable
> him to travel. He would certainly become a second Wolfgang Amadeus Mo-
> zart if he progresses as he has begun.[68]

When Mozart died in 1791, Beethoven was twenty-one years old, and his
creative career had not been nearly so exceptionally precocious as Mozart's. But at that time it was Mozart's creative genius, in all the originality
and variety of his accomplishments, that was at the heart of the mourning
and regrets of all those who imagined what the composer's destiny might
have been had the Viennese patrons supported him in his last, so fertile
and yet so financially difficult years. Here we see the power of the mechanism that is triggered by regret, and that sets in motion a train of counterfactual reasoning: The idea that things might have been different leads to
the causal inference according to which Mozart's destiny, at this point in
his career, was largely dependent on the support of patrons who ultimately
let him down. But the feeling of regret that could prompt a biased interpretation of the past also acts, of course, on choices regarding future action

and on the emergence of behavioral norms.[69] As Lockwood reminds us, a feeling of an incalculable loss prevailed, concerts and editions of Mozart's works proliferated, commemorations and the first biographies attested to the intensity of the feeling of loss, and to the fear of the artistic void that only a new composer as powerfully original and universal as Mozart could fill, in order to become the hero of a new age. That was the gamble made by Count Waldstein, one of whose distant relatives, Prince Lichnowsky, was to be Beethoven's chief patron during his first years in Vienna after having been one of Mozart's patrons as well,[70] and that was also Archduke Max Franz's project:

> The original plan was that Beethoven would study with Haydn, perfect his craft, and eventually return to Bonn, where Max Franz dreamed of fame, with Beethoven as the Electorate's star. As it turned out, the political avalanche that buried the Bonn court cut Beethoven off from any possible return, even supposing that he intended one.[71]

The economy of social capital as DeNora invents it leads her to imagine a "programming" of Beethoven's success by conferring on those holding social power in Bonn an ability to act with unprecedented effectiveness and lucidity. The portrait of musical life in Bonn and of its main protagonists brings out quite different characteristics: high-level professionals, opportunities for training and learning through practice in contact with teachers and instrumentalists whose value and careers were connected with numerous other musical centers, a complex of the usual motives for supporting music in conformity with investments in the arts made by the leading aristocracy of the court cities, and of individual patrons who had personal connections with the most celebrated composers and with the most emblematic genius of the time, Mozart, a situation of competition for positions and support that concentrated investments and gambles on a small number of musicians and apprentice composers. Given this situation, which placed Bonn rather high among the musical centers that could promote a composer's career, but in no way gave it a crushing advantage over other cities and courts, what was it that favored Beethoven? Lockwood outlines a line of reasoning analogous to that which, in DeNora's work, seeks to compare two composers placed on the same starting line, but the comparison takes an entirely different turn. Here it is based on a given context, and not, like DeNora's comparison of Beethoven with Dussek, on a given creative potential. Anton Reicha and Beethoven were the same age; Reicha was the nephew of Joseph Reicha, a noted cellist who joined the court orchestra of Bonn in 1784 and assumed the direction of the court opera in 1790. Anton arrived in Bonn at the age of fourteen, and like

Beethoven, he was Neefe's pupil. Fellow students and friends, Beethoven and Anton Reicha both registered for study at the faculty of philosophy in Bonn in 1789. But Reicha had an entirely different career as a composer, teacher, and theorist in France. Lockwood describes this way the stimulating power of the musical world into which the two young classmates were plunged:

> That the Bonn orchestra rehearsed and played every day, providing a wealth of exposure to contemporary styles, is not just a reasonable assumption, but is confirmed by witnesses, including Anton Reicha, perhaps the young Beethoven's worthiest peer. Brimming with expectations of a musical career, Reicha was exposed to exactly the same musical environment but eventually showed that his talents lay more in theory and pedagogy than in composition, despite his many finished works. Reicha later said of his years in Bonn that "playing and hearing good music every day, instrumental and vocal, I became completely devoted to music. . . . Up to then, I had been a simple performer and quite an ordinary musician; now the passion for composition came over me and became a veritable fever."[72]

The comparison makes it clear that an artistic milieu not only has the power to stimulate but also makes a selection in function of what is revealed by the situation of apprenticeship and the first manifestations of creative aptitude. This comparison orients the investments made by patrons in accord with a very ordinary cost/benefit logic, in function of the principal variable of the competition, which is the hoped-for value of the creative talent of the person who is exposed to repeated situations of testing, relative comparison, and elevation or revision of anticipations regarding his chances of success.

Between Bourgeois and Aristocrats: Beethoven the Musician among His Peers

Was Beethoven a partly uncontrollable product of bourgeois emancipation, or the protégé of Viennese aristocrats who secured leadership by supporting an exceptionally talented musician? But do we have to limit ourselves to hovering between Adorno's arguments (and, in more mechanistic versions, those of Hauser or Raynor[73]) and those of DeNora's constructionist sociology? Just as Ernst Gombrich or Millard Meiss challenged the deterministic analyses that made the style and successes of a given painter or school of painting causally dependent on social factors reduced to the class position of sponsors,[74] Charles Rosen, in a severe critique of DeNora's work, has raised a series of strong objections.[75] Two of them are, for my purposes, particularly significant: (1) the complexity of the relations between artists and aristocratic patrons, and (2) the neglect of a crucial category of actors in the analysis of networks of influence and control over musical life, that of the professional musicians themselves.

In Beethoven's behavior with regard to his patrons, we find an unstable compound of a request for protection and a refusal to subordinate himself, in the name of the artist's self-affirmation and of the superiority of talent over inherited wealth. The ways of denying the subordinating relationship of protection illustrated by the chronicle of Beethoven's escapades with respect to high society are part of repertory of the manifestations of the artistic genius's rebellious temperament that has been well known and often commented upon since Michelangelo. In reality, Charles Rosen emphasizes,

> [T]he relation of a high classical art and the artist as genius to an aristocratic society is a very complex one, in which the artist's genius is a trophy for the court that hires him but also a protest against, and an undermining of, the aristocratic authority that finances art. . . . The shock of alarm and indignation followed by fascination was the basis for Beethoven's reputation.[76]

As the most stimulating studies in the social history of art show, current distinctions among the systems for organizing artistic life that seek to measure the degree of formal or real freedom that each of these systems provides artists proceed from overly simple stylizations. They neglect in particular an essential factor that confers a degree of freedom on the activity of certain artists in any system of organization whatever: the influence that their reputation gives them. The power of negotiation and acting that the artist can use to extend his control over his activity increases as his value is celebrated. The modalities of this differ from one system of creation to another, of course, since the formation of reputation is not governed by the same rules in the context of aristocratic or royal patronage, a mercantile system, public patronage, or control by an academy or professional union that holds a monopoly on the attribution of rewards, titles, and official positions. But in all cases, the efforts and struggles in which the innovative artist engages in order to assert himself involve the quest for an advantage that escapes the strict rules of the dominant system concerned.

In a patronage system, a famed artist may be able to successfully negotiate the price and availability of his talent; he recovers, in a competitive market system, a temporary monopoly power because of the increased sensitivity of demand with regard to the differences in quality of artworks and artists, which leads to a part of the demand greater than is proportional to the difference in quality being concentrated on the most famous: The artist can play a double game to loosen the stranglehold of a totalitarian political system and escape its control.[77] This quest for freedom, from the machinery of artistic life and from the constraints that it imposes on original ways of working, may be based in particular on the fact that systems for organizing artistic life, far from simply succeeding one another, can coexist more or less long-term. As Raymonde Moulin has written:

> None of the modes of the professionalization of the artist includes, at a given moment, the whole of the population that is engaged in artistic practice, to precisely the same extent that the mode of professionalization is, in each period, one of the major stakes in the competition among artists for social recognition and the means of existence.[78]

The relations between Beethoven and his patrons are asymmetrical in the exchange of economic support for the creator against the hope of a social return on a good investment in patronage, but the two parties to the exchange have good arguments for seeking to succeed together in their quest for fame and prestige. This is a positive-sum game, it is cooperative, and not merely antagonistic, because the patron's hopes of gain would be reduced if the artist did not have a sufficient chance of expressing his intrinsic talent: It is the competence of both the artist and the patron that is the condition of the success of their association and that makes the relationship profitable. The idiosyncrasies of genius and the combination of "a shocking and even alarming originality of improvisation and composition with a brilliant and imperious virtuoso style of performance"[79] that characterize Beethoven demonstrate the creator's margin of negotiation rather than his imprisonment in a situation of alienating control.

In his preface to DeNora's book, the musicologist Howard Robbins Landon does not bother with subtle sociological models: According to him, Beethoven made very practical use of the financial security that the Viennese nobility offered him without demanding a *quid pro quo,* and took advantage of it to learn how to free his art from any confinement:

> Having been put on the right track, so to speak, Beethoven was free to develop his talent. His mind soon soared. . . . With the *Eroica,* he left the brilliant world of eighteenth-century Viennese salons and suddenly found himself in a world of his own: violent, rhapsodic, explosive.[80]

Let us extend Charles Rosen's analysis. Several complexities disrupt the schema that makes artistic success the true "product" of a collective labor of social mobilization and construction: the missing causal impulse concealed by the determinist reading of social history; the combination of roles and resources, with the relations of interdependency that are attached to them; the mobilization of a network of actors more heterogeneous than the struggle between social classes or social groups assumes.

Beethoven the Superior Calculator: The Paralogisms of the Counter-Mythology

For the artist, what does it mean to accumulate and mobilize social capital, and in what direction does the causal relation act? Is it in function of his talents, musical or other, that the composer wins the favor of powerful protectors and assures himself a reputation by means of a classical mechanism of the self-reinforcement of success—success eliciting the support that strengthens the probability of succeeding? Or is it in function of his initial capital of connections that the composer benefits from support that subsequently raises the level of the demands put on him and leads him to develop talents he could not have known he had before forging them in the uncertainties and the process of learning that characterize creative labor?

This kind of question seems to point to the ultimate foundation of a deterministic causal argument in the attempt to explain exceptional talent: The answer obviously cannot be found, because the question is badly framed. The most spectacular solution would be to overthrow the legend of the inspired, free artist, indifferent to the management of his interests, preoccupied with his art and the salvation of humanity through the sacrifice of his person in the service of art in a society doomed to fail to understand the profound meaning of the universal aesthetic challenge that he poses. To this spectacular "overthrow" corresponds the portrait of a Beethoven who is a supreme strategist, a kind of Shumpeterian innovator who is very determined from the outset (he has "programmed" himself) to acquire by any means the independence necessary for taking aesthetic risks. His relationship with Haydn would then correspond to a supremely calculating scheme of docility followed by emancipation,[81] and his admiration for Bach and the energy put into the publication of some of his musical works would have permitted Beethoven himself to grow, while his false pretension to nobility would have as its goal to "renegotiate his status with respect to his patrons" and "to innovate on the social level," and the manipulation of publishers who might publish his new musical works would make Beethoven a "pioneer in the use of commercial tactics in music."

The interactions between the factors of success are too complex for it to be possible to reduce all behaviors and situations to a naive calculation of the benefits expected from every interaction, and for the intrinsic motives of action to be exhausted by the hypothesis that there are extrinsic goals that are ideally calculable. Beethoven's biographers,[82] while listing for each of his activities the particulars of his ways of operating (the fiery performer, the touchy teacher, and such), stress the growing diversity of the ways of controlling the artist in his rising career and at the same time the growing security in the negotiation of his independence with respect to his patrons. The interlacing of the demand for protection and entrepreneurial activism constantly thwarts the traditional schemas. On the one hand, Beethoven is often inclined to think himself badly off, prey to financial difficulties, and to assume that he has great needs, whereas his very simple and increasingly slovenly way of life seems to require very little. On the other hand, the patrons are willing to provide him with an income over several years without receiving anything in exchange, to commission musical works from him, to help promote private concerts, and to contribute to the success of his profit-making public concerts. And beyond these bilateral patronage relationships, there is the constitution of the network of all the professionals in the musical world who entered into business relationships with Beethoven, and who set the price, thus giving rise to a continual flow of transactions and cessions of rights for the publication or distribution of this or that group of musical works on the national or international level.[83]

It is much more difficult, then, to reduce the course of a composer's activity, with its constraints and margins of uncertainty, to a simple formula, to an organizing principle whose terms are supposed to vary little over time. The composer learns to exploit the margins of freedom in terms of the power that his reputation gives him, just as he can vary his behavior and put mercenary work (arrangements, harmonizing folk songs, composing commissioned occasional works) in the service of much more uncertain projects.

One of the indices of this complexity has to do with what usually concerns the sociography of the artist's life, the resources that the creator procures for himself. But the resources are only the bottom line of a set of transactions negotiated and priced in various ways, and of a combination of activities and professional roles. This involves simultaneous negotiations between the level of gain, the degree of constraint in the execution of the artwork, the time reserved for oneself, and the positive and negative nonmonetary dimensions of the act of labor. It also involves the establishment of relationships with various categories of partners during these transactions, in which the degree of control that each person seeks to obtain over the course of his activity is always at stake.

At the end of the eighteenth century, apart from the support sought from the aristocracy, Mozart's career, and still more that of Beethoven, were constructed on the basis of a diversification of the sources of gain and the combination of professional roles (performer, composer negotiating commissions and publication rights, teacher, organizer of concerts to promote musical works, occasional consultant for this or that publisher or instrument maker, and so on).[84] It is clear that thanks to this combination of roles, which changed in the course of his career, Beethoven obtained the means of weaving together multiple connections with professional musical circles and the patrons, and of rapidly establishing his reputation—the heart of this diversity being, at the outset, constituted by the accumulated profits from his twofold activity as a virtuoso pianist and as a powerfully original creator. These combinations of roles are certainly not peculiar to Beethoven's career, but they allow us to better understand how formulas of professional independence are composed, here, in a historical situation of a twofold system of organization of musical life.

It would be risky to correlate these well-known ways of holding several positions at once with the composer's capacity for aesthetic innovation. This play of multiple positions and their transformations characterize, first of all, the system of organizing musical activities and its developments. But it is important to observe that the celerity of Beethoven's accumulation of reputation can be explained in part by the interdependence of the roles he played and by his success in dovetailing the advantages that could be obtained by combining them. The reputation capital that the artist accumulates subsequently allows him to better manage this diversity of activities, in order to eliminate constraints and guarantee himself relative control over his career and his social and professional environment. In other words, different ways of professional doubling-up do not have the same characteristics, depending on whether they are dictated by economic constraints and the difficulties of exercising the activity known as a "vocation" or whether they accompany and express the extension of the famous creator's artistic power.[85]

The Viennese Aristocracy and Its Patrons: Networks and Advisers

To endow the aristocracy as a class with an intentionality and strategic behaviors designed to allow it to maintain control over musical life in a period when an avalanche of changes was occurring is to suppose that all members of the class acted in a way that was homogeneous, coordinated, and systematic. The sociohistorical approach to art should lead to more differentiated weightings. Recourse to historical investigation allows us to characterize Beethoven's most active supports according to their social identity, but it definitely does not authorize us to make them the actors by proxy for the whole fraction of the aristocracy identified, since the preference for Beethoven was far from being shared by all the members of that fraction. That would suppose that a microsociological analysis of the mobilization of resources and the support networks can be perfectly superimposed on the macro-sociological analysis of social classes conceived as homogeneous, collectively acting entities. The variable identifying individuals through the lens of their social position, which must enter into an explanatory model as an analytical variable, is converted into a historical actor, and individuals become merely substitutable embodiments of class: Both the configuration of their relations and the motives of their behavior lose their particular contextual determinations. Conversely, a sociology of actors and networks of actors leads to embodying social forces in precise individuals and to endowing them with intentionality and a capacity for action as soon as it is a matter of grasping episodes of interaction with the composer—negotiations, demands, conflicts, exchanges of honors, dedications—such that they can be attested by the available documents. In Beethoven's support networks, the number of participants acting directly is particularly limited: It is easy for Charles Rosen to point out that the whole Viennese aristocracy did not follow Beethoven in his enthusiasm for difficult and "through-composed" music.[86] It then becomes particularly important to explain the involvement of Beethoven's principal patrons, such as Count Waldstein (in Bonn), Prince Lichnowsky, Archduke Rudolf, Prince Lobkowitz, Prince Kinsky, and Baron van Swieten (in Vienna). And the major role played by some of them can disrupt the elementary explanatory schema based on class position. For example, Baron van Swieten played a key role in the propagation of the aesthetic canon of serious music. However, he does not exactly belong to the old aristocracy: His personality is more complex than is suggested by the claim that he is the pure representative of a fraction of the aristocracy, inasmuch as the fraction from which he came was inferior in status to the one to which he is supposed to be one of the most reliable cultural guides.

Let us try to apply a line of reasoning similar to the one that seeks to test the influence of social capital on the career of two composers of equal abilities or the influence of talent on the career of two composers whose social origins closely resemble each other. Given a comparable social position and equivalent resources, why does one aristocrat engage in the patronage of serious music, and why does another, who is socially equivalent to him, not do so? There are only two possibilities. Either the hypothesis of interindividual differences in competence and talent is refuted by the study of the patrons as well as by that of the creators, and in that case, the explanation of the joint success of Beethoven and his patrons becomes increasingly abstract and hollow by invariably referring to the support of socially dominant groups. Or the activity of certain patrons brings out differences in aptitude, whether they are a matter of artistic flair, a deep comprehension of music, entrepreneurial virtuosity, or some other quality that is unequally distributed within the group of patrons. In this latter case, the patrons most active on Beethoven's behalf were not simply the possessors of social, economic, and cultural resources (other patrons who also had them made less good artistic choices), but they appear to have been endowed with superior clear-sightedness or superior strategic abilities, that is, with talents that the constructionist analysis wanted precisely to exclude as hypotheses. Whence the curious effect that would be produced by an explanation that challenged the notion that there is a difference in talent between Beethoven and his less glorious rivals: It would be the patrons who become geniuses by knowing how to raise a composer of indeterminate value to absolute success.[87]

The solution proceeds in reality from a deeper analysis of what talents are and from a more attentive examination of the patron's chances of success. The analysis of the network of family ties and social relations among patrons, as it appears fleetingly in DeNora, offers a path to be followed in an investigation that is complex, to be sure, but is not beyond the scope of social historians.[88] But we must also examine with particular care the role of musicians, artists, and men of letters at the very heart of the networks and activities of patronage. Charles Rosen emphasizes the determining role of the musicians who advised the few aristocrats financing Beethoven by telling them where to put their money to make the best cultural investments.[89] Rosen also emphasizes the essential role played by literary groups of poets and novelists in supporting Beethoven and in acclimating music as a great art, Haydn's work having already provided an internationally famous model of cultural greatness. Visible aristocratic patronage came to terms with what Philippe Urfalino has called "hidden patronage" based on evaluations made by professionals, peers, partners, and competitors.[90]

Historical research on musical salons has provided, for its part, a quantity of materials that suggest that one might see in these salons organizations playing multiple roles—social, political, professional, and aesthetic. We can compare them to social credit banks, to borrow Max Weber's characterization of such groups. It is important to identify, in the "production" of these salons, the successful gambles on and investments in artistic talents that are rapidly if not durably canonized, as well as the failures and the unfortunate choices that shed a bright light on the unequal clear-sightedness of the elites. And we should analyze how patrons manage these investments—in prudent, diversified, or specialized ways—all through the life cycle of these particular organizations. Then a competitive space is revealed, a competition internal to the salons, between their members or between factions that confront each other within them, and competition between salons. In this space, composers and musical performers obtain revenues, symbolic credits, supports in high society and officialdom, and negotiate parts of their public careers: Competition is there to incite them never to be completely dupes nor completely insincere in managing their social relations. The new forms of organizing the production and public dissemination of artworks, which are largely dependent on initiatives on the part of musicians and networks of actors acting in concert, have as their central characteristic that they multiply the mechanisms of comparison and selection that structure competition for success. On what tests is the competitive game based? Instead of offering a statistical analysis in terms of the mobilization of capital and the engagement of investments that are supposed to obtain a durable advantage in competition, I will conclude my analysis by sketching the contours of a dynamic analysis of talented success.

Neither Given nor Constructed: The Amplification of Indeterminate Differences in Talent to the Celebration of Genius

The central point of my analysis is to discover how to account for exceptional talent. Up to this point, I have presented and discussed two kinds of explanation. The first maintains that the individual in question is exceptional either because he has exceptional aptitudes or because his social origins make him unclassifiable, and that for that reason he produces exceptional artworks. According to the second explanation, there is, at the outset, nothing exceptional about the individual of genius, he is no more talented than others, but he is supported by social forces that allow him to have an exceptional career. And I have criticized these two lines of argument. It is time to propose a solution. We have no absolute proof of the presence or absence of talent because we do not know exactly what talent is, because we do not know how to measure it independently of what it produces—artworks—and because measuring the value of artworks is not a natural and simple process that is endowed with an incontestable objectivity. Evaluations diverge, they change, the value of artists can be revised upward or downward, and so forth.

So how should we proceed?

Can we dispense with the hypothesis that makes exceptional talent a crushing advantage in the competition for success and the origin of a genius's career? It suffices to make a slight modification of the hypothesis to find the solution. I refer to the theoretical model set forth in the preceding chapter, which explains considerable differences in reputation and gains by a mechanism of amplifying differences that may very well be initially indeterminate.

As I theorized in the preceding chapter, we can assume that at the outset there is only a very small difference in talent between two artists, one of whom will become what we call a genius, but we have to assume that this difference is perceived quite early by those who make comparisons (critics, musicians, audiences), and then we have to explain why this difference will suffice to concentrate, on the artist who is judged to be a little more talented, most of the demand and thus to give him a reputation very superior to what his real advantage in artistic value might be. But two conditions are required for this model to have genuine analytical power. We have to acknowledge this perceptible difference in quality that appears in the judgments that are made initially by professionals and based on multiple relative comparisons. And we have to conceive a space of competition, along with the mobility of opinions and evaluations that characterizes it. In each trial of competitive comparison, this perceptible difference, whether small or large, acts to guide the judgments and investments of the system's actors, the artist's teachers, professional musicians, patrons, concert entrepreneurs, critics, and audiences. Now, on these two points the constructionist analysis examined above was incorrect.

The schema of dynamic amplification that serves me as a solution here suggests how the careers of two artists originally close to each other can diverge radically. Depending on the projects and evaluations, this mechanism of self-reinforcement or cumulative advantage permits an artist whose abilities are best mobilized to obtain a greater variety of commissions, to explore more new solutions, to acquire better opportunities for collaboration with outstanding professionals, and to feel the mixture of growing self-esteem and perpetually renewed challenge that results in the growth of his reputation.

Competition and the uncertainty that persistently govern creative activity preserve the dynamic tension of the testing to which talent is subjected. It is on this basis that the analysis of differences in success makes the network of relationships established by the artist play a determining role. Whether it is a matter of the patrons, instrumental partners, or various categories of professionals with which Beethoven established ties of labor and collaboration, his networks of activity are organized in accord with a formula of assortative matchings. When artistic labor is no longer grounded in the permanent connection with an employer within a stable organization, as was, for example, the case for the employment of the music director in a princely court, the career is constructed from one project to another, in relations of negotiation and cooperation in which the partners—musicians, concert organizers, patrons, publishers, critics, musical instrument makers, writers and poets, and such—are co-opted in terms of their level of reputation and their artistic and social influence. The dynamics of the successful creative career is this movement of rising mobility within a stratified world of networks of people who know each other, and of collaboration: When talent is a complementary factor of production and not an additive factor,[91] the combination of talents of approximately equivalent level, each in their respective function (interpretation, organizational mediation, editing, fundraising) has a multiplicative effect on a given project's chances for success and on the project collaborators' chances of accumulating reputation.[92]

Among the benefits drawn from this hierarchization of matching networks, not the least is the mutual learning seen, for example, in the many cases of fertile collaboration between the most talented composers and the most famed performers, and here, between Beethoven and the celebrated performers (Clement, Duport, Kreutzer, Rode, Schuppanzigh, Stich, and others) with whom he worked. By means of these collaborations, artists increased their chances of developing their competences through contact with equally talented partners, and they could more easily engage in demanding creative projects. This allows us to better understand how, on the basis of classifications by reputations, whose initial metrics is often crude (promising or minor talent, a first-rate or second-rate artist, valuable artworks or mediocre ones, and so on), a subtly graduated hierarchy is constituted that can, of course, always be contested because it is subject to the tests of interindividual competition, but that leads to very unequal chances for the blossoming of creative talent.

At this point, I can bring together the two sides of the analysis. The intrinsic power of individual talent and the segmentation of the market for creative labor, prompted by the mechanism of assortative matchings, constitute, in a dynamic interaction, the two forces whose combination produces the considerable variance in reputations and leads, when the statistical distribution of aptitudes is completed, to the exception that is called genius. However, exceptional talent still requires a terrain for aesthetic reception: that is the object of an analysis of the matrix in which "greatness" is elaborated as a canonical aesthetic value, and it is the other point of difference from the constructionist analysis of the elevated style in music, which proceeds in accord with an exhaustive reduction of levels of meaning to pure social power relationships. Here the works of Carl Dahlhaus, Lydia Goehr, Leonard Meyer, and Charles Rosen are the best guides.[93] The notion of a musical art that is sophisticated or elevated must be connected with the aesthetic that was developed in the second half of the eighteenth century and was given its most profound formulation by Kant, and with its Romantic posterity: Musical creation, having become the paradigm of art, is supposed to be achieved only when it is liberated from its extramusical uses and meanings, in order to acquire universality and spirituality and at the same time the intelligibility of an expressive construction strictly evaluated by the yardstick of its formal coherence, which is the guarantee of its universalizing acontextuality. But artistic creation is also evaluated by the yardstick of its originality in making use of new compositional formats in accord with a competitive game that compels composers to ensure the viability of their works on the music market through the economic and social exploitation of their durability. The "matrix" of the elaboration of the value of greatness is henceforth also the evolution of the size of concert halls, the size of orchestras, the new equilibria of sound implied by the recourse to larger orchestras, and the heterogeneity of concert audiences that include listeners with very different levels of competence. All of these are realities that have encouraged the composition of longer, more massive, more contrastive musical works, whose complexity of structure, texture, and orchestration obliges the composer to highlight the striking individualization of expressive ideas and climaxes, and to seek to achieve integration through an increased tonal differentiation. Analytical levels of musical greatness multiply, even on the terrain of social symbolics, where the attraction of greatness, of the sublime, and of signs of transcendence can be related to a pact of aesthetic communication, to a redistribution of the forms of consumption more than to a hypothetical benefit of control providing a rampart against cumulative changes.

The very dynamics of increasing the status of sophisticated, elevated, and serious music incorporates these different dimensions all the more directly because the terms of the professionalization of artists change with the competition between two systems of organizing professional activity (subordinate salaried work, independent activity) and with the combinations that can be practiced. The adoption of categories that hierarchize genres and styles leads to the composer's increasing his power of negotiation with his partners and his most influential audiences. In this evolution, the categories of greatness or sophisticated, serious art, along with that of genius, have a long history forged by the development of a language, and complex and highly specialized compositional techniques, that form the necessary conditions for the identification of music with an extraordinary creative knowledge.[94] But these values of seriousness, greatness, and difficulty must also be examined as part of a professional rhetoric intended, as the sociology of professions has taught us, to distinguish an elite of musicians who claim a superior knowledge and competence from a less cultivated base occupied with more common activities. Rosen thus reminds us that the first labor union for musicians, founded in Vienna in the early 1780s, refused to allow dance musicians to join: This point indicates the kind of resource the qualification of levels of practice can offer in the competition that accompanies the expansion of a professional market.

Conclusion

For someone seeking to conceive the world of art as an arena in which the distribution of the resources provided by the social positions occupied spread to artistic destinies and to the contents of innovation, competitive struggles are a zero-sum game: Everything gained by some individuals is lost by others. Thus everything that Beethoven managed to acquire thanks to the connections he established first with the Bonn nobility, and then with the Viennese nobility, is supposed to act as a mechanism for concentrating the means of success. The same is supposed to go for patrons and audiences: Everything that is under the control of the former is equivalent to a power of social domination over the latter. The patron has the superiority over the artist that is conferred on him by his social and economic power; the artist takes advantage of his sources of support to forge a reputation with audiences that are persuaded to support his audacities. One of the radical conclusions that some draw on the basis of this kind of explanation of success is that admiration for Beethoven underestimates the social violence that made his career possible.

The constructionist destabilization, which seeks to present itself in the guise of a healthy demystification of sacred greatness, thus ends up gradually transforming all the content of sophisticated culture into a gigantic negative social accounting.

What argument can be opposed to this enterprise of reducing the values and meanings of art to pure power relationships and manifestations of social violence? The answer that was long proposed is contained in the argument for a relative autonomy of art, and in the argument for the socially exceptional nature of the great artist, as I first examined it.

If individual achievement in creative activities were no more than a zero-sum game, we could no longer understand why the considerable inequalities in reputation, whatever their determinants and longevity, are so legitimate that they transform the artworks emerging from all the competitions into public goods in halls of fame such as museums and other organizations financed by the collectivity to preserve, study, disseminate, and make known the winners of competitions for celebrity. Genius, as the manifestation of an exceptionally superior aptitude, could not be found in a society in which it was omnipresent, totally "democratized" as a manifestation of a lack of interindividual difference in a society in which each individual is endowed with equal capacities for self-realization in all sorts of activities and could actualize them without limits or competitive confrontation. In short, a super-abundance of talents would be required to do away with the interindividual differentiation of which the genius is the hyperbolic embodiment. That is one of the deepest contradictions of the social critique of art that emerges here: Differences in talent, and all the inequalities to which they give rise and which they legitimate, would lose their influence and their importance only if no resource were any longer really rare.

Profiles of the Unfinished

Rodin's Work and the Varieties of Incompleteness

A N ARTWORK is usually conceived in the fine arts as a finished, lasting reality, complete, never changing—a candidate for material and cultural eternity. What happens to it later is separate, something completely formed being pulled into a turbulent future. Diverse viewpoints, readings, and incompatible interpretations give it multiple meanings. Diverse formats of exhibition, "publishing," and diffusion create new connections, putting the artwork into changeable contexts where its meanings will be seen from new perspectives. Reproduction, in media which may not transmit all its original characteristics, or restoration, will subject it to an unforeseeable flow of uses and manipulations. The artwork is what, in this Heraclitean flux, remains the same, still itself, with its name, its title, its inventoried characteristics, and the list of its physical movements and transfers between owners.

But what happens to an unfinished artwork? The history of art is full of unfinished artworks—sculptures by Michelangelo or Rodin; canvases by Leonardo de Vinci, Turner, or Picasso; symphonies by Schubert, Bruckner, or Mahler; operas by Berg or Debussy; novels by Kafka, James, or Musil; philosophical works by Pascal or Nietzsche; and such poetic embodiments of Balzac's *Chef-d'œuvre inconnu* as Mallarmé's *Livre,* or detailed descriptions of the creator's wanderings such as those found in Ponge's *Pour Malherbe.* Such works are puzzling when we know nothing about the interrupted course of their creation. Their author may have told themselves they could not be completed, because they had been a hundred times begun and a hundred times given up. They may have been put away, then rediscovered by the artist or by posterity and put into circulation, with or without the explicit assent of the artist (Kafka was, happily for us, betrayed by his friend and executor Max Brod). Their making may have been brutally interrupted by the death of the artist—among the most moving cases is the last page of *The Art of the Fugue,* where Bach signs his extraordinary composition by introducing the four notes that spell his name to form the second subject of the triple fugue, whose development was suddenly stopped by the composer's death.

This inquiry will focus on Rodin's work. Sculpture is an art whose production can be tracked mainly upstream, penetrating the mental and material workshop of the artist. By contrast, music and the other performing arts also generate a whole set of transformations downstream, due to the mediating and creative activity of the performers. So we need to take an extended look at the issue of unfinishedness.

We start with three examples that suggest the variability of Rodin's practices and the analytic challenges his work poses.

- In her book *Rodin,*[1] Antoinette Le Normand-Romain (1997) describes three versions of *La Méditation:* a large-scale plaster model, unfinished and without arms, dating from approximately 1896–1899,[2] a small plaster model from, roughly, 1895,[3] and a bronze of the small version from, also roughly 1887–1897.[4] We learn that the version of *La Méditation,* which appears as a muse in the monument to Victor Hugo (first project, fourth model), came from the left panel of *La Porte de l'Enfer,* and that it was later completed and modified to become an independent figure.
- *L'Homme au nez cassé (The Man with the Broken Nose),* carried out at the age of twenty-three and widely considered Rodin's first masterpiece, resulted from an accident: The terra cotta figure presented at the Salon of 1864 was the mask that survived the accidental breaking of the complete head Rodin had initially modeled. Steinberg, who points out that Michelangelo, emblematic figure of the art of the sculpture, also had a broken nose, also notes that "twenty years later, Rodin produced a smaller replica of the *Nez cassé,* which he wanted to include in the *Porte de l'Enfer,* and this new version testifies to the direction of his thought: The malleability of the nose provoked by unhappy circumstance had become the determining characteristic. From now on, the entire face was an unstable medium, a roiling sea."[5]

• The third example is *La Porte de l'Enfer,* which seems to embody the story of Balzac's *Chef-d'œuvre inconnu*. Rodin worked some twenty years on this piece until its exhibition in 1900. By then it had been stripped of the bunches of figures that had been suspended in front of its panels. *La Porte de l'Enfer* resulted from a public commission, and its long gestation gave rise to a public chronicle of unfinished-ness, newspaper stories that featured the bluffs and signs of impotence of the creative genius. The paradox is that this artwork, which symbolizes Rodin's failure to finish his greatest project, constituted the generative matrix of smaller, individual artworks to which Rodin owed his considerable popularity at the end of the nineteenth century. As Judith Cladel writes, "*La Porte* occupies, from several points of view, a place of capital importance in his work as a whole. The something like two hundred figures it included constituted a fund from which he was continually drawing; his most celebrated statues and groups were taken from it and adapted, transformed, 'enlarged.' They were at the disposal of the great dramatist of visual art: a troupe of experienced actors. *Le Penseur, Les Ombres, La Cariatide, La Femme accroupie, Les Métamorphoses, Les Faunesses, La Belle Heaulmière,* the group *Le Baiser,* the figures of *Adam* and *Eve* and many others—they are all fragments of *La Porte.*"[6]

Rodin's work seems to thwart the most patient and scrupulous attempts at classification. Sculpture, in the hands of Rodin and his many assistants, is no longer simply an art of creating single specimens or of casting series from a stable, finished prototype. It is also a gigantic reservoir made up of all the sketches and conceivable incarnations of the creative process and its prolongations, fragments, assemblages, replicas, works with missing, mutilated, or dismembered parts—all reworked at variable intervals of time. The "games" Rodin played with the finishing of artworks also reflect highly variable motives and intentions: from obsessively preserved documents of the successive stages of work on a particular piece, which were then sold off, or given away, or donated to an institution; to the reuse or recycling of earlier stages—previously considered unfinished but declared complete after (or sometimes without) modification; to reworkings intended to satisfy the request of a collector dissatisfied with the state of an artwork or a collector interested in an explicitly defined variation; to the dismantling of groups in order to extract elements or to adapt them to a new iconographic plan; to, finally, uncertainties about the classification of the various genetic states of many of Rodin's creations, which often took several completed forms between the sketch, the initial study, and drafts.

These different states appeared throughout the production process, which was rarely linear.

Playing with Completeness: Uniqueness, Multiplicity, Plurality

Genette, following Goodman, distinguishes two modes of existence of artworks, *autographic* and *allographic,* distinguishing arts according to whether they give rise to the production of a materially unique physical object (painting, "'chiseled' sculpture") or of an ideal "object" then produced as copies or multiples (literary works, musical scores, cast sculptures).[7] Genette scrupulously elaborates and deepens this distinction to create a continuum of the many intermediate, mixed, and ambiguous cases that blur this initial classificatory opposition: Sculpture, for instance, occupies several positions on the continuum, according to the type of practice considered. But Genette wraps this dualistic ontology in a distinction between two possible modes of existence of an artwork. The autographic and allographic regimes specify only one of these modes: that of the immanence of the artwork or, put differently, the artwork regarded as embodied in an object (material or ideal, but always complete and well defined). In contrast, what Genette calls the transcendent mode refers to everything that occurs or can occur subsidiary to the immanence of the artwork: the plurality of versions (as distinguished from the multiplicity of identical copies),[8] the partiality of the fragmentary artwork, the multiplication of the artwork through its readings, and through the shifting context of its reception. Immanence is the dominant mode of existence, Genette tells us. It is logically and ontologically first. The transcendence that affects these avatars of immanence is only a derivation of the first mode: There is no conceivable artwork without a defined object already in existence—no artwork that begins with the plural or the fragmentary.

The interest of this exploration is to do justice to everything that can affect the artwork in its initial form. Our goal is to give full aesthetic significance to all the "games" played with the immanence of the artwork. Let us distinguish two categories of games.

The first is based on the derivation, from the complete artwork, of multiple versions, whose closeness to the original varies subtly or considerably, depending on many differentiating factors. What do we find in Rodin's *oeuvre?* Following Genette's classification of types of immanence, we find a superabundance of versions (varying in their degree of difference) derived from the same artwork. Some are replicas produced in response to the popularity of certain artworks, or "versions" reworked to satisfy a patron dissatisfied with a detail (a broken nose or a bust without arms). Others involve making the artwork larger or smaller, often to create a range of formats for commercial purposes, but sometimes to compare and evaluate the same figure in several sizes or to create variant themes (often by making marginal additions and subtractions to a piece, accompanied by a change in the title); or "alterations," small additions and variations made in the production of multiple examples, which redifferentiate the artwork; or the serial exploration of thematic or formal motifs in new artworks, inspired by the artist's obsession with a particular set of concerns, but made without copying an earlier artwork.

In many of these cases, we are left in permanent indecision: Where, for example, do we draw the line between copies or derivations, dependent on an original model, and autonomous artwork or original reelaboration? Typically, the multiplication of distinctions, which has obvious analytical virtues, reinforces the hypothesis that we are dealing with a continuum of practices and solutions—between "the same" and "the new," or plurality and singularity. The fine points of differentiation among them offer arbitrary and shifting possibilities for characterizing such artworks, and opportunities for aesthetic games. What is important, for our purposes, is that they offer the same resources to the creator of the artwork, who can employ them to virtuoso effect.

The second type of "game" takes us to the other side of the artwork: While the idea of an artwork as a matrix for the production of variations presupposes a definite and stabilized, if not definitive, original artwork, here we are more concerned with states of the artwork which are incomplete, filled with gaps, partial, fragmentary. In theory—or rather, following good taxonomic practice—we should, like Genette, separate the drafts, outlines, and other preparatory states, which must be referred to a completed artwork (which are its genesis, "upstream" from the finished result), from what Genette calls partial manifestations, which include the various modes of incompleteness that occur "downstream" from some real or hypothesized more complete version of the artwork we know.

The difference between, and the proximity of, these modes of unfinishedness depend on the teleological assumptions we make about the artwork: "Draft" and "outline" make sense only in reference to the artwork's final state; the fragment with missing parts makes sense only in reference to a previous, supposedly more complete, state. In the first case, we make ourselves, as we contemplate and examine the drafts, part of the genesis of the artwork; in the second case, the artwork bears witness to its history, the different forms it has taken. The distinction seems simple: Either we are inside the creative process, in possession of successive traces related to the end point of the completed artwork, or we are outside this process, but in touch with the historical density of the artwork's career, traceable through the absences, mutilations, and accidents that have undermined its integrity.

Nonetheless, here again intermediate or mixed cases proliferate, and the distinction is muddied: For example, Rodin made multiple outlines and sketches, some of which were shelved, others given away, while others were put into circulation and thus considered authentic artworks by the sculptor—even when they obviously weren't finished. Can't we just place such artworks in the category of the *non finito,* to rid them of the stigma of unfinished sketches? From another perspective, that of the result which has been established as the end point of the creative process, the simple case of artworks that are incomplete because of excisions or involuntary accidents, which were never accepted by the artist because they occurred after his death, concern a finished artwork; but the unfinished state certified *a posteriori* is far from having always the unhappy simplicity of these cases of destruction followed by the dispersal of the fragments. Making a case for an artwork being unfinished requires knowing, one way or another, what the complete artwork should have been. But this claim, which makes incompleteness an *a posteriori* subtraction, does not depend on the evidence. Uncertainty about the "internal clues of incompleteness," as Genette puts it, grows as the aesthetic standards relevant to the characteristics of the production of the artwork are called into question. And the subsequent uses of such uncertainties increase apace. Thus, Rodin's fragments—which at first were only detached pieces (a hand, foot, or arm) intended to be integrated into a larger figure through an assemblage of available elements and other pieces newly made—can be recharacterized as an autonomous artwork, and equipped with eloquent symbolism, as in the case of the hand. The model for an aesthetic characterization of the fragment as a totality was provided in an early commentary by Rilke, who was employed for several years by Rodin in Paris, and who delivered a reading inspired by Rodin's creative practices:

> It is given to the artist to form one thing out of many or to shape a world from the smallest part of one thing. There are hands in Rodin's work: small independent hands which live without belonging to any body. Hands which leap up, irritated and spiteful; hand whose five bristling fingers seem to bellow like the five throats of a hell-hound. Hands that walk, sleeping hands, and hands that awaken. Criminal hands, cursed with heredity, and those that are tired, that no longer want anything, that have laid themselves down in a corner like sick animals who know that no one can help them. But hands are already a rather complicated organism, a delta into which much life has flowed from distant origins to bathe in the great stream of action. There is a

history of hands; they have, indeed, their own culture and their particular beauty, and one must concede to them the right to their own evolution, their own wishes, feelings, moods, and romances.[9]

One must always specify the point, on the dimension that runs from finished to unfinished, where intentions, decisions, and opportunities branch. As his artwork evolved, Rodin habitually preserved the successive stages of his clay and plaster models, in order to visualize, as in a film, the fruitfulness of the transformations, or to experiment with the multiple branchings made possible by the larger pieces into which he integrated his figures, or perhaps because of his obsession with conserving every piece of his creative work. His Meudon workshop was filled with these "sculptured people," in whom he enjoyed seeing the materialization of his modeling and combinatorial genius. For each unfinished specimen, the reasons for saving it as a sketch, or for recharacterizing it as an autonomous artwork, varied. Some contributed to a reservoir for possible artworks to come, others belonged to temporarily suspended projects to be taken up again later, while still others formed a ready reserve of salable pieces in the event of success, a friendly request, or the patrimonialization of his own *oeuvre* into a private or public museum (perhaps someday his own museum, le *musée Rodin*).

This abundance of provisional states (always capable of being made eternal by a later redefinition by the artist or by a posterity seduced by the cult of the unfinished and the fragmentary) launches a superabundance of possible interpretations of artworks as, variously, intentional, compulsive, strategic, calculated, neglected, forgotten, artisanal, or grandiosely megalomaniacal. The periodization of the artist's actions in regard to incompleteness and fragmentation only adds a longitudinal dimension of complexity to the interpretive project. The key point then is to know whether the taste for the fragment became systemic, even a well-used license for invention, and whether the fragmented sculptures are not, in fact, defaced sculptures, which would reverse the meaning of being fragmented and incomplete: A completed sculpture, later deliberately defaced, would be a perfectly finished form in the artistic game involving the completeness of the figure, and no longer an interruption of the aesthetic gesture in its early stages. The question then is of the analysis of practices of defacement and dismemberment: Can one un-finish a defacement?[10]

Genette observes that the modern taste for the fragment and the unfinished, by rehabilitating states of artworks that were only preparatory, "is . . . clearly a betrayal or high-handed violation of the author's intention, which defines the status of the work." But he immediately concedes that:

But this founding or legitimizing intention is not always certain. When an artist leaves a manuscript, painting, or sculpture behind, whether at his death or in order to turn to another work, he does not attach a certificate to it attesting that it is finished or unfinished, so that posterity will not be left in doubt as to its intentional status: Thus it is not entirely certain how Picasso regarded, from this standpoint, "Les Demoiselles d'Avignon."[11]

Rodin's case brings this remark into spectacular relief. In every way, the dream of the genetic specialist who inquires into the creative process via the analysis of sketches is too richly fulfilled by Rodin, who is, in effect, his own "geneticist." He constitutes and preserves his work permanently for himself, and delivers to posterity a complete, or overcomplete, genetic dossier of the states of incompleteness of his own productions. Not that the enigmas disappear: Rodin did almost no dating of his artworks, which is the icing on the cake.

Inquiry into the intention of the artwork and of its many forms, insufficiently covered by the sole notion of *oeuvre*, comes up against the profound elasticity of the criteria Rodin used in his practice. The reception of Rodin's *oeuvre* can be seen as a real-life experiment on responses to incompleteness and about its acceptability, an experiment as important as that which affects the course of the artworks' production and its multiple branchings. As for the spectators—expert art critics, collectors, art lovers, the broader public, public opinion informed by the press of Rodin's time, contemporary opinion—the reception of Rodin's *oeuvre* integrates as of its permanent lines of force what Genette nicely calls the "public's operative tolerance, . . . the capacity of a generation to accept as a version of a work what the preceding generation would have perhaps considered a simple genetic document, or even simply thrown in the trash."[12] The strongly contrasting reactions to Rodin's practices and his use of all the fragments they produced, in turn fed the press, diverse aesthetic quarrels, and ultimately led to the charge that Rodin practiced incompleteness in reverse—finishing artworks, and then fragmenting them to make his mark as the master of the *non finito*. This "operative tolerance" of the creative freedom of the artist varied greatly in the twentieth century: Rodin's powerfully disturbing games with completeness had much to do with this.

The Meaning of the Unfinished

The quality of being unfinished can thus be related to multiple dimensions of operative plurality, according to whether they are versions or variants of an artwork, responses, adaptations, amendments, sketches, or any number of lacunal, fragmentary, defaced, or scattered forms.

But what happens, then, to the principle that gives logical and ontological precedence to activity directed to the production of finished artworks—artworks that are materially stable and, ideally, immutable? Because the plurality attached to the transcendent mode of existence is, for Genette, only a derived state, a supplementary form that assumes an ontologically self-sufficient artwork. In taking this position, the theorist subordinates his taxonomy to the massively dominant practice of artists and art worlds, which generally recognize only finished artworks. Nevertheless, the manifestations of this transcendent plurality proliferate, changing over time without ceasing to multiply and diversify, and are embodied in formulas that can make playing with the object's status a central variable of the creative act. It is in this sense that Krauss takes Rodin's practice as the perfect springboard for deconstructing the logical and ontological precedence of the artwork over its avatars, in order to regard the latter as demonstrations of an irreducible and primordial plurality rather than as accidents.[13]

The first disturbing effect of the irruption of the unfinished into the analytical and interpretative game is this: What ontology of art resists the multiplication of its modes of existence? Or the transformations, innovations, and developments that take as their basis the totality of the possible states of the artwork, rather than a single determination of its final state?

And wouldn't it be legitimate to subject finishing itself to questioning, to put off assuming a necessary closure of the creative process in an immutable form and object, in order to understand that finishing is, first of all, a decision in a labor process that follows an uncertain course, and that it is not a question of a simple application of a standard, such as prevails in the world of objects that have specific functions, which holds that useful objects can do what they are supposed to do only when they are fully made?

How can an artist finish with an artwork, if we admit that Picasso's dictum—"the most difficult thing is to know when to stop"—goes beyond his specific case? And how can the creator play with the requirement of completion? Green notes that, for certain creators, not finishing becomes a mode of behavior, motivated by anxiety that their creative capacity may dry up.[14] Evaluating what they produce, they see in the completion of each artwork the possible end of the whole process, their total exhaustion, the risk of an unbearable decline. Because experience repeats itself, and because each artwork frees its maker to the degree that it endangers him, the trick for the creator is to stay "on the threshold, short of full achievement, [in order to] to save oneself from the anguish of the most unforgivable sanction, the one that one imposes on oneself."[15] The artist prudently transfers to the spectator the definitive or defining task of attributing meaning to the artwork. The artwork can then seem complete to the spectator, and yet remain unfinished in the mind of the artist, who is the ultimate arbiter of this protective illusion. Alternatively, the artist asks the public to tolerate the unfinished artwork inasmuch as it is only a trace of a process, and only the process, in its progressive achievement, makes sense of and does justice to the artist's meaning.

But then, it's the question of the meaning of any artwork that is displaced by the always-open possibility, variously solicited and used, of not finishing, and the tricks that make not finishing more or less obvious. As Baxandall notes, when Picasso declared the *Demoiselles d'Avignon* unfinished, the problem posed by the artwork was not so much solved as announced:[16] How not to see in this determined interruption of the creative act, and in its closure by the words of the artist, a splendid analysis of the complexities of deciphering creative labor? Because the failure to finish thus indicates the ambivalence of any interpretive approach to the artwork.

On the one hand, beginning with an object with fixed contours and limits makes interpretation of the artwork's meaning and the artist's intention (because the signs can be found there) stabilized and available for investigation. On the other hand, the artist's labor, as it is deposited in such and such an artwork, only makes complete sense when located in the broader course of its production and in relation to the contemporary or former productions to which it can be connected. We place ourselves here both upstream and downstream from the artwork, seeing in it the dynamics of the creative process that gave birth to it. We deny the closure of an artwork in order to place it in a flow of creation and in a relational context of differences and similarities that form a tangible universe of reference, in an ensemble of possibilities in relation to which the artist chooses.

The unfinished artwork offers privileged access to the very dimension of labor that the artistic act conceals. Granger points out that "*qua* work, aesthetic creation is one of our attempts to overcome the impossibility of theoretically grasping the individual":[17]

the general thesis is that the object individuates when several concurrent structurations are simultaneously possible—and not only increasingly fine or encapsulated structurations, so to speak, but also overlapping structurations, superimposed structurations, some partial and others global for a given object. Just as the stereoscopic effect is obtained by the conjunction of two disparate images, "the effect of individuation" is, in the same way, born from this virtuality of multiple structures. We of course do not claim to give an account of metaphysical individuation, enunciating the character of its being. Nor do we describe a feeling. The thesis advanced here relates to the relationship between man, seeking to know and to act, and the experience of the world which he constitutes through objects. Epistemological individuation is thus defined only in and by a practice. We will observe once more that one of the movements of science—its "mathematical" component—consists precisely in being unaware of individuation, insofar as it chooses and privileges such and such a type of structuration. At the same time, an opposite movement—its "historical" component—pushes it to move disparate structurations toward convergence, toward the determination of the here and now, in short toward the speculatively inaccessible ideal of a knowledge of the individual.[18]

Doesn't the unfinished artwork place us in the tension between the dynamics of the production of form and content, and the individuating closure of the thing created? The diverse possible forms of the unfinished—the interruption of the act, the fragmentation or reelaboration of a state of the artwork presented previously or elsewhere as complete, the sudden accident that is accepted and preserved as the intervention of chance in the course of the activity, as well as the various intentional positions on not finishing (the product of a decision, a negotiation, or a constraint, the ratification of a situation by the artist, or by others with or without his agreement, and so forth) —bring about the emergence of multiple lines of creative practice, grasped in their uncertain course, revisable, and shaped by ceaseless interactions with other people and the environing situation.

Thus, we no longer consider the creative act as the revelation of a hidden thing-in-itself or, following Aristotle's analysis, as the extraction of the artwork from the husk that completely contains it, in virtual form. It is rather a question of finding, in the uncertain manifestation of the realization and closure of the artwork, a way of accessing the process of its production.

Here we must take account of two analytical perspectives that make it possible to describe this immersion of the artwork in the uncertainty of its end. Chastel wants to distinguish, in the art of the Renaissance, three "ways of disarticulating and compromising the integrity of form": the *unfinished* and two forms associated with the *non finito*, the *fragment* and the *hybrid*.[19] He saw in the "dynamic play of the unfinished and the finished" and in the "pulling form out of the opacity of the material" the expression of the artist's new awareness of the established relation between matter, imagination, and spirit—an awareness created by the very act of production. The higher value given to the artistic process, and to its successive stages, lets us evaluate the various phases of this "reflexive" appropriation of the material, even at the risk of seeing analogies to the torments of the heart struggling with its own complexities.

Nevertheless, a quasi-longitudinal analysis using the intermediate states of an artwork to document the creative process must, logically, be based on a fixed term. The meaning of being unfinished is dialectically dependent on the existence of an outcome, a finished state. If the outlines, sketches, versions, or proliferating transformations of a figure sculpted by Rodin enrich our comprehension of the resulting artwork which the artist has declared finished (and our analysis of its production), it is because they provide access to what, without these early trials, later surpassed in the making of the artwork, would otherwise remain locked up in the artist's mental laboratory; namely, the working out of the alternatives deployed by invention and creative research and gradually pared down by the creative intelligence to the preferred solution. That is one of the secrets we seek to learn when, to understand an artwork better, we scrutinize the branching of this singular decision tree, the creative act. There has indeed been calculation and decision in this process, and not simply uncontrolled passion. The evidence lies precisely in the alternatives left behind along the way, which, like so many beacons that seem unimportant from the perspective of the final result, enlighten us *because* of that teleological conclusion.

The Burden of Choice

Let us clearly understand the dialectic at work here, putting aside cases in which creative labor is so narrowly constrained as to seriously limit the artist's initiative (these cases are rare, in any event, since the rise, on the one hand, of art which has no practical function and the aesthetic value of originality, and, on the other hand, of the legal and socioprofessional means with which the artist can control his creative autonomy). In all other cases, the result is not predetermined by a clear end that could have been conceptually specified from the start (which would have rendered the act of creation purely functional, fully shaped by this representation of the goal). The creative act is thus teleologically directed, but it cannot be organized or appraised according to a functionally optimizing account of the relationship between means and ends. Nevertheless, the production of the artwork remains under the control of the creator, starting from his evolving vision of its internal organization, and at the same time under the control of the various constraints the creator must take into account—constraints of intelligibility, of "exhibitability," of material stability, of reproduction (for allographic arts)—in other words, a range of conventional limits, always manageable and revisable, but at a cost.

Thus, although creative labor is oriented according to choices carried out among an ensemble of initially unspecified alternatives, it operates in a structured and limiting space. In his analysis of "editing," Becker shows that "an art work [takes] the form it does at a particular moment because of the choices, small and large, made by artists and others up to that point":[20] choices between multiple possibilities of subject, format, stylistic treatment, material, and assembly; between various techniques, whether new for the artist or previously employed; choices involving direct negotiation, confrontation, or collaboration with various others, or choice made by anticipating the preferences, objections and evaluations of these others through the dialogical construction of imagined alternatives and test cases; and they include conscious choices, automatic selections, and choices which are not fully conscious.

Becker's description[21]—of how acts of choice and the accumulation of the results of micro- and macro-decisions in the creative process involve collective action—can be broken up into four arguments:

- The number of choices made is considerable, but it is absurd to imagine that they are all conscious: The energy invested in weighing them would devour and paralyze the artist. Whence the assumption of a distribution of choices dominated by those made below the level of consciousness and, as a corollary, of a relative inability to justify even the most obvious choices;
- The infinity of choices to be made is based on the artist continually shifting his point of view, as a result of encounters with his partners and on the usable experience that proceeds from them. Decisions flow continuously from this mental to-and-fro, in which the artist convenes an interior dialogue of various categories of actors situated in his network of interaction and cooperation;
- Just as the great majority of choices are difficult to verbalize, anticipating the opinions and evaluations of others (by imagining their viewpoints on the work in progress) is both necessary and quite imperfect. The artist can nevertheless limit the space of choice by calculating the probabilities of successful completion and presentation of the artwork—especially when such reasoning is elementary or intuitive. A new musical work for string quartet, for example, is likely to be played more frequently than a sonata for bassoon and viola;
- The completion of the artwork is generally not clearly given, as the artist is not unambiguously informed that the end has been reached. Modifications are always conceivable and practicable, and the exact

point of equilibrium where the artwork must stop evolving ("neither more nor less") cannot be calculated, because the hoped-for result can't be determined in advance. The answer comes from external constraints (a deadline for publication, an exhibition or performance on a particular date), the environment (the artwork is complete in the eyes of those partners the artist decides to listen to), and the direct costs and opportunity costs of drawing out the artwork (for example, a delay in the release of a film can run up production costs, push back payment of personnel, and—less directly—adversely impact the visibility and reputation of the artist by preventing him from moving on to another film or to another job).

It certainly would be simpler to stick to an intellectualized description of creation as the resolution of problems, and to the analysis of its halting progress as an exploratory process of trial and error, brought to an end by the more or less complete success of the enterprise. In this context, a failure to finish would indicate that the problem could not be fully solved, but it would also provide intermediate and preparatory materials that, thanks to the celebrity of the artist, could be turned into documents or artworks themselves—imperfect, of course, but more exciting than completed artworks by less inventive and talented artists. The contemporary cult of authenticity surrounding artworks and interpretations in fact brings about the digging up and circulation of the whole corpus of artwork by the greatest creators, with an ever more inclusive appreciation of sketches and incomplete versions.

As Baxandall observes, however, the relevance of such a comparison between creative activity and the resolution of a problem is quite relative: Undoubtedly, without an initial plan that could serve as a guiding principle for the project (intention, project, broad design, diagram, schema, among others), the creative process has neither substance nor a real chance to get off the ground.[22] But how can one delimit this initial impulse? And how can one grasp the trial-and-error exploration and approximation involved without falling into a naive descriptive view of creative production? For Popper, who uses the language of the "problem to be solved" and the "specifications" of a project, this strain is simply the dynamic of creative labor itself, with its feedback loops between the originally conceived model and the progress of the artwork, which makes it possible to concretize and gradually specify the original intuition or intention.[23]

The conception which distinguishes, in order to point to the tension between them, the initial design phase of a project from the innumerable and unprogrammable choices and inventions that progressively give it form collapses into one or the other only in extreme cases. This is the case, for example, with commissioned work that is so thoroughly specified that the artist is little more than an executant, his actions subordinated to external ends. The execution of such a project will be more or less skillful, but the creative practice is "defined" and thus routinizable. At the other extreme is experimentation that tries to be purely random—automatic writing, algorithmic composition, "dripping" without the work of editing—in which the arbitrary character depends, finally, on an initial determination to use only the least considered gestures and to correct or eliminate nothing. A final borderline case, one could argue, is that of the completely fragmentary artwork, whose progress obeys no initial formula nor any progressive striving toward coherence. We might include, in this category, a collection of correspondence or a private diary whose chronological thread takes the place of an ordering principle, and which would be fed by a continuous flow of decisions to consign facts and thought to writing but not governed by macro-level decision making. In the latter two cases, the artwork cannot be unfinished by being "incomplete," because the interruption, voluntary or involuntary, represents a cut-off in an indefinite flow. In the first case, finishing is, in principle, programmable, and thus not finishing logically consists of a gap that can always be filled later by someone acting in the artist's place.

In all the other cases of creation that constitute the canon and are the objects of the most attentive and widespread evaluations (themselves the products of inegalitarian chance), the value of what we see as the success of an artwork is always double. First of all, the end result was unforeseeable—originality is the signature of surprise, it is a cardinal value, considerably esteemed in our culture. Further, the successful artwork imposes a sense of inevitability, in that it cannot be imagined otherwise.

The Artwork: An Unforeseeable and Inevitable Outcome

The two values must coexist: Alone, inevitability would transform creation into a closed process; unpredictability, for its part, would transform creation into a chance activity, subjectively and objectively a lottery. But to be *co-possible*, these two values must still be understood in a way that allows their joining.

What would happen if the value of inevitability indicated a necessity that was logical—formally, historically, or socially logical? This would lead to the triumph of a conception of artistic labor as constrained, given a starting point and an impulsion: Either the original motivation for the creative act is an artistic problem to be solved, and the choices then follow inevitably, or the creative process again follows an inevitable logic but one whose terms the artist does not know and whose course he cannot control, because he is in the grip of forces whose strength he can at best measure but whose deeper nature is beyond him. Thus, two contrasting images of inevitability: the one of rational and axiomatizable computation, the other of the unconscious. In the second case, three types of unconscious can vie for precedence in the etiology of inevitability: the unconscious of psychoanalysis, that is, the personal unconscious of the artist; the historical unconscious, which makes the artist dependent on social forces whose expressive representative he becomes; and the unconscious of the language of the specific art under study and of the constraints of formal work. But to conceive inevitability as purely logical would reduce to zero the component of unpredictability, which gives meaning to the ideas of invention and originality.

Symmetrically, what would happen if the unpredictability of the making of the artwork were conceived as objectively random, something occurring in the flow of matters largely outside the control of the artist? That would be the case, for example, if the production of the artwork depended entirely on chance: The chance distribution of the genetic factors supposedly responsible for artistic talent, the chance meetings and opportunities that make it possible for such talent to express itself in a creative project, on accidental inventions, or on the random alignment of circumstances favorable to the reception of the artwork. As Kris and Kurz showed us, this is one of the classic ways of weaving the legend of the artist's life—a life made of innate gifts, fortuitous meetings, and providential interventions supporting the expression of those gifts.[24] But in this case, the component of inevitability simply disappears and the artist seems to be the plaything of indecipherable natural laws and the random intersections of those lines of causality that determine all things.

In fact, we need to work toward a double specification of unpredictability and inevitability: the unpredictable conceived in a framework of subjective probability, and inevitability comprising an element of evaluation. To conceive the creation of an artwork and its reception as imperfectly foreseeable does not make the creative act an inaccessible black box. Rather, it fully assimilates artistic production to a labor process: The artist evaluates (by a probabilistic balancing of the items submitted to his judgment) the preferable course of his activity, according to the degree of control he can exercise, and the preferred outcomes of his interactions with others. These probabilistic evaluations are subject to experience which, through the emission, reception, acquisition, and reinterpretation of information, causes the artist to move from initial distributions of subjective probabilities to revised probabilities based on the new information. This Bayesian behavior gives a dialectical character to the formation of the judgments by which the artist directs his action. It is there that the conscious constraints on the artist meet his capacity for initiative and invention.

As for the value of inevitability, the idea is compatible with that of unpredictability only if it is based on a judgment: To say that the configuration of the artwork as it is presented to us was inevitable is to hypothesize, as Meyer argues,[25] that there was no outcome preferable to the one actually chosen, and that the result is, temporarily or definitively, the optimal solution.

Such a hypothesis accentuates a central characteristic of both the perception and the appreciation of any artwork. These do not result, as Meyer reminds us,[26] simply from grasping the possibilities and probabilities effectively realized in the artwork, but also from understanding what could have developed differently in the formal organization of the artwork, out of its implicit structure, and from our idea (based on knowledge, intuition, or our learned ability to understand a style) of the options available to the creator, with due regard for the constraints of the style employed.

Our interest in studies, drafts, sketches, outlines, and other preparatory states of the most admired artworks lies precisely in the access they seem to give us to versions of what could have been: They make available to us alternatives that enrich our knowledge and evaluation of what exists, by a kind of probabilistic enrichment, and bring us closer to the creative act considered as a process incarnated in the structure of the artwork.

Which Analytical Approaches? Rodin and the Pluralities of Interpretation

Rodin preserved and used an exceptionally large number of creative states located on the longitudinal axis of the creative process. He thus gives us not only documents of his activity, but also the materials of an investigation to be carried out in many different registers, so that we can approach the creative act, and even the form and transformation of the artworks. I can only enumerate here a few of these registers, keeping their full development for a work in preparation.

Which Rodins should we refer to in the game of deciphering and interpreting his artworks? In the absence of the complete analysis, I will mention here the three pillars of Rodin's variety that bring us closest to the analysis of the artwork itself.

Sculpture and Flights of Originality

Rodin is the practitioner of an art, sculpture, which offers, by virtue of its techniques and materials, a wide range of possibilities, unavailable in painting, for multiplying stages of the creative process which can be described and reelaborated: Casting a clay original by the lost wax process (in which the original model is destroyed) or with a solid core (the model can then be preserved and reused); the variety of materials (clay, plaster, bronze, marble, and so on); and the diversity of the techniques (modeling, molding, layering); the possibility of varying the scale when making a model into an artwork. We can thus locate the sculptor's labor in a multidimensional universe of invention, which demands—and risks exhausting—the concept of originality. As Gaborit writes:

> one of the major difficulties encountered when one first studies sculpture is to locate it in the slow development process which makes it possible for the sculptor to arrive at the completed work. The concept of original work in sculpture is particularly fleeting. Between the unique, original work and the simple commercial reproduction, there exists a whole range of possibilities which have no rigorous equivalent in the field of painting.[27]

The reconstitution of the genealogy of *Balzac* and the analysis of the techniques Rodin used, as they appear in the exhibition catalogue of *1898: Le Balzac de Rodin*,[28] provide an impressive demonstration of Rodin's prolific use of this profusion of sculptural processes.

The Process before the Artwork

Three essential components of Rodin's art are rooted in the unfinished and its combinatorial resources: defective creation, hybrid assemblages, and plural creation. What we call defective creation in Rodin (unfinished, defaced, and broken figures) draws on glorious examples from the past practice of the *non finito*, particularly in the *oeuvre* of Michelangelo,[29] but also that of ancient statuary, many of these artworks having come down to us incomplete. The fragmentary state of the *Torso du Belvédère* has fascinated and inspired large numbers of sculptors since the Renaissance. As Chastel points out, the Renaissance reserved allegorical and moralizing functions for the anatomical pieces and the *mises en scène* of the fragments of the living.[30] The practice of hybridizing partial figures in composite assemblages has the same beginnings: Chastel reminds us that its importance in the Renaissance coincided exactly with the discovery of the *non finito*, before finding a home, above all, in Mannerism. Rodin's deficiencies can be seen as a systematic exploration of these three resources by which Renaissance artists "compromised the integrity of form," as Chastel puts it.[31] But incompleteness per se is not a Renaissance ideal, while for Rodin it becomes a systematically exploited aesthetic principle, and acquires the strengths of a style.

Aesthetic analyses of Rodin's use of the unfinished emphasize the way this formal resource finally became self-conscious, and thus was no longer treated as an accidental and uncertain discovery, as with Michelangelo, but as a decisive step toward the revelation of the essence of the sculptor's art. Freed from the anecdotal and the constraints of having to imitate reality—especially from the reality par excellence of the human form—the sculptor's art moves toward the progressively abstract treatment of forms taken from the human body (which by long tradition constituted an aesthetically indivisible totality, except in the case of deliberate grotesqueries). As marks of artistic modernity, unfinishedness and the freedom to ignore the unity of the human body are central in the development of a self-conscious approach to formal elements. This was already one of the leitmotivs of Malraux's aesthetic analyses, which cited Baudelaire and his remarks on Corot ("a work that is done is not necessarily finished, nor a finished work necessarily done"), and it is the keystone of the reevaluation of Rodin and the celebration of his modernity, even of his archmodernity, by the critic Leo Steinberg in the 1960s and 1970s—beginning with the reversal of critical responses to Rodin's works: The best-known artworks (for example, *Le Baiser, Le Penseur, L'Eternel Printemps*) were now considered too sentimental, too accessible, too expressive, too illustrative, too rhetorical), and the grandeur and the modernity of Rodin were seen to lie in the fragmentary, the incorporation of accidents, the unfinished artworks, and finally in those sculptures, his "best [works], which have as their subject the materials of which they are made and the process that created them." From then on, the aestheticians who modernized Rodin systematically insisted on this strange turning of the artwork in on itself, in which "the way the work is produced (through its dependence on chance, error, discovery, failures, and corrections) constitutes a history which tends to become the essential topic of Rodin's work," the climax of his personal confession, so much "more honest than any manifest erotic content."[32] Belting systematizes this aesthetic proposition when he argues that the *non finito*

became the most convincing manner of dealing with absolute art. Not only did the artist refuse to complete a work, he actually intended that every work should be surpassed by its idea. Rodin's confessional torso is a new mask of the masterpiece that is only completed in our imagination. With Cézanne the creative process never arrived at a result: no single work was so perfected as not to lead to further works in an attempt to do better. The *eros* of the gaze sometimes led both artists to uncompromising self-censorship, or drove them to an act of self-liberation from the work itself.[33]

Here, interpretation draws the artist toward a negative ontology of the absence of artworks as a result of an excess of "will-to-expression" or "will-to-perfection." The odd thing, however, lies in the way the artist skirts this absolutist void and this overabundance of sequences embodied in pieces considered, more or less provisionally, unfinished. The situation becomes highly undecidable for the hermeneutic analyst, who would prefer to find a simple and unique generative principle for the artist's activity: Because, faced with the impossibility of creating a masterpiece, or with the failure of the artwork to express its idea (of which it would only be a defective embodiment), how can we think about the proliferation of artworks or attempted artworks without reducing them to the nothingness of creative impotence? Our modernity can work both sides of the street here, using both the absence and the abundance of artworks to celebrate the artist's originality. To describe the imperfect states, it is necessary and sufficient to convert the movement toward the final state into so many evidences of creative tension. This is the diffusion or halo effect of the value of originality, as Chatelain suggests in his examination of the uses of this value:

> Since it is the creative gift that makes the artist, it is by its innovative nature that a work of art is to be characterized. A true work of art is one which has never been done before: in short, an original work. Likewise, everything which bears witness to the creative steps of the artist will become a work of art. Since the modern artist no longer makes replicas, for to do so would be inconsistent with his very nature, each time he returns to the same subject or theme—be it twice, ten times, or a hundred times—he brings to it variations and subtleties which make the product an original work. . . .
>
> On the other end of this fertile chain of production, the rough outlines and sketches, hitherto considered incomplete forms of a work undertaken by the artist, become witnesses to this creative process. They are all the more moving and important as they are more rudimentary and spontaneous; so they too are considered original works, worthy of being preserved and admired.[34]

While exploiting the multiple resources sculpture offers as a compound and editable art (through the production of series), Rodin also multiplied the institution of originality by using his deliberate, trial-and-error creative method as a productive resource. His descendants in the second half of the twentieth century made these effects the basis of a triumphantly modern practice, all the while pushing his strategic games with originality and scarcity to new lengths, as Raymonde Moulin so brilliantly showed.[35]

The Phenomenology of the Profile
and the Ontology of Multiplicity

Rodin had only one aesthetic creed: an obsession with closeness to nature. But the applications of this creed in the visual arts are so varied, and lend themselves to such different readings, that the creed functions more like a transcendental proposition, a super-rule informing all possible outcomes. Simmel and Rilke, for example, saw Rodin as the sculptor of life, of the flux of life, of living matter put into movement by the vibration of its surfaces, in the tension between complete, partial, and hybrid forms, in the surge of form out of formlessness. Matter is less substance than it is Heraclitean flux, and Rodin's worship of nature departs completely from the simplistic naturalism that is basely mimetic and, therefore, for Simmel, deeply antimodern.

How to give flesh to this inaccessible ideal of restoring movement to the most obstinately material art, the art of clay, plaster, marble, stone, and bronze? Rodin seems to have tried everything, from fanatic exactitude in observing and rendering the human body (which earned him the accusation of having molded *L'Âge d'airain* directly from the body of its model), to the formula, borrowed notably from Michelangelo, of having the form and the figure surge out of formless matter (a block of stone or partially cut marble from which the carved subject emerges). Add to this his proliferating experiments on the movements of bodies, limbs, and torsos, by means of assemblages, fragmentations, and recompositions, all duly documented, filed, even photographed. It is a little as if Rodin, like a new Etienne-Jules Marrey, produced—with his fingers, the scissors of his assistants, and the cameras of his photographers—the film of his creative practice.

In Rodin's several interviews (to which we owe his only quasi-systematic written examples of self-analysis and clarification), he outlines the principle involved: an asymptotic approximation to the subject and model. Simply put, this approximation operates in time, not by simple processual gradations, but through several stages of perception and correction of the artwork, in a way that resembles the phenomenological analysis of perception.

Auguste Rodin: When I begin a figure, I look initially at the face, the back, the two right and left profiles—in other words, the profiles from four angles; then I set up the mass of clay as best I see it and as exactly as possible. Then I form the intermediaries, which provide three-quarters views of the profiles; then, successively turning my clay and my model, I compare and refine them.

Henri Dujardin-Beaumetz: But what do you mean by "profiles"? It is always important to define terms precisely . . .

Auguste Rodin: In a human body, the profile is given by the place where the body ends; it is thus the body that makes the profile. I place the model so that the light, coming from behind, clarifies this profile. I model it, I turn my platform and my model's, I thus see some other profile, I turn some more, and thus make a full circle of the body.

I start again; I close in on the profiles, and I purify them. Just as the human body has profiles ad infinitum, I multiply them as much as I can or as much as I judge useful.[36]

It would be easy to reconcile, using selective quotations, this dynamic description of the serial acts of observation and the Husserlian conception of the perceptive act, in which the object is grasped through a flow of silhouettes, profiles that are given to the perceptive consciousness. The dynamic character of the perceptive act, concentrated in the flux of experiences constituting the object (thing, human being, mental reality, or imaginary content) and its intentional correlate, the ensemble of the innumerable "drafts" or "silhouettes" of the object (in the vocabulary of phenomenology itself) are grasped through a constant process of corrections and additions: The acts of perception have a time dimension, in that the retention of the immediately perceived and the anticipation of the to-be-perceived are woven into the changing flow of the successive perspectives on the object. These acts are directed relations, givers of meaning in the linked orders of perception, memory, imagination, and judgment.

I will go no further in this game of analogies, since I'm not concerned here with testing how well Rodin's practice lends itself to phenomenological analysis.[37] The point of interest, rather, is this: Rodin's creative practice contains, at its heart, a postulate that makes possible the proliferation of sketches and experiments. The question remains: Is Rodin's proliferating flux of production the logical consequence of a fully controlled aesthetic innovation, applied with full knowledge of the facts (after an initial vivid intuition), or an empirical recipe founded on a stubborn artisanal practice that respects the most ancient principles of sculpture?[38]

In his statements, Rodin repeatedly describes at least four aspects of his ways of working: (1) the meticulous observation of "nature" and the life it conceals; (2) the lessons of the Ancients; (3) chance of every kind (accidents, lucky finds, unexpected opportunities); and (4) the fruitfulness of enduring and perfectible labor. The whole makes for a rather pedestrian equation: truth, simplicity, observation, and labor. If we stick to the letter of this "program," which is far from a subtly worked-out aesthetic, we underestimate the engine of Rodin's creative activity: The composition of repertoires of acts whose interconnections are impossible to place in a simple causal sequence, even though the individual elements are completely banal.

The way this assembling of behaviors has no stable formula, how the process is effectively kept open by the very act of creative labor and by the variable contexts in which it takes place—Rodin repeatedly and quite willingly provides a clue to all this instability when he describes what might be called reasoning by *imitative recovery*. His reasoning is roughly this: (1) the secret of art is to reconstitute nature truthfully; (2) the sculptors of Antiquity knew how to make an art which is simple and true, founded on the proper rendition of nature; (3) good artistic practice thus consists of following the lessons of Antiquity and, in that way, coming as close as possible to Nature. Now Rodin continuously emphasized that for him, as for anyone who wants to be a sculptor, knowledge of Antiquity leads to nothing if study and work are not first divorced from a connection to Antiquity. It is by independent progress that one needs, by exploration of the past or by coincidence, to find the principles of the previous millennia. Rodin's doctrines, which appear banally imitative and which seem to provide guarantees ratified by the eternal beauty of Greek art, are (as Marx might say) little more than summarily "naturalist," at a time when the choice between realistic art and abstraction had no meaning.

To complicate things, one could apply the notion of capturing profiles to the argument for fidelity to the ancient art of sculpture, just as the "ancients studied everything via the profile—by all the profiles, successively,"[39] Rodin himself is compelled to approach Greek art, the art of Michelangelo, or that of sculptors of the Middle Ages, only from their profiles. This is a kind of circular fidelity, based on an impossibly totalizing, inevitably selective, perspective.

The theme of the profile and the multiplication of profiles has two opposed meanings: fragmentation and totalization, which it connects through a kind of spiral dynamic, a creative process that experiments by multiplying instantaneous and partial perspectives.

In this association of singular and plural, is the naturalist evidence of the world simply better assured by the creative act, at least more completely approached by it, or does this evidence escape ordinary categories modeled on the stable, fixed, and limiting substance of objects and beings grasped by the artist in their atemporal poses? There is no single answer to this question because Rodin's practice is variable: Thus, in a number of his artworks, it is either the very absence of a model (as in the case of *Balzac*) which often makes Rodin's work branch out, leading him to a result nothing like that of a "naturalist" investigation, to the point of causing one of the biggest of the many controversies in the sculptor's career; or the use of a duplicated figure which, through assemblage, leads to a literal staging of the method of profiles (the *Trois Faunesses* and the three *Grandes Ombres* are famous examples of this) but multiplying the figures instead of condensing the profiles into a single figure;[40] or, again, the reuse of all or parts of existing artworks which, by combination, produce a new group or, by the dismemberment, hybridization, and recombination, generate figures or groups that depart completely from any "naturalist" postulate. Conversely, in other cases, the asymptotic approximation to a visual truth of the model is so obsessive that it gives rise to conflicts with the model, as in the case of the bust of Clémenceau;[41] or it generates incidents like that of the Italian model who posed for Eve and who, in the course of the sessions, gradually changed in appearance due to pregnancy, thus providing Rodin with a perfect little story illustrating his scrupulous respect for the reality of nature, as it appears in the flow of perceptions. Rodin suggested that one can see in this last case a highly symbolic encounter between two key values of his naturalism: the tightest possible perceptive grasp of the reality "to be copied," and the intervention of chance, which is only another manifestation of nature in the form of an intersection of independent causal series.[42]

The Variability of Creative Activity in the Face of Multiple Reality

Gradually, the suspension of belief in the stable identity of the things and people to "copy" is communicated to the creative activity itself: Can we assign only one form of creative behavior to an artist who makes such diverse demands on cardinal artistic values like completion and originality? Historians of art and aestheticians tend to give three answers:

- One which privileges the artist himself who, questioned rather late in his career, reflected back on it and emphasized some fundamental principles, generally as simple as they are timeless—sincerity, the lesson of antiquity, and respect for the truth of nature. Paradoxically, Rodin is not the least concerned with change or multiplicity in his work;
- One which makes Rodin the deconstructor par excellence of the substantialist ontology of the world, and which provides the matrix

for a general reading of his *oeuvre* or of its most significant part: The essence of Rodin's art, once it was completely formed, could be defined as a rejection of uniqueness, systematically and in all its dimensions. This is the thesis of Krauss[43] and Steinberg;[44]

- One which analyzes the evolution of Rodin's creative work and which identifies periods, turns or changes of direction in it, a common procedure in the study of artists' careers. Multiplicity is thus chronologically ordered in connected and graduated sequences, according to various (and unequally harmonious) profiles.[45]

To these diverse and not mutually exclusive scenarios, we can add a fourth, more preferable, which in my view represents the possible contribution of a sociology of art confronted with the artwork in its multiple states. The various forms that Rodin's creative activity takes cannot all be interpreted in the same terms, depending on whether one sees him as: an inventive craftsman; an obstinate defender of a singularly emancipated naturalist aesthetics; an experimenter who proceeds by trial and error and lets chance enter in the course of an activity directed toward a particular end-state (which is nevertheless not foreseeable); a creator trapped in the torment of the creative process, as has been described by psychoanalytic theory; an entrepreneur managing a firm, who responds attentively to a vigorous demand for his product, and who puts considerable energy into multiple negotiations and transactions with private individuals, patrons, dealers, and institutions, in France and abroad, in order to promote his work; a social being with two faces—eager for honors, government commissions, public recognition, and the social immortality that could be produced by the creation of a public museum devoted to his *oeuvre;* and a secret, tireless, obsessive, worker—sometimes ready to confront public opinion, sometimes inclined to compromise, to accommodate his own research to contractual obligations to complete an artwork; an artist fascinated by the glory and undying reputations of his predecessors—such great creators of his own idolatrous century as Balzac, Hugo, and Baudelaire, as well as such great predecessors as Michelangelo, Dante, and Phidias; and, what fascinated the powerful people of his time, a charismatic master who devoured the energy of his collaborators and assistants, who was accused of "vampirizing" the talent of some of his colleagues (Camille Claudel, Medoardo Rosso), and who constructed the images of his grandeur by means of artists devoted more or less briefly to his cause (Rilke, Steichen).

The point of this list, which could be lengthened even further, is certainly to suggest that the exceptional artist has multiple faces and multiple roles, and that the creator who attains international fame modifies his activity in proportion to the inextricable interweaving of the causes that reinforce his growing self-esteem, the artistic and social power that accompany lasting success, and the more complex management of an activity of production that moves between research into new methods and the exploitation of proven solutions—duly patented as immediately recognizable stylistic processes. But the multiplicity of the profiles of his work and career are also concretely expressed in the multiplicity of the meanings and the values of the finished and the unfinished. If our hypothesis is fruitful, we need to see in Rodin's supposed "duality" (for example, Krauss's opposition between the audacious Rodin who makes completion of his artworks a problem, and the obliging Rodin, inclined to produce in series) a reduction of this multiplicity to a too-convenient polarization. The corollary assumption of the priority of the plural over the singular surely singles out a characteristic of the creative material and the system of production of artworks inherent in the compound arts,[46] nothing less than one of the marks of originality of Rodin's poetics. But what a sociology of the artwork must propose (other than an aesthetic ontology, however deconstructive) is exactly the analysis of a completely deployed space of games, in the precise sense offered by game theory, in which the production, definition, evaluation and commercialization of artworks, in their various possible states of uniqueness and multiplicity, of being finished or unfinished, of being "produced" versus being "reproduced" (repetition, transposition, reuse, and so on) are the subject of a remarkably open ensemble of procedures of experimentation and negotiation.

Endings and Unendings: The Trade, Modernity, and Purposefulness of Creative Behavior

The Business of the Geniuses' Production

Increasingly, experts and scholars, but also collectors, music lovers, and several kinds of cultural consumers have been interested in collecting the whole range of the greatest artists' works. This has to do, of course, with how our admiration and fascination for these artists converts every piece of handmade, signed, and authenticated output into something to be added to the catalogue of an artist's *oeuvre*. Sacralization of genius and attempts to overcome the "scarcity limit" are clearly at stake. In the visual arts, for example, since museums and foundations have pumped more and more masterpieces out of private collections, and out of the market, scholars, curators and critics have been interested, each for his own reasons (and more often than not hand-in-hand), in exploring what the storehouse of a great artist contained. Rodin's studio in Meudon, which is now an annex to the main building of the Rodin Museum in Paris, holds an impressive number of pieces of every kind that Rodin himself gathered in order to control his own museification.

But the same happens in every art world in which most of what is of greatest value belongs to the achievements of the past. In the classical music world, the repertoire phenomenon has tended to cannibalize contemporary music, which, in turn, has been more and more radical and esoteric, as long as the avant-garde spirit was equated with the break with that damned, admired, and overconsumed past. But once performers began to dominate the musical sphere, by programming over and over again the same masterpieces, a new game surfaced: Performers began competing to establish new standards of interpretation, of bringing performance in line with artistic and cultural truth and fidelity to a great composer's historical situation, intentions, meanings, and the means at his disposal. And since everything a great artist spits is taken for art, to quote Kurt Schwitters's provocative statement, an enormous industry of musicological research and editorial production has been set in motion in order to go back to Urtexts, to historical authenticity, to genuine styles of interpretation, to instruments used at the time, and so on. Operatic productions are a good case in point. Works entering the canonical repertoire have been able to deliver an indefinite flow of aesthetic, financial and scholarly services, thus becoming durable intermediary goods, only by remaining subject to ceaseless interventions. And famous, nearly finished works arouse special interest, as the search of the true motive for their incompleteness repeatedly sparks controversial interpretations and tentative endings.[47]

So, due to the process of unearthing and completing whatever a great master had left sketched, unfinished, or planned, a considerable number of artworks have been detected, discovered, recertified, redignified, and presented as embodiments of a master's genius. This is the cultural business story, which relies on the supply-and-demand mechanics of rediscoveries, completions, and supplementations.

Our Modernity and the Relativization of Finishedness

As Gombrich writes somewhere, "imperfection of perfection is a discovery of the 19th century." A good way to understand that paradox is to trace it back to Baudelaire's definition of modernity, and to its four criteria.[48]

The first criterion is the *non-fini*, the *unfinished:* This is an anti-academic stance, a criticism of the "polished" character of academic painting. As Boime notes, at the end of the eighteenth century, and more and more in the nineteenth, not only have sketches been reevaluated, but also the sketch-like technique that preserves the flow of spontaneity and inspiration, and arouses a sense of unpredictable dialog between reality and its representation.[49]

Baudelaire's second criterion is that the *fragmentary* has true aesthetic value, as opposed to the enormous organic painting "machines" (history painting, and the like), where each detail had a minute functional location and a predictable signification.

Third, Baudelaire described *insignificance* as a value resulting from the combined virtues of fragmentation and incompleteness: As he says, "cut something into several pieces and each of them may well exist apart, attract interest and stand on its own." This is especially true for the noblest subject of classical painting, the human body. The classical aesthetic convention of harmonious composition was, exactly, based on the human body's perfection as an organic whole.

Finally, Baudelaire recognized *reflexivity* and *self-criticism* as the new bases of the artist's behavior and world vision.

Taken together, these criteria help to understand why modernism is so interested in the appraisal of the fragment, in the valuation of incompleteness, and why modernist scholarship has been obsessed with reevaluating the early signs and manifestations of incompleteness; and also with the positive appraisal of failure, trial, and error as admirable signs of the artist's dedication to his painful and sometimes even life-threatening work. Yet, this last issue remains an intriguing one: How can imperfection, failure, and powerlessness be turned into heroism, challenge, and mastery of a superior kind?

The Work Process and Its Multiple Results as a Laboratory for the Study of Creativity and the Power of Invention

Once we question completeness as a conventional sign of perfection, the black box of the artist's unique abilities is easier to open. Instead of habits, bits of learned techniques, fidelity to reality, and inherited constraining conventions, the artistic realm becomes more and more that of individualistic originality and competition for innovative output. Note a dramatic paradox here: Competition via less conventional originality is accompanied by a growing insistence on personal sincerity, on individual fidelity to one's inner world of feeling and experience (rather than to inherited and imposed criteria), in a word, with insistence on authenticity. But how can an artist guarantee his sincere dedication to his art, when he simultaneously moves away from the conventional ideal of a perfect achievement, of a significantly polished contribution to the arts, when he becomes increasingly critical, self-critical, idiosyncratic, nihilistic, minimalist, unpredictable, radical, even up to the point where the artwork itself disappears, as in many Duchamp-like and conceptual experiments leaving the artist's critical intention as the only evidence of his meaningful creative process?

The growing value attached to the labor process, and not only to the end result, arises from this paradox. "Open work" in literature, hypertext fiction, improvisation in music, and performance in the visual arts are aesthetically challenging stances of incompleteness, instances of a puzzling mix of indeterminacy and variability in the creative process, but also of the predetermination of a creative protocol. They are challenges for both the creative artist and the audience, who are asked to bring to the artwork more imagination, more active involvement, and more information about the positional value of a new creative proposal. In a sense, more verifiable justifications of the artist's dedication to his work may help to sustain such an inducement to shared creativity. In fact, as artworks play with completeness as a revisable convention, the claim that work is behind the work, to echo Robert Faulkner's statement,[50] has to be strengthened.

Since museums, libraries, and shelves of classic music records are filled with artworks considered to be paradigms of finished perfection, a new modernist cult of accident, chance, open-ended labor, improvisation, and interactive performance has to challenge the inevitable suspicion that artists who work in this way lack artistic power, are simply lazy, or without skill and inspiration, yet nevertheless claim to be authentically expressive. Aesthetic canons tailored for the appreciation of self-sufficient artworks may well not apply convincingly to artworks whose fragmentary or incomplete shape are not attached to great names. Other guarantees are necessary to convince audiences that art, up even in its most radical and nihilistic expressions, is still a serious matter of skill, knowledge, and involvement, an expert activity over which the artist and his co-workers justifiably claim jurisdictional control.

Thus, a kind of moral responsibility goes along with the ethics of authenticity, and the individualistic game of creativity is both a search for innovation and an aim for self-expression in its truest and highest significance.

Insistence on the creative process might turn out to be a deceptive one if artists were unable to demonstrate the seriousness of their striving for originality, or if their creative behavior were severely constrained by some strategic game that would rule the field and yield mechanistic runs of innovation by trial and error. Maybe the more widely shared desire to look at the artist's mental laboratory as well as at the numerous tangible proofs of his strivings conveys the sense that art can then be seen as a serious game, that of creativity, even if many of the innovative artworks artists produce may look frivolous and meaningless for a while. Thus, one way to give credit to that game is to consider seriously the characteristics of art as a labor process. Examples of artists showing themselves as obsessive, workaholic, and ruminating beings are countless. I should cite artists as different as Beethoven, Baudelaire, Schoenberg, Kafka, Musil, Paul Valéry, Matisse, Cézanne, or, even if of a quite opposite type of creativity, Picasso.[51] In fact, that bundle of names remains meaningless until we explore each case carefully. However, what these artists have in common, and many others with them, is not only that they consider completion of an artwork as a nonnatural process, but also that they display a reflexivity that shows how creative labor strives hard for invention.

Upstream–Downstream

There are important differences between the arts. In the visual arts, films, and literature, an artwork has, in theory, a unique shape and substance, once it has been released, exhibited, or displayed: One can explore the different phases of its production process, and accept some by-products as valuable, and even collectable and marketable. In the case of the greatest artists, the whole range of the intermediary products that survive—preparatory material, more or less successful trials, more or less elaborate sketches—have become evidence, fetishes, sacred pieces emanating from the godlike hero. In that case, we move upstream, back from the end result, and penetrate the mental and material workshop of the creative artist.

In other cases, for the performing arts, and especially music, which is the concern of the majority of our papers, the multiple embodiments and the completeness versus incompleteness issue apply additionally, mainly downstream, once a musical work has to be performed.

Yet things are not so simple. Innovation may lie in the way artists transform the labor process of the first type into an open-ended, or two-stage, process of the second type: Think of hypertext fiction, or of visual artists today performing artistic events in galleries, in contemporary art centers, and in museums. In that case, artistic achievement as an artwork, as a stable and substantial end result whose identity can be strictly determined, vanishes more or less entirely.

The difference between upstream and downstream kinds of incompleteness also refers to a situation of control, cooperation, and competition.

For example, composers have increasingly tried to control the conditions under which their musical works are performed, by using increasingly precise notation systems, and giving more and more instructions to performers and conductors; but, as a result, they may have spent more and more time producing sketches and revising the score. Baroque composers left scores amazingly short of interpretative instructions, and often adapted their work to the constraints of each specific situation, so that we are left with musical works, notably operas and oratorios, which have many different scored embodiments.

Jazz plays both sides of the street: A successful improvisation can be scored and its essential parts standardized and reused, thus giving rise to a set of endless variations, and arousing the improvisatory spirit, on the exploratory side. One example might be James Moody's improvisation on "I'm in the Mood for Love," which became "Moody's Mood," and a basis for improvisation in its own right.[52]

Moving Purposefully toward an Unspecified End

Access to the mental life of the creative artist seems easier when originality tends toward experimentation and systematic innovation. But easier access to the black box and its contents still does not explain achievement. Envisioning art as a labor process seems to bring into play the sense of a purposeful activity led by a flow of intentions, choices, and decisions. These notions have to be questioned, as shown by the above discussion of Baxandall's analysis of the patterns of intention and of Becker's chapter on editing in his *Art Worlds*. What should be emphasized is that the situation of creative invention is that of striving to an end, which, even if it is impossible to specify and plan, is in a sense directing the process. Uncertainty and variability of that process are both the motor of the invention engine and the obstacle to an easy and straightforward decisional process.

The signature of creative activity is well known, though hard to describe precisely: It is the invention and testing of multiple possibilities. But what remains obscure is how the choice proceeds, given that the end result remains uncertain and is sometimes amazingly impossible to fix until the deadline is reached, at least in the case of the most innovative achievements. Bringing to light the alternatives and scraps of the labor process (sketches, proofs, unfinished artworks, failures, alternative takes, editings, and so on) has a crucial role, that of materializing the labor process, even if only a small part of the whole range of the actual simulations and trials appears. In a sense, through them we learn how the artist talks to himself, how intention operates. Far from being a kind of efficient cause leading from a clearly viewed goal to a controlled process of creating the artwork by making the decisions it requires, intention might be better conceived as "a way to understand the thing done, of describing what happens."[53]

Doing things, trying alternatives, sketching bits of realization and having that at hand make one aware of what is going on. Why? Perhaps because artists must choose between countless possibilities, and they cannot envision every possibility: They move forward by setting down, step by step, what their internal discourse, partially not consciously controlled, suggests to them. Here I should mention the "Zeigarnik effect" (named after Kurt Lewin's student who first tested the idea), according to which people often become obsessed with incomplete tasks, coming back to them again and again, while forgetting things that are completed. Our memory for unfinished tasks is certainly greater than for those that are finished, to which correspondingly less memory is devoted. Performing an action thus tends to erase the memory of the intention that lay behind it. If people often forget tasks simply because the tasks have been completed, this signals a loss of contact with their initial intentions once actions are over, and thus a susceptibility to revised intentions.[54]

Is that process mainly a learning process? To be sure, feedback loops, like those stemming from a trial-and-error learning situation, act as selection devices. But they are mixed with reflexive evaluation: During the creative act, artists have to maintain a sense of variability, not putting the process solely under the influence of the self-reinforcing trial-and-error process.

That's why we have to distinguish so clearly the creative process from the learning process, and also have to find which of the different learning theories best describe the part of the creative process that involves learning sequences.

In sum, the multiple branchings along which a process of creative labor moves are both the signature of an uncertain course (the skeleton of its directionality) and the support of an extensive learning process. Consider again Rodin's *Balzac*, a famous artwork whose creation was long and complex: The Rodin Museum's curators have been able to reconstitute its genetics, that is, to identify more than ninety different steps and to show how each branching generated dead ends or fertile side developments Rodin could use again in another setting. In fact, some important artworks act as matrices, allowing the artist to draw on them for a long series of new pieces. Rodin's *Porte de l'Enfer* played that role: This masterpiece was never finished, and became a widely publicly discussed testimony to Rodin's genius and difficult strivings. Such examples are numerous: For instance, Wagner's *Tannhäuser,* which was constantly revised and changed each time Wagner staged it, and which was the only work Wagner declared unfinished, has been similarly the matrix of many of his later operas. In each case, the seminal, unfinished artwork relates to so many following pieces that one can easily see and analyze the full set as a hypertext-like creation.

Conclusion

AT THE END of the six chapters of this book, what does creative activity look like? In Chapter 6, I quoted Gilles-Gaston Granger's remark that "*qua* work, aesthetic creation is one of our attempts to overcome the impossibility of theoretically grasping the individual." This statement can serve to underline my reason for seeking to shift the focus of the analysis from employment and the artistic professions to the act of invention and its essential uncertainties.

The general arc of the analysis structuring this book led me to lay the basis for a conception of action, and then to extract from it properties indispensable for the qualification of labor, for the expressive value of labor, and for a reinterpretation of the opposition between work and leisure. I then showed how artists work and behave under uncertainty. Uncertainty acts as a necessary condition for innovation and self-realization in the creative act, but also as a delusion, because of the overestimation of the chances of success that it can trigger. As a result, learning by doing plays a decisive role. Inequalities in this professional world are greater than in other professional categories. To what should these inequalities be attributed? The argument from talent (or genius) hardly advances us if we make it an initial capital that is easily detectable and that procures elevated guarantees of success for those who are endowed with it. The forms taken by competition within art worlds, and the means of assessing the value of artworks and artists through incessant relative comparisons, tell us that interindividual differences have to be examined differently. Can they be reduced to so little that a democracy of genius would be possible, and would be impeded only by today's excessively competitive and mercantile organization of artistic activities? But the argument that reduces interindividual differences to zero leads us straight to a dead end. It is possible to construct an explanatory model of the disproportions between differences in success and differences in underlying quality that will enable us to isolate creative labor's coefficient of individualization and originality, while at the same time immersing it in the network of interindividual relationships of collaboration and evaluation that endows it with its social and economic properties, without cancelling the fundamental given, the artist's, his partners', and his audience's uncertainty with regard to the quality of what might be new, different, original, and convincing. Creative labor can then be integrated into the labor market, with its networks, spatial concentrations, mechanisms of public policy, and its tensions between the functional requisite of autonomy (of productive indifference with respect to demand) and the allocation of a social and historical depth (of a meaning, an expressive and symbolic value), that makes the artwork more than a contingent and ephemeral product of a fertile individual imagination.

Having thus broadened my approach from individual behavior to the functioning of labor markets in the arts, I would like to conclude this book by returning to the result of creative labor, the artwork. I have shown how the production of artworks, all through the creative process, results from the combination of three factors—labor, talent, and chance. Labor signifies effort and endurance, knowledge acquired and implemented, the trials and errors of invention, the accumulation of experience, the constraints to which one must adjust, the intrinsic motivation of the engagement, and the proven solutions that can be relied upon. Talent is this gradient of interindividual differentiation (the unpredictable surging up of individuation to which the spontaneity of the imagination is assimilated) that emerges by originality from the competition: It makes it possible to derive a greater benefit from labor as productive effort. The coefficient of chance designates the increased sensitivity of the system of action represented by creative labor with properties that are unpredictable or cannot be controlled by its environment. Paul Valéry offered a probabilistic definition of creative labor that connects effort with chance and interweaves the motifs of reflexive control and inventive spontaneity:

> What a poem aims at is to give the impression of coming from a loftier source than its maker. All his labors, sacrifices, artifices are directed to this end, naïve and primitive no doubt, but perhaps not false.
>
> One may have noticed in one's own experience the chance effect of a "heaven-sent" situation or a happy turn of speech.

By dint of work and art this author whom we presume to be, or to command, is made to become an almost supernatural being. The aim of art and the
poet's labors is to juggle with the spontaneous and the serial, since the series of
bright ideas always falls far short of the hoped-for series of winning coups. So
we try to build up a lucky series *artificially* by a long, patient exercise of trial
and error. Art and labor are devoted to creating a language that no real man
could either improvise or keep up, and the semblance of flowing freely from a
source is imparted to a piece of writing that is richer, more strictly ordered, better balanced and composed than anyone could count on if he depended on the
immediate promptings of his natural self. Such writing we call "inspired." A
piece of work that has taken a man three years of gropings, prunings, amendments, excisions, sortileges, is read and appraised in thirty minutes by another
man. And this reader forms a mental picture of the author as a man who was
capable of writing it all straight off, spontaneously—an infinitely "unlikely"
sort of author. This author within the author used to be styled his "Muse."[1]

I sought to discover what the artwork and the steps in its creation, in
their materiality, can tell us about this interaction of three factors when I
asked in Chapter 6 how the artist goes about completing an artwork, ter-
minating a project, in order to put the final touches on a performance. I
will deal with this question of labor on the artwork itself more fully in a
forthcoming book.

If I consider the artwork as the result of a creative process, I can situate
myself in a longitudinal analysis of the act of creation. Before arriving at
the closed and stable state of a distinctly identifiable and catalogable artwork, creative labor has passed through successive states that give the act
of labor a profile that is often much more complex than that of a linear process of the optimal selection of the most appropriate solutions and of rejecting the insignificant debris left over from creative experimentation. When it
is accessible to us, the archived documentation of these successive states
leads us to suspend the distinctive identity of the artwork: The artwork is
multiplied in its progressive transformations (the documentation of its creation can provide us with the sketches, corrections, revisions, and sometimes radical transformations), and the artwork is enveloped in a set of
conceivable scenarios, some of which, at least, could have occurred had the
course of the activity of creation and the choices made been different. In the
modern era, the reality of the creative labor has been increasingly documented with care by artists, first in the visual arts, and then, especially since
the nineteenth century, in literature and music, through the preservation
and study of manuscripts, sketches, drafts, and revisions. It has given rise to
the hope that philology could be transformed into a science of artistic creation by becoming a genetics of texts and artworks. I note here chiefly that
the envelopment of the artwork in the possible, but not realized, courses of

its production and completion is connected with a probabilistic qualification of the creative act, and might be inscribed in an ontology of possible art worlds to which counterfactual investigations seem to provide access.

The seductiveness of an ontology of possible art worlds must not be underestimated. The artist's intervention can be the object of an emplotment, because it acquires the dynamic properties of a shift into a space of choices and constraints, of decisions and revisions, whose detail cannot, *stricto sensu,* be represented, but whose contours and some of whose contents are visible and attest to a permanent mechanism of action and intervention by the creative subject on himself and on the material of his creative imagination. It is in this way that the figure of the worker-creator emerges: ruminating, enduring, experimenting, struggling with himself and apt to reject, through the exercise of judgment, infertile paths. Artistic activities and, in different proportions, scientific work, have the particularity of involving two forces whose combination is usually described as the couple that is the motor of creativity: the faculty of invention, for its properties of tearing itself away from the base of known and already produced realities, and the patient and permanent control of the course of invention, for its properties of selection and optimization on the basis of a schema of evaluation and correction.

The artist is not the only one who acquires prominence in the development of the uncertain course of creative action. The person (genetic philologist, historian, aesthetician) who examines the archive and develops the counterfactual reasoning regarding what could have been a possible course of creation immerses himself in the creative act at the points of bifurcation he deems crucial, in order to project the artist and the artwork into a possible world. In that world, he can obtain the rank of co-creator or editor, and he interprets not the text, the musical score, or the canvas as they are, but as another course of creation would have established them: either to indicate how much the distance from the realized artwork validates the creator's choices; to explain the proven failure of a given project; to change the assessment made on the hierarchy of the artist's works; to try to resolve the enigma of uncompleted artworks; or again, to do justice to artworks that the intervention of a publisher, a merchant, or a producer who have a power of control and intervention have diverted from the foreseeable course of the artworks' completion.

The increased value set on creative work elicits a demand and a market. The seductiveness of projecting an artwork into an ontology of possible worlds has long been attested by the multiplication of exhibitions in which the presentation of artworks is accompanied by drafts, preliminary versions, sketches, studies, revelations of pentimenti, and reworkings. The considerable philological and genetic industry seeking authenticity in the interpretation of medieval, baroque, or classical music provides an infinite number of hypotheses for the reinterpretation of artworks and the reevaluation of their degree of stability. Technologies elicit multiple procedures of interaction between users and artworks, and of intervention on the artworks. Films sold on DVDs are accompanied by their bonuses and their "making-of" features. The publication and reading of a digital book propels the artwork into a hypertextual network in which the text is connected with an unlimited network of contents, those of its own genesis (we can imagine how Musil might henceforth be read), and those of books, documents, and libraries of knowledge to which it can be referred.

In all these cases, it is no longer a matter of a simple scholarly production that provides the carefully arranged materials of a demonstration ending with the assertion of the superiority of the *ens realissimum* that is the artwork thus documented. It is also a matter of procuring for everyone the hope or the means of identifying with the artist, or of entering into dialogue with his artwork, by taking up residence in the artist's internal discourse and in the mental and material workshop where his decisions, considered, improvised, unpredictable, corrected, or assumed, are made, or even by reappropriating his artwork in order to lower the costs of one's own invention.

The notion of the artwork is changing. Its classical figure is preserved for us by the immense apparatus of heritage formation and management that has consecrated the artwork and cultural goods as durable goods par excellence, products of a singular imagination raised to the rank of public goods, and ideally candidates for universal and perennial admiration. A whole legal and economic apparatus has supported the construction of the modern figure of the author at the same time that it defined the material and immaterial integrity of the artwork as a commodity, as a vector of symbolic communication, and as the basis for the exercise of a property right attributed to the author and his legal successors. But contemporary technologies for digitizing contents, with their avalanches of innovations, easily inscribe each artwork in a network of transactions, uses, appropriations, and possible transformations that rapidly come to affect the received definition of the artwork. They shatter the architecture of rights and responsibilities in the production and appropriation of the artwork. They announce the advent of another world: In the uncertain horizon outlined by technological innovations, the notion of the artwork is rapidly being transformed.

Notes
Acknowledgments
Index

Notes

1. Time, Causes, and Reasons in Action

1. Jon Elster, *The Cement of Society* (Cambridge: Cambridge University Press, 1989); Jean-Pierre Dupuy, *Introduction aux sciences sociales: Logique des phénomènes collectifs* (Paris: Ellipses, 1992).

2. See Gary Becker's interview in Richard Swedberg, *Economics and Sociology: Redefining Their Boundaries: Conversations with Economists and Sociologists* (Princeton: Princeton University Press, 1990), 27–45.

3. Pierre Bourdieu, *Pascalian Meditations* (Stanford: Stanford University Press, 2000).

4. There is more than one species of determinism. Gigerenzer et al. distinguish five:

- metaphysical determinism, which posits that every given event or state of affairs had to happen and that past and future are symmetrical: every past event had only one possible future and every future event will prove to have had only one possible past;
- epistemological determinism, which refers to our ability to predict and retrodict; it augments metaphysical determinism by specifying the principle of our capacity to know;
- scientific determinism, which specifies that to correctly exercise our power of prediction we use the general laws that govern the world of observable phenomena, laws determined by scientific theories. A description of the world in terms of these laws may be as complete as desired, as long as the theories specify (1) a set of basic characteristics for the objects observed that uniquely

determine all their observable properties, and (2) the laws governing the manifestation of those characteristics in time;

- methodological (or pragmatic) determinism, holding that the incompleteness of our current knowledge does not invalidate scientific determinism: in cases of deficient explanation, the right method is to seek to enrich knowledge with deterministic hypotheses rather than turn to indeterminism;
- effective determinism, which requires distinguishing between several levels of scientific theorization. Determinism is valid for one of these levels, but this understanding tolerates recourse to nondeterministic hypotheses in the study of another level of phenomena. A macro-development may be subject to strict causal determinism, whereas specific, unforeseeable developments and properties slip the grip of deterministic explanation. However, the deterministic postulate remains dominant in that it orients the analysis.

See Gerd Gigerenzer, Zeno Swijtink, Theodore Porter, Lorraine Daston, John Beatty, and Lorenz Krüger, *The Empire of Chance* (Cambridge: Cambridge University Press, 1989), 276–279.

5. In his study of the antinomies of classical sociological thinking, Jeffrey C. Alexander (in *The Antinomies of Classical Thought: Marx and Durkheim* [London: Routledge and Kegan Paul, 1982]) offers a detailed analysis of the modulations in Durkheim's determinism as discernible across his writings. The first type, mechanistic determinism, was based on the theoretical schema of the agent's strict adaptation to his environment via the strength and resonance of habits developed through repeated actions, each of which is undertaken to reestablish equilibrium with his milieu. This environment is populated by other agents, and equilibrium can only be reached by postulating an integrative collective consciousness. With the theory of increasing differentiation of labor and personal identities and increasing density of interactions, Durkheim went beyond establishing an opposition between mechanism and organicism, the two dominant forms for organizing interindividual relations. Durkheim's basic model was gradually overtaken by its increasingly voluntarist understanding: The sphere of the agent's autonomy grows, and the characteristics that individualize action come into active play; the margin for personal expression in action widens, while actor interdependence comes to be organized in accordance with a complex model of differentiation within the social totality. The central argument, however, does not change: Though the source of the collective order has shifted, that order remains the guarantor of the functional equilibrium of interdependencies.

6. François Bourricaud, *L'individualisme institutionnel: Essai sur la sociologie de Talcott Parsons* (Paris: Presses Universitaires de France, 1977).

7. Ibid. Bourricaud claims that Parsons's refusal to assimilate structural functionalism to strict determinism—that is, culturalism or behavioralism—led him to make a probabilistic, "interactionist" correction that complexified functionalism, thereby revealing the theoretical tension that inventories of local deviations may inflict on systemic ideas of global order. This "generous" interpretation of Parsons's thought (Bourricaud's qualifier) implied a detailed examination of all the probabilistic injections that work to preserve the concept of action in Parsons's work while being nonetheless constrained by the (Parsonian) necessity of equilibrating the so-

cial system. It is worth noting that dialogue with economic analysis is of no help here. François Chazel ("Théorie économique et sociologie: Adversaires ou complices? La réflexion d'un 'classique': Talcott Parsons," *Sociologie et sociétés* 21[1] [1989]: 39–53) shows that for Parsons, economic analysis of action could hardly provide a means of integrating functionalist and individualist approaches: In order for such analysis to satisfy the functional criteria for attaining social equilibrium, it would have to be purged of its individualist and utilitarian aspects.

8. Pierre Bourdieu with Loïc Wacquant, *Réponses* (Paris: Seuil, 1992), 108–109; my italics.

9. Ibid., 109.

10. Ibid., 111.

11. "To the extent that practical activity is meaningful, sensible, reasonable— that is, engendered by habituses that are adjusted to the immanent tendencies of the field—it transcends the immediate present by practically mobilizing the past and practically anticipating the future inscribed in the present as objective potential. Because the habitus implies practical reference to the future implied in the past that produced it, it becomes temporalized in the very act by which it is enacted" (Bourdieu, *Réponses*, 112–113).

12. François Héran, "La seconde nature de l'habitus," *Revue Française de Sociologie* 28(3) (1987): 393–394.

13. Bourdieu, *Réponses*, 114.

14. Raymond Boudon and François Bourricaud, *Critical Dictionary of Sociology*, trans. Peter Hamilton (Chicago: University of Chicago Press, 1989).

15. Peter L. Berger and Thomas Luckmann refer, for example, to a "secondary socialization" in their influential *Social Construction of Reality: A Treatise in the Sociology of Knowledge* (Garden City, NY: Doubleday), 1966.

16. Raymond Boudon, *Effets pervers et ordre social* (Paris: Presses Universitaires de France, 1977).

17. Blumer summarizes the four central conceptions in symbolic interactionism thus:

> (1) People, individually and collectively, are prepared to act on the basis of the meanings of the objects that comprise their world; (2) the association of people is necessarily in the form of a process in which they are making indications to one another and interpreting each other's indications; (3) social acts, whether individual or collective, are constructed through a process in which the actors note, interpret and assess the situations confronting them; and (4) the complex interlinkages of acts that comprise organizations, institutions, division of labor, and networks of interdependency are moving and not static affairs. (Herbert G. Blumer, *Symbolic Interactionism* [Berkeley: University of California Press, 1969], 50)

18. Ibid., 53.

19. Edmund Husserl, *Cartesian Meditations,* trans. Dorion Cairns (The Hague: Martinus Nijhoff, 1960); *On the Phenomenology of the Consciousness of Internal Time,* trans. John Barnett Brough (Dordrecht: Kluwer, 1991).

20. Jacques Derrida, *Speech and Phenomena, and Other Essays on Husserl's Theory of Signs,* trans. with an intro. by David B. Allison (Evanston, IL: Northwestern University Press, 1973), 65.

21. Husserl writes: "Within my ownness and moreover within the sphere of its living present, my past is given only by memory and is characterized in memory as my past, a past present—that is: an intentional modification. The experiential verification of it, as a modification, then goes on necessarily in harmonious syntheses of recollection; only thus does a past as such become verified. Somewhat as my memorial past, as a modification of my living present, 'transcends' my present, the appresented other being 'transcends' my own being (in the pure and most fundamental sense: what is included in my primordial ownness). In both cases the modification is inherent as a sense-component in the sense itself; it is a correlate of the intentionality constituting it. Just as, in my living present, in the domain of 'internal perception,' my past becomes constituted by virtue of the harmonious memories occurring in it and motivated by its contents, an ego other than mine can become constituted" (*Cartesian Meditations*, 115).

22. Anselm L. Strauss, *Mirrors and Masks* (Glencoe, IL: Free Press, 1959).

23. Donald Davidson, *Essays on Actions and Events* (Oxford: Clarendon, 1980), 316ff.

24. Ibid., 239.

25. C. Wright Mills, "Situated Actions and Vocabularies of Motive," *American Sociological Review* 5(6) (1940): 904–913.

26. Ibid., 905–908.

27. Harold Garfinkel, *Studies in Ethnomethodology* (Englewood Cliffs, NJ: Prentice-Hall, 1967). For a helpful synthesis of Harold Garfinkel's work and commentary on the opposition between ethnomethodology and structural functionalism, particularly with regard to the dimensions considered here, see John Heritage, *Garfinkel and Ethnomethodology* (Cambridge, UK: Polity Press, 1984).

28. See, for example, Thomas Schelling's notions of *self-command* and metapreferences ("Self-Command in Practice, in Policy and in a Theory of Rational Choice," *American Economic Review* 74[2] [1984]: 1–11) and Jon Elster's discussion of analyses of weak will, with his celebrated example of Ulysses chaining himself to the mast to avoid succumbing to the irresistible siren song (Jon Elster, *Ulysses and the Sirens* [Cambridge: Cambridge University Press, 1979]).

29. Jon Elster, ed., *The Multiple Self* (Cambridge: Cambridge University Press, 1985).

30. Anselm L. Strauss, Introduction to George Herbert Mead, *On Social Psychology* (Chicago: University of Chicago Press, 1956).

31. Erving Goffman, *Encounters* (Indianapolis: Bobbs-Merrill, 1961), 117, 123.

32. Anselm L. Strauss, *Negotiations: Varieties, Processes, Contexts, and Social Order* (San Francisco: Jossey-Bass, 1978).

33. Michel Crozier and Erhard Friedberg, *Actors and Systems: The Politics of Collective Action,* trans. Arthur Goldhammer (Chicago: University of Chicago Press, 1980).

34. Elster, *Ulysses and the Sirens;* see also Philippe Van Parijs's discussion of the opposition between deterministic and intentionalist models in his book *Le modèle économique et ses rivaux* (Geneva: Droz, 1990).

35. Mead's pragmatist theory of action (George Herbert Mead, *The Philosophy of the Act,* ed. Charles W. Morris [Chicago: University of Chicago Press, 1972])

already provided the basis for this understanding in its explicit rejection of an exclusively continuist temporalization of action. For Mead it is the constant combining of the continuity characterizing a series of events with the discontinuity of the present and the novelties it brings that makes it possible both to experience temporal continuity altogether and to apprehend the newness of the present situation. Continuity is thus not simply given to the actor but is the product of a reconstruction by means of which the actor realigns his experiences within a comprehensible totality, while being confronted with discontinuous elements brought to light by unexpected experiences. This idea would obviously not make sense if the present of an action-interaction situation did not contain emerging, *new* elements that the actor has to react and adjust to. In other words, it is the emerging newness of the situation that elicits realignment of the various pasts and that moves the actor to process them by means of symbolic reconstruction so that the new situation can be understood and hypotheses formulated, anticipations made and objectives for the future chosen.

36. Howard S. Becker, *Art Worlds* (Berkeley: University of California Press, 1982).

37. Robert Redfield, "The Folk Society," *American Journal of Sociology* 52(4) (1947): 293–308.

38. David K. Lewis, *Convention: A Philosophical Study* (Cambridge, MA: Harvard University Press, 1969).

39. On this self-splitting of self, see Dupuy, *Introduction aux sciences sociales,* 75–76.

40. Quoted by Vincent Descombes, *Les institutions du sens* (Paris: Minuit, 1996), 225.

41. Dupuy, *Introduction aux sciences sociales.*

42. This is the subtle, counterintuitive example of "sunspot equilibrium" models proposed by Cass and Shell and Azariadis and Guesnerie. See David Cass and Karl Shell, "Do Sunspots Matter?" *Journal of Political Economy* 91(2) (1983): 193–227; Costas Azariadis and Roger Guesnerie, "Sunspots and Cycles," *Review of Economic Studies* 53(5) (1986): 725–738.

43. Kenneth J. Arrow and Gérard Debreu, "Existence of an Equilibrium for a Competitive Economy," *Econometrica* 22(3) (1954): 265–290; Kenneth J. Arrow and Frank Hahn, *General Competitive Analysis* (San Francisco: Holden-Day, 1971).

44. Gilles-Gaston Granger, *Essai d'une philosophie du style* (Paris: Colin, 1968), 223.

45. See, for example, Pierre Bourdieu in *Distinction,* trans. Richard Nice (Cambridge, MA: Harvard University Press, 1984), 165–166: "What the competitive struggle makes everlasting is not different conditions, but the difference between conditions . . . The structural gap and the corresponding frustrations are the very source of the reproduction through displacement which perpetuates the structure of positions while transforming the 'nature' of conditions . . . Competitive struggle is the form of class struggle which the dominated classes allow to be imposed on them when they accept the stakes offered by the dominant classes. It is an integrative struggle and, by virtue of the initial handicaps, a reproductive struggle, since those who enter this chase, in which they are beaten before they start, as the constancy of

the gaps testifies, implicitly recognize the legitimacy of the goals pursued by those whom they pursue, by the mere fact of taking part."

46. For an effective, useful presentation, see François Bourguignon, Pierre-André Chiappori, and Patrick Rey, *Théorie micro-économique* (Paris: Fayard, 1992), 322ff.

47. Edmond Malinvaud, *Théorie macroéconomique, vol. 1.* (Paris: Dunod, 1981), 363.

48. See Jean-Michel Grandmont, *Temporary Equilibrium: Selected Readings* (New York: Academic Press, 1987).

49. Bernard Walliser, *Anticipations, équilibres et rationalité économique* (Paris: Calmann-Lévy, 1985).

50. Sanford J. Grossman, "An Introduction to the Theory of Rational Expectations under Asymmetric Information," *Review of Economic Studies* 48(4) (1981): 541–559.

51. In game theory, these deviations instantly weaken the forecasting power of the economic models, since much of that power is due to the fact that the models situate transactions and equilibrium attainment within a competitive environment that actors are perfectly informed about. As Gérard-Varet reminds us, "To this day there is no model more powerful [than Walras's] when it comes to taking into account market power and private information: Market power introduces strategic uncertainty, and private information introduces uncertainty about participant characteristics themselves" (Louis-André Gérard-Varet, "Pouvoirs de marché et informations privées en équilibre général. La théorie peut-elle avoir un pouvoir prédictif?" *Recherches Économiques de Louvain* 55[4] [1990]: 1–26).

52. Among the classical presentations and surveys of game theory, see in particular Hervé Moulin, *Game Theory for the Social Sciences,* 2nd and revised ed. (New York: New York University Press, 1986), and Roger Myerson, *Game Theory: Analysis of Conflict* (Cambridge, MA: Harvard University Press, 1991). Interestingly enough, as Richard Breen puts it, "[while] in the past fifty years game theory has swept all before it in many social sciences, most notably in economics, but also political science, law and social psychology . . . in sociology it has not attained anything like a dominant position and continues to be a minority interest," despite Elster's claim that "if one accepts that interaction is the essence of social life, then . . . game theory provides solid microfoundations for the study of social structure and social change" (Jon Elster, "Marxism, Functionalism and Game Theory," *Theory and Society* 11[4] [1982]: 477, quoted by Richard Breen, "Game Theory," in *Handbook of Analytical Sociology,* ed. Peter Hedström and Peter Bearman [Oxford: Oxford University Press, 2009], 619).

53. Paul Valéry, *Cahiers,* vol. 1 (Paris: Gallimard, Pléiade, 1983), 531.

54. Bourdieu, *Pascalian Meditations,* 135–136.

55. Gilles-Gaston Granger, *Méthodologie économique* (Paris: Presses Universitaires de France, 1955).

56. Héran, "La seconde nature de l'habitus."

57. Charles Taylor, *The Explanation of Behavior* (London: Routledge and Kegan Paul, 1964). Let us follow here Ernst Nagel's clarification:

It is a mistaken supposition that teleological explanations are intelligible only if the things and activities so explained are conscious agents or the products of such agents.

Thus, in the functional explanation of lungs, no assumption is made, either explicitly or tacitly, that the lungs have any conscious ends-in-view or that they have been devised by any agent for a definite purpose. In short, the occurrence of teleological explanations in biology or elsewhere is not necessarily a sign of anthropomorphism. On the other hand, some teleological explanations patently do assume the existence of deliberate plans and conscious purposes; but such an assumption is not illegitimate when, as in the case of teleological explanations of certain aspects of human behavior, the facts warrant it. It is also a mistake to suppose that, because teleological explanations contain references to the future in accounting for what already exists, such explanations must tacitly assume that the future acts causally on the present. Thus, in accounting for Henry [VIII]'s efforts at obtaining an annulment of his marriage, no assumption is made that the unrealized future state of his possessing a male heir caused him to engage in certain activities. On the contrary, the explanation of Henry's behavior is entirely compatible with the view that it was his existing desires for a certain kind of future, and not the future itself, which were causally responsible for his conduct . . . By giving a teleological explanation one is therefore not necessarily giving hostages to the doctrine that the future is an agent of its own realization. (Ernst Nagel, *The Structure of Science: Problems in the Logic of Scientific Explanation* [London: Routledge and Kegan Paul, 1961], 24)

58. Paul Ricoeur, *Oneself as Another,* trans. Kathleen Blamey (Chicago: University of Chicago Press, 1992), 81ff.

59. Vincent Descombes, "Le pouvoir d'être soi," *Critique* 529–530 (1991): 545–576.

60. Vincent Descombes, "L'action," in *Notions de philosophie, vol. 2,* ed. Denis Kambouchner (Paris: Gallimard Folio), 158 and 166.

61. Ibid., 168–169.

62. Descombes, "Le pouvoir d'être soi," 573.

63. Granger, *Méthodologie économique,* 161.

64. Gilles-Gaston Granger, *Pensée formelle et sciences de l'homme* (Paris: Aubier, 1967), 104.

65. Gilles-Gaston Granger, *Essai d'une philosophie du style* (Paris: Colin, 1968), 294.

66. Ibid.

67. Jean-Claude Passeron, "Weber et Pareto. La rencontre de la rationalité dans les sciences sociales," in *Le modèle et l'enquête,* ed. Louis-André Gérard-Varet and Jean-Claude Passeron (Paris: Editions de l'EHESS, 1995), 37–137.

68. Jean-Claude Passeron, *Le raisonnement sociologique: Un espace non popperien de l'argumentation, Nouvelle édition revue et augmentée* (Paris: Albin Michel, 2006).

69. Claude D'Aspremont, Rodolphe Dos Santos Ferreira, and Louis-André Gérard-Varet, "Fondements stratégiques de l'équilibre en économie: Coordination, rationalité individuelle et anticipations," in *Le modèle et l'enquête,* ed. Louis-André Gérard-Varet and Jean-Claude Passeron (Paris: Editions de l'EHESS, 1995), 449.

2. Is Working to Achieve Self-Fulfillment Rational?

1. On the introduction of the vocabulary of talent into the management of human resources and into the systems of "High Performance Work Systems," see Ed

Michaels, Helen Handfiel-Jones, and Beth Axelrod, *The War of Talent* (Boston: Harvard Business School Press, 2001); Dick Grote, *Forced Ranking. Making Performance Management Work* (Boston: Harvard Business School Press, 2005); Robert E. Lewis and Robert J. Heckman, "Talent Management: A Critical Review," *Human Resource Management Review* 16 (2006): 139–154; and Brian E. Becker, Mark A. Hauselid, and Richard W. Beatty, *The Differentiated Workforce. Transforming Talent into Strategic Impact* (Boston: Harvard Business Press, 2009).

2. Bernard Gazier, *Économie du travail et de l'emploi* (Paris: Dalloz, 1991), 152.

3. As Daniel Hamermesh and Albert Rees suggest (*The Economics of Work and Pay* [New York: Harper and Row, 1988]), these two components can be seen as the extremities of a continuum, and the acquisition of human capital specific to the vocation, the investment peculiar to the sector of employment, and the different factors responsible for variations in the supply and demand for skills on the local labor market can be situated on this continuum.

4. Jacob Mincer, preface to Solomon Polachek and Stanley Siebert, *The Economics of Earnings* (Cambridge: Cambridge University Press, 1993), xiii.

5. The argument can be made here with a constant type and context of employment, without taking into account two other essential sources of the increase in individual salary, promotion to a new position and a voluntary change from one enterprise to another, and without referring to either the differences in the rate of remuneration that may result from imperfections in the competitive market, such as the differences in remuneration between industrial sectors (analyzed, for example, by Lawrence Katz and Lawrence Summers in "Industry Rents: Evidence and Implications," *Brookings Papers: Microeconomics* [1989]: 209–229) or the more complex case of a change in vocation. For a presentation of the various models for explaining salaries, see Robert Willis, "Wage Determinants: A Survey and Reinterpretation of Human Capital Earnings Functions," in *Handbook of Labor Economics Vol. 1*, ed. Orley Ashenfelter and Richard Layard (Amsterdam: North-Holland, 1986), 525–602; Polachek and Siebert, *The Economics of Earnings*.

6. George A. Akerlof and Janet L. Yellen, eds., *Efficiency Wage Models of the Labor Market* (Cambridge: Cambridge University Press, 1986).

7. Edward Lazear, "Why Is There Mandatory Retirement?" *Journal of Political Economy* 87(6) (1979): 1261–1284; Robert Hutchens, "Seniority, Wages and Productivity: A Turbulent Decade" *Journal of Economic Perspectives* 3(4) (1989): 49–64; Gérard Ballot, "La théorie des contrats à paiement différé," *Travail et Emploi* 54(4) (1992): 60–71.

8. Adam Smith, *An Inquiry into the Nature and Causes of the Wealth of Nations* (London: Strahan, 1776), book 1, chap. 10.

9. Solomon Polachek, "Occupational Self-Selection: A Human Capital Approach to Sex Differences in Occupational Structure," *Review of Economics and Statistics* 63(1) (1981): 60–69.

10. The relation between autonomy and intrinsic motivation in an activity is well analyzed by Frank Baron and David Kreps in *Strategic Human Resources* (New York: John Wiley and Sons, 1999), 326–327. These authors also emphasize the reason that autonomy creates difficulties not only for certain workers who demand monetary compensations for being exposed to stressful situations of respon-

sibility, but also for the organization if the latter does not succeed in using the habitual mans of control when confronted by salaried workers who turn their autonomy into resistance to the hierarchy.

11. On this point, see the works by John H. Goldthorpe and Keith Hope, *The Social Grading of Occupations. A New Approach and Scale* (Oxford: Clarendon, 1974); Donald J. Treiman, *Occupational Prestige in Comparative Perspective* (New York: Academic Press, 1977); Christopher Jencks, Lauri Perman, and Lee Rainwater, "What Is a Good Job? A New Measure of Labor-Market Success," *American Journal of Sociology* 93(6) (1988): 1322–1357; Christine Chambaz, Éric Maurin, and Constance Torelli, "L'évaluation sociale des professions en France: Construction et analyse d'une échelle des professions," *Revue française de sociologie* 39(1) (1998): 177–226.

12. Mark Killingsworth and James Heckman, "Female Labor Supply: A Survey," in *Handbook of Labor Economics Vol. 1,* ed. Ashenfelter and Layard, 140–141.

13. Boyan Jovanovic, "Job Matching and the Theory of Turnover," *Journal of Political Economy* 87(5) (1979): 972–990.

14. Rosen, "The Theory of Equalizing Differences," 642.

15. See James M. Malcomson, "Contracts, Hold-Up, and Labor Markets," *Journal of Economic Literature* 35(4) (1997): 1916–1957; Olivier Godechot, "Hold-up en finance: Les conditions de possibilité des bonus élevés dans l'industrie financière," *Revue française de sociologie* 47(2) (2006): 341–371.

16. Rosen, "The Theory of Equalizing Differences," 677.

17. Willis, "Wage Determinants," 555–556.

18. Michael Spence, *Market Signaling* (Cambridge, MA: Harvard University Press, 1974).

19. Bernard Walliser and Charles Prou, *La science économique* (Paris: Seuil, 1988).

20. Rosen, "The Theory of Equalizing Differences."

21. The theory of human capital has assimilated the act of consumption to a process of domestic production: The act of consuming requires that the individual or the household assign time to the choice and use of goods and services, and that they mobilize, in addition to monetary expenditure, resources of their own for appropriating the objects of their consumption (the resources used varying with the characteristics of the individuals—educational level, socioprofessional position, age, health, family size, living conditions, environmental factors). The combination of these factors produces final goods that provide the consumer with the satisfaction sought. The way is thus opened to an analysis of the heterogeneity of behaviors of consumption and of the shaping of individual choices, but always on the hypothesis of the consumer's strict rationality and perfect information. In later theoretical analyses, notably Lancaster's, the study of consumption is no longer complicated solely on the side of individual consumers, but also on the side of the objects of consumption. In the "new theory of the consumer," each good can be described as a constellation of "characteristics" of diverse orders from which the consumer's utility derives. If we correct the hypothesis of the consumer's perfect information regarding the state of the market and the whole range of products on offer, choices and decisions to purchase assume the acquisition of

information, and thus the costs of examining the market and evaluating the qualities of the goods.

22. Kelvin Lancaster, *Variety, Equity and Efficiency* (New York: Columbia University Press, 1979), 326–327.

23. Ibid., 327.

24. Ibid., 327–328.

25. Émile Durkheim, *The Division of Labour in Society*, trans. W. D. Halls (New York: Free Press, 1984 [1893]).

26. This functionalist argument has had a considerable effect on later sociology. For example, it was adopted by James D. Thompson in his classic work *Organizations in Action: Social Science Bases of Administrative Theory* (New York: McGraw-Hill, 1967), 105:

> If the modern society is to be viable it must sort individuals into occupational categories; equip them with relevant aspirations, beliefs and standards; and channel them to relevant sectors of "the" labor market. On those dimensions most relevant to jobs as defined technologically, each occupational category is relatively homogeneous, and it is this relevant uniformity which enables individuals and organizations to meet in the labor market.

27. Ibid., 13.

28. Ibid., 338.

29. Émile Durkheim, *Suicide*, trans. John H. Spaulding and George Simpson (New York: Free Press, 1951 [1897]): 250–251. The sociology developed by Bourdieu, which has incorporated part of Durkheim's heritage, has sought to challenge this separation between the hereditary distribution of gifts and the equalization of chances in social competition, and art has been one of the favorite terrains for this deconstruction.

30. John Rawls, *Theory of Justice* (Cambridge, MA: Harvard University Press, 1971), 414.

31. Ibid., 413.

32. Ibid., 443–444.

33. Ibid., 428.

34. Ibid., 429.

35. Ibid., 448.

36. Ibid., 457–458.

37. Ibid., 523.

38. Jean-Pierre Dupuy, *Le sacrifice et l'envie* (Paris: Calmann-Lévy, 1992).

39. Rawls, *Theory of Justice*, 441.

40. Ibid., 529.

41. Ibid., 565.

42. Dupuy, *Le sacrifice et l'envie*, 187–188.

43. Pierre Aubenque, *La prudence chez Aristote* (Paris: Presses Universitaires France, 1963).

44. Aristotle, *Nicomachean Ethics*, trans. Harris Rackham (Cambridge, MA: Harvard University Press, 1968).

45. In her typology of careers, Rosabeth Moss Kanter writes: "If the key resource in a bureaucratic career is hierarchical position, and the key resource in a

professional career is knowledge and reputation, then the key resource in an entrepreneurial career is the capacity to create valued output" ("Career and the Wealth
of Nations: A Macro-Perspective on the Structure and Implications of Career
Forms," in *Handbook of Career Theory,* ed. Michael B. Arthur, Douglas T. Hall,
and Barbara S. Lawrence [Cambridge: Cambridge University Press, 1989], 516).
What establishes a parallel between types 2 and 3 is the necessity of developing
abilities in a riskier environment, under the external pressure of market uncertainties and the internal pressure of interindividual competition, up to the point where
the acquisition of a permanent status makes it possible to reduce the uncertainty
about individual reputation, as is pointed out by Joel Podolny in *Status Signals: A
Sociological Study of Market Competition* (Princeton, NJ: Princeton University
Press, 2005).

46. Thompson, *Organizations in Action,* 105–116. Thompson offers the following definition:

> One significant dimension on which jobs, considered as action spheres, can vary is the
> *opportunity to learn* skills, data, and attitudes which are appropriate for other, better
> jobs. The "assistant-to" position (Whistler, 1960, for example), or the management
> trouble-shooting job (Dill et al., 1962) affords the individual opportunities to interact
> with others in more advanced positions and to observe the requirements and behavior
> patterns for a variety of managerial positions. They provide considerable opportunity to
> learn from the successful and unsuccessful performances of others. Not all jobs provide
> such opportunities or provide them in such degree. (106)

47. Peter Cappelli ("Talent Management for the Twenty-First Century," *Harvard
Business Review* [March 2008]: 1–2) sums up the successive stages in the management of very skilled personnel in American business that have led to the management of talents:

> Internal development was the norm back in the 1950s, and every management develop-
> ment practice that seems novel today was commonplace in those years—from executive
> coaching to 360-degree feedback to job rotation to high-potential programs. Except at
> a few very large firms, internal talent development collapsed in the 1970s because it
> could not address the increasing uncertainties of the marketplace. Business forecasting
> had failed to predict the economic downturn in that decade, and talent pipelines con-
> tinued to churn under outdated assumptions of growth. The excess supply of manag-
> ers, combined with no-layoff policies for white-collar workers, fed corporate bloat.
> The steep recession of the early 1980s then led to white-collar layoffs and the demise
> of lifetime employment, as restructuring cut layers of hierarchy and eliminated many
> practices and staffs that developed talent. After all, if the priority was to cut positions,
> particularly in middle management, why maintain the programs designed to fill the
> ranks? . . .
> The alternative to traditional development, outside hiring, worked like a charm
> through the early 1990s, in large measure because organizations were drawing on the
> big pool of laid-off talent. As the economy continued to grow, however, companies
> increasingly recruited talent away from their competitors, creating retention problems.
> Watching the fruits of their labors walk out the door, employers backed even further
> away from investments in development. I remember a conversation with a CEO in the
> medical device industry about a management development program proposed by his
> head of human resources. The CEO dismissed the proposal by saying, "Why should we
> develop people when our competitors are willing to do it for us?" By the mid-1990s,

virtually every major corporation asserted the goal of getting better at recruiting talent away from competitors while also getting better at retaining its own talent—a hopeful dream at the individual level, an impossibility in the aggregate. . . . Outside hiring hit its inevitable limit by the end of the 1990s, after the longest economic expansion in U.S. history absorbed the supply of available talent. Companies found they were attracting experienced candidates and losing experienced employees to competitors at the same rate. Outside searches became increasingly expensive, particularly when they involved headhunters, and the newcomers blocked prospects for internal promotions, aggravating retention problems. The challenge of attracting and retaining the right people went to the very top of the list of executives' business concerns, where it remains today.

3. Rationality and Uncertainty in the Artist's Life

1. Ernst Kris and Otto Kurz, *Legend, Myth, and Magic in the Image of the Artist: A Historical Experiment,* trans. Alastair Laing and Lottie M. Newman (New Haven: Yale University Press, 1981 [1st German ed.: 1934]).

2. Randall Filer, "The 'Starving Artist': Myth or Reality? Earnings of Artists in the United States," *Journal of Political Economy* 94(1) (1986): 56–75.

3. William Baumol and William Bowen, *Performing Arts: The Economic Dilemma* (New York: Twentieth Century Fund, 1966); Baudoin Seys, "Les groupes socioprofessionnels de 1962 à 1985," in *Données Sociales* (Paris: INSEE, 1987), 37–72; Glenn Withers, "Artists Subsidy of the Arts," in *Governments and Culture,* ed. Richard Waits, William Hendon, and Harold Horowitz (Akron, OH: Association for Cultural Economics, 1985), 154–163.

4. Withers, "Artists Subsidy of the Arts."

5. Karla Fohrbeck and Andreas Wiesand, *Der Künstler-Report* (Munich: Hanser Verlag, 1975); Filer, "The 'Starving Artist.'"

6. Christian Baudelot, "Les carrières salariales," in *Données Sociales* (Paris: INSEE, 1984), 132–138.

7. Tom Bradshaw, "An Examination of the Comparability of 1970 and 1980 Census Statistics on Artists," in *The Economics of Cultural Industries,* ed. William Hendon, Nancy Grant, and Douglas Shaw (Akron, OH: Association for Cultural Economics, 1984), 256–267.

8. Gail Graser, "Manpower and the Arts: A Growth Area in Canada," in *The Economics of Cultural Industries,* ed. William Hendon, Nancy Grant, and Douglas Shaw, 245–255.

9. Seys, "Les groupes socioprofessionnels"; Pierre-Michel Menger, "Les artistes en quantités: Ce que sociologues et économistes s'apprennent sur le travail et les professions artistiques," *Revue d'Economie Politique* 120(1) (2010): 205–236.

10. Raymonde Moulin, Jean-Claude Passeron, Pascaline Costa, and Danièle Hanet, *Les recensements et les enquêtes sur les artistes plasticiens* (Paris: Ministère de la Culture et Centre de Sociologie des Arts, multigr., 1986).

11. Mark C. Berger, "Cohort Size and the Earnings Growth of Young Workers," *Industrial and Labor Relations Review* 37(4) (1984): 582–591; Filer, "The 'Starving Artist.'"

12. For an economic assessment of the professions of ballet dancer and singer, see F.P. Santos, "Risk, Uncertainty and the Performing Artist," in *The Economics*

of the Arts, ed. Mark Blaug (Boulder: Westview, 1976), 248–259. For a detailed analysis of the impact of most of the factors above on three sets of artistic professions, see Fohrbeck and Wiesand, *Der Künstler-Report.*

13. Milton Friedman, *Price Theory* (New York: Aldine, 1976); Walter Fogel, "Occupational Earnings: Market and Institutional Influences," *Industrial and Labor Relations Review* 33(1) (1979): 24–35; Peter B. Doeringer, "Internal Labor Markets and Noncompeting Groups," *American Economic Review* 76(2) (1986): 48–52.

14. John E. Cairnes, *Some Leading Principles of Political Economy Newly Expounded* (New York: Harper and Brothers, 1874), 66ff.

15. Michel Gollac and Baudoin Seys, "Les professions et catégories socioprofessionnelles: Premiers croquis," *Économie et statistique* 171–172 (1984): 97.

16. Ibid. The circularity of this argument is even more obvious if we take into account the high rate of social self-reproduction of the "artist" category, as highlighted in the various monographic studies available.

17. Fohrbeck and Wiesand, *Der Künstler-Report;* Brian Taylor, "Artists in the Marketplace: A Framework for Analysis," in *Artists and Cultural Consumers,* ed. Douglas Shaw, William Hendon, and Richard Waits (Akron, OH: Association for Cultural Economics, 1987), 77–84.

18. Edward Arian (*Bach, Beethoven and Bureaucracy* [Tuscaloosa: University of Alabama Press, 1971]) interprets the reactive behaviors of orchestra musicians—greediness, union combativeness, rebellions against conductors, strict bureaucratic definition of working conditions, among others—as a form of goal substitution that may help reduce the tensions which stem from professional frustration.

19. Dominique Schnapper, *L'Épreuve du chômage* (Paris: Gallimard, 1981).

20. Friedman, *Price Theory.*

21. Pierre Bourdieu, "The Market of Symbolic Goods," in *The Field of Cultural Production: Essays on Art and Literature* (New York: Columbia University Press, 1984).

22. Jon Elster, *Sour Grapes: Studies in the Subversion of Rationality* (Cambridge: Cambridge University Press, 1986). In his discussion of Paul Veyne's and Pierre Bourdieu's analyses of the fundamental property of behavior rationality, according to which "in many cases, the lack of instrumental calculation is a condition for instrumentally defined success" (69), Elster shows that the creation of an artwork is an intentional action, a series of choices oriented toward a goal, but that the artist fails if he is deflected from his true goal—if he deliberately seeks material success or the esteem of others. According to this analysis, success can only be the by-product of creative action. The question is even more profound than that of financial success or reputation, because it touches on the fundamental properties of creative invention. Elster asks: How can one want that which cannot be wanted? How can one seek inspiration and spontaneity without destroying them in the very act of pursuing them? As is well known, one of the most important arguments in all of philosophical aesthetics is the dual nature of creative forces: on the one hand, imaginative or unconscious spontaneity, and, on the other, the labor of testing and reworking that which the initial movement of inspiration—the flash of brilliant invention—has caused to surge up immediately and spontaneously. This argument

can be analyzed as a remarkable illustration of the paradoxes inherent in finding a balance between the values of spontaneity and immediacy, on the one hand, and those of deliberation and calculation, on the other—a balance that is at the heart of the general analysis of action and behavior.

23. Max Weber, *Economy and Society: An Outline of Interpretative Sociology,* vol. *1* (Berkeley: University of California Press, 1978).

24. Jean-Paul Sartre, *The Family Idiot,* trans. Carol Cosman (Chicago: University of Chicago Press, 1994), 107.

25. Ibid., 136–137.

26. Thus, regarding the conception of artistic labor that was shared by mid-nineteenth century writers and poets who inherited the legacy of Romanticism, Sartre writes:

> We shall note, first of all, the most obvious contradiction: the artist is called upon to found his aristocracy or his superhumanity on his incapacity to live, or, more precisely, to take pleasure and to act. Action in all its forms is *alien* to him; only on this condition can he attempt to write. But what will the accomplished work be if not the result of an activity? To be sure this determination of praxis—like all others—has its particular structures; it is a matter not of satisfying a need, of gratifying a real desire, of modifying the structure of our practical field, but of producing, through the organization of a discourse, a center of unrealization. Be that as it may, the motivations are there, the concrete end, which is the finished work in its totalizing unity and its complexity; the raw material, language, presents itself as a field of possibles, with its primary instrumentality and its coefficient of adversity. From this starting point, the end will recruit its means, the means will define the end. There is no doubt we are dealing with an enterprise. Yet the work must in no way seem to be a *practical* result. To those who will soon be its authors, it claims never to be a *product:* it will shine through its gratuitousness, issuing from that "gratuitous act" which is not an act but a nontemporal creation. (Ibid., 164)

27. Bourdieu, "The Market of Symbolic Goods."

28. Sartre, *The Family Idiot.*

29. Paul Bénichou, *The Consecration of the Writer 1750–1830* (Lincoln: University of Nebraska Press, 1999).

30. Daniel Kahneman, Paul Slovic, and Amos Tversky, *Judgment under Uncertainty: Heuristics and Biases* (Cambridge: Cambridge University Press, 1982).

31. Santos, "Risk, Uncertainty and the Performing Artist."

32. Following Charles Taylor (*Hegel* [Cambridge: Cambridge University Press, 1975]), we can trace the elaboration of this model to Johann Gottfried von Herder (*Ideen zur Philosophie der Geschichte der Menschheit* [Munich: Hanser, 2002]; see also Isaiah Berlin, *Vico and Herder: Two Studies in the History of Ideas* (London: Hogarth, 1976), and locate its immediately pre-Marxian theoretical milestones in Hegel, the Romantic philosophy of Schelling (whose first philosophical system culminated in a metaphysics of the Beautiful) and Feuerbach. We can then, following Jürgen Habermas (*The Philosophical Discourse of Modernity* [Cambridge, MA: MIT Press, 1990]), study the extension of this model into its twofold, contemporary legacy: (1) Husserl-inspired constructivist sociology, which Peter Berger and Thomas Luckmann developed most systematically (*The Social Construction of Reality* [Garden City, NY: Doubleday, 1966]); and (2) a set of Marx-inspired critical

philosophical works, ranging from the Frankfurt School's writings on art to Hannah Arendt's thesis on human work (*The Human Condition* [Chicago: University of Chicago Press, 1959]). See also Eliot Freidson, "L'analyse sociologique des professions artistiques," *Revue française de sociologie* 27(3) (1986): 431–443.

33. Karl Marx, *Economic and Philosophic Manuscripts of 1844* (Amherst, NY: Prometheus, 1988).

34. Adolfo Sanchez-Vázquez, *Art and Society: Essays in Marxist Aesthetics* (New York: Monthly Review Press, 1973).

35. In addition to Marx, a variety of authors and schools of thought have attributed this role to artisanal production: from Romantic writers to English reformers who were contemporaries of Marx—such as Ruskin and Morris—all the way to Hannah Arendt. The more he developed his philosophy of historical materialism, the less Marx referred to the expressivist model, as attested by the dwindling presence of the vocabulary of alienation in his work. Yet, as Habermas suggests (*The Philosophical Discourse of Modernity*), even though Marx came to see the model of artisanal and undividable labor as a regressive utopia and eventually abandoned it (after having used it heuristically), the first concept of *praxis* continued to haunt his labor theory of value. We might also extend our investigation of the role played by the artisanal mode of production in the history of thought to Durkheim's analyses in *The Division of Labor in Society* (New York: Free Press, 1984), through focusing on the model of the corporative organization of professions. In the works of Marx and Durkheim, the reference to artisanal labor is a response to the same problem: How can we develop a model of social organization that simultaneously preserves the freedom of each and the equality (or just inequality) of all, or, in Durkheimian terms, one that guarantees the full development of individualization *and* interindividual cohesion in complex and differentiated societies? Both authors highlight the same internal contradiction at work in society: The ferment of civilizing progress is also that which causes social decay.

36. Charles Lalo (*L'Art et la vie sociale* [Paris: Doin, 1921]) recalls how much the idealization of the artisanal mode of production and the nostalgic praise for premarket systems for the organization of artistic activities (guilds, academies) ignore all the imperfections and contradictions that led, precisely, to the historical overcoming of these successive stages of artistic life. For Lalo as for Durkheim, evolution is, indeed, marked by internal contradictions. It has led art to increasingly differentiate itself from crafts, and has enabled the imperative of originality to prevail; yet the development of a market supplied with ever more individualized artworks and talents has also given rise to the dilemma inherent in the modern condition of the artist. Lalo observes that (1) competition between artists has increased; (2) the intensification of this competition, in some ways, plays the role of selecting and filtering talents—a role formerly assumed by crafts training in the guilds; (3) differences in remuneration and wealth between the most established artists (and entrepreneurs) and all the rest have grown steadily; (4) a schism has been created between the production of artworks for a small audience and a high-investment, high-profit business whose mode of operation brings art closer to industry: "a condition which disfavors originality—which is nevertheless the source of life and evolution for art" (83). Yet one of the most interesting aspects of Lalo's

argumentation is that he still views as progress the historical movement of differentiation between art and crafts, as well as the growing division of labor within the "relatively autonomous" (as he puts it) sphere of artistic production. In his final assessment of the merits and drawbacks of the main systems of organization of artistic life—guilds, academies, personal patronage, the market—he reminds us that the organization of the medieval guild was not the pure model of egalitarian community: Hierarchies were established, obscure tasks were assigned to the collaborators of the master, and prestige went to the latter. Moreover, whenever it prevailed, the confusion between art and crafts "was always an instrument for preserving outdated traditions and routines, and an obstacle to any progress. It was the advent of new forms of division of labor that contributed to the greatest aesthetic reforms" (41). The systems that gradually supplanted the guilds seemed like many instruments of liberation that later proved inadequate, for they inevitably ended up becoming constraining as well. With the foundation of the academies, artists freed themselves from the tyranny of the guilds, while simultaneously making themselves dependent on the king: "Despite the way we might perceive them today, the academies responded to the same need to free original personalities and guarantee the possibility of a truly artistic life alongside the simple crafts of the guilds" (44–45). Moreover, the same evolutionary mechanism later shaped the destiny of the academies: "In our time, it is academicism that has become oppressive. Innovative artists instinctively turn to new forms of professional affiliations in order to defend their innovations" (47).

37. Raymonde Moulin, *The French Art Market: A Sociological View* (New Brunswick, NJ: Rutgers University Press, 1987), 133.

38. Weber, *Economy and Society*.

39. Arthur Stinchcombe, *Constructing Social Theories* (Chicago: University of Chicago Press, 1968).

40. Ibid., 263.

41. This is why Marx's peculiar comparison between the activity of Milton writing *Paradise Lost* and that of a silkworm spinning its cocoon is completely misleading, as shown by Jon Elster in his essay on Marx, *Making Sense of Marx* (Cambridge: Cambridge University Press, 1985).

42. Howard S. Becker, *Art Worlds* (Berkeley: University of California Press, 1982).

43. Albert O. Hirschman, "Against Parsimony: Three Easy Ways of Complicating some Categories of Economic Discourse," *Economics and Philosophy* 1 (1985): 7–21.

44. A long tradition of analysis has emphasized the quasi-functional character of manic-depressive states among artists. Originating with Aristotle, this tradition exerted decisive influence during the Renaissance, notably in Marsile Ficin's neoplatonic theory of artistic creation, and found its most striking formulations and examples in the Romantic period. As Hershman and Lieb have noted, the Romantic conception of genius is a catalogue of manic-depressive symptoms. These lead the artist to alternate between manic periods of highly intense intellectual labor—which common sense refers to as inspiration—and depressive episodes. The former, often pursued and prolonged through the use of substances such as drugs and

alcohol, are characterized by a profusion of ideas, an expanded imagination, and a sense of creative urgency; the latter, by contrast, offer the benefits of reflexive control over the artwork. "The grandiosity of the manic, so long as it does not destroy his critical judgment, drives him to attempt to surpass not only others', but also his own, past achievements. . . . Depression makes different contributions to the pursuit of excellence. When it is not severe enough to reduce intellectual functions, it can improve creative work. It supplies the critical judgment needed to correct the extravagances of mania. It also promotes the calm, patient, disciplined effort, the revision and polishing, that is an essential ingredient in most kinds of creative work" (Jablow Hershman and Julian Lieb, *The Key to Genius* [Buffalo, NY: Prometheus, 1988], 16).

45. Santos, "Risk, Uncertainty and the Performing Artist"; Richard Waits and Edward McNertney, "Uncertainty and Investment in Human Capital in the Arts," in *Economic Policy for the Arts,* ed. William Hendon, James Shanahan, and Alice MacDonald (Halifax: Abt Books, 1980), 200–208.

46. Adam Smith, *An Inquiry into the Nature and Causes of the Wealth of Nations* (London: Strahan, 1776), book 1, chap. 10.

47. Alfred Marshall *Principles of Economics,* 8th ed. (London: Macmillan, 1920).

48. Friedman, *Price Theory.*

49. Sherwin Rosen, "The Economics of Superstars," *American Economic Review* 71(5) (1981): 845–858. I will examine Rosen's model in greater detail in Chapter 4.

50. Raymonde Moulin, "Le marché et le musée," *Revue française de sociologie* 27(3) (1986): 369–395.

51. The lottery analogy can suggest any of the following: The realization of an artistic masterpiece is entirely random; the relation of uncertainty must be viewed from the perspective of the artist who, confronted with the multiplicity of possibilities open to him, does not know how to complete his work or how to devise a solution that will bring him admiration and fame; uncertainty pertains to the individual preferences of consumers, which are too unpredictable and volatile for evaluations to crystallize into stable rankings that might inform the artist about his chances of attaining long term success or of remaining lastingly in the pantheon of consecrated values. Furthermore, this analogy can be interpreted to mean either that nature is the source of unpredictability and that chances for success are devoid of any direct relation with the number of players involved (as in Smith's example of the gold digger or professional gambler who fights nature by playing games of chance), or that the number of participants mathematically affects each individual's probability of gain.

52. Marshall, *Principles of Economics,* 518.

53. For analyses of reputation, brand, and signature style as tools for reducing uncertainty in a market for strongly differentiated goods whose qualities are imperfectly known or not easily perceived *a priori,* see George Akerlof, *An Economic Theorist's Book of Tales* (Cambridge: Cambridge University Press, 1984). For an application of this type of analysis to the arts, see Roger McCain, "Markets for Works of Art and Markets for Lemons," in *Economic Policy for the Arts,* ed. William

Hendon, James Shanahan, and Alice MacDonald (Halifax: Abt Books, 1980), 122–138.

54. Max Bazerman, *Judgement in Managerial Decision Making* (New York: Wiley, 1986); Kahneman, Slovic, and Tversky, *Judgment under Uncertainty;* Richard Nisbett and Lee Ross, *Human Inference* (Englewood Cliffs, NJ: Prentice-Hall, 1980); Bernard Walliser, *Anticipations, équilibres et rationalité économique* (Paris: Calmann-Lévy, 1985).

55. Boyan Jovanovic, "Job Matching and the Theory of Turnover," *Journal of Political Economy* 87(5) (1979): 972–990; Jacob Mincer and Boyan Jovanovic, "Labor Mobility and Wages," in *Studies in Labor Markets,* ed. Sherwin Rosen (Chicago: University of Chicago Press, 1981), 21–64.

56. Robert Miller, "Job Matching and Occupational Choice," *Journal of Political Economy* 92(6) (1984): 1086–1120.

57. The advantage of this indicator is that it allows us to inquire about income in terms that are sufficiently general to overcome the reluctance of respondents faced with an information request which is particularly difficult to meet when earnings are irregular, originate from diverse sources, and above all, are likely to go undeclared—as is often the case with freelance professionals (on this point, see Moulin, "Le marché et le musée"; Filer, "The 'Starving Artist'"). Yet the significance of this indicator is problematic in that the estimation of the threshold of economic independence and needs satisfaction greatly varies depending on the individual and his position in the life cycle.

58. Raymonde Moulin, "De l'artisan au professionnel, l'artiste," *Sociologie du travail* 25(4) (1983): 388–403; Bruno Frey and Werner Pommerehne, *Muses and Markets: Explorations in the Economics of the Arts* (Oxford: Blackwell, 1989).

59. For the musicians, actors, and dancers questioned by Baumol and Bowel (*Performing Arts: The Economic Dilemma*), the contribution of the domestic partner far exceeded, on average, the income derived from the artist's secondary job or activity. According to a study by the American Writers Guild (cited in Lewis Coser, Charles Kadushin, and Walter Powell, *Books: The Culture and Commerce of Publishing* [New York: Basic Books, 1982]), this contribution represented, on average, two-thirds of household resources for American authors living exclusively by their pen.

60. It is worth noting that this investment will be managed differently depending on whether the beneficiary is a man or a woman. As a general rule (see François de Singly, *Fortune et infortune de la femme mariée* [Paris: Presses Universitaires de France, 1987]), investing in a marriage or domestic partnership increases the probability of success for men, but penalizes women artists in their careers. In the latter case, we can take full measure of the ambivalence inherent in some of the investments that reduce the risks associated with the artist's life. Marriage constitutes for women artists one of the means of material support for their artistic vocation, and can thus compensate for the handicap their gender identity signifies in most artistic professions (the only exceptions being certain specialized segments such as novel writing and, above all, activities based on a gendered division of labor such as acting, singing, or dancing). Yet paradoxically, marriage also presents drawbacks for the artistic careers of women: the greater the economic advan-

tages in marriage, the greater the drawbacks. Marrying into wealth causes women artists to be rapidly discounted as professionals, making them appear as dilettantish amateurs whose husbands are funding their whims and illusions (Michal McCall, "The Sociology of Female Artists," *Studies in Symbolic Interaction* 1 [1978]: 289–318; Dominique Pasquier, "Carrière de femmes: L'art et la manière," *Sociologie du travail* 25[4] [1983]: 418–431). According to a French study on visual artists by Raymonde Moulin, Jean-Claude Passeron, Dominique Pasquier, and Fernando Porto-Vazquez (*Les Artistes* [Paris: La Documentation Française, 1985]), marriage into wealth is four times more likely for women painters than for their male counterparts.

61. Pierre-Michel Menger and Marc Gurgand, "Work and Compensated Unemployment in the Performing Arts: Exogenous and Endogenous Uncertainty in the Artistic Labor Markets," in *Economics of the Arts,* ed. Victor Ginsburgh and Pierre-Michel Menger (Amsterdam: Elsevier, 1996), 347–381. The French unemployment system put in place for artists and technical workers in the performing arts since the 1960s (which has no equivalent anywhere else) performs two different functions: (1) that of providing earnings replacements which reduce the compensating pay differential associated with the risk of unemployment and uncertainty about lifetime earnings—in fact, the position on the contingent labor market may be optimized so that each individual permanently combines fees and unemployment benefits; and (2) that of subsidizing nonworking time which can be used as leisure time, as training time for a future, demanding job, or as time spent searching for a new job. In the former function, unemployment is seen as a constraint on individual behavior via a labor-demand explanation, whereas in a labor-supply explanation, unemployment can be interpreted as the outcome of a worker's choice with regard to his job search. The compensation scheme designed to fit the requirements of contractual flexibility ran into financial problems because compensated unemployment grew more rapidly than paid work. Employment has indeed been allocated quite exclusively in the form of contingent jobs and short-term hirings, which typically spread the available work among a growing number of agents. Thus the performing arts sector expanded by having an increasing portion of the income required to attract workers paid through unemployment benefits. In aggregate, the amount of unemployment benefits paid to those workers today in France represents more than one-half the amount of their total wages and fees. See Pierre-Michel Menger, *Les intermittents du spectacle: Sociologie du travail flexible* (Paris: Editions de l'EHESS, 2011).

In their survey of unemployment insurance, Robert Topel and Finis Welch ("Unemployment Insurance: Survey and Extensions," *Economica* 47[187] [1980]: 351–379) noted that "to the extent that workers take future unemployment benefits into account when evaluating a job offer, this effect must be ambiguous. While workers will certainly be more selective with respect to job offers if benefits are increased, the value of any particular job must be comprised of both income from working and benefit income from contingent unemployment. The increase in benefits will allow firms to offer the same value of an employment contract with a lower wage" (354). Much less ambiguous are the effects on employers, who are able to exploit asymmetrical information on their work and job allocation agenda in order to include entitlement to unemployment benefits in their wage bargaining with their contingent employees. Firms also collude with their employees by hiring them repeatedly for short periods in order to secure a kind of internal labor market without bearing the full cost of long-term relationships. In presence of asymmetrical information and moral hazard in insurance, the implementation of an experience rating formula is the only way to make employers responsible for the impact of their hiring decisions on the fund's finances.

62. Pierre-Michel Menger, "L'État-providence et la culture," in *Pratiques culturelles et politiques de la culture,* ed. François Chazel (Bordeaux: Presses Universitaires de Bordeaux, 1987), 29–52; Moulin, "De l'artisan au professionnel, l'artiste."

63. Kenneth Arrow, *Essays in the Theory of Risk-Bearing* (Amsterdam: North-Holland, 1969); Michael Block and John Heineke, "The Allocation of Effort under Uncertainty: The Case of Risk-Averse Behavior," *Journal of Political Economy* 81(2) (1973): 376–385.

64. Three factors must be taken into account in assessing portfolio risk, and hence in optimizing diversification: (1) the risks associated with each portfolio asset; (2) the correlation among the assets' returns; and (3) the number of portfolio assets (Bertrand Jacquillat and Bruno Solnik, *Les marchés financiers et la gestion de portefeuille* [Paris: Dunod, 1987]). The capacity to diversify is assuredly more limited for human capital than it is for physical capital. Jacques Drèze offers the following comments on the idea that the individual can diversify risks through using labor rather than capital resources (as a firm would do):

There exists a marked difference between the risk-sharing opportunities applicable to human capital, which are narrowly limited; and those applicable to physical capital, which are quite extensive. . . . Unlike human capital, financial assets are divisible and free of transportation costs. This opens up opportunities for diversification which are substantial (although still imperfect). . . . As noted by Meade ("The Theory of Labor-managed Firms and of Profit-sharing," Economic Journal 82[325] [1972]: 402–428): 'While property owners can spread their risks by putting small bits of their property into a larger number of concerns, a worker cannot put small bits of his effort into a large number of different jobs. This presumably is a main reason why we find risk-bearing capital hiring labour rather than risk-bearing labor hiring capital.' . . . For these reasons, I believe that risk tolerance is greater:

- For owners of non-human capital than for owners of human capital;
- For corporations than for the self-employed;
- For firms than for workers.

(Jacques Drèze, "Human Capital and Risk-bearing," in *Essays on Economic Decisions under Uncertainty* [Cambridge, UK: Cambridge University Press, 1987], 349–350)

65. Freidson, "L'analyse sociologique des professions artistiques."

66. Anselm Strauss, "The Art School and Its Students: A Study and An Interpretation," in *The Sociology of Art and Literature,* ed. Milton Albrecht, James Barnett, and Mason Griff (London: Duckworth, 1970), 159–177; Judith Adler, *Artists in Offices* (New Brunswick, NJ: Transaction, 1979).

67. Bernard Rosenberg and Norris Fliegel, *The Vanguard Artist* (New York: Arno, 1979); Barbara Rosenblum, "Artists, Alienation and the Market," in *Sociologie de*

l'art, ed. Raymonde Moulin (Paris: La Documentation Française, 1986); Sanchez-Vázquez, *Art and Society.*

68. Paul Claudel, quoted in Christophe Charle, "Le champ de la production littéraire," in *Histoire de l'édition française, vol. 3,* ed. Roger Chartier and Henri-Jean Martin (Paris: Promodis, 1985). This belief typically derives from Romantic ideology, whose neoaristocratic undertone Sartre brought to light in his important book on Flaubert. In order to affirm the autonomy of literature, Romantic writers conceived of creative activity as the opposite of a profession—of bourgeois activity:

> The writer must produce without counting on the public's favor, which, in any case, is nowhere to be found; and above all, writing cannot become his profession. In other words, working in the *belles-lettres* will be noble, provided the writer does not live by his pen. Hence the writer must imperatively provide for his own material independence. He can only achieve this, though, in one of three ways: by practicing a secondary profession that will function as his livelihood; by accepting a state pension or sinecure; or by being sufficiently wealthy to live from his property and investments. (Sartre, *The Family Idiot*)

Is Alfred de Vigny, in the preface of his play *Chatterton* (New York: Griffon House, 1990), thinking of the condition of rentier or the virtues of extreme deprivation—a type of rent as pure as it is suicidal—when he writes that "the original genius" needs "to *do nothing,* in order to do something in his art"?

69. Becker, *Art Worlds.*

70. Thus, Raymonde Moulin (*De la valeur de l'art* [Paris: Flammarion, 1995], 100) recalls that "commercial art is the secondary activity of novice painters, whereas it is one of the primary activities of successful ones."

71. Fohrbeck and Wiesand, *Der Künstler-Report.*

72. Erving Goffman, *Asylums: Essays on the Social Situation of Mental Patients and Other Inmates* (Garden City, NY: Anchor, 1961).

73. Randall Filer, "The Price of Failure: Earnings of Former Artists," in *Artists and Cultural Consumers,* ed. Douglas Shaw, William Hendon, and Richard Waits (Akron, OH: Association for Cultural Economics, 1987), 85–100.

74. Alan Peacock and Ronald Weir, *The Composer in the Marketplace* (London: Faber, 1975).

75. Dennison Nash, "The Career of the American Composer," in *The Sociology of Art and Literature,* ed. Milton Albrecht, James Barnett, and Mason Griff (London: Duckworth, 1970), 256–265.

76. Pierre-Michel Menger, *Le Paradoxe du musicien* (Paris: Flammarion, 1983); Pierre-Michel Menger, *Les Laboratoires de la création musicale* (Paris: La Documentation Française, 1989). On the importance of teaching careers for artists holding a university degree in the United States, see in particular Judith Adler (*Artists in Offices*); on visual artists and composers see Jann Pasler (*Writing through Music: Essays on Music, Culture and Politics* [Oxford: Oxford University Press, 2007], chap. 11, "The Political Economy of Composition in the American University, 1965–1985").

77. Menger, "L'État-providence et la culture."

78. Cesar Graña (*Bohemian versus Bourgeois* [New York: Basic Books, 1964]) described the main characteristics of this demographic influx. The absence of visible

barriers to entry in the literary world rendered the writing profession exceptionally attractive. As a unique embodiment of the self-made man, and in the absence of any univocal professional practice or certified skills requirement, the writer seemed entirely free to define himself as creator. In a society wherein access to professions of comparable prestige was governed by strict educational or social selection mechanisms (wealth, relational capital, social heredity), the possibility of acceding fully to a domain in which success was both spectacular and unpredictable made the literary world a zone of apparent social indeterminacy. As such, this world had all that was needed to attract a heterogeneous, socially mobile population: students discouraged by failure, but also candidates for social promotion who had come from the provinces to the big city (Paris) and turned their back on stable yet routine or less accessible professions. These swelled the population of writers in search of rapid success as well as declassed individuals tempted by the marginality of the artist's life.

79. Paul Hirsch, *The Structure of the Popular Music Industry* (Ann Arbor: University of Michigan Press, 1969); Paul Hirsch, "Processing Fads and Fashions," *American Journal of Sociology* 77(4) (1972): 639–659.

80. Hirsch, *The Structure of the Popular Music Industry.*

81. Howard S. Becker, "Distributing Modern Art," in *Doing Things Together: Selected Papers* (Evanston, IL: Northwestern University Press, 1986).

82. Stinchcombe, *Constructing Social Theories.*

83. Becker, "Distributing Modern Art."

84. Muriel Cantor and Anne Peters, "The Employment and Unemployment of Screen Actors in the United States," in *Economic Policy for the Arts,* ed. William Hendon, James Shanahan, and Alice MacDonald (Halifax: Abt Books, 1980), 210–218.

85. Robert R. Faulkner, *Hollywood Studio Musicians* (Chicago: Aldine, 1971).

86. Robert R. Faulkner, *Music on Demand: Composers and Careers in the Hollywood Film Industry* (New Brunswick, NJ: Transaction, 1983).

87. René Bonnell, *Le cinéma exploité* (Paris: Le Seuil, 1978).

88. Robert Escarpit, "Succès et survie littéraires," in *Le littéraire et le social,* ed. Robert Escarpit (Paris: Flammarion, 1970).

89. See Harrison C. White and Cynthia A. White's pioneering essay (*Canvases and Careers* [New York: John Wiley, 1965]) on the evolution of the painting world and the collapse of the academy system in the nineteenth century. The authors analyze, in particular, the demographic aspects of the increasingly poor adjustment between the recruitment, training, and professionalization of painters.

90. To the organizational inertia of the education system, we must add factors linked to the specific conditions prevailing in certain artistic training programs. For instance, precocious and lengthy training in ballet or classical music have two major consequences. First, given the prolonged duration of the selection period, the chances for success of the students who are brought together in training programs are revealed to be unequal at a relatively advanced point in time; second, their career prospects can radically change over the ten-to-fifteen-year period required for complete training. As I have indicated above, the more that training is technical and specialized, the poorer the conditions are for potential retraining. Yet the young

age of this population, the slow and gradual selection of talent, and the high proportion of students without a professionalization project also work to ensure the existence of a vast market for teaching jobs. Therein lies one of the conditions for the perpetuation or slow resolution of the crises of artist overpopulation. This becomes particularly clear in the case of music, as shown by Cyril Ehrlich's study of the evolution of the music professions in England (*The Music Profession in Britain Since the Eighteenth Century* [Oxford: Clarendon, 1985]).

91. Raymonde Moulin, "Architecte: Le statut d'une profession," *Encyclopedia Universalis,* 1977.

92. Bernard Haumont, "Les débouchés de l'architecture: Un nouveau paysage," *Le Monde,* December 3, 1987.

93. The number of architects in France went from 9,000 in 1950 to 14,500 in 1970, and then to around 40,000 in the early 2000s. Meanwhile, according to INSEE data, activity in the construction sector more than quadrupled in volume between 1949 and 1973, and stagnated after the first oil shock of 1973; since then, it has been fluctuating without ever again reaching its early 1970s peak. See Nicolas Nogue, *Les chiffres de l'architecture: Populations étudiantes et professionnelles* (Paris: Éditions du Patrimoine, 2002).

94. Raymonde Moulin, Françoise Dubost, Alain Gras, Jacques Lautman, Jean-Pierre Martinon, and Dominique Schnapper, *Les Architectes* (Paris: Calmann-Lévy, 1973).

95. *Les débouchés de l'architecture,* a study by *Monde Campus* and the Conseil de l'ordre (*Le Monde,* December 3, 1987). For a survey, see Florent Champy, *Sociologie de l'architecture* (Paris: La Découverte, 2001).

96. Nisbett and Ross, *Human Inference.*

97. This concern for the well-being of future generations is of course one of the main economic justifications for the rationality of supporting the subsidization of the arts by the welfare state. See *The Economics of the Arts,* ed. Mark Blaug (London: Martin Robertson, 1976).

4. Talent and Reputation

1. In the United States, for example, the number of artists rose 78 percent from 1980 to 2000. In France, at constant scope, the total number of persons in artistic professions rose 50 percent from 1990 to 2005—four times faster than the active population at large. Visual and applied arts professionals constitute the largest category, accounting for one-third of all artistic professionals. In this category, the sub-subcategory of *"stylistes-décorateurs"*—designers, graphic artists, fashion designers, interior designers (in graphic arts, fashion, and decoration)—predominates. Performing artists make up both a smaller and a more homogeneous category. The same hierarchy is observed for the United States.

2. On musicians' careers and earnings by sex, see Hyacinthe Ravet and Philippe Coulangeon, "La division sexuelle du travail chez les musiciens français," *Sociologie du Travail* 45(4) (2003): 361–384.

3. The surveys take into account the characteristics of individual workers, including sex, age, place of residence, family situation, and nationality, as well as

characteristics more directly predictive of expected earnings, such as level of education or qualification and professional experience. The earnings function allows one to measure the opportunity cost of choosing an artistic profession, that is, the negative gap between the average income an individual can expect to earn in an artistic profession and the income he could earn from the best alternative solution available to him in the labor market, given his personal characteristics.

4. Neil Alper and Greg Wassall, "Artists' Careers and Their Labor Markets," in *Handbook of the Economics of Art and Culture, vol. 1*, ed. Victor Ginsburgh and David Throsby (Amsterdam: Elsevier, 2006), 813–864.

5. Paul Kingston and Jonathan Cole's study of American writers' income in the late 1970s (*The Wages of Writing: Per Piece, Per Word, or Perhaps* [New York: Columbia University Press, 1986]) likewise found that earnings equations are poorly adjustable for artistic professions.

6. Stith Bennett analyzed the behaviors associated with learning by doing: "Apparently the musical expertise which is created during the period of transition from *non-musician* to *rock performer* cannot be explained through conventional patterns of teaching and pedagogy. Although some enterprising schools of popular music have sprung up in large urban areas, and some long-standing colleges and universities have admitted the study of popular music through 'appreciation' and history courses, rock musicians typically combine the availability of instrumental lessons from a private instructor (usually at a music store) and some formal art music instruction (perhaps in high school or at a local college) with the more important resource of a group relationship as the source of skills" (Stith Bennett, *On Becoming a Rock Musician* [Amherst: University of Massachusetts Press, 1980], 5). The key component of skills acquisition here is a kind of collective learning based on listening to records and partaking in ongoing discussions ("shop talks") on how to produce the identified sound effects. One might wonder whether "self-teaching" is still the appropriate term for this informal structure which is grounded in the group and imposes itself on individuals who, nevertheless, have extremely diverse musical skills and backgrounds. "Without someone to show them how rock musicians learn to make music together by talking about 'getting a group together,' by finding places to practice, by talking about instruments and equipment and acquiring what materials they consider necessary, by setting gigs, by gaining access to compositions and learning how to play them, and, most importantly, by ceaselessly assessing who and what 'sounds good'" (p. 5). For recent analyses of the world of popular music in France, see Morgan Jouvenet, *Rap, techno, electro . . . Le musicien entre travail artistique et critique sociale* (Paris: Editions de la MSH, 2006), and Marc Perrenoud, *Les musicos: Enquête sur des musiciens ordinaires* (Paris: La Découverte, 2007).

7. Notes to a recording of Brahms's D major Concerto, Nathan Milstein violin, Vienna Philharmonic Orchestra conducted by Eugen Jochum (LP, DGG 2530 592).

8. The history of doctrinal conflict around the twofold source of artistic creation— divine inspiration (*"Poeta nascitur, non fit"* ["The poet is born, not made"], declared a commentator of Horace's *Ars poetica*) and training, wherein the trainee learns to master techniques and to develop conscious control of his creative activity by means of acquired science—is about as old as the philosophical genres of poetics

and aesthetics. Edward Lowinsky recalls a few key moments of this history in his two-part essay, "Musical Genius—Evolution and Origins of a Concept" (*The Musical Quarterly* 50[3] [1964]: 321–340 and *The Musical Quarterly* 50[4] [1964]: 476–495). The Romantic doctrine of artistic genius, which received decisive impetus from the many writings in aesthetics published in Europe in the second half of the eighteenth century, stressed the authentic artist's power of self-teaching and self-creation. In this understanding, the value of the artwork's originality—its ability to create itself out of nothing—is conferred on the individual creator who detaches himself from tradition or from conventions organized around imitation—a distancing that is both deliberate and impossible to achieve through the application of rules.

9. Robert Merton, *Sociological Ambivalence and Other Essays* (New York: Free Press, 1976), 4–5. It is interesting to analyze the wide variety of instruments employed in the academic world to reduce this ambivalence: incentives for students to seek their first job outside of the university they attended; prolonged training in research through having students work on other teams (postdoctorates); collaboration between students and their mentors in coauthored articles; the importance of placement records in establishing professors' reputations and enabling them to attract the best students. The size and organization of the job market, as well as the conditions of competition for renown, are essential in determining whether or not the master-apprentice relationship remains a zero-sum game (that is, anything transferred from the former to the latter increases the probability of the latter eliminating the former), or if providing the apprentice with optimal training actually enhances the master's reputation, in what becomes a positive-sum game. It is significant that the two quotations discussed in this section are from musicians. Of all the artistic disciplines, art music offers the most developed and selective system of initial training. Competition in this art involves a selection process similar to that of the scientific career. Moreover, an important component of professionalization in the composition of art music entails specialized technical training, which enables composers to teach as a complementary source of employment. For a general analysis of teaching as the organizational linchpin of professions involving intense, highly selective initial training, see Andrew Abbott, *The System of Professions* (Chicago: University of Chicago Press, 1988).

10. Pierre Boulez, *Conversations with Célestin Deliège* (London: Eulenburg, 1976), 36.

11. Pierre Boulez, *Orientations,* trans. Martin Cooper (Cambridge, MA: Harvard University Press, 1986), 418–419.

12. Paul Watzlawick, Janet Helmick Beavin, and Donald Jackson, *Pragmatics of Human Communication* (New York: W.W. Norton, 1967).

13. Quoted by Anthony Storr in *The School of Genius* (London: Andre Deutsch, 1988), 169.

14. In the *Critique of the Power of Judgment,* Kant formulates the relation between the mastery of rules required for practicing an art (one of the fine arts, says Kant) and the "natural endowment" of genius: "*Genius* is the talent (natural gift) which gives the rule to art. Since the talent, as an inborn productive faculty of the artist, itself belongs to nature, this could also be expressed thus: *Genius* is the inborn

predisposition of the mind *(ingenium)* **through which** nature gives the rule to art. . . . For every art presupposes rules which first lay the foundation by means of which a product that is to be called artistic is first represented as possible. The concept of beautiful art, however, does not allow the judgment concerning the beauty of its product to be derived from any sort of rule that has a **concept** for its determining ground, and thus has as its ground a concept of how it is possible. Thus beautiful art cannot itself think up the rule in accordance with which it is to bring its product into being. Yet since, without a preceding rule, a product can never be called art, nature in the subject (and by means of the disposition of its faculties) must give the rule to art, that is, beautiful art is possible only as a product of genius" (Immanuel Kant, *Critique of the Power of Judgment,* § 46, trans. Eric Matthews [Cambridge: Cambridge University Press, 2000], 186).

15. In his critical sociology, Pierre Bourdieu *(Distinction: A Social Critique of the Judgment of Taste* [Cambridge, MA: Harvard University Press, 1984]) criticizes the identification of genius with natural dispositions and the Kantian theory of aesthetic judgment. The questions raised by Kant regarding creative activity are as follows: the distribution, in a given population, of the rarest qualities; the impossibility of determining criteria for producing and assessing originality; and the infraconscious nature of creative activity (which in German Romantic thinking became a theory of the creative unconscious). These three questions are also three ways of characterizing the radical indeterminacy of creative invention as well as its irreducibility to deterministic analysis.

16. Barbara Rosenblum, *Photographers at Work: A Sociology of Photographic Styles* (New York: Holmes & Meier, 1978).

17. Charles Kadushin, "The Professional Self-Concept of Music Students," *American Journal of Sociology* 75(3) (1969): 389–404.

18. Pierre-Michel Menger, *La profession de comédien. Formations, activités et carrières dans la démultiplication de soi* (Paris: La Documentation Française, 1998).

19. Raymonde Moulin, *L'artiste, l'institution et le marché* (Paris: Flammarion, 1992), 312.

20. Judith Adler, *Artists in Offices* (New Brunswick, NJ: Transaction, 1979), 133 and 136.

21. Ibid., 136–137.

22. Initial training is the only aspect of artistic training examined here. In the arts, as in other areas, professional activity is marked by periods of continuous training and formal learning. One example is opera: It is common, if not necessary, for opera singers to work with a teacher throughout their careers to keep their voice or body in shape and to rehearse roles and scores. While regularly consulting teachers to resolve this or that difficulty can undoubtedly be compared to a form of continuous training, it is not always easy, however, to distinguish between that which constitutes training and that which simply follows the logic of employment in the arts. As Ruth Towse remarks in *Singers in the Marketplace* (Oxford: Clarendon Press, 1993), preparing with a teacher is a normal component of work in opera singing. Familiarizing oneself with new technologies is another example of artists' investment in in-depth training, as I showed in *Les laboratoires de la création musicale* (Paris: La Documentation Française, 1989).

23. The assistant conductor offers a case wherein prolonged learning fuses with initial professional practice. This type of learning follows initial in-depth training in the disciplines of writing, analysis, and in many cases composition, as well as in the practice of one or several instruments. It can consist of a long period of training with one or several seasoned professional conductors, which combines learning by imitation and absorption, collaboration in preparing and rehearsing with an orchestra, and the development of one's first personal contracts.

24. Paul Valéry, "Pièces sur l'art," in *Oeuvres* (Paris: Gallimard, 1960), vol. 2, 1358.

25. Richard E. Caves, *Creative Industries: Contracts between Art and Commerce* (Cambridge, MA: Harvard University Press, 2000), 24–25.

26. In their analysis of the functional properties of the artist's manic-depressive state, Jablow Hershman and Julian Lieb (*The Key to Genius* [Buffalo, NY: Prometheus, 1988], 14–15) highlight that the strong sense of self-confidence that stems from the manic dimension of behavior protects the artist in periods of discouragement, financial difficulties, or failure. A grandiose self-image and the belief systems associated with it—for instance, mystic faith in one's creative vocation—are necessary conditions for defying authority and tradition, developing a spirit of competition, and maintaining one's taste for oversized undertakings. Colin Camerer and Dan Lovallo have sought to show experimentally that excessive self-confidence and optimism, which lead massive numbers of individuals to enter fields wherein success is highly uncertain, may be due to the fact that these fail to take into account the reference group of their competitors, each deeming himself good enough to succeed. This argument may be generalized: Overconfidence, which amounts to rejecting others' opinions and maximizing the value placed on the future, is the type of behavior necessary for the optimal development of high-risk businesses and professions. See Colin Camerer and Dan Lovallo, "Overconfidence and Excess Entry: An Experimental Approach," *American Economic Review* 89(1) (1999): 306–318.

27. Since Max Weber, the economic condition of artists has been examined not as a simple problem of adding up sources of income, but as the association between anti-economic behavior (which guarantees the charismatic practice of the activity) and economic solutions (a subsistence job). In *Economy and Society: An Outline of Interpretative Sociology Vol. 1* (Berkeley: University of California Press, 1978), Weber offered a definition of charisma and charismatic domination that applied notably to religious prophets, warrior heroes, and political leaders, and also to artists. Pure charisma constitutes a "vocation" in the sense of a "mission," an "inner calling." It "disdains and repudiates economic exploitation of the gifts of grace as a source of income," though, Weber adds, "this often remains more an ideal than a fact." In order to disdain "traditional or rational everyday economizing, the attainment of a regular income by continuous economic activity devoted to this end," one must resort to other means: "Support by gifts, either on a grand scale involving donation, endowment, bribery and honoraria, or by begging, constitute the voluntary type of support. On the other hand, 'booty' and extortion, whether by force or by other means is the typical form of charismatic provision for needs. From the point of view of rational economic activity, charismatic want-satisfaction

is a typical anti-economic force. It repudiates any sort of involvement in the every-day routine world. It can only tolerate, with an attitude of complete emotional in-difference, irregular, unsystematic acquisitive acts" (244–245). As Weber observes, in addition to patronage, solutions for the provision of basic needs include rents (which guarantee one's economic independence) and any kind of side job.

28. David Throsby, "Disaggregated Earnings Functions for Artists," in *Economics of the Arts,* ed. Victor Ginsburgh and Pierre-Michel Menger (Amsterdam: North Holland, 1996).

29. The disaggregation of artist activity into three components has been tested in empirical studies of the profession; see Catherine Paradeise's *Les Comédiens* (Paris: Presses Universitaires de France, 1998) and my own study, *La profession de comédien.*

30. Neil Alper and Ann Galligan, "Recession to Renaissance: A Comparison of Rhode Island Artists, 1981 and 1997," *Journal of Arts Management, Law and Society* 29(3) (1999): 178–203.

31. Arthur L. Stinchcombe, "Some Empirical Consequences of the Davis-Moore Theory of Stratification," *American Sociological Review* 28 (1963): 805–808, re-published in *Stratification and Organization* (Cambridge: Cambridge University Press, 1986).

32. David Jacobs, "Toward a Theory of Mobility and Behavior in Organizations," *American Journal of Sociology* 87(3) (1981): 684–707; James Baron and David Kreps, *Strategic Human Resources* (New York: John Wiley and Sons, 1999).

33. Alper and Wassall, "Artists' Careers and Their Labor Markets."

34. In France, this law of inequality is illustrated by available statistics on the income that visual artists and authors (such as writers, photographers, composers) earn from their creative activities, as declared to the social security agencies with which they are affiliated. In 2005, 10 percent of visual artists obtained 45 percent of all distributed income, while 10 percent of authors received half of all distrib-uted income. Likewise, 10 percent of performing artists (principally, actors, musi-cians, dancers, and circus artists)—very broadly defined as those affiliated with the profession due to having received at least one payment in the year considered (2004)—concentrated 44 percent of earnings from the activities considered (ex-cluding sources of income unrelated to employment contracts in the sector). See Éric Cléron and Frédérique Patureau, "Ecrivains, photographes, compositeurs: Les artistes auteurs affiliés à l'AGESSA in 2005," *Culture Chiffres* 5 (2007) and "Pein-tres, graphistes, sculpteurs: Les artistes auteurs affiliés à l'AGESSA en 2005," *Culture Chiffres* 6 (2007).

35. Howard S. Becker, *Art Worlds* (Berkeley: University of California Press, 1982), 363ff.

36. A recording company that resorts to payola provides financial compensation to radio and television stations (direct payments, royalties on the sale of planned CD recordings, share offers, the purchase of advertising slots during relevant musi-cal programming, gifts to programmers, and such) in order to get its recordings on the air. Here, contrary to paid advertising, the audience remains unaware of the transaction. The public may then assume that the programmers' choices were made independently, as a function of their tastes and opinions. Long practiced in the

United States, payola was declared illegal in 1960 on the grounds that it distorted competition; however, it has not ceased to exist and is even considered by some to be inevitable in one form or another. See Ronald Coase, "Payola in Radio and Television Broadcasting," *Journal of Law and Economics* 22(2) (1979): 269–328; Marie Connolly and Alan Krueger, "Rockonomics: The Economics of Popular Music," in *Handbook of the Economics of Art and Culture Vol. 1,* ed. Victor Ginsburgh and David Throsby (Amsterdam: Elsevier, 2006), 667–719; Caves, *Creative Industries,* chap. 18.

37. For an assessment of the stability of great painters' reputations over the long term, see, for example, Victor Ginsburgh and Sheila Weyers, "Persistence and Fashion in Italian Renaissance Art from Vasari to Berenson and Beyond," *Poetics* 34(1) (2006): 24–44.

38. One of the consequences of this is that artists and artworks of the past may persist in competing with those of the present. The field of art music (symphonic, instrumental, and lyrical), with its classics and established repertoire, has expanded *toward* the past, favoring a great number of rediscoveries. A spectacular example of this is the movement of baroque music interpretation with instruments from the original musical period. See Pierre-Michel Menger, *Le paradoxe du musicien* (Paris: Flammarion, 1983) and Caves, *Creative Industries,* chap. 22.

39. Francis Haskell analyzes these rediscoveries along with their various motives in *Rediscoveries in Art* (London: Phaidon, 1976).

40. Becker, *Art Worlds,* 368.

41. Ibid.

42. Ibid.

43. Howard S. Becker, private letter.

44. Ian Hacking, *The Social Construction of What?* (Cambridge, MA: Harvard University Press, 1999).

45. Howard S. Becker, "Distributing Modern Art," in *Doing Things Together: Selected Papers* (Evanston, IL: Northwestern University Press, 1986), 76–77.

46. Harriet Zuckerman, *Scientific Elite: Nobel Laureates in the United States* (New York: Free Press, 1977).

47. James English, *The Economy of Prestige: Prizes, Awards and the Circulation of Cultural Value* (Cambridge, MA: Harvard University Press, 2008).

48. Tyler Cowen, *What Price Fame?* (Cambridge, MA: Harvard University Press, 2000). Cowen describes the functioning of cultures and societies heavily focused on fame, opposing them to the ideals of merit-based reward for artistic value. He also inventories the many procedures that produce and amplify fame through activating the mechanisms of contagion in fan groups, intensifying promotion via advertising, seeking a vertical integration of literary criticism, and exploiting various forms of praise for sale. In contrast to Robert Frank and Philip Cook, the authors of a critical essay on the expansion of winner-take-all markets (*The Winner-Take-All Society* [New York: Free Press, 1995]), Cowen maintains that the growing celebrity industry is generating increasing benefits in terms of diversity and innovation, though he offers no proof of this claim. In a critical review of Cowen's book ("Tyler Cowen, What Price Fame?" *Journal of Cultural Economics* 25[2] [2001]: 151–155), Sherwin Rosen holds that the author's notion of fame is overly vague,

which enables him to praise the benefits of the commercial expansion of cultural markets in spite of the many ways in which the allocation of fame is manipulated. Rosen reminds us that advertising was previously the subject of the same debates: While it is considered a useful means for diffusing information, advertising is also viewed as a device for manipulating people's tastes. The growing importance of advertising spaces for the financing of freely distributed, digital cultural platforms should grasp our attention for a renewed focus on this ambiguity.

49. See, for example, Connolly and Krueger, "Rockonomics: The Economics of Popular Music."

50. Cowen, *What Price Fame?* 105. See also Alan Collins and Chris Hand, "Vote-clustering in Tournaments: What Can Oscar Tell Us?" *Creativity Research Journal* 18(4) (2006): 427–434. The authors examine the probability for a given film to accumulate awards in American film competitions (the Golden Globe and the Oscar); they also observe that the resulting distribution follows Yule's law (that is, success is cumulative), as does the highly skewed distribution of film proceeds.

51. Stephen Cole and Gary S. Meyer, "Little Science, Big Science Revisited," *Scientometrics* 7(3–6) (1985): 443–458.

52. See Joseph Ben-David and Awraham Zloczower, "Universities and Academic Systems in Modern Societies," *European Journal of Sociology* 3(1) (1962): 45–84; republished in Joseph Ben-David, *Scientific Growth* (Berkeley: University of California Press, 1991).

53. Derek J. de Solla Price, *Little Science, Big Science* (New York: Columbia University Press, 1963).

54. Jonathan Cole and Stephen Cole, *Social Stratification in Science* (Chicago: University of Chicago Press, 1973), chap. 8.

55. Robert Merton, "Singletons and Multiples in Scientific Discovery: A Chapter in the Sociology of Science," *Proceedings of the American Philosophical Society* 105(5) (1961): 470–486.

56. Ibid., 484.

57. Cole and Cole, *Social Stratification in Science,* 231. In a later study ("Little Science, Big Science Revisited"), Cole and Meyer proceeded to estimate the outcomes of both the growth in the number of young physicists beginning their university careers in the 1960s and the decrease in the rate of incoming students in the first half of the 1970s. If Price's hypothesis and the conclusions the Coles drew from the invalidation of the "Ortega hypothesis" were correct, then the proportion of young scientists who obtained at least one citation of their works in the two major physics journals under study should increase as the number of scientists decreases, and vice versa; this is because the number of researchers recognized as the most innovative (that is, those who are most often cited by their colleagues) should vary in far more limited proportions than the total number of publishing researchers. Yet the data show, on the contrary, that the proportion remains fairly constant: The number of young physicists who make noteworthy and frequently cited contributions at the beginning of their careers increases and decreases just as does the total number of students in the different incoming cohorts over the years. In other words, according to the study, the fluctuation in the number of young "talented" scientists depends on the available employment opportunities and corresponding

career choices. But this fluctuation can also reflect the deferred consequences of variations in the job supply: In a period of strong growth in recruitment, qualitative dispersion may increase, just as may the number of valuable scientists driven to join less prestigious university departments.

58. Derek de Solla Price, "Some Remarks on Elitism in Information and the Invisible College Phenomenon in Science," *Journal of the American Society for Information Science* 22(2) (1971): 75.

59. Caves, *Creative Industries,* 3 and passim. There are other sectors to which one can apply the uncertainty principle, with its inegalitarian correlate of a Paretian distribution of material and symbolic remunerations. Frank and Cook (*The Winner-Take-All Society*) note that the spectacularly inegalitarian mechanisms for rating talents and remunerating reputations that prevail in sports and in the arts are also becoming apparent in journalism, publishing, fashion, design, the legal profession, business management, consulting, medicine, university research, finance, and advertising.

60. See, for example, Eric von Hippel, *Democratizing Innovation* (Cambridge, MA: MIT Press, 2005).

61. It is interesting to note that the current technological revolution gives new life to the arguments of those who, at the beginning of the nineteenth century, opposed the legislation on literary and artistic property. In an essay that has remained famous to this day, *Les Majorats littéraires* (2nd ed., intro. by Dominique Sagot-Duvauroux [Paris: Presses du Réel, 2002]), Proudhon pursued his socialist critique of property on the level of intellectual production, and contested the principle of ownership over intellectual works. He disputed, namely, the assimilation of exploitation rights to absolute, exclusive, enduring, and even perpetual property rights—an assimilation founded in the philosophical and legal tradition of possessive individualism that originated with Locke. On this point, see Laurent Pfister's law thesis, *L'auteur, propriétaire de son oeuvre: La formation du droit d'auteur au XVIè siècle à la loi de 1957* (Strasbourg, 1999).

62. Jon Elster, *Making Sense of Marx* (Cambridge, UK: Cambridge University Press, 1985).

63. Ibid., 103.

64. Luc Boltanski, *Love and Justice as Competences,* trans. Catherine Porter (Cambridge, UK: Polity Press, 2012), 137.

65. Gerald Cohen, *Karl Marx's Theory of History,* revised ed. (Oxford: Oxford University Press, 2000), 345–346.

66. Quoted in Elster, *Making Sense of Marx,* 89.

67. Ibid., 523–524.

68. John Rawls, *Theory of Justice* (Cambridge, MA: Harvard University Press, 1971), 471.

69. Ibid., 448.

70. Ronald Dworkin, *Sovereign Virtue: The Theory and Practice of Equality* (Cambridge, MA: Harvard University Press, 2000).

71. Ibid., 253.

72. Kwame Anthony Appiah, "Equality of What?" *New York Review of Books* 48(7) (2001).

73. Kant, *Critique of the Power of Judgment,* 186. Kant also considered that there is but a slight difference in the sciences between the greatest inventor and the most laborious imitator and disciple. Kant likened the phenomenon of artistic geniality to a mechanism of random distribution of innate dispositions. Under the law of this mechanism, the essence of each gifted artist's creative work forms a self-enclosed totality, and deposits itself in an artistic legacy, and not—as in the sciences—in a body of communicable knowledge. In economic language, we would say that the artwork is a final good (and a durable one, since its production is not governed by the aspiration to reach a predetermined end), while scientific knowledge is an intermediate good—transmittable, transmutable in the advancement of knowledge, and thus, destined to become obsolete.

74. Entrepreneurship has related to risk and uncertainty as soon as the term "entrepreneur" was coined in early economic thought. Most famous for his insistence on ability to face uncertainty as the defining characteristic of entrepreneurship is Frank H. Knight, in his *Risk, Uncertainty and Profit* (Boston: Houghton Mifflin, 1921). Knight's well-known analytic distinction between risk and uncertainty has proved to be of lesser importance, as Parker shows in his excellent survey—Simon C. Parker, *The Economics of Entrepreneurship* (Cambridge, UK: Cambridge University Press, 2009).

75. This strategy of overproduction, which prevailed in the so-called predigital age of cultural production, is illustrated by the following example from the French music industry: "[The unpredictability of success] encourages firms to produce a great number of artists—which proves fairly inexpensive because the bulk of fixed costs per album are incurred only after recording (in promotion and distribution)—and then to promote a selection of those for whom there seems to be a demand. The star system thus consists in trying to concentrate demand on a few stars in order to increase economies of scale. The 10% of artists who achieve commercial success are enough to compensate for the losses incurred with the rest of the catalogue. . . . This tendency to concentrate commercialization efforts on a small number of titles is consistent with the structure of the retail market. In 2004, 39% of CD sales occurred in specialized mega-retailers, and 37% took place in hypermarkets; in the latter, however, the number of titles available is one-tenth to one-twentieth what it is in the specialized FNAC and Virgin Records stores" (Nicolas Curien and François Moreau, "L'industrie du disque à l'heure de la convergence télécoms/médias/internet," in *Création et diversité au miroir des industries culturelles,* ed. Xavier Greffe [Paris: Ministère de la Culture/Documentation Française, 2006], 78).

76. Charles Lalo, *L'art et la vie sociale* (Paris: Doin, 1921).

77. There exist innumerable historical examples of this excess supply of artists: the increase in the number of painting careers in the Netherlands in the seventeenth century; the profusion of composers in late-eighteenth-century Vienna; the influx of novelists and poets in Paris and other major European cities beginning in the 1830s which resulted in the formation of Bohemian literary and artistic circles; the inability of the French academy system to provide for the careers of the innumerable painters trained in a growing number of art schools in the nineteenth century; the influx of musicians contending for professional status in London in

the second half of the nineteenth century. These examples are drawn from the following studies: John Michael Montias, *Le marché de l'art aux Pays-Bas, XVe–XVIIe siècles* (Paris: Flammarion, 1996); William Baumol and Hilda Baumol, "On the Economics of Musical Composition in Mozart's Vienna," in *On Mozart,* ed. James Morris (Cambridge, UK: Cambridge University Press, 1994); Cesar Graña, *Bohemian versus Bourgeois* (New York: Basic Books, 1964); Robin Lenman, "Painters, Patronage and the Art Market in Germany 1850–1914," *Past and Present* 123 (1989): 109–140; Harrison C. and Cynthia A. White, *Canvases and Careers: Institutional Change in the French Painting World* (New York: John Wiley, 1965); Cyril Ehrlich, *The Music Profession in Britain since the Eighteenth Century* (Oxford: Clarendon, 1985). For a theoretical treatment of the phenomenon of excess supply in the arts, see my contribution, "Artistic Labor Markets: Contingent Work, Excess Supply, and Occupational Risk Management," in *Handbook of the Economics of Art and Culture Vol. 1,* ed. Victor Ginsburgh and David Throsby (Amsterdam: Elsevier, 2006), 765–806.

78. See Françoise Benhamou, *L'économie de la culture* (Paris: La Découverte, 2008); Connolly and Krueger, "Rockonomics: The Economics of Popular Music"; Nicolas Curien and François Moreau, *L'industrie du disque* (Paris: La Découverte, 2006); Xavier Greffe and Nathalie Sonnac, eds., *Culture Web: Création, contenus, économie numérique* (Paris: Dalloz, 2008); David Hesmondhalgh, *The Cultural Industries* (London: Sage, 2002); and "Cultural Industries: Learning from Evolving Organizational Practices," *Organization Science* 11(3) (2000).

79. Barry Nalebuff and Adam Brandenburger, *Co-opetition* (New York: Doubleday, 1996).

80. As David Hesmondhalgh recalls in chapter 5 of his study, *The Cultural Industries.*

81. See notably Paul Lopes, "Innovation and Diversity in the Popular Music Industry, 1969 to 1990," *American Sociological Review* 57 (1992): 56–71; and Caves, *Creative Industries,* on the evolution of the music industry since Richard Peterson and David Berger's foundational study "Cycles in Symbol Production: The Case of Popular Music," *American Sociological Review* 40 (1975): 158–173.

82. James Rosenbaum, "Tournament Mobility: Career Patterns in a Corporation," *Administrative Science Quarterly* 24 (1979): 220–241, and *Career Mobility in a Corporate Hierarchy* (New York: Academic Press, 1984). These studies focus primarily on career management in organizations, and show how mechanisms of tournament and selection are deployed to handle upward mobility in organizations that insist on the nonobjectifiable productivity factors of talent and potential—that is, on quality differentials that are visible only through tournaments of relative comparison. In *L'économie du star-system* (Paris: Odile Jacob, 2002), Françoise Benhamou explores in detail the economic literature that seeks to account for the disproportionate gaps in earnings and fame, and provides a full set of French data to substantiate the models presented. She studies competitive tournaments such as contests and rankings in the arts, basing her analysis on Sherwin Rosen's valuable model ("Prizes and Incentives in Elimination Tournaments," *American Economic Review* 76[4] [1986]: 701–715). My own use here of sociological and economic studies on ranking mechanisms informs the construction of an integra-

tive model that I will present at the end of this chapter. This explains in part why I attribute greater reach to the tournament model over that of awards and rankings in my characterization of artistic careers.

83. John Huber considers talent (manifested in productivity over a given time period—such as yearly productivity) and tenacity (manifested in the longevity of production) to be the two principal determinants of success in a scientific career. Moreover, he hypothesizes that the distribution of these two qualities in a given population of scientists is highly skewed, and creates the observed Pareto-type inequalities. See John C. Huber, "A New Method for Analyzing Scientific Productivity," *Journal of American Society for Information Science and Technology* 52(13) (2001): 1089–1099. Michèle Lamont and her colleagues conducted studies on the peer-review process for social science grant applications. Here, the originality criterion plays an important role. But can it be universalized in keeping with the Mertonian ideal? These authors argue that multiple psychological, moral, and cultural considerations slip into the evaluation and serve to define the degree of originality of a given research project. See Joshua Guetzkow, Michèle Lamont, and Grégoire Mallard, "What Is Originality in the Humanities and the Social Sciences?" *American Sociological Review* 69(2) (2004): 190–212; Michèle Lamont, Marcel Fournier, Joshua Guetzkow, Grégoire Mallard, and Roxane Bernier, "Evaluating Creative Minds: The Assessment of Originality in Peer Review," in *Knowledge, Communication and Creativity,* ed. Arnaud Sales and Marcel Fournier (London: Sage, 2006), 166–182.

84. See the studies collected by Robert Sternberg in *Handbook of Creativity* (Cambridge: Cambridge University Press, 1999) and Mihaly Csikszentmihalyi in *Flow: The Psychology of Optimal Experience* (London: Harpers, 1991).

85. It is in the United States that we find the most abundant scholarly research—but also the highest number of best sellers and works intended for a broad readership—on creativity, exceptionally gifted individuals, and geniuses. A much greater degree of tolerance for inequality and the valorization of spectacular success in the United States are anchored in meritocratic individualism, which sees exceptional talent as a sign of the ultimate indeterminacy of success. For a nicely presented analysis of the "ingredients" for success—in a book that itself became a best seller—see Malcolm Gladwell's *Outliers: The Story of Success* (London: Little, Brown, 2008).

86. Glenn MacDonald, "The Economics of Rising Stars," *American Economic Review* 78(1) (1988): 155–166. MacDonald's model was tested, for instance, by Mark Fox and Paul Kochanowski in "Multi-Stage Markets in the Recording Industry," *Popular Music and Society* 30(2) (2007): 173–195. Using data on the American sound recording market from 1958 to 2001, the authors show how the market success or failure of singles acted as an elimination filter that allowed only a certain percentage of candidates to record entire albums, as the production of these required far greater investment. They also show that quality (measured unidimensionally) is not the only explanatory criterion, and that several sociodemographic variables can account for certain inequalities in success.

87. Oddly, in his essay *What Price Fame?* Tyler Cowen views this amalgamation of critical appraisal and "praise for sale" as a welcome tool for diffusing informa-

tion that might favor innovation and diversity, before the work of gatekeeper critics starts shaping the fame agenda following a conservative logic of risk aversion
and consolidation of established reputation.

88. Raymonde Moulin, *L'artiste, l'institution et le marché,* 212ff.

89. James Rosenbaum, "Organization, Career Systems, and Employee Misper-
ceptions," in *Handbook of Career Theory,* ed. Michael Arthur, Douglas Hall, and
Barbara Lawrence (Cambridge: Cambridge University Press, 1989), 337–338.

90. Sherwin Rosen, "The Economics of Superstars," *American Economic Review* 71(5) (1981): 845–858.

91. Sherwin Rosen, "The Economics of Superstars," *The American Scholar* 52(4)
(1983): 455.

92. Ibid., 455. Rosen's model has been applied to various professions and sectors
of activity. Among recent applications is an ingenious study by Xavier Gabaix and
Augustin Landier on the remuneration of American CEOs. The authors demonstrate that when CEOs are ranked by level of talent, replacing the top CEO at the
head of the corporation with the CEO who ranks in the 250th position would only
result in the firm losing 0.016 percent of its value, despite the fact that the top
CEO is paid more than five times the salary of the CEO in the 250th position. The
explanation for this lies notably in the intensity of firms' demand for CEOs, and in
the fact that growth in firm size leverages the increase in general remuneration levels
for CEOs. See Xavier Gabaix and Augustin Landier, "Why Has CEO Pay Increased
So Much?" *Quarterly Journal of Economics* 123(1) (2008): 49–100.

93. Rosen, "The Economics of Superstars" (1983), 453.

94. William Goode, *The Celebration of Heroes: Prestige as a Social Control
System* (Berkeley: University of California Press, 1979).

95. Ibid., 68.

96. Intrigued by this model, a number of researchers decided to test it empirically and sought out ways of measuring talent and differences in talent. Thus, William Hamlen equated the quality of pop and rock music singers with the quality of
their voices. He performed a spectrum analysis on the voices of close to one hundred singers to determine the richness of their high-frequency harmonics. Other
variables were taken into account (for example, career length, sex, ethnic group,
whether or not the singer was also the songwriter, adjacent film career, and so
forth) to explain the sales of single records. Career length proved to have the strongest explanatory power. Of all factors with a significant effect, vocal quality had
the weakest correlation with success; in this case, the gaps in success levels were
never more than proportionate to the gaps in quality thus measured. These results,
of course, would seem to counter Rosen's analysis. In a second article, which distinguishes between the two main recording formats in the market (singles and albums), Hamlen observed that quality plays no significant part in the sales of albums (as opposed to singles). Singles act as a selective filter, retaining a small
number of singers from a vast population of candidates for success. Only the candidates who have completed this stage will compete for enduring success (through
the production of albums), in accordance with MacDonald's dynamic model of
selection by elimination examined earlier. Vocal quality no longer plays a role in
this second stage, because defining it by the richness of voice harmonics no longer

suffices. Other qualities, which pertain both to songs and to the artist's characteristics, are just as essential. Talent proves to be particularly difficult to define and measure, except by resorting to multidimensional and comparative methods. Moreover, the fame an artist acquires after the initial elimination tournaments acts as a quality signal that segments the market. See William Hamlen Jr., "Superstardom in Popular Music: Empirical Evidence," *Review of Economics and Statistics* 73(4) (1991): 729–733, and "Variety and Superstardom in Popular Music," *Economic Inquiry* 32(3) (1994): 395–406.

97. See Alan Bowness, *The Conditions of Success: How the Modern Artist Rises to Fame* (London: Thames and Hudson, 1989).

98. Benhamou, *L'économie de la culture,* 89; Raymond Boudon, "L'intellectuel et ses publics," in *Français, qui êtes-vous?,* ed. Jean-Daniel Reynaud and Yves Grafmeyer (Paris: La Documentation Française, 1981); Bowness, *The Conditions of Success.*

99. Philip Nelson, "Information and Consumer Behavior," *Journal of Political Economy* 78(2) (1970): 311–329.

100. Albert O. Hirschman, *Shifting Involvements: Private Interest and Public Action* (Princeton, NJ: Princeton University Press, 1982).

101. Kee Chung and Raymond Cox, "A Stochastic Model of Superstardom: An Application of the Yule Distribution," *Review of Economics and Statistics* 76(4) (1994): 771–775.

102. Ibid., 772.

103. Ibid.

104. Matthew Salganik, Peter Dodds, and Duncan Watts, "Experimental Study of Inequality and Unpredictability in an Artificial Cultural Market," *Science* 311 (2006): 854–856.

105. Ibid., 855.

106. Ibid., 856.

107. A simple definition of an informational cascade is a situation in which "it is optimal for an individual, having observed the actions of those ahead of him, to follow the behavior of the preceding individual without regard to his own information. . . . [The authors argue that] localized conformity of behavior and the fragility of mass behaviors can be explained by informational cascades" (Sushil Bikhchandani, David Hirshleifer, and Ivo Welch, "A Theory of Fads, Fashion, Custom, and Cultural Change as Informational Cascades," *Journal of Political Economy* 100[5] [1992]: 992–1026). See also Abhijit Banerjee, "A Simple Model of Herd Behavior," *Quarterly Journal of Economics* 107(3) (1992): 797–817; Sushil Bikhchandani, David Hirshleifer, and Ivo Welch, "Learning from the Behavior of Others: Conformity, Fads, and Informational Cascades," *Journal of Economic Perspectives* 12(3) (1998): 151–170; Christophe Chamley, *Rational Herds: Economic Models of Social Learning* (Cambridge: Cambridge University Press, 2004). For an application of this model to movie consumption, see Arthur De Vany, *Hollywood Economics: How Extreme Uncertainty Shapes the Film Industry* (London: Routledge, 2004), chap. 6.

108. Marcel Proust makes light of these disparities in *Remembrance of Things Past.* He describes the "experiments in the lighter side (or what was to Swann the

lighter side) of sociology" which Swann conducts in his soirées by composing "social nosegays [with] heterogeneous elements" (Marcel Proust, *Remembrance of Things Past,* vol. 1, *Within a Budding Grove* [Hertfordshire: Wordsworth Editions, 2006], 483). In *Cities of the Plain,* Madame de Cambremer, during a soirée at the Verdurins, asks the pianist to play a reduction of Debussy's *Fêtes.* However, since he knows only the opening notes, "in a spirit of mischief, without any intention to deceive, [he] began a March by Meyerbeer. Unfortunately, as he left little interval and made no announcement, everybody supposed that he was still playing Debussy, and continued to exclaim 'Sublime!' " (Marcel Proust, *Remembrance of Things Past,* vol. 2, *Cities of the Plain* [Hertfordshire: Wordsworth Editions, 2006], 303).

109. Georg Simmel, "On the Concept and Tragedy of Culture," in *The Conflict in Modern Culture: And Other Essays* (New York: Teachers College Press, Columbia University, 1968); Gabriel de Tarde, *The Laws of Imitation* (New York: Henry Holt, 1903); Bourdieu, *Distinction: A Social Critique of the Judgment of Taste.*

110. Moshe Adler, "Stardom and Talent," *American Economic Review* 75(1) (1985): 208–212; "Stardom and Talent," in *Handbook of the Economics of Art and Culture vol. 1,* ed. Victor Ginsburgh and David Throsby (Amsterdam: Elsevier, 2006), 895–906.

111. George Stigler and Gary Becker, "De gustibus non est disputandum," *American Economic Review* 67 (1977): 76–90.

112. It would be reductive to transform such learning behavior into a process of pure knowledge accumulation, which would, to use Jean-Claude Passeron's terms, reduce *"esthèse"* to *"ascèse"*—aesthetic pleasure to its knowledge content—as is the case in a strictly intellectualist conception of aesthetic competence. On this point, see Passeron, "L'œil et ses maîtres," afterword to the catalogue for the exhibition *Les jolis paysans peints* (Marseille: Musée des beaux-arts and Imerec, 1990) and Pierre-Michel Menger, "L'un et le multiple. Sur la sociologie de la culture et de l'expérience esthétique dans les travaux de Jean-Claude Passeron," *Revue européenne de sciences sociales* 34(103) (1996): 99–108. One way to analyze this point empirically is to examine consumption careers. In a study I conducted on the audiences of concerts featuring France's most important contemporary music orchestral ensemble, I examined the behaviors of lasting adherence or disaffection in relation to new, difficult-to-grasp musical works of unequal interest. These works have a heightened "disappointment potential," to cite Hirschman's aforementioned formulation. The stable core of listeners presents the remarkable particularity of remaining faithful, even when faced with musical works that elicit strong and lasting perceptive perplexity. They assume that it is they—and not the composers—who are responsible for the failure in aesthetic communication. Moreover, they attribute sufficient value to the musical works to wager on the benefits of prolonged attendance, which they believe will help them overcome the gap between the limits of their current perception and the satisfactions to be gained from competent perceptive grasp. This tendency—based on the anticipation of future satisfaction—resonates in some way with one of the motives for socializing creative risk; namely, drawing on the uncertainty of immediate aesthetic evaluations while counting both on time and on *a posteriori* revelations of artworks' actual value to turn contemporary art into a public good. This attitude is especially prevalent among art

world professionals present in the audience, and among teachers responsible for the production and diffusion of knowledge. See Pierre-Michel Menger, "L'oreille spéculative," *Revue française de sociologie* 27(3) (1986): 445–479.

113. Ken Hendricks and Alan Sorensen, "Information and the Skewness of Music Sales," *Journal of Political Economy* 117(2) (2009): 324–369. Using a sample of 355 musicians, the authors examined the impact of publishing a new album on the sales of musicians' previously and subsequently produced CDs. They observed significant backward spillover, that is, consumers' discovery of an artist's earlier production based on the knowledge they obtain from purchasing a recent album by that same artist. The advertising value an artist's recent production represents for his earlier works is all the stronger when the success of the recent album is greater. This constitutes a sort of retroactive cumulative advantage, which adds to the cumulative advantage that offers a novice (yet sufficiently famous) artist a greater probability of achieving substantial sales for his subsequent production. The authors thus estimate, via a counterfactual calculation, that sales for an artist's second album will be 25 percent higher than for his first album. It should be noted, however, that the probability of recording a second album is correlated with the success of the first; this is equivalent to an elimination tournament that excludes a portion of the cohort of novice musicians, and thus affects the counterfactual estimate.

114. This is, in fact, a central argument in Kant's *Critique of the Power of Judgment.* Béatrice Longuenesse analyzes the pleasure of communicating and sharing with others one's attitude toward a beautiful object: "According to Kant, the pleasure we experience in apprehending the object we judge to be beautiful is twofold. It is the first-order pleasure we take in the mutual enlivening of imagination and understanding in an act of apprehension and reflection that is not bound by the rule of any universal or particular concept. That is what Kant calls the 'free play' of imagination and understanding. But that pleasure on its own would not yet be sufficient to constitute our experience of what we call aesthetic pleasure of reflection, pleasure in the beautiful. Another constitutive feature of aesthetic pleasure is the sense that the mutual enlivening of imagination and understanding in apprehending the object, and the first-order pleasure it elicits, could and ought to be shared by all. This sense of a universal communicability (capacity to be shared) of a pleasurable state of mutual enhancement of imagination and understanding is the source of the second-order pleasure that results in the aesthetic judgment: 'this is beautiful.' This is why the pleasure includes the peculiar kind of longing (the demand we make upon others, to share in the pleasure we experience and to agree with the judgment we ground on that pleasure, 'this is beautiful!') that is characteristic of the aesthetic experience" (Béatrice Longuenesse, *Kant on the Human Standpoint* [Cambridge: Cambridge University Press, 2005], 278).

115. Under the stimulus of marketing research, an increasing number of studies have been conducted to estimate the respective weight of these various sources of information and influence. For example, Morris Holbrook and Michela Addis ("Art versus Commerce in the Movie Industry: A Two-Path Model of Motion-Picture Success," *Journal of Cultural Economics* 32 [2008]: 87–107) have compared the two main categories of film success: artistic excellence (founded on criti-

cal recognition and on professional prizes and awards) and commercial appeal (measured in terms of box office as well as video rentals and sales). The first category of success is based on the evaluations of critics and consumers: Predictably, these evaluators react negatively to information on the film's production budget, the number of opening screens, and the opening box office—all of which are advertising techniques aimed at signaling the (commercial) quality of films in the mass market. In the latter market, by contrast, popular buzz and journalistic reviews directed at target audiences are heavily influenced by marketing strategies that highlight the ingredients of production (blockbuster budgets, stars, mass programming, and such). The authors, however, say nothing about the uncertainty of success in each of these market segments.

In a study of moviegoers' viewing decisions, Enrico Moretti ("Social Learning and Peer Effects in Consumption: Evidence from Movie Sales," *Review of Economic Studies* 78[1] [2011]: 356–393) examines how consumers learn to adjust to uncertainty about quality. He traces how they react to information constituted by the gap between a given movie's expected performance (estimated by the number of screens on which it is shown) and actual observed performance (measured by box-office sales for the movie's first week of release). Unexpected success (higher box-office sales than could be expected from the number of screens dedicated to the movie) has a positive effect: The information it contains leads potential viewers to revise their appraisal of the movie's quality, and provokes an increase in ticket sales in the second week, which is consistent with the social learning mechanism analyzed in the study. This effect is stronger on viewers who had indeterminate expectations and information regarding the movie, and who then decide to go see it. It is also stronger on viewers who have an extensive social network (this indirect argument is based on the hypothesis that adolescents, who react more strongly to a better-than-expected success, have a wider social network).

116. Salganik, Dodds, and Watts, "Experimental Study of Inequality and Unpredictability in an Artificial Cultural Market," 856.

117. See notably Theodor Adorno and Max Horkheimer, *Dialectic of Enlightenment* (Palo Alto, CA: Stanford University Press, 2007); Theodor Adorno, *Introduction to the Sociology of Music,* trans E.B. Ashton (London: Continuum, 1988).

118. On this point, see Claude Grignon and Jean-Claude Passeron, *Popular Culture in Modern France: A Study of Cultural Discourse* (London: Routledge, 1991); see also Passeron's preface to the work of Richard Hoggart, *La culture du pauvre* (Paris: Editions de Minuit, 1970), the French translation of *The Uses of Literacy: Aspects of Working-Class Life* (London: Chatto and Windus, 1957).

119. See Pierre Bourdieu, "The Market of Symbolic Goods," in *The Field of Cultural Production: Essays on Art and Literature* (New York: Columbia University Press, 1984).

120. Narasimhan Anand and Richard Peterson studied the use and evolution of methods and technologies for analyzing sales and constructing performance charts in the music industry. They showed how "*Billboard*'s agency in creating the 'Hot 100' chart in 1958 focused the attention of artists, record label executives, retailers, jukebox operators, radio programmers, and the like on a single summary measure of performance in the field. In the field of commercial music, the creation and

weekly dissemination of information showing the relative success of the most popular phonograph records made it possible for field participants to structure their beliefs about success or failure of particular recordings, artists, and sub-genres by reading the performance charts . . . [and] began using chart information . . . to make sense of past track records and future potential of individuals and organizations" (Narasimhan Anand and Richard Peterson, "When Market Information Constitutes Fields: Sensemaking of Markets in the Commercial Music Industry," *Organization Science* 11[3] [2000]: 281). The authors specifically examined the impact that the innovation of real-time information had on record sales beginning in the 1980s, with the introduction of product barcode scanning by SoundScan. The measurement of actual record sales enabled by this new technology effectively ousted relative rankings based on preestablished charts, increased the control of the business sector over the art sector, and modified marketing strategies by having promotional efforts precede the release of records (once it became apparent that a record's fate played out shortly after its release, and no longer following the gradual conquest of an audience). As for the impact of these innovations on the structure of the competition, the authors noted that they could at once reinforce the concentration of sales to the benefit of large labels and consolidate market niches by enabling better-informed producers to exploit specific segments of creation and consumption more accurately.

121. Alan Sorensen ("Bestseller Lists and Product Variety," *Journal of Industrial Economics* 55[4] [2007]: 715–738) estimated the impact on sales generated by the appearance of books on *The New York Times* best-seller list, and hence the influence that success signals (provided by other consumers' purchasing behavior) exert on a given consumer. He based his analysis on the discrepancy between the publication date of a book, sales curves in the initial weeks following its publication, and the moment when a well-selling book is placed on the best-seller list. His analysis indicated that (1) on average, the best-seller list has but a marginal impact on the sales of books whose success it reveals; (2) this impact, nonetheless, is selective and far more marked for certain books (notably those by novice writers) than others; and (3) the observed increase in sales is important mainly during the week in which a book enters the list. Sorensen, moreover, estimated the specific impact that the diffusion of such lists may have on the consolidation of consumer choices, and hence on the diversity of literary production. He concluded, more cautiously, that the publication of best-seller lists does not seem to increase the sales of books signaled as successful to the detriment of other books in a given genre. There would thus seem to exist a relation of complementarity rather than substitution (or holdup) between best sellers and other books in the same genre.

122. Moulin, *L'artiste, l'institution et le marché*.

123. Buzz is a marketing technique that takes advantage of the contagious nature of information propagation through interpersonal networks of communication and exchange of information and opinion. In *The Anatomy of Buzz* (New York: Doubleday, 2002), Emanuel Rosen details the mechanisms of optimized buzz management: the selection of products with strong potential for information contagion; the use of techniques for unleashing and accelerating contagion through product overexposure at strategic points of interpersonal networks, as well as

through recourse to viral marketing on the Internet; the invention of good stories (storytelling) around the product to be publicized and their gradual leakage to preserve both the mystery and the scarcity value of the good in question; and so forth. In many respects, buzz represents the large-scale application of the results of studies on networks of communication and interpersonal influence and on mechanisms of innovation diffusion, which figure among the social science advances of the last half-century.

124. These markets operate on the following principle: A platform producing goods or services brings into contact two categories of agents by courting each in such a way that the numbers of customers on both sides develop interdependently. For example, a video game platform selling game consoles requires a large enough number of players who use them to incite video game producers and developers to configure their products for those game consoles. Similarly, a television network offers programs to consumers while selling advertising slots as a function of the number of viewers it attracts. This is the network externalities mechanism, whereby "a product is best viewed as a platform on which different groups of users meet or trade. . . . The externalities that benefit to one group typically originate in the number of participants from the other group: network externalities cross from one side to the other" (Jean Gabszewicz and Xavier Wauthy, "Platform Competition and Vertical Differentiation," *CORE* working paper [Université de Louvain, September 2012], 1). Thus the number of users impacts the perceived quality of the product: "as a result, consumers' willingness to pay for a product, say A, whose number of consumers exceeds that of a competing product B, is larger than that of B" (ibid.). The development of multisided markets in the cultural sector brings to light the key role of advertising and audience-targeting technologies made possible by network platforms such as Web 2.0: Seemingly free access to an increasing quantity and variety of content, notably via the development of community Internet sites, is backed by the spectacular development and refinement of advertising technology. On multifaceted and multisided markets, see Jean-Charles Rochet and Jean Tirole, "Platform Competition in Two-Sided Markets," *Journal of the European Economic Association* 1 (2003): 990–1029.

125. Are economic returns on sequels lower than they are on the parent film, or are they higher than they are on non-sequels? The former will be posited if one believes in the intrinsic power of originality, and the latter will be if one assumes success to have branding and reputation effects. In "Fast and Frequent: Investing Box Office Revenues of Motion Picture Sequels" (*Journal of Business Research* 61 [2008]: 798–803), Suman Basuroy and Subimal Chatterjee show that both mechanisms are at work: A sequel replicating the formula of an initial success will be less successful than the parent film, but it will succeed better than a non-sequel, especially when it is produced rapidly.

126. Hesmondhalgh, *The Cultural Industries*. This sociological work is entirely built around the question of the degree of autonomy of artists and creation in firms and in the cultural industry system.

127. In his pioneering article "Processing Fads and Fashions" (*American Journal of Sociology* 77[4] [1972]: 639–659), Paul Hirsch showed how cultural industries hire contact men so as to exert influence over media gatekeepers (such as artistic

directors, programming directors)—a practice that allows for circumventing the recourse to payola.

128. Michael Storper, "The Transition to Flexible Specialisation in the Film Industry," *Cambridge Journal of Economics* 13(2) (1989): 273–305. For a critical discussion of Storper, see Asu Aksoy and Kevin Robins, "Hollywood for the 21st Century: Global Competition for Critical Mass in Image Markets," *Cambridge Journal of Economics* 16(1) (1992): 1–22; see Michael Storper's reply, "Flexible Specialisation in Hollywood: A Response to Aksoy and Robins," *Cambridge Journal of Economics* 17(4) (1992): 479–484; see also Joseph Lampel and Jamal Shamsie, "Capabilities in Motion: New Organizational Forms and the Reshaping of the Hollywood Movie Industry," *Journal of Management Studies* 40 (2003): 2189–2210.

129. Caves, *Creative Industries*. See also Paul DiMaggio, ed., *The Twenty-First Century Firm: Changing Economic Organization in International Perspective* (Princeton, NJ: Princeton University Press, 2003); John Roberts, *The Modern Firm: Organizational Design for Performance and Growth* (Oxford: Oxford University Press, 2007); Oliver Williamson and Sidney Winters, eds., *The Nature of the Firm* (Oxford: Oxford University Press, 1993).

130. Thomas DiPrete and Gregory Eirich, "Cumulative Advantage as a Mechanism for Inequality," *Annual Review of Sociology* 32 (2006): 271–297.

131. Robert Merton, "The Matthew Effect in Science," *Science* 3810 (1968): 56–63; "The Matthew Effect in Science, II: Cumulative Advantage and the Symbolism of Intellectual Property," *Isis* 79 (1988): 606–623.

132. Cole and Cole, *Social Stratification in Science,* 220–221.

133. Joel Podolny, *Status Signals: A Sociological Study of Market Competition* (Princeton, NJ: Princeton University Press, 2005), chap. 2, especially pp. 26–27.

134. Merton, "The Matthew Effect in Science," 57.

135. Zuckerman, *Scientific Elite*.

136. On this point, see for example Cole and Cole, *Social Stratification in Science,* 68ff. The authors recall the unfruitful results of tests that measure the correlation between the IQ of researchers and the scientific value of their production (as measured by the rate of citation of their works). The correlation is positive for the probability of obtaining a PhD; however, among those holding a PhD, the measurement of abilities via IQ provides no additional information. To state it simply, measurable intelligence is a necessary but insufficient condition. Nevertheless, the positive correlation between the IQ levels of researchers and the prestige of the university departments that house them allows the authors to identify the indirect role played by differences in cognitive ability in a given population of researchers.

137. For the arts, in addition to the studies I cite later in the text, I can mention the study of Kees Van Rees and Jeroen Vermunt, "Event History of Author's Reputation: Effects of Critics' Attention on Debutants' Careers," *Poetics* 23 (1996): 317–333. The authors examine whether or not there exists a cumulative effect in the attention that critics give to writers whose earlier books received moderately or highly favorable reviews. The hypotheses they tested are as follows: (1) Attention increases when the writer is published by a reputable publishing house and has received good reviews for his earlier books; (2) as time goes by and the writer produces a series of new books, the attention and critical coverage diminish because

the effects of discovery and excitement wear off. The data used by the authors confirm these hypotheses, but also show that the most renowned writers are better protected from this erosion process. The case of Romain Gary—whose identity split I discuss at the end of this chapter—provides support, in the form of a natural experiment, to this statistical analysis.

138. Zuckerman, *Scientific Elite,* 250.

139. Cole and Cole, *Social Stratification in Science,* chap. 9.

140. Ibid., 235.

141. Paul Allison, Scott Long, and Tad Krauze, "Cumulative Advantage and Inequality in Science," *American Sociological Review* 47(5) (1982): 615–625.

142. With respect to scientific invention, Dean Simonton (*Scientific Genius: A Psychology of Science* [Cambridge: Cambridge University Press, 1988]) sought to more clearly define the phasing model said to derive from the description Henri Poincaré made of his own work on Fuchsian functions in his 1908 essay "Mathematical Discovery" (reprinted in Henry Poincaré, *Science and Method* [Mineola, NY: Courier Dover, 1914]), and from the usage Jacques Hadamard then made of Poincaré's description in his *Essay on the Psychology of Invention in the Mathematical Field* (Princeton, NJ: Princeton University Press, 1945). Poincaré's key phrase was "to invent is to discern, to choose" from among the numerous ideas generated by intensive work on a given subject, and from among the many associations and collisions between previously disconnected ideas. In keeping with an evolutionist epistemology developed by Donald Campbell ("Blind Variation and Selective Retention in Creative Thought as in Other Knowledge Processes," *Psychological Review* 67[6] [1960]: 380–400), Simonton conceives of genius as a powerful "generator of chance permutations"—that is, ordered combinations of previously unrelated ideas. Among these combinations, a small number prove capable of surviving the selection process that tests their fruitfulness and of forming stable configurations that are preserved and further elaborated for communication; a last selection process then leads the scientific community to accept some of those configurations. In this model, chance lies at the heart of inventive combinations, and genius distinguishes itself by the very high volume of ideas it produces and incorporates into the movement of unpredictable associations and collisions out of which emerges a discovery. Robert Merton was himself sufficiently fascinated by the element of lucky chance in the process of discovery to devote, with Elinor Barber, an entire book to the phenomenon and genealogy of the curious concept of "serendipity"—a mixture of inspiration, tenacity, and good fortune or lucky chance. See Robert Merton and Elinor Barber, *The Travels and Adventures of Serendipity,* 2nd ed. (Princeton, NJ: Princeton University Press, 2006).

143. Robert Faulkner's study of the careers of music composers for Hollywood movies (*Music on Demand: Composers and Careers in the Hollywood Film Industry* [New Brunswick, NJ: Transaction, 1983]) and William and Denise Bielby's analysis of the careers of scriptwriters for films and television shows ("Organizational Mediation of Project-Based Labor Markets," *American Sociological Review* 64[1] [1999]: 64–85) demonstrate the extent to which reputations are sensitive to the impact of artists' most recent success or failure. They also show, in a more counterintuitive fashion, how participation in a series of successful projects over

several years may become a negative signal in an industry whose genre and content turnover is very rapid.

144. For an analysis of the role of serendipity in the careers of women orchestra conductors, see Cora Diaz de Chumaceiro, "Serendipity and Pseudoserendipity in Career Paths of Successful Women: Orchestra Conductors," *Creative Research Journal* 16(2–3) (2004): 345–356. For an analysis of women's musical careers that reveals the reverse side of chance—that is, the discrimination against women in the recruitment of instrumentalists for symphonic orchestras—see Claudia Goldin and Cecilia Rouse's methodologically rigorous and highly original study "Orchestrating Impartiality: The Impact of 'Blind' Auditions on Female Musicians," *American Economic Review* 90(4) (2000): 715–741. The introduction of screens to conceal candidates' identity during recruitment auditions has led to the increased hiring of women musicians. The point was to eliminate a "chance" factor—the discriminatory bias of evaluators' gendered preferences—which varies by orchestra and is sometimes surprisingly entrenched. The latter is the case with the Vienna Philharmonic Orchestra, which is one of the most reputed in the world, but also the last of the great orchestras to admit women into their ranks.

145. The disasters that marred the shooting of the film Terry Gilliam sought to produce, based on Cervantes' *Don Quixote,* caused the misery of the director, film crew, and producer. However, these catastrophes spurred the delight of those who were present to observe and film this resounding failure; they themselves produced a film, *Lost in La Mancha,* which went on to attain unexpected success.

146. On the analysis of chance and coincidences in the social sciences (in addition to the previously cited work of Merton and Barber), see Albert Bandura, "The Psychology of Chance Encounters and Life Paths," *American Psychologist* 37(7) (1982): 747–755; Howard S. Becker, "*Foi por acaso:* Conceptualizing Coincidence," *Sociological Quarterly* 35(2) (1994): 183–194; David Krantz, "Taming Chance: Social Science and Everyday Narratives," *Psychological Inquiry* 9(2) (1998): 87–94 (as well as the commentaries on this article that appear in the same issue of the journal).

147. Victor Ginsburgh and Jan van Ours, "Expert Opinion and Compensation: Evidence from a Musical Competition," *American Economic Review* 93(1) (2003): 289–296.

148. This role of chance might echo Machiavelli's formulation whereby half of the Prince's political successes are explained by *virtù* (strength, aptitude, intrinsic qualities) and half by *fortuna* (uncontrollable chance, which upsets all rational order). The reference to Machiavelli figures in Stephen Turner and Daryl Chubin, "Chance and Eminence in Science: Ecclesiastes II," *Social Science Information* 18(3) (1979): 437–449. The authors of this constructionist critique refute the notion that science is a robust system of stratification that relies on an established standard of valuation of scientific productions, and leads to an inegalitarian allocation of reputations and rewards based on differences in the productivity of researchers and in the importance of their contributions. Instead, they invoke the role of chance to suggest that the inegalitarian machinery of science constitutes in fact a massive institutional production of differences whose amplification and structuration mask a partially random distribution of opportunities for action among

competitors. Nonetheless, the authors should recall that the Prince's art consists entirely in his capacity to prepare himself for the disruption of his actions by *fortuna,* and to react accordingly by seizing the power of chance and redirecting its action in his favor.

149. De Vany, *Hollywood Economics,* 239–242.

150. Ibid., 241.

151. This results from the equation: $P(x > x_o) = (x_o/x)^a$, where x_o is the number of films already produced, x is the number greater than x_o, and the exponent a is the power coefficient that captures the effect of Pareto's law; in De Vany's calculation, a is equal to 1.5. Thus, for a director who has made four films, we find that the probability he will make a fifth film or more is $(4/5)^{1.5}$, or 0.71. See De Vany, *Hollywood Economics,* 241–242.

152. For a detailed study of the French labor market in the performing arts and its skewed distribution of earnings, see my book *Les intermittents du spectacle: Sociologie du travail flexible* (Paris: Éditions de l'EHESS, 2011).

153. Faulkner, *Music on Demand.*

154. De Vany, *Hollywood Economics,* 239.

155. See Moulin, *L'artiste, l'institution et le marché.*

156. Artists are quick to claim that they work more than ordinary wage earners and invest themselves completely in the act of creative labor, even though they obtain only modest income. Such perception of the puzzling relationship between effort and its monetary value fuels the multiple forms of artist protest against what is perceived as a kind of exploitation and self-exploitation. This necessarily rests upon a normative economy of creation, itself based on the hypothesis that the social value of art can replace the criterion of demand intensity. In the late 1960s, artists in France regularly denounced the market-based, capitalist exploitation of art. Visual artists in the ephemeral group *Support-Surface* (considered to have formed the last artistic avant-garde in France, before the very notion of avant-garde and collective mobilization around its ideals faded away) sought to set the price of their artworks as a function of what it cost to produce them. They suggested calculating this price by multiplying the quantity of labor by an hourly wage, to which would be added material expenses and fixed costs (such as the cost of renting a studio, the costs of exhibiting in a gallery, among others). Yet, in doing so, they only shifted the problem to defining which criteria to use in establishing the rate of remuneration for creative labor.

157. Bruno Frey and Werner Pommerehne, *Muses and Markets* (Oxford: Blackwell, 1989).

158. In *Talking Prices* (Princeton, NJ: Princeton University Press, 2005, chap. 7), Olav Velthuis studies price differences as quality signals, as well as the effects of falling prices on the painting market. He highlights that price is not only a vector of information about quality, but also a feature of the painting market organized as a system of hierarchized positions among painters and collectors. Velthuis's analysis is in line with Harrison White's theoretical works on markets conceived as networks (*Markets from Networks* [Princeton, NJ: Princeton University Press, 2002]). For a general economic analysis of the relation between price, quality, and reputation, see especially Sanford Grossman and Joseph Stiglitz, "Information and

Competitive Price Systems," *American Economic Review* 66(2) (1976): 246–253; Carl Shapiro, "Premiums for High Quality Products as Returns to Reputations," *Quarterly Journal of Economics* 98(4) (1983): 659–680; Joseph Stiglitz, "The Causes and Consequences of the Dependence of Quality on Price," *Journal of Economic Literature* 25(1) (1987): 1–48.

159. In *Analyse économique de la valeur des biens d'art* (Paris: Economica, 2000), Nathalie Moureau suggests applying Rosen's superstar model to the visual arts.

160. A famous example of this is Giorgio de Chirico's artistic production, which followed the brief phase of innovation constituted by his metaphysical paintings. See John Henry Merryman, "Counterfeit Art," *International Journal of Cultural Property* 1(1) (1992): 27–78.

161. Robert Merton, "The Matthew Effect in Science, II: Cumulative Advantage and the Symbolism of Intellectual Property" and "'Recognition' and 'Excellence': Instructive Ambiguities," in *Recognition of Excellence,* ed. Adam Yarmolinsky (New York: Free Press, 1962), republished in Robert Merton, *The Sociology of Science* (Chicago: University of Chicago Press, 1979), chap. 19.

162. Cole and Cole, *Social Stratification in Science,* 112ff.

163. Dominique Lafourcade, "L'insertion professionnelle des instrumentistes diplômés du conservatoires national supérieur de musique et de danse de Paris," Diplôme d'Etudes Approfondies (DEA) degree paper (Paris: EHESS, 1996).

164. As Raymonde Moulin has shown in *Le marché de l'art: Mondialisation et nouvelles technologies* (Paris: Flammarion, 2003), the globalization of art markets has significantly contributed to enlarging the existing pools of artists. One of the latest pools to be exploited by the market is that of Chinese visual artists, whose success is due to the development of a sufficient critical mass of wealthy collectors who embody the rise of Chinese capitalism and know how to activate the levers of the international art trade. Art dealers, art schools, art collectors, public institutions, and private organizations draw on such pools of artists to fuel their speculative wagers on which talented individuals to train, launch, and valorize in a coordinated fashion. It would be interesting to estimate the impact of these growing pools of artists and increasingly interdependent local art systems on career length and on the distribution of success by age.

165. David Galenson, *Painting outside the Lines: Patterns of Creativity in Modern Art* (Cambridge, MA: Harvard University Press, 2001).

166. Ibid., 18.

167. Fabien Accominotti, "Creativity from Interaction: Artistic Movements and the Creativity Careers of Modern Painters," *Poetics* 37 (2009): 267–294. Using a different model for analyzing Galenson's data, Accominotti uncovered a factor that might influence the value assigned to the precocity of "conceptual" innovators: their frequent membership in an aesthetic group or movement. This factor may help explain the enhanced interest in artworks produced by painters during the period in which they fully identified with an innovation introduced by the movement under consideration. The market valuation of innovative artists who belong to an aesthetic movement draws on their double identity: Their name is attached to a remarkable collective innovation, yet they are viewed as more than cogs in a col-

lective enterprise. Impressionism, cubism, fauvism, and the like, are extremely powerful aesthetic labels used in art history, in scholarly discourse, and in the most effective lay categorizations of cultural consumption. These labels increase the average value of all artists who belonged to such groups, while also exerting a considerable lever effect on the reputations of a group's major artists and on the prices their artworks command. Michael Farrell (*Collaborative Circles: Friendship Dynamics and Creative Work* [Chicago: University of Chicago Press, 2001]) has studied the formation and life course of these aesthetic movements and artist groups. Following in the tradition of psychosociological analysis of small group dynamics, he breaks down the life course of a collaborative circle into several stages: formation, rebellion, collectively negotiated quest for a shared vision, creative work, collective action (organized by a leader), group disintegration, and nostalgic reunion. However, as Randall Collins highlights in a review of Farrell's work ("Collaborative Circles: Friendship Dynamics and Creative Work," *Social Forces* 83[1] [2004]: 433–436) that rests on his own studies in the sociology of philosophy (*The Sociology of Philosophies* [Cambridge, MA: Belknap Press, 1998]), this analysis puts forward a causal explanation for the formation of such circles which is overly conventional: It would be because they are marginal that artists and innovative creators find in collective collaboration the resources necessary to organize their innovative breakthrough. In fact, the notion of marginality is debatable and imprecise. Moreover, there are numerous counterexamples of artists and researchers located at the heart of art or science systems who position themselves in competitive struggles by forming a group through which they can mobilize resources and create actor coalitions. It would be more interesting to study the unequal gains that different group members obtain from collaborating with each other, as well as the erosion of the benefits derived from collective action.

168. According to Curien and Moreau ("L'industrie du disque à l'heure de la convergence télécoms/médias/internet"), the major firms spend 20 percent of their resources on talent search; the figure for independent producers is 60 percent.

169. In other words, the scenario for abolishing Pareto's law amounts to rejecting the conventional definition of an artwork as the product of a strict division of labor between the creator and consumers. It would call for a radical restructuring of the apparatus of laws and conventions that have organized the market economy of artistic production and exchange centered around the artwork conceived as the monopoly of an innovator, as a reservoir of value, and as the source of a potentially everlasting flow of artistic services linked to the work's durability.

170. Chris Anderson, *The Long Tail: How Endless Choice Is Creating Unlimited Demand* (New York: Random House, 2007).

171. Anita Elberse, "Should You Invest in the Long Tail?" *Harvard Business Review* (July–August 2008): 88–96.

172. Anita Elberse and Felix Oberholzer-Gee, "Superstars and Underdogs: An Examination of the Long Tail Phenomenon in Video Sales," *MSI Reports: Working Paper Series* 4 (2007): 49–72.

173. The conclusion of a study based on French data and conducted by Pierre-Jean Benghozi and Françoise Benhamou ("The Long Tail: Myth or Reality," *International Journal of Arts Management* 12[3] [2010]: 43–53), further emphasizes

the sales dispersion that is rendered possible by an incomparably more-abundant supply (which Elberse also noted). This dispersion does not, however, upset the Paretian concentration on a narrow proportion of artists and artworks, nor does it make a long-tail business model (fragmentation into multiple niche markets) seem viable as things stand. See also Erik Brynjolfsson, Yu Hu, and Duncan Simester, "Goodbye Pareto Principle, Hello Long Tail: The Effect of Search Costs on the Concentration of Product Sales," MIT Sloan School of Management Working Paper (2007).

174. See John B. Thompson, *Merchants of Culture. The Publishing Business in the Twenty-First Century* (Cambridge: Polity Press, 2010).

175. On the relationship between hierarchical position in a given organization and the multiplicative effect of ability gradients on productivity in the highest position, see Sherwin Rosen, "Authority, Control and the Distribution of Earnings," *Bell Journal of Economics* 13(2) (1982): 311–323. On the assortative matching model, see Michael Kremer, "The O-Ring Theory of Economic Development," *Quarterly Journal of Economics* 108(3) (1993): 551–575.

176. Faulkner, *Music on Demand*.

177. Fabien Accominotti, "Marché et hiérarchie: La structure sociale des décisions de production dans un marché culturel," *Histoire & Mesure* 23(2) (2008): 177–218.

178. Arthur L. Stinchcombe, *Constructing Social Theories* (Chicago: University of Chicago Press, 1968), 264–265.

179. Niklas Luhmann, *Trust and Power* (Chichester: Wiley, 1979).

180. See Harrison White, *Careers and Creativity* (Boulder: Westview, 1993), chap. 3.

181. Podolny, *Status Signals,* 19. The distinction between reputation and status is at the heart of Podolny's analyses.

182. Roger Gould, "The Origins of Status Hierarchies: A Formal Theory and Empirical Test," *American Journal of Sociology* 107(5) (2002): 1143–1178. Fabien Accominotti has judiciously remarked that, with his model, Gould aims to explain moderate status inequalities within small social groups, and endows individuals with a preference for reciprocal exchange that would enable them to counteract the highly inegalitarian effects of an unbridled mechanism of cumulative advantage à la Merton. One possible point of disagreement between Gould's model and mine pertains to my integration of the theoretical argument of assortative matching into the analysis. In Merton's model, individuals benefit from associating with better-reputed professionals early in the cumulative advantage process, whereas in the theory of assortative matching, collaborative relations are established between individuals of comparable reputation and status. The difficulty can be resolved if we allow that the high status of an artist or researcher guarantees him a reputation, but does not guarantee that what he produces will invariably be considered of the highest quality. Careers have a peak, variations in intensity, and a declining slope. Despite the gap in reputation or status, an experienced and renowned colleague can hope to benefit from collaborating with a promising young colleague who potentially represents a future researcher of high repute. It may therefore be in the best interest of a reputed artist or scientist to diversify his investments in col-

laborative work. However, the difference in age or career advancement is not the only issue. Uncertainty also derives from the complex function of production that characterizes activity in a team or in a project-by-project organization: The cases of failure in live performances, concerts, or films that bring stars together demonstrate that the aggregation of talents does not guarantee successful teamwork. Lastly, one must acknowledge that the rule of optimal association with a colleague of superior status is more difficult to apply at the top of the pyramid, where the limited number of professionals exerts a structural constraint on the possible range of association.

183. DiPrete and Eirich, "Cumulative Advantage as a Mechanism for Inequality," 290ff.

184. Gould, "The Origins of Status Hierarchies: A Formal Theory and Empirical Test," 1146–1147.

185. A natural experiment is an economics method modeled on controlled studies in therapeutic clinical trials. In order to validate the effectiveness of a medical procedure (treatment or medication), one group is administered an active treatment, while the so-called control group is given an inactive treatment. All individuals in both groups display the same characteristics relevant to the experiment, and the highest guarantee—randomization—is provided by the chance distribution of individuals among the two groups. This method has been adopted in economics, under the name of natural experiment, in order to measure the effectiveness of a given instrument of economic policy by comparing its effect on one human group to another, "untreated" group of identical make-up.

186. See www.mercuredefrance.fr/gary-ajar.htm. See also Juliette Cerf, "De Gary à Ajar: Double Je chez Gallimard," *Les mots du cercle* 26.

187. Romain Gary, "The Life and Death of Emile Ajar," appendix to *King Solomon* (New York: Harper and Row, 1983).

188. See Michel Lafon and Benoît Peters, *Nous est un autre: Enquête sur les duos d'écrivains* (Paris: Flammarion, 2006). The work most notably includes the results of a quantitative linguistic study by Dominique Labbé, which measured the degree of similarity in the vocabulary and style of Gary and Ajar's novels. Labbé's conclusion reveals a three-point configuration: Romain Gary had two styles of writing and narrative construction (which coexisted rather than succeeded each other in his career), and Émile Ajar adopted a third style that, according to the proposed statistical analysis, was closer to one of the two styles developed by Gary. Dominique Labbé's updated version of this study, "Romain Gary et Émile Ajar" (2008), can be consulted and downloaded at http://hal.archives-ouvertes.fr, reference hal-00279663.

5. How Can Artistic Greatness Be Analyzed?

1. Lydia Goehr, *The Imaginary Museum of Musical Works* (Oxford: Oxford University Press, 1992).

2. The ambivalence of the now-obsolete and discredited term *patronage* (sponsorship, protection, and control all combined in a duly contractualized service relationship) must be preserved, because it reminds us of the dimension of control

better than does the term *mécénat,* whose present usage retains first of all the liberal side of support, as a result of the successful emancipation of artists with regard to past formulas of direct control.

3. Gérard Lebrun, *Kant et la fin de la métaphysique* (Paris: Armand Colin, 1970); Edward Lowinsky, "Musical Genius—Evolution and Origins of a Concept—I&II," *The Musical Quarterly* 50(3) (1964): 321–340, and 50(4): 476–495; Roland Mortier, *L'originalité* (Geneva: Droz, 1982); Rudolf Wittkower, "Genius: Individualism in Art and Artists," in *Dictionary of the History of Ideas: Studies of Selected Pivotal Ideas,* vol. 2, ed. Philip P. Wiener (New York: Charles Scribner's Sons, 1973), 297–312.

4. Theodor Adorno, *Beethoven: The Philosophy of Music,* trans. Edmund Jephcott (Cambridge, UK: Polity Press, 1998); Theodor Adorno, *Introduction to the Sociology of Music,* trans E. B. Ashton (New York: Seabury, 1976).

5. Norbert Elias, *Mozart: The Sociology of a Genius,* trans. Edmund Jephcott (Cambridge, UK: Polity, 1994).

6. Tia DeNora, *Beethoven and the Construction of Genius: Musical Politics in Vienna, 1792–1803* (Berkeley: University of California Press, 1995).

7. Lucien Goldmann, *The Hidden God: A Study of Tragic Vision in the Pensees of Pascal and the Tragedies of Racine,* trans. Philip Thody (London: Routledge, 1976), 17.

8. On this point, see Walter Jackson Bate, *The Burden of the Past and the English Poet* (Cambridge, MA: Belknap Press, 1970); Harold Bloom, *The Anxiety of Influence: A Theory of Poetry* (Oxford: Oxford University Press, 1973).

9. See Robert Klein, "L'éclipse de l'oeuvre d'art," in *La forme et l'intelligible* (Paris: Gallimard, 1970), 403–410.

10. "[T]here are specific categories of labour which, from the outset, represent a higher value than others, so that the individual achievement within one category requires neither more effort nor more talent than is contained within another order, nonetheless, to acquire a higher status. We are well aware that countless work activities in the 'higher professions' in no way place higher claims on the subject than they do in lower ones; that workers in coal mines and factories must often possess a circumspection, a capacity for resignation, a defiance of death which raises the subjective value of their achievement far above that of many bureaucratic occupations or those requiring education; that the achievement of an acrobat or juggler requires exactly the same perseverance, proficiency, and talent as that of some pianists who do not ennoble their manual dexterity with an admixture of spiritual depth. Nonetheless it appears to be the case not only that we reward the one category of labour much more highly in relation to the other, but also that in many cases a socially unprejudiced sense of value goes in the same direction. With full awareness of the same or higher subjective labour that a product requires, one will nonetheless award the other a higher status and value so that it at least appears as if other elements than the amount of labour determine its evaluation" (Georg Simmel, *The Philosophy of Money,* trans. Tom Bottomore and David Frisby [London: Routledge, 1978], 419).

11. Ibid., 420.

12. Raymonde Moulin, *The French Art Market. A Sociological View,* trans. Arthur Goldhammer (New Brunswick, NJ: Rutgers University Press, 1987).

13. Simmel, *The Philosophy of Money,* 418–419.

14. Adorno, *Introduction to the Sociology of Music,* 211.

15. Ibid., 176.

16. Adorno, *Beethoven.*

17. Adorno, *Introduction to the Sociology of Music,* 209.

18. Ibid., 213.

19. Ibid., 209.

20. Ibid., 213.

21. Ibid., 68.

22. Ibid., 215.

23. See in particular Charles Lalo, *L'art et la vie sociale* (Paris: Doin, 1921).

24. Pierre Bourdieu, *The Rules of Art,* trans. Susan Emanuel (Stanford: Stanford University Press, 1996).

25. The concept already appears in Lalo, *L'art et la vie sociale.*

26. Bourdieu, *The Rules of Art,* 111.

27. Ibid., 103.

28. On this scheme of commutation, the reversal of the active into the passive, and on its presence in Bourdieu's theory of *habitus* in the wake of Husserlian phenomenology, see François Héran's penetrating analysis, "La seconde nature de l'habitus," *Revue française de sociologie* 28(3) (1987), already quoted in Chapter 1.

29. The description that Adorno gives of authentically innovative artists who bear the truth about the social world in the midst of this same world that continues to lose itself in "satanic catastrophes of capitalism" reminds us how much the romanticization of the genius has persisted, even in the authors most aware of the ideological manipulation of aesthetic arguments.

30. See the works of John Michael Montias on Dutch painting and the emergence of the art market in the seventeenth century (*Artists and Artisans in Delft. A Socio-Economic Study of the Seventeenth Century* [Princeton: Princeton University Press, 1982]), as well as his very meticulous investigation of Vermeer's career (*Vermeer and His Milieu: A Web of Social History* [Princeton: Princeton University Press, 1989]). Studying the same artistic world, Svetlana Alpers (*Rembrandt's Enterprise: The Studio and the Market* [Chicago: University of Chicago Press, 1988]) saw in Rembrandt an innovator who used the emerging system of the art market to free himself from patronage and impose his ideas and his autonomy.

31. See Martin Warnke (*The Court Artist: On the Ancestry of the Modern Artist,* trans. David McLintock [Cambridge: Cambridge University Press, 1993]) on the competition between cities and courts in the governing of painters' careers from the Renaissance to the seventeenth century.

32. Harrison C. White and Cynthia A. White, *Canvases and Careers: Institutional Change in the French Painting World* (Chicago: University of Chicago Press, 1993).

33. Frederik Antal, *Florentine Painting and Its Social Background* (London: Routledge, 1948); Arnold Hauser, *The Social History of Art* (London: Routledge and Kegan Paul, 1951).

34. Elias, *Mozart,* 10.

35. *The Sociological Review* 42(3) (1994): 588–589. Of course, Elias died before he could complete his work, and only his reputation and the inclusion of this study

in his work as a whole seemed to DeNora to justify the publication of such an imperfect manuscript. But the problem raised is more profound than that of the lack of completion, and it has led to frequent disputes regarding sociological work on the arts: Can a famous theorist really engage in an exercise in interpretation on the basis of a compilation of a few works that are supposed to have waited, as it were, to deliver up its loftiest secrets, the surplus value of an unprecedented theoretical framework and an inspired reading, thereby exempting this theorist from having to subject them to a substantial historical investigation provided with original hypotheses and new empirical proofs? The criticism regarding the lack of empirical evidence becomes still more acute when the sociologist is not a "great theorist" but a simple manipulator of paradigms considered reductive and mechanistic. Art historians have often complained that sociologists simplify historical reality, and some of these complaints are still famous, such as Millard Meiss's indictment of Frederik Antal, the author of *Florentine Painting and Its Social Background* (see Millard Meiss, review of *Florentine Painting* by Frederik Antal, *Art Bulletin* XXXI [1949]: 143–150), or that of Ernst Gombrich directed against Arnold Hauser's Marxist sociology of art (see Ernst Gombrich, *Meditations on a Hobby Horse* [London: Phaidon, 1963]). More recently, Antoine Schnapper, in the introduction to his vast, two-volume investigation of French collectors of artworks and curiosities (*Le géant, la licorne et la tulipe* [Paris: Flammarion, 1988]; *Curieux du Grand siècle* [Paris: Flammarion, 1994]), contrasted the rigor and fertile modesty of the historian's empirical work to the empty and monotonous simplifications of "sociologism." Fortunately, there are counterexamples, such as the generally warm reception given the work of Harrison and Cynthia White, *Canvases and Careers,* one of the rare examples of the sociological modeling of a historical transformation of artistic production and of the conditions for the emergence of an innovation, impressionist painting, as Jean-Paul Bouillon reminds us in his preface to the French translation, *La carrière des peintres au XIXe siècle* (Paris: Flammarion, 1991).

36. Wolfgang Hildesheimer, *Mozart,* trans. Marion Faber (New York: Farrar, Straus, Giroux, 1982).

37. In *Quarter Notes and Bank Notes. The Economics of Music Composition in the Eighteenth and Nineteenth Centuries* (Princeton: Princeton University Press, 2004), the economist Frederic Scherer shows that if employment in courts and chapels was in fact the main component of the labor market for composers, freelance activity had emerged long before Mozart, and its importance grew gradually, usually by supplementing stable jobs and playing an increasing part in the combination of sources of remuneration.

38. DeNora, *Beethoven.*

39. To cite only a few works, see Henry Raynor (*A Social History of Music: From the Middle Ages to Beethoven* [London: Barrie & Jenkins, 1972]), Maynard Solomon (*Beethoven* [Oxford: Oxford University Press, 2000]), and Lydia Goehr (*The Imaginary Museum of Musical Works,* rev. ed. [New York: Oxford University Press, 2007]). All mention the inventions and ruses Beethoven used to have it both ways, to get paid twice, and to take advantage of his popularity in the markets for both art music and popular genres. Thus Lydia Goehr speaks of a "two-sided autonomy," (211) that consists in pledging allegiance to two contradictory ideals: art

for art's sake, the idealism of detachment from the world, on the one hand, and the democratic ideals of the composer laboring on behalf of the emancipation of humanity in need, on the other. These authors also mention the errant aspect of this multiplication, that of Beethoven's duplicity; he was capable, for instance, of promising a manuscript to a whole series of editors at once. A famous case of this is that of the *Missa Solemnis,* in which Beethoven negotiated with five publishers at virtually the same time that he was preparing to sell copies of the musical work to potential subscribers in courts all over Europe. Another often-cited case is his departure from Vienna to take a position as musical director at Kassel that he had been promised by Jérôme Bonaparte, and that he pretended to accept in order to obtain from his Viennese patrons an increase in his annual pension; another item in the repertory of Beethoven's clevernesses or half-clevernesses is his addition of the preposition "van" to his name, which allowed him to pass himself off as an aristocrat until the trick was discovered . . .

40. Pierre Bourdieu, "Bref impromptu sur Beethoven, artiste entrepreneur," *Sociétés & Représentations* 11 (2001): 17.

41. Alpers, *Rembrandt's Enterprise.*

42. Julia Moore, *Beethoven and Musical Economics,* Ph.D. diss., University of Urbana/Champaign, 1987.

43. Christoph Wolff, *Johann Sebastian Bach. The Learned Musician* (Oxford: Oxford University Press, 2000). Between the fifteenth and seventeenth centuries, a significant number of the greatest painters were able to take advantage of all the prerogatives of court painters without experiencing the latter's situation of subordination. At the courts, along with titles and honors they obtained a regular flow of lucrative commissions that provided them with most of their income, and the security connected with an eminently reliable demand, but also a prestige that could assure them a reputation and commissions on the international scale, and a greater freedom to innovate since, as Martin Warnke tells us in *The Court Artist,* persons at the court who commissioned artworks were more likely to be looking for something extraordinary, for novelty, for originality, and did not fear departures from tradition, as sponsors or officials in the city, who had more conservative expectations, often did. But these illustrious painters usually lived in cities, in order to preserve their area of freedom from the control of official organization, while at the same time freeing themselves from dependency on urban corporations and the constraining rules and taxes that the latter imposed on ordinary painters in the city. It was because of their exceptional reputation that these painters were able to doubly emancipate themselves by playing a double game that was, however, not equivalent to a position of stable equilibrium between two systems of organization. It was the system of court commissions that prevailed, and it was primarily through it that independence was assured. Analyzing the situation of Dürer, and comparing it to those of Rubens, Titian, and other artists, Warnke shows that it was fame at court that secured independence for them in the city.

44. This empirical density is very largely due to the works of Julia Moore and Mary Morrow, who are so abundantly cited and used by DeNora that her work might appear to be a collective production, were she not ultimately responsible for the interpretive coherence of the whole. See Moore, *Beethoven and Musical*

Economics; Mary Morrow, *Concert Life in Haydn's Vienna: Aspects of a Developing Musical and Social Institution* (New York: Pendragon, 1989).

45. DeNora, *Beethoven,* 50.

46. Ibid., 45.

47. Ian Hacking, *The Social Construction of What?* (Cambridge, MA: Harvard University Press, 1999).

48. Karl Mannheim, "Das problem einer Soziologie des Wissens," *Archiv für Sozialwissenschaft und Sozialpolitik* 53 (1925): 577–652.

49. Paul Ricoeur, *Time and Narrative,* trans. Kathleen McLaughlin and David Pellauer (Chicago: University of Chicago Press, 1984), vol. 1, 183.

50. Raymond Williams, *Keywords: A Vocabulary of Culture and Society* (Oxford: Oxford University Press, 1985).

51. Peter Kivy, *The Possessor and the Possessed: Handel, Mozart, Beethoven and the Idea of Musical Genius* (New Haven: Yale University Press, 2001), 178.

52. "The crux of the problem with most Beethoven literature as it addresses the composer's reputation is that, to varying degrees, that literature consists of retrospective accounts that isolate the quality of Beethoven's works as the cause of his recognition. In these accounts, greatness emerges out of a kind of temporal conjuring trick" (DeNora, *Beethoven,* 5).

This argument has been exploited by various authors who have seen in the recent evolution of musicological studies devoted to Beethoven the true ideological matrix of a mythological invention of musical genius. For instance, in a long essay on Josquin des Prez, Paula Higgins seeks to demonstrate that Josquin suddenly became a genius starting in the 1970s, as the result of a veritable mythological construction founded largely on the example of Beethoven, in the wake of the decisive moment marked by the celebration of the bicentenary of Beethoven's birth and the acceleration of his transformation into a mythical hero of modern civilization. See Paula Higgins, "The Apotheosis of Josquin des Prez and Other Mythologies of Musical Genius," *Journal of the American Musicological Society* 57(3) (2004): 443–510.

53. DeNora, *Beethoven,* 189.

54. See Solomon, *Beethoven;* Barry Cooper, *Beethoven* (Oxford: Oxford University Press, 2000); Lewis Lockwood, *Beethoven: The Music and the Life* (New York: W. W. Norton, 2003).

55. DeNora, *Beethoven,* 187–188.

56. Moore, *Beethoven and Musical Economics,* 420, quoted in DeNora, *Beethoven,* 58.

57. DeNora, *Beethoven,* 58.

58. See Marc Vignal, *Joseph Haydn: Autobiographie. Premières biographies* (Paris: Flammarion, 1997), quoted in DeNora, *Beethoven,* 102.

59. DeNora, *Beethoven,* 61.

60. Ibid., 69.

61. Ibid., 142.

62. Ibid., 188.

63. Ibid.

64. Ibid., 71.

65. DeNora's chapter on Beethoven's relations with Haydn after he settled in Vienna attacks the mythology of Beethoven's genius constructed on the basis of an overexploitation *a posteriori* of documents and declarations celebrating Beethoven's exceptionally promising talent: "My purpose is to point out that the telling and retelling of a story about Beethoven's potential was a condition of his eventual success. The anecdote provided a particular type of publicity, and it created a resource for the subsequent favorable reception of Beethoven's works; recounting the story of Beethoven's talent, in other words, was a means of dramatizing Beethoven as someone who had received approval and acceptance from a famous teacher" (Ibid., 84).

66. Quoted from Lockwood, *Beethoven,* 50.

67. Ibid., 30.

68. Quoted in ibid., 34.

69. On this point, see Daniel Kahneman and Dale Miller, "Norm Theory: Comparing Reality to Its Alternatives," *Psychological Review* 93(2) (1986): 136–153; Neal J. Rose, "Counterfactual Thinking," *Psychological Bulletin* 121(1) (1997): 133–148.

70. Barry Cooper also notes that the feeling of shame at not having given Mozart more help at the end of his life might have made Prince Lichnowsky's feeling of responsibility more acute with regard to supporting the nascent career of the very promising young Beethoven in Vienna. See Cooper, *Beethoven,* 41.

71. Lockwood, *Beethoven,* 52.

72. Ibid., 40–41.

73. Hauser, *The Social History of Art;* Raynor, *A Social History of Music.*

74. Gombrich, *Meditations on a Hobby Horse;* Meiss, review of *Florentine Painting,* 143–150.

75. Charles Rosen, "Did Beethoven Have All the Luck?" *New York Review of Books,* November 14 (1996): 57–63; rpt. in Charles Rosen, *Critical Entertainments* (Cambridge, MA: Harvard University Press, 2000), chap. 8.

76. Rosen, *Critical Entertainments,* 111–112, 118.

77. One of the most discussed and most enigmatic cases of this kind of aesthetic double game is certainly that of Dimitri Shostakovich, whose work and career seem to be an inextricable tangle of submission to the Stalinist order and to the most brutal forms of totalitarian terror, more or less persistent adhesion to, but not the application of, some of the ideals that this system promoted, and critical resistance to totalitarian domination. The analysis of Shostakovich's musical works and the exegesis of his writings, declarations, and correspondence, along with the reconstruction of his biography, provide one of the best examples of half-academic, half-political dispute regarding an artistic creator: The fabrication of the enigma is all the more fascinating because this composer was long scorned and excluded from the pantheon of modernity before undergoing a spectacular reevaluation that converted all the signs of conformism into manifestations of critical irony or painful testimony to the trials imposed on the all-too-human artist by history, by its tragedies, violence, and conflicts beyond human measure.

78. Raymonde Moulin, "De l'artisan au professionnel: L'artiste," *Sociologie du Travail* 25(4) (1983), rpt. in Raymonde Moulin, *De la valeur de l'art* (Paris:

Flammarion, 1995), 94. Among the works that have emphasized artists' ability to change the rules of the game as soon as their reputation makes them in demand and desired, we may mention Martin Warnke, who provides, in his book *The Court Artist,* a fine analysis of the artist's strategic inscription of his activity in a double system that allowed him to exploit his reputation, that is, to benefit from the competition among those whose sought his artworks and services, and thus to give his activity more independence than subordination.

79. Rosen, *Critical Entertainments,* 118.

80. Howard Robbins Landon, preface to Tia DeNora, *Beethoven et la construction du génie,* trans. Marc Vignal (Paris: Fayard, 1998), 11.

81. As I indicated in Chapter 4, the complexity of the relations of apprenticeship in the world of artistic creation very often produces double-bind situations. The pupil has to try to benefit from the competences of those who know more than he does by accepting the master's authority, but he also has to try to avoid allowing himself to be sterilized by the latter's power of inculcation. For his part, the master can shape his disciples in his own image and see in them no more than imperfect replicas of his genius or instruments for propagating his reputation. Or else he can teach them not to submit, because he knows that creative originality cannot be taught, or because he is annoyed by the apprentice's possible theft of his ideas and personal inventions. See also Pierre-Michel Menger, "La formation du compositeur: L'apprentissage de la singularité et les pouvoirs de l'établissement," in *Le Conservatoire de Paris, 1795–1995,* ed. Anne Bongrain and Yves Gérard (Paris: Buchet/ Chastel, 1996), 321–343.

82. See Solomon, *Beethoven;* Cooper, *Beethoven;* Barry Cooper, ed., *Dictionnaire Beethoven* (Paris: Jean-Claude Lattès, 1991).

83. Beethoven considered his economic situation more unstable and precarious than it actually was. This pessimism can be explained in several ways: It expresses a behavior of obsessional concern confronted by the variations in fortune related to his own creative difficulties and the effects of economic situations (the impact of inflation on the level of his revenues). But it also expresses the uncertain relation between creative effort and the material basis for independent activity. In an economy of the cessions of rights, remunerative commissions, and profit-making concerts, the economic evaluation of the artwork in progress comes down to making the creative act a function of quantities that are fluctuating and negotiable in transactions whose terms are specific in each case. Inversely, in a rentier economy, like the one provisionally and partially established in Vienna in 1809 by the financial support of three princes, Beethoven's reputation assured him an income stream independent of his productivity and of the intensity, measured at every moment, of demand.

84. For a limited sample of famous composers born between 1650 and 1850, Frederic Scherer carried out a statistical analysis of their sources of income and the development of their combinations for the different cohorts of composers studied. The boom in freelance careers is connected with a multiplication of the various possible sources of remunerations connected with the activity of composing music. The constitution of a publishing market provides revenues directly connected with the exploitation of original artworks and increases the demands for artworks

commissioned—pedagogical products, arrangements, orchestrations, or abridgments of original artworks, among others. The composer's knowledge and reputation can be exploited in activities of private or public education. The entrepreneurial initiatives multiply with the rise of the market for concerts and musical publication, and more and more composers include them in their portfolios of activities. See Scherer, *Quarter Notes and Bank Notes,* chap. 3.

85. This point was taken up earlier, in Chapter 3.

86. Rosen, "Did Beethoven Have All the Luck?"

87. The argument can be generalized to include the mercantile system: When differences in talent between artists are set aside, a decisive role has to be accorded to differences in talent between the enterprises (publishing houses, galleries, recording companies, producers and distributors of films, audiovisual firms) that "patronize" the artist. Some entrepreneurs are not simply more powerful, or endowed with larger networks, but also have a flair, a culture, a superior talent for discovery, or, to follow Joseph Schumpeter's *Theory of Economic Development,* trans. Redvers Opie (New York: Oxford University Press, 1961), it is the most brilliant innovators who know how to combine the necessary resources in a superior way. For how can we describe the ability of the patron or merchant who chooses the right artist to defend once it is admitted that among patrons as among artistic entrepreneurs there is competition and failure as well as success? Expelled on the side of the artist, talent returns on the side of the innovative entrepreneur.

88. The work of John Padgett and Christopher Ansell ("Robust Action and the Rise of the Medici, 1400–1434," *American Journal of Sociology* 98[6] [1993]: 1259–1319) on the rise of the Medicis in Florence offers an excellent example of the scope of an analysis of social networks that puts the emphasis on the ambiguity and heterogeneity of behaviors rather than on their deliberate and purely self-interested planning.

89. Rosen, "Did Beethoven . . . ," 61.

90. Philippe Urfalino, "Les politiques culturelles: Mécénat caché et académies invisibles," *L'Année Sociologique* 39 (1989): 81–109.

91. On this point, see Arthur L. Stinchcombe, *Stratification and Organization* (Cambridge: Cambridge University Press, 1986); Michael Kremer, "The O-Ring Theory of Economic Development," *Quarterly Journal of Economics* 108(3) (1993): 551–575; Richard Caves, *Creative Industries* (Cambridge, MA: Harvard University Press, 2000).

92. Among the studies based on this kind of analytical perspective, we may mention Robert R. Faulkner, *Music on Demand* (New Brunswick NJ: Transaction, 1983); and William Bielby and Denise Bielby, "Organizational Mediation of Project-Based Labor Markets," *American Sociological Review* 64(1) (1999): 64–85.

93. Carl Dahlhaus, *Die Musik des 19. Jahrhunderts* (Wiesbaden: Athenaion, 1980); Goehr, *The Imaginary Museum* (1997); Leonard B. Meyer, *Style and Music* (Philadelphia: University of Pennsylvania Press, 1989); Charles Rosen, *The Classical Style: Haydn, Mozart, Beethoven,* expanded ed. (New York: W. W. Norton, 1998).

94. For an analysis of Beethoven's heroic style, as it was forged by the composer, as it was received by successive generations of listeners, and as it has become a

cultural value, see Scott Burnham, *Beethoven Hero* (Princeton: Princeton University Press, 1995).

6. Profiles of the Unfinished

1. Antoinette Le Normand-Romain, *Rodin* (Paris: Flammarion, 1997).

2. Ibid., 80.

3. Ibid., 106.

4. Ibid., 155.

5. Leo Steinberg, *Le retour de Rodin,* trans. Michelle Tran Van Khai, rev. ed. Leo Steinberg (Paris, Macula, 1997), 10–11.

6. Judith Cladel, *Rodin,* trans. James Whitall (New York: Harcourt, Brace, and Co., 1937), 76–77.

7. Gérard Genette, *The Work of Art: Immanence and Transcendence,* trans. G. M. Goshgarian (Ithaca, NY: Cornell University Press, 1994).

8. Genette provides the following characterization of "plural immanences":

> the feature common to all these forms is that the work immanates in several nonidentical objects, or, more exactly (since, strictly speaking, no two objects in this world are absolutely identical), in two objects *not deemed to be* identical and interchangeable, in the sense in which we generally assume that two casts of a cast sculpture *are.* This proviso, let us recall, underlies the distinction between multiple and plural objects. A cast sculpture or a print is (generally speaking) a multiple work (a work with multiple immanence); the works we are now about to consider are works with plural immanence. (163)

But Genette relativizes the impact of his distinction, specifying that it is more cultural than ontological and more gradual than categorical. Taking the example of engraving, he makes the point that prints are seen as multiple copies and not as plural versions (since the differences between two prints are generally caused by the defects of the process, and are therefore involuntary). But cases of voluntary differences exist: The continual gradation between multiplicity and plurality is located precisely in this possibility. And this is what is exploited in Rodin's work.

9. Rainer Maria Rilke, *Rodin,* trans. Robert Firmage (Salt Lake City: Peregrine Smith, 1979), 35–37.

10. In his biography of Rodin, Frederic Grunfeld (*Rodin* [New York: Henry Holt, 1987]) provides a brief glimpse of the declarations, anecdotes, and journalistic interventions—benevolent and violently polemical—that signal the growing interest of the sculptor in the fragment.

11. Genette, *The Work of Art,* 196.

12. Ibid., 205.

13. Rosalind Krauss, *Passages in Modern Sculpture* (New York: Viking, 1977).

14. André Green, "Vie et mort dans l'inachèvement," *Nouvelle Revue de Psychanalyse* 50 (1994): 155–183.

15. Ibid., 180.

16. Michael Baxandall, *Patterns of Intention* (New Haven: Yale University Press, 1985).

17. Gilles-Gaston Granger, *Essai d'une philosophie du style* (Paris: Armand Colin, 1968), 8.

18. Ibid., 203.

19. André Chastel, "Le fragmentaire, l'hybride et l'inachevé" (1957), in *Fables, formes, figures,* vol. 2 (Paris: Flammarion, 1978).

20. Howard S. Becker, *Art Worlds* (Berkeley: University of California Press, 1982), 194.

21. Ibid. See, in particular, pages 198 to 204.

22. Baxandall, *Patterns of Intention.*

23. At least for those artists who appear to him to proceed by tests, errors, corrections, and the dynamics of self-criticism—in opposition to a second category of creators producing above all at the "first stab without drafts or final improvements." Karl Popper, "Rôle de l'auto-critique dans la création," *Diogène* 145 (1989): 38–48.

24. Ernst Kris and Otto Kurz, *Legend, Myth and Magic in the Image of the Artist,* trans. Alastair Laing and Lottie M. Newman (New Haven: Yale University Press, 1979).

25. Leonard B. Meyer, *Style and Music* (Philadelphia: University of Pennsylvania Press, 1989). Meyer reminds us, à propos of the stylistic analysis and appreciation of musical works, that the use of such a notion has an evaluative—not logical—quality.

> The notion that musical relationships are, or should be, inevitable has a pernicious effect on analysis and criticism. This is the case because the valuing of inevitability directs attention almost exclusively to those possibilities that are actualized. But, as argued here, a full appreciation of a relationship involves an understanding of its implied structure as well. The tacit line of argument would seem to run somewhat as follows: The best relationships are necessary (inevitable) ones; hence the best compositions exhibit a high degree of inevitability. Since we customarily study and criticize excellent compositions, what happens in them must be inevitable, and for this reason, we need not trouble ourselves with unrealized possibilities. (33, note 71)

26. Ibid., 32–33.

27. Jean-René Gaborit, "Sculpture, matériaux et techniques," in *Encyclopedia Universalis,* vol. 20 (Paris, 1996), 767.

28. Antoinette Le Normand-Romain, ed., *1898: le Balzac de Rodin* (Paris: Editions du Musée Rodin, 1998).

29. Rodin said of Michelangelo: "He held out his powerful hand to me." André Chastel commented thusly on the influence of Michelangelo:

> Beginning with the first works like *l'Homme au nez cassé* (1864)—therefore before his voyage in Italy, he shows that the strong and battered contours of Michel-Ange attracted him. *L'Age d'airain* (1876) still confirms it. But it is especially after 1880, in the cycle born around the *Porte de l'Enfer,* with *Adam,* the *Eros,* the *Trois Ombres,* the *Penseur* . . . that the adhesion to his grand style shown itself in detail. Here, in the option and in the treatment of forms, is the great justification of Rodin, which tends, as with the Master, toward a kind of complete animation of the block. And the major analogy is in the rediscovery of the *non finito,* this principle of contrast that all experts and artists up to that point had to excuse. Rodin understood it as the essential spring of an art attentive to the movement and the shivering of forms, to the point of suggesting their appearance and their dissolution. The recourse to the incomplete, which is directly inspired in Rodin by the study of Michelangelo, is the key to a strange, complex style, where it is as if force is seized by a vibration that retains it and threatens to destroy it; the works, according to

Rodin, seem 'ready to break' under their anxious tension. (André Chastel, "Michel-Ange en France" [1966], in André Chastel, *Fables, formes, figures,* vol. 2 [Paris: Flammarion, 1978], 306)

30. Chastel, "Le fragmentaire, l'hybride, l'inachevé."

31. Chastel contrasts the three methods of figural disorder:

The incomplete, the fragmentary and the hybrid are three manners of disarticulating and compromising the integrity of forms. Wölfflin could justifiably define the style of the Renaissance by the desire to push as far as possible for clarity, articulation, and the precision of forms. He only omitted the counterpart of this effort, which is more visible today to us now that emphasis is placed on anticlassical currents and on the spiritual complexity of the Renaissance. The hybrid, even if consigned to the decorative (which often escapes its limits), supposes a perception of chaos which resists reasonable definitions, which escapes from standards and objectivity, and which can go from the horrible to the marvelous: it is a negation of the "finished" and of "truth" via error and excess. The fragmentary is the ruin of those ideals by accident, and introduces not the fascination of the formless, but distress—impotence—in the face of deterioration and death and the difficulty of maintaining the integrity of the "completed" and the "realized." These two forms are thus easily associated with the *non-finito* itself, especially if one extends it, as we propose, to certain rustic effects in architecture. Thus the hermès caryatides, which are torsos, sometimes seem absorbed in the indecision of the raw material. The incomplete—the form in draft state—completes the series of negative reactions to the order and the clearness of the images by obliging one to seize the tension that governs their appearance and that sometimes doesn't come to an end. (Chastel, "Le fragmentaire, l'hybride et l'inachevé," 44)

32. Steinberg, *Le retour de Rodin.*

33. Hans Belting, *The Invisible Masterpiece,* trans. Helen Atkins (London: Reaktion, 2001), 202.

34. Jean Chatelain, "An Original in Sculpture," in *Rodin Rediscovered,* ed. Albert Elsen (Washington: National Gallery of Art, 1980), 275–276.

35. Raymonde Moulin, "La genèse de la rareté artistique," *Ethnologie Française* 8(2–3) (1978): 241–258, reprinted in R. Moulin, *De la valeur de l'art* (Paris: Flammarion, 1996).

36. Auguste Rodin, *Eclairs de pensée. Ecrits et entretiens* (Paris: Editions Olbia, 1998), 85.

37. This kind of investigation should lead us to wonder, for example, about the common foundations (perhaps banal ones) of a poetics of figuration and a philosophy of knowledge rooted in the act of perception or judgment. It should direct us toward the kind of research carried out especially in the second half of the nineteenth century on the analysis of the forms and movement, and toward the consequences of the invention of photography (think of the possible rapprochements between some of Rodin's experiments and Etienne-Jules Marey's research on movement. In her essay on *La Porte de l'Enfer,* Rosalind Krauss *(Passages in Modern Sculpture)* connects Rodin's practice with the Husserlian theory of the ego and the interplay between the ego and alterity in the formation of the self. She does this in order to read Rodin's sculpture in terms of a phenomenology of bodily experience and thereby to challenge the ordinary causal/temporal schema in which the artist draws on his former experience (perceptive, imaginary) in order to "express himself." But the idea that an experience can be conceived without relation to a

retained past, or to an anticipated future, goes directly against the phenomenology of perception and consciousness. Krauss actually wants to deconstruct the notion of a consciousness turned back on itself and its stock of experiences, in favor of an image of the creative act as produced in its own unfolding.

38. Rodin's declarations tend toward the modesty of an obstinate naturalist and a laboriously perfectionist craft ethic:

> In sculpture, beautiful execution lies in the profile; in volume. If one sketches well, one finds it when it is sincerely sought, as part of a violent desire to make things true. But if one is satisfied with a result that appears satisfactory, one never achieves more. How many times have people told me: Stop there. Don't touch it again. And sometimes with reason. But I continued, intending to go further.
>
> I often made ten starts on the same bust. I made their multiple aspects and various expressions; in the end, what a joy of seeing and understanding! Wanting to do better, one sometimes demolishes what one did well; but it is necessary to be possessed by the demon of perfection. If it misguides us one day, it takes its revenge by leading us further. (Rodin, *Eclairs de pensée*, 130)

39. Ibid., 39.

40. This process of plastic creation, diverging from the tradition of group composition, becomes a pivotal issue in the reinvention of Rodin as a modernist: The aesthetic treatment of the multiplicity is located among the many means used by the sculptor to dramatize the process of production of his artworks (as Krauss points out in commenting on the position of Leo Steinberg, inventor of modern Rodin):

> At that point Rodin's frequent practice of composing a figure by what Leo Steinberg has called multiplication becomes extremely interesting to consider. The plasters, cast from the clay models, which had before Rodin been the formally neutral vehicle of reproduction, became for him a medium of composition. If there can be, must be, one plaster, why not three? And if three . . . Thus the multiple, we could say, became the medium. . . .
>
> In its effort to rescue Rodin's art from the enthusiasm of sentiment and make it available to the rather sterner assessment of modernism, Leo Steinberg's reading of this manipulation of sameness regards the phenomenon of multiplication through the lens of process. The revelation of process works to expose the means of representation; in formalist terms, it bares the device. It is the intentional, shocking construction of a surface that will report not on "the secrets of sculpture," but on the banalities of making: In addition to sheer multiplication, there is the whole panoply of casting "error" courted and magnified by Rodin, as there is also the phenomenon of modeling strategies (like the little clay pellets added to a given plane to further the buildup of the form) left in their most primitive state to be recorded by the final cast. (Rosalind Krauss, *Originality of the Avant-Garde and Other Modernist Myths* [Cambridge, MA: MIT Press, 1985], 185–186)

41. The Rodin Museum holds more than thirty successive versions; see Le Normand-Romain, *Rodin*, 127.

42. The account of this incident perfectly condenses a number of the characteristics around which interpretations of the intentionality and the modernity of Rodin are deployed:

> Then I worked on my *Eve* statue. I saw my model changing, without knowing the cause; I modified my profiles, naively following the successive and expanding transformations of the forms. One day, I learned that she was pregnant; I understood everything. The profiles of the belly had changed in a barely perceptible manner; but one could see to what ex-

tent I had copied nature with sincerity by looking at the muscles of the loins and the sides.

Henri Dujardin-Beaumetz: It is absolutely clear that your statue gives the impression of a primitive woman, mother of humanity.

Auguste Rodin: I certainly had not thought that translating Eve required a pregnant woman as a model; it was a happy chance, and it singularly contributed to the character of the figure. But soon my model became more sensitive, and found that the workshop was cold; she spaced out the meetings, then did not come back. That is why my *Eve* is unfinished. (Le Normand-Romain, *Rodin,* 124–125)

43. Krauss, *Originality of the Avant-Garde and other Modernist Myths.*

44. Steinberg, *Le retour de Rodin.*

45. The artist's notoriety can continuously increase whereas the "quality" of the artworks (a compound of originality, invention, innovation, and commercial value expressing the fluctuations of demand) moves according to different variables related to the behavior of the art market (in its totality and its various segments), and to the career of the artist's works in this market. For an artist of continuously rising reputation, this will cause variable valuations according to a range of factors, including the period of manufacture of the artwork—see, on this subject, David Galenson, *Painting Outside the Lines: Patterns of Creativity in Modern Art* (Cambridge, MA: Harvard University Press, 2002).

46. Krauss, drawing on the analyses of Jean Chatelain, remarks:

This is a question of what could be called an "irreducible plurality"—a condition of multiplicity that will not reduce to the unit *one,* to the singular or unique—a condition that is inside the very existence of the unique or singular instance, multiplying it. Under this condition the compound arts are, simply, compound and no amount of systematic rarefaction will change this. The transfer of the idea from medium to medium in the production of the final "original" guarantees that inside that ultimate oneness is such a state of fission that the locus of singularity keeps receding from us. (Krauss, *Originality of the Avant-Garde and Other Modernist Myths,* 181)

47. Famous examples include Verdi's *Don Carlo,* Berg's *Lulu,* Mussorgski's *Boris Godunov,* and Puccini's *Turandot,* whose new completion by Luciano Berio enabled the publishing house Ricordi to extend its copyright far beyond the normal time limit. See Pierre-Michel Menger, "Le travail à l'œuvre: Enquête sur l'autorité contingente du créateur dans l'art lyrique," *Annales HSS* 65(3) (2010): 743–786.

48. Antoine Compagnon, *Les cinq paradoxes de la modernité* (Paris: Seuil, 1989).

49. Albert Boime, *The Academy and French Painting in the Nineteenth Century,* 2nd ed. (New Haven: Yale University Press, 1986).

50. As Robert Faulkner notes in his essay on the work process in jazz:

The interplay of exploitation and exploration has relevance not only in the community of jazz musicians but in other occupations as well. The shed is ubiquitous. Examination of practicing may inform the work behind the work not only of sculptors, musicians, and dancers but also of test pilots, air traffic controllers, military strategists, baseball players, accountants, and surgeons. Like surgeons, musicians trying something new get worse before they get better (Gawande 2002, 60). In medicine you practice on people, your patients (Gawande 2002). In music you practice on an instrument, your horn. In accounting you practice on double-entry ledgers, your books (Carruthers and Espeland 1991). (Robert R. Faulkner, "Shedding Culture," in *The Art from Start to Finish,* ed. Howard S. Becker, Robert R. Faulkner, and Barbara Kirshenblatt-Gimblett [Chicago: The University of Chicago Press, 2006], 115)

51. It is well known that Picasso's *Les Demoiselles d'Avignon* was the end product of a series of some 500 sketches, studies, preparatory drawings, and trials, but still Picasso has insisted that this major painting was unfinished. See William S. Rubin, Hélène Seckel, and Judith Cousins, *Les Demoiselles d'Avignon: Studies in Modern Art* (New York: Museum of Modern Art, 1995).

52. See Paul F. Berliner, *Thinking about Jazz: The Infinite Art of Improvisation* (Chicago: University of Chicago Press, 1994); Robert R. Faulkner and Howard S. Becker, *"Do You Know . . . ?": The Jazz Repertoire in Action* (Chicago: University of Chicago Press, 2009).

53. Stanley Cavell, *Must We Mean What We Say?* 2nd ed. (Cambridge: Cambridge University Press, 1976), 230.

54. Daniel Wegner, *The Illusion of Conscious Will* (Cambridge, MA: MIT Press, 2000).

Conclusion

1. Paul Valéry, *The Collected Works of Paul Valéry, Vol. 14, Analects,* ed. Jackson Mathews, trans. Stuart Gilbert (Princeton: Princeton University Press, 1970), 237–238.

Acknowledgments

Among my colleagues in sociology with whom I have maintained close ties throughout the pursuit of the research program that led to this book, I would like to express my particular gratitude to Raymonde Moulin and Howard Becker.

I would never have embarked upon the research on artistic labor of which this book supplies a good overview had I not benefited from several months of complete freedom from work and study to become familiar with the economic analysis of risk and uncertainty. My position as a researcher at the Centre National de la Recherche Scientifique allowed me this period of learning and investment. I was able to gauge the benefit of this by seeing that the article "Rationalité et incertitude de la vie d'artiste" that I wrote at that time, and which appears here as Chapter 3 of this book, constituted a matrix for later works, because it seemed to me that the theoretical framework it developed could be applied both to the analysis of certain important mechanisms in creative activity and to the functioning of the labor market in the various arts.

I have taught the sociology of labor and that of the arts at the Ecole des Hautes Etudes en Sciences Sociales since the mid-1990s. Much of the material presented in this book was the subject of seminars, and it benefited from exchanges with my students and doctoral candidates. It was also presented in colloquia and research seminars in France and abroad, often with the support of the EHESS. In my view, the EHESS's most original feature is that it makes it possible to form relationships of collaboration, exchange, and friendship beyond the boundaries of one's discipline. I owe a great deal to my colleagues who are economists, and first of all to Christophe Chamley, Roger Guesnerie, and André Masson, and also to the late Louis-André Gérard-Varet, to my colleagues in history, and especially to Jacques Revel and Pierre Rosanvallon, and to my colleagues in philosophy, especially Vincent Descombes.

The errors that may result from this (lack of) discipline remain my own, but the risk was taken with pleasure, and for me it was a profound lesson concerning work in the social sciences. From September 2006 to July 2007, I was a fellow at the Wissenschaftskolleg in Berlin, where I had the advantage of exceptional research conditions and countless opportunities for exchange with marvelous companions in free research, philosophers, biologists, psychologists, historians, archeologists, jurists, anthropologists, musicologists, and artists. Among them, I would like to mention particularly Béatrice Longuenesse, as well as Joseph Bergin, Toshio Hosokawa, Helmut Lachenmann, Wayne Maddison, Georg Nolte, Marta Petrusewicz, Frank Rösler, Paul Schmid-Hempel, Alain Schnapp, and Andreas Vosskuhle, without whom these months of studious freedom would not have had the same intensity. I also want to express my gratitude to all the staff and the marvelous organization of the Wiko. I devoted part of my year in Berlin to working on a question—"What does it mean to complete a work?"—to which I have tried to provide an actual in the present volume, while continuing to work on the book on completion as such.

During 2008, I was a visiting scholar in the department of sociology at Columbia University in New York, where I was studying the academic labor market in the United States, the mechanisms of competition and mobility, and the relations between inequalities of reputation and inequalities in salary. Despite the difference in the subject, the long Chapter 4 draws part of its material from the exchanges I had there and from the lectures I gave there. I thank Peter Bearman, Patrick Bolton, Alan Brinkley, Pierre-André Chiappori, Thomas DiPrete, Priscilla Ferguson, Fred Neuhouser, Kristina Orfali, Emmanuelle Saada, Bernard Salanié, Seymour Spilerman, Diane Vaughan, and Harrison White, of Columbia University; Augustin Landier, Xavier Gabaix, and Thomas Philippon, of New York University; Paul Benacerraf, of Princeton University; and Barry Loewer, of Rutgers University.

Finally, in writing the long fourth chapter of this book I benefited from the comments and valuable suggestions made by Fabien Accominotti and from numerous conversations with Béatrice Longuenesse. I thank them most warmly.

The translation for this book has been performed by several translators: Steven Rendall translated the Introduction, Chapters 2 and 5, and the Conclusion; Amy Jacobs translated Chapter 1; Arianne Dorval and Lisette Eskinazi translated Chapters 3 and 4; and Emmanuelle Saada and Joe Karaganis translated Chapter 6. With his keen eyes and sharp mind, Ian Malcolm, my editor at Harvard University Press, provided me with invaluable help to improve and smooth out the end result.

SEVERAL CHAPTERS in this book were originally published as articles or contributions to essay collections and have been revised for inclusion here:

"Le génie et sa sociologie: Controverses sur le cas Beethoven," *Annales HSS* 4 (2002): 967–999.

"Profiles of the Unfinished: Rodin's Work and the Varieties of Incompleteness," in H. S. Becker, R. R. Faulkner, and B. Kirshenblatt-Gimblett, eds., *Art from Start to Finish* (Chicago: University of Chicago Press, 2006), 21–68.

"Rationalité et incertitude de la vie d'artiste," *L'Année sociologique* 39 (1989): 111–151.

"Temporalité de l'action et différences interindividuelles: L'analyse de l'action en sociologie et en économie," *Revue française de sociologie* 38(3) (1997): 587–633.

"Est-il rationnel de travailler pour s'épanouir?" in Louis-André Gérard-Varet and Jean-Claude Passeron, eds., *Le modèle et l'enquête. Les usages du principe de rationalité dans les sciences sociales* (Paris: Editions de l'EHESS, 1995), 401–443.

Chapter 6 previously appeared in *Art from Start to Finish: Jazz, Painting, Writing, and Other Improvisations* published by the University of Chicago Press © 2006 by the University of Chicago.

Index

Abbott, Andrew, 349n9

Académie Française, 167, 212

Accominotti, Fabien, 222, 226, 370n167, 372n182

accountability, 31

action, 16, 26; Aristotle's philosophy of, 99; phenomenological analysis of, 19; as process, 65–66; rationality of, 94–95; temporality of, 15

actors, 36, 55; beliefs and representations of, 29; cooperation among, 25; as generic beings, 69; income inequalities among, 159; initiatives of, 105; "macro-actors," 237; multiplication of self and, 28; networks of, 240; rationality of, 40, 53; in sequential games, 57–58. *See also* agents

Adam (Rodin), 287, 383n29

Adler, Judith, 150–151

Adler, Moshe, 198

Adorno, Theodor, 237, 239, 375n29; on Beethoven, 244–249, 257, 271; social classes as main actors in narrative of, 255

advertising, 171, 186, 203, 355n59; consumers influenced by, 192; functions of, 204; talent-makers and, 206

aesthetics, 165, 309

Âge d'airain, L' (Rodin), 305, 383n29

agents, 19, 50, 51, 185; access to information by, 41, 68; competition and, 21, 42; defined by otherness, 34; general equilibrium theory and, 40, 43–44, 46; intentionality of, 62; learning by, 52; neoclassical theory and, 39; shared information and, 29; social condition of, 8; temporary equilibrium and, 48, 49; uncertainty and, 47. *See also* actors

Alexander, Jeffrey C., 326n5

Allison, Paul, 213, 216, 230

Alper, Neil, 155, 159

Alpers, Svetlana, 254

American Idol (U.S. TV show), 222

analytic philosophy, 26, 65

Anand, Narasimhan, 363n120

Anderson, Chris, 224

Anscombe, Gertrude Elizabeth, 65

Antal, Frederik, 252, 376n35

anthropology, 37

Appiah, Kwame Anthony, 176

apprenticeship, 82, 148, 157, 226, 270, 380n81

architects, 139–140, 347n93

Arendt, Hannah, 162, 339n35

aristocracy, 115, 239, 240, 246, 263; as Beethoven's patrons, 255, 265, 267; decline of, 256; in mechanistic Marxist